G000099795

Henry Disney was born in 1938 and was separated from his parents for part of the War; while his wife-to-be had to be dug from the remains of her home following a bombing raid. After the War he was partly brought up in the Sudan, he served on active service in Cyprus during his National service in 1958, and he carried out research in the rain forests of Belize and Cameroon, as well as on a three month expedition to Indonesia. He was in charge of a Field Centre and National Nature Reserve in Yorkshire before moving in 1984 to become a researcher at the University of Cambridge. He has been author or co-author of about 600 scientific publications, with his co-authors being from more than 50 countries across the world. He has served on various public bodies as well as being a churchwarden. He has previously published ten collections of poetry, many reflecting on his position as a scientist and 'Lapsed atheist'.

In gratitude for the life of my wife

AUDREY DISNEY

22 January 1928 – 1 March 2012

(We were married on 23 November 1963)

and

For our children

TRUDIA, ADRIAN and RACHEL

and

Our grandchildren

ALISTAIR, SAMANTHA, ZOE and MAX

Dr Henry Disney

REGAINING LIFE'S WINDING TRAIL

AUSTIN MACAULEY
PUBLISHERS LTD.

Copyright © Dr Henry Disney (2017)

The right of Dr Henry Disney to be identified as author of this work has been asserted by him in accordance with section 77 and 78 of the Copyright, Designs and Patents Act 1988.

All rights reserved. No part of this publication may be reproduced, stored in a retrieval system, or transmitted in any form or by any means, electronic, mechanical, photocopying, recording, or otherwise, without the prior permission of the publishers.

Any person who commits any unauthorized act in relation to this publication may be liable to criminal prosecution and civil claims for damages.

A CIP catalogue record for this title is available from the British Library.

ISBN 9781786127976 (Paperback)
ISBN 9781786127983 (Hardback)
ISBN 9781786127990 (E-Book)
www.austinmacauley.com

First Published (2017)
Austin Macauley Publishers Ltd.
25 Canada Square
Canary Wharf
London
E14 5LQ

All royalties for
MEDECINS SANS FRONTIERS (UK)
Lower Ground Floor, Chancery Exchange, 10 Furnival Street, London EC4A 1AB
www.msf.org.uk
(Charity number 1026588)

PREFACE

I have been urged many times to compile an autobiography, but have persistently declined as indicated in this poem first published in 2005.

AUTOBIOGRAPHY (RE)

When urged to write account of life
I've spent, by friend who thinks there's tale
That's worth the telling, laughter's smiles
At once engulfed my thoughts. It seems
A glossy cover leads astray.
The pages they enclose are just
A catalogue of routine years.
I'll grant I've worked in places few
Have seen, apart from those for whom
It's home. I've done some things that few
Have done. I've been involved in rare
Events that seem like extracts torn
From novel's page. But none were planned.
To me it's more a case of storms,
Or days in sun, that came and went,
While I just carried on as though
Each day was normal gift. At times
I've had a close exchange with death,
But soon escaped to live again.
I've met a rich array of men
And women drawn from diverse walks
Of life, both high and low. With some
I've clashed. With most I've relished each
As I've beheld the child behind
The mask. The only tale I'll tell
Is one of thanks for love for wife,
For children too, for theirs as well.

I later referred to this poem when I reinforced its message:

RIPOSTE (CW)

I wrote a simple poem as
To why I shunned suggestion made
To me that varied life required
I tell my tale. My mind forbade
I so embark in genre by which
Selection mints a fiction more
At odds with truth than novels built
From fancy's whims. I still ignore
Request. The only tale I'll tell
Is poems dropped to litter world,
With many contradictions plain
For all to read. When death has furled
My life on earth then some, at least,
Of poems will remain, I more
Than hope. With few, but common, themes,
A shallow, clever critic's sure
He'd spotted flaw. Recurring themes,
He ruled, are just a bore. And yet
He gave unqualified assent
When pundit praised Beethoven's set
Of great symphonic works because
Of way the master made a tune
Recur, but often giving fresh,
Surprising shifts. It's like our moon.
Despite relentless wax and wane
A dance of passing clouds ensures
It never seems the same. Delight
Persists. Indeed it never bores.
I will admit my total haul
Is curate's egg. If some survive
When I am dead I'll be content
If read as though they're still alive.

This message had been reinforced as follows:

SELECTED DATA (RE)

I sometimes wish this life was just
A set of proofs I can amend
Before it goes to press. But no,
Because it would become a tale
Evading truths instead. To tell
My story straight, in full, cannot
Be done by anyone but me;
But I resist the urging friend
Who wished I'd try. I know too well
I'd edit out the darker parts,
Enhance my role at times of gain,
And twist account until it came
To be a novel not report.
And so I leave the yarn to fool
Who'd reconstruct it, bit by bit,
From scraps of litter by the way
I wandered in a daze without
A plan. I've slowly learned to love,
With help of wife who's stuck with me
Despite my many faults, and so
This golden thread is all that needs
Recall when I am gone ahead
To what awaits beyond demise.

In short there is always the risk that 'The life of a person is not what happened, but what he remembers and how he remembers it' (Gabriel García Márquez, quoted in the Financial Times in 2015).

Most of my poems deal with public events, political comment, people and events I have encountered or read about in the press, reflections on the meaning of life, etc. However, my 'autobiography' already existed as a subset of my poems that originated as reflections on events and relationships in my life. A friend who urged me to write the story of my life had added that I would have to call it a work of fiction, as nobody would believe it otherwise. She had a point:

FICTION'S TRUTH (MC)

I lose myself in novel's world
Of make believe that seems as real
As daily life or more. I feel
I've met these folk before or heard
Of them from friend who talks of time
He was abroad. Indeed I find
They're closer than the folk who live
Next door. I greet them daily when
We coincide, but hardly know
What's in their minds or how they spent
Their youth. But those in book reveal
Their inmost thoughts, their doubts, their hopes.
I know their secret loves and deeds,
Both black and white. Despite their sins
I feel compassion slowly grow.
I sense that's how our Lord knows us.
He sees the hidden glow. His love
Desires to fan it into flame,
If we will only let Him so.
His fire will burn away the night
And lead us to eternal light.

However, despite my reservations, I have given in at last to the urging by family, friends and colleagues that I put together an account of my unusual life. My life seems to be perceived as 'unusual' from two viewpoints. Firstly (for me) my good fortune in marrying Audrey, who so many people considered to be one of the kindest people they had ever met. Secondly, how come, that never having been a research student, I have been so productive of scientific publications? The short answer to the latter is that I tackled situations where our ignorance was great so that adding to knowledge was inevitable, even for an old fashioned naturalist!

Rather than a formal autobiography, I have set out instead to document seemingly significant incidents and aspects of my life. However, I was urged by colleagues to include sufficient selected summaries of my scientific contributions (with citations of their key publications) to illustrate the sort of advances in knowledge I have achieved. Both these components are illustrated by poems that were initiated by reflection on these strands of a life of the unforeseen.

I have indeed encountered an extraordinary range of people from the famous to the infamous. Nevertheless, I have resisted the temptation to name most and to comment on their characters. My purpose is more limited. I have attempted to present landmarks in what has proved to be an unpredictable life more varied than I had even imagined when a child. I have minimized formal comments on these events in favour of poems that have sprung from them. Indeed my method of working has been to select poems that were prompted by significant events in my life and I have then added the context and such additional comments on these events as considered necessary or desirable. I leave the reader to judge whether these prose pieces are more 'truthful' than the poems!

The end result of the above approach is less a formal autobiography and more a set of reflections in my anecdotage interspersed with illustrative, rather than strict reportage, poems. These included poems (comprising not quite a quarter of my total of published poems) reflect real experiences but need considering in the light of the warning I gave at the beginning of my 8th collection: I herewith 'present for inspection imaginary gardens with real toads in them' (From Marianne Moore's original version of her poem POETRY).

The letters in brackets after the titles of the poems (e.g. CW, MC and RE after the titles of the poems above) refer to the collections listed at the end of these selections. In most cases poems had been published elsewhere before being included in one of these compilations. These prior publications are listed in the relevant collection. Thus the poem AUTOBIOGRAPHY was first published in an Anchor Books anthology in 2005 but was reproduced in my 2011 collection (RE).

My late wife, Audrey, had being putting together some memories for our grandchildren when she unexpectedly died. I have included these compilations by her (chapters 4 and 5) but have added a little to Audrey's memories, mainly to provide some additional explanations or contexts.

Before proceeding the reader should be warned that my conceptual framework is that of a deeply committed scientist who is also a Christian. With regard to the latter I am best characterized as a lapsed atheist (see poem of this title in chapter 3) who is allergic to fundamentalists – be they religious or atheist fundamentalists. The following poem introduced my 2004 collection.

STATUTORY HEALTH WARNING (CO)

My sole kaleidoscopic self
Launched on life as son and brother.
But soon I came to be a friend,
An uncle, a husband for she
Who merits medal for coping
With my Legion self, who became
A dad of two lovely daughters
And a son, whose paraplegic
Accident has anguished my heart.
The tiresome youth to mellowed man
Had grown; and as a grandad see
Me quite sentimental become;
And more frequently be patient
In doctor's waiting room or just
Impatient in a queue for stamps.
I may be all of these at once,
It seems, without adverse comment
From Boojum nerds. But just declare
Myself a scientist, a poet
And a follower of Christ, without
Confessing discord from these facts,
Then disbelief elicits charge
Of dire mental confusion. For
An Art and Science are not
Supposed to share a bed. But worse,
Religion's known as choice of folk
Who should be sidelined in a place
Reserved for those of no account.
My faith is viewed as QWERTY quirk
That still survives on the keyboard
Of my wondrous desktop PC,
Despite its rationale that died
When I shed my ancient heavy
Typewriter in a skip. But I
Recall in youth my faith had pulled
Me through when army two reports
Confused. As punishment for deeds
Another man had done, I'd found
Myself in Cyprus on active
Service in the ranks and despair.
A gentle grace restored my hope.

My fickle faith has been through fire,
Both then and many a night since.
But confronted with latest sheaf
Of poems to peruse, craven
Critics mostly declare the brew
Is marred by toxin of my faith
And decline to review. One crank,
With carapace of atavist
Beliefs of fundamentalist
Persuasion, trampled my pet pearls
In mud of 'heresy' on grounds
That unread Darwin is devil
Disguised. But C. D. and Jesus
Are my lights. One scribbler, for whom
Both God and Science are threats
To his nihilistic views, carped
"His poems are derived from mind
Disengaged from today's concerns
And expressed in metric forms long
Abandoned by those freed from past's
Restrictive shackles" – I presume
He meant those fetters forged and honed
By greatest masters of my art!
So do not claim you've not been warned.

As this compilation progressed it seemed to be more and more dominated by recurring references to my understanding of the Christian Gospel, to the extent that at times it seemed increasingly like a meandering sermon. An element of repetition results. I attempted some pruning, but it proved to be too difficult to decide as to what should go and what survive. I decided instead to leave readers to skip what they will. I will just add this quote from The Guardian: 'Most people ignore most poetry because most poetry ignores most people' (Adrian Mitchell). I hope my poems are not thus ignored!

CHAPTER 1

CHILDHOOD

My Family and Birth

My paternal grandfather was Henry William Disney, a lawyer, stipendiary magistrate and recorder judge. He died before my birth. My grandmother was Isabel Weymss Power, a headmistress and Scottish. My maternal grandfather was Hope Wadell Kelsall, a colonel in the Royal Engineers (in practice engaged in civil engineering building bridges in difficult mountainous terrain) in India and married to Jean Hope Mitchell. The Kelsalls and Mitchells are Scottish families, so I suspect I am three quarters Scottish. It is essentially only my surname that links me back to Norman forebears.

My parents were Anthony Weymss Moore Disney, who served in the Sudan for most of his career. He married Joan Hope Kelsall, (who was born in Burma) a maths teacher.

I was born on 27th December 1938 in the remote hamlet of Chalbury to the north of Wimborne Minster in Dorset. I was not intended to be born there. My mother had booked a quiet Christmas, away from the need for the normal business of Christmas, with the intention of returning to home in time for my expected arrival. However it snowed and the road out became hazardous. Consequently I was born in Chalbury.

I was named Ronald Henry Lambert. Ronald was after my mother's brother who had died in a riding accident when serving as an army officer in India. Henry recalled my deceased grandfather. Lambert refers to my remote ancestor who came from Normandy, from today's Ile d'Isigny. Following the conquest in 1066, he became Lord of the Manor of a village south of Lincoln, today known as Norton Disney. Surnames generally only gradually came into use in the 12th Century and initially referred to one's trade (baker, smith, tailor, etc.), a feature of one's appearance (short, etc.), place of origin or whatever. The surname did not necessarily imply heredity rather, as in the case of the Disneys, referred to the ancestor's origin before the Conquest. So the surname was initially more a clan name than necessarily implying immediate family. The surviving records refer to my ancestors being from d'Isigny, but being also written as De Isney and de Iseinni, before being contracted to Disney (see Hugh Disney, 2002. Disneys of Norton Disney 1150-1461. Hugh Disney, ISBN 0-9525908-1-6).

In Cromwell's time my ancestor (along with the ancestor of Walt Disney's branch of the clan) moved from Lincolnshire to Ireland.

Being three quarters Scottish (see above) means it is essentially only my surname that links me to the Disney clan. Whether I inherited any of Lambert's genes is highly questionable! One's ancestors may be of interest but, not as one or two of my relatives thought, a source of pride and an indication of 'superiority'!-

SHOULD I RETURN? (TL)

Decanting tube of insects sent
From garden in Zimbabwe's sun,
I soon delight in finding fly
That's undescribed, despite it seems
It's common there when fruits are ripe
And fall to ground to make a feast
For it to breed. But soon I think
My pleasure blind to pain that stalks
That land. Its crazed dictator adds
To fears that drought inflicts on those
To whom a daily meal becomes
The main concern as harvests fail.
He mouths his racist bile against
The farmers born and raised on land
Their forebears settled long ago.
Whatever crimes were then involved,
In stealing what was not for grabs,
Cannot condone Mugabe's thugs
In flouting law with bloodied hands.
When history's page is claimed to be
Enough to justify attacks,
That render brutes appear benign,
Then terror reigns. Should I return
To France from whence, in Norman times,
Ancestor came to seize some fields
A Saxon owned? The sins of past
Are no excuse for blaming those
Who now produce the crops that feed
A modern nation's needs. By slow
Degrees, within the law, the cake
With fairer cuts can be restored
To many hands devoid of blood.
For otherwise resentment thrives
And creeping trouble lies ahead

Awaiting chance to show its head.

1938-1957 – Childhood and Schooling.

My father worked in provincial government service in the Sudan. As the War progressed people left the service to join the war effort. My father's medical category was not eligible for conscription at that stage as he had lost his vision in one eye as a boy through an infection (there were no antibiotics then and the infection was prevented from spreading by the use of leeches to suck out the poison). Those remaining in the Sudan increasingly had to take on greater responsibilities. When returning from leave in 1942 my mother accompanied my father to help him with the move to offices in a new location and that covered a larger area of responsibility. The separation from her children for a time was not then perceived to be such an odd occurrence. Especially for someone like my mother, who was the daughter of parents serving in India. Indeed she had been packed off for schooling in England, and the care of an aunt, at an early age. The principal concern of my parents, therefore, was who would care for us during her absence. As my maternal grandmother in Broadstone (Dorset) was unable to help (the house being too small and my grandfather having Parkinson's disease) my mother left my older sister Katharine, myself and my younger sister, Diana, in the care of a Miss Wild in Wimborne Minster. Miss Wild was also providing similar temporary care for another family. The expectation was that both the mothers would return in a few months. However, while on the ship out the Government announced there would be no further such passages for families to and from Africa, as too many ships were being sunk by the German U-boats. So Miss Wild was stuck with us for the duration of the War. Subsequently we became the origins of a school started by Miss Wild – The Manor House School!

My Aunt Sheila, who was a teacher in a school on the edge of Cardiff, was nominated as my guardian in case of any crises needing referral by Miss Wild. Aunt Sheila was a formidable character. During air raids on Cardiff she drove ambulances at night. In the holidays she returned to her home (up a ladder to two rooms above today's boathouse at the quayside) in Overy Staithe on the north Norfolk coast. During these vacations in the War she helped out on a farm.

At Miss Wild's.

During the War I was the only boy of my age at Miss Wild's. Katharine made friends with Patricia, the daughter of the other family. Due to her age Diana needed constant care, mainly from what would now be called a nursery nurse. Katharine and I were old enough to feel the shock of being separated from our mother. Initially I was very weepy. I found myself often left to my own devices. It was thus I began an interest in natural history. Indeed on one

20

occasion I could not be found and panic ensued. Eventually I was discovered sitting among the cabbages watching the caterpillars chewing away. I kept collecting specimens – snail shells, odd stones, fir cones, etc. So Miss Wild emptied one of the cupboards on the landing and designated it my museum!

We made occasional visits to our maternal grandparents in Broadstone. An unexpected consequence was that she became upset at hearing me being called 'Ronnie', as it recalled the untimely death of Uncle Ronald. So it was agreed that in future I would be called by my second name – Henry. Very confusing! Still my two teddy bears remained as my constant companions at night! Not infrequently, however, they could not be found at bedtime as Katharine and her friend Patricia (the daughter of the other family left in Miss Wild's care) liked to tease by hiding them! They then blamed their disappearance on a flying monster called Shakay (= the 'sha' sound of Patricia and 'kay' from Kay, which was what many called Katharine) and they would point out the window to a distant black blob in the sky (a distant bird in reality)! Katharine later confessed that this teasing derived from having been told by our mother to "look after" me and her feeling of not being up to the task, as she felt she herself needed as much looking after when our mother departed for the Sudan. Miss Wild made sure we regularly 'contributed' to letters to our parents. But they steadily became a distant abstraction rather than real people.

When the Germans discovered that Poole Harbour (due south of Wimborne Minster) had acquired several additional jetties and had become a major refuelling station for ships, and that it was also a base for flying boats, they launched a series of bombing raids. When planes started coming our way we had to go to the Anderson shelter that had been constructed just beyond the front door. One night a plane that had been hit crashed into some trees just beyond the Manor House. It was decided to evacuate us to Devon until the raids on Poole Harbour abated. My abiding memory of this was banks of primroses beside the roads in Devon.

Another memory was the build up to D-Day. Lorries of equipment, tanks, etc. as well as allied soldiers from several nations streamed past the school gates. We quickly learned that if we smiled and waved at the Americans they would throw us sweets (candies)!

Towards the end of the War the food and clothes rationing became ever an increasing problem. Miss Wild insisted we all have an apple a day. One day she managed to procure some rice. This was made into a rice pudding, which was served as a great treat. I took one spoonful but ejected it with a grimace and declared I didn't like it. Miss Wild would have none of it and I was firmly told to stay at the table until I had eaten it all. I stubbornly resisted for most of the afternoon, but in the end grudgingly ate it up – slowly! On another occasion I wore through the seat of my much worn brown corduroy shorts. With insufficient coupons to procure a replacement Miss Wild contacted Aunt Sheila, who was on holiday at Overy Staithe at the time. She was a regular scourer of the high tide line on Scolt Head Island and frequently obtained items (such as a case of margarine on one occasion) from ships that had been casualties of the War. She was pondering Miss Wild's request for help when she came across a large bale of brand new brown corduroy washed up on the beach! I not only got a new pair of shorts but brown corduroy featured in a range of garments for several people! The other material that was increasingly made into items of clothing (especially under clothes) was discarded parachutes.

Reunion with parents.

After the war our Father transferred to the Political Service in Khartoum (eventually becoming Director of Economics and Trade). In August 1945 my parents returned from the Sudan on leave and I and my sisters were re-introduced to them as though they were strangers, along with our new sister Halcyon (born in Kenya in 1944). We stayed in temporary rented accommodation in rooms in a large country house. Here the gardener, discovering my interest in natural history, used to get me to sit quietly beside him and he would call birds to him and give them food. My increasing interest in natural history further manifested itself in that I started a collection of pressed wild flowers.

We embarked for the Sudan later in the year of 1946. This entailed flying in a converted Dakota bomber with wooden seats. We refuelled in the south of France and proceeded to Malta where we spent the night. Next day we flew on to Cairo where our plane journey terminated. After a day or two, during which we met up with a wealthy Egyptian family with whom we survived an interminable meal with too many courses and an excess of opulence. We also attended a lavish Egyptian wedding. The contrast with wartime rationing back home was astonishing. Furthermore the gap between the wealthy and the rest in Cairo was extreme at this time. This was strikingly illustrated by a parade of Egyptian soldiers we watched. It seemed one's rank was a function of one's girth. The privates were exceedingly thin but the general had such an enormous belly that he couldn't see his own toes! For me a most memorable sight was looking out of our hotel window onto a roof below where a pair of hoopoes had established their nest.

Leaving Cairo we went by steamer up the Nile until we reached the cataracts. Two memories stand out. A pair of wagtails had established a nest on the steamer. When they flew to the shore to forage for insects they had to frantically relocate the steamer after each excursion. Secondly we stopped off at Abu Simbel, which was then in its original location before its removal following the later development of Lake Nasser. This visit sparked off an interest in archaeology. At the cataracts we transferred to a train to Khartoum.

In the New Year my mother, my sisters and I returned to England. We stayed on a farm on the Dorset-Wiltshire border. On the farm I relished the animals and the country life. Instead of school our mother taught us at home.

One day I had the fright of my life. I was collecting mushrooms in a field when a large snorting bull came charging at me. I dropped the basket of mushrooms and did an Olympic level gate vault to exit the field! The bull did a flying leap over the hedge beside the gate. However, it had not realized that the hedge was atop a steep drop to the lane below. It landed with a tremendous thud on the lane and was clearly somewhat shaken. As it turned its head down the slope of the lane and started moving that way I raced off up the slope in the opposite direction. The bull was eventually recaptured in the main street of the nearby village!

We later moved to the Dorset village of Lytchett Matravers. Before returning to the Sudan my father had negotiated with the owner of an orchard in this village for the erection of a bungalow. The owner was a bricklayer and laid out the foundations. My further had bought a small wooden hut, a garage and a cricket pavilion. These were dismantled and reassembled as a bungalow – named Apple Orchard. In contrast to all mod cons in Khartoum, there were no mains supplies. Rainwater butts supplied water for washing. Baths were in water heated in a Calor gas copper and decanted into a metal bath tub. Cooking was by means of Calor gas and lighting by Calor gas, candles and paraffin lamps. Drinking water came from a well that the orchard owner had located at the bottom of the slope by water divination discovering an underground stream. In the great drought of 1948 only two wells in the village were still providing water – ours and that supplying the mediaeval village pump. The toilet was an Elsan bucket system which was emptied onto a heap beside the vegetable garden, the contents covered with a layer of soil and a layer of bracken (it being one of my chores to collect the bracken). The following year the well-rotted heap provided excellent manure for growing potatoes.

In the summer term of 1947 I attended the village school in Lytchett Minster. Mixing with other boys of my age was a novel experience. My principal memory of this episode is of the playground being divided down the middle with separate halves (and doors) for boys and girls!

In the summer holiday we helped out at harvest time by gathering sheaves for stooking (combined harvesters not yet being part of the farm machinery) and by gleaning spilled grain, as with rationing still in force waste was not acceptable.

1947-1953 – Boarding Schools

In the autumn of 1947 I was dispatched to boarding school – The Dragon School in Oxford. After gradually getting to know my parents again since 1946 this came as a shock. This manifested itself in that for the first year I came bottom of the class in all subjects! Furthermore, despite there being a few girls (mainly sisters of some of the boys) at the school, I was now suddenly surrounded by boys by day and at night for the first time in my life. While there had been mild teasing at Miss Wild's, some boys at the Dragon went further.

The teachers seemed largely unaware that bullying and physical assault were not infrequent. My poem LOVE WITHHELD (TL) incorporates the following true episode based on my own experience:

LOVE WITHHELD (TL)

As babe neglect was what he knew;
And thus he early learned to stare
But make no sound. As lad his lack
Of height had picked him out in eyes
Of bigger bully boys, until his life
Was hell. His temper's fuse now shrank
Until the day they'd knocked him down
And piled upon his prostrate form
In heap. He bit the nearest leg
To hand. The largest jackal's yelp
Unmasked their yellow fear. They fled.
And from that day a wary pack
Engaged in war of taunts instead.
It's thus he'd learned to walk alone.

See also my poem EXCLUDED below. Furthermore some teachers maintained discipline by means now forbidden. The use of a cane or a strap across the hands was employed on occasions. One teacher hurled a wooden backed blackboard rubber at you if he thought you were not paying attention. It certainly hurt if it found its target. The result of these unpleasant experiences was to channel my energies and emotions more strongly into my spare-time activities.

The contrast with the caring set up at Miss Wild's resulted in a growing shyness and reluctance to follow the crowd. A similar friend had an aunt who lived in north Oxford and we used to visit her on Sunday afternoons for tea and listening to gramophone records, requiring regular manual winding up. Also the steel needles needed frequent replacement.

Natural history became an ever more important interest. Indeed I was eventually nominated as the boy curator of the little natural history museum in the school. I also took on a small patch of garden. Indeed I won a prize for the result.

GROWING UP (TL)

At school I had a tiny patch
Of earth to cultivate as I
Would wish. I nursed a range of plants,
From leeks to lilies. Ordered ranks
And lack of weeds proclaimed my care.
I won a prize, and preened my pride.
Today our garden's scene of war,
As thistles, nettles, ragwort thrive
Along with random growth of blooms
We'd carefully sown in hope.
A jungle's come to town. It seems
Our youthful dreams of ordered life
Have suffered just the same. But look!
Our present garden's much more fun,
And many weeds are little gems.
Perhaps we should accept control
Is out of reach and come to terms
With what we get when good intent
Is mixed with other wilful ways -
As when we raised our kids and found
Them straying from our dreams but still
A source of strange delight and love.

One day I was cycling with two companions along the main highway towards the city centre when one boy suddenly swerved towards me causing me to fall sideways onto the road. As I started to get ready to get up a passing car missed my head by less than a foot!

I was late in learning to swim, as I tended to suffer inflammation in my ears that was aggravated if I got water down them. Indeed when on holiday in the Sudan one Christmas I had to be admitted to Khartoum Hospital with acute ear inflammation. My principal memory of this episode was of a friendly Sudanese boy of about my age who was employed to sweep the ward each day. When he discovered me trying to do a 1000 piece jigsaw puzzle he did his sweeping in an extra fast time and then sat on my bed and we tackled the puzzle together. However, after a day or two when we were getting on fine a supervisor intervened and ordered the lad to get back to work. I thought he should have been congratulated for taking my mind off the pain in my ears!

After acquiring earplugs I started to learn to swim. The teacher had been an NCO in the Boer War. His method was unusual. He had what looked like a very robust fishing rod with a belt instead of the hook. One strapped the belt round one's waist and jumped in the river Cherwell while the ex-soldier bore one's weight. When one had progressed he inserted a wedge at the back of the belt so one could not tell when he was not bearing one's weight. He would then announce "well done lad, you just did three lengths without me taking any of your weight"!

Following the birth of my brother John in 1948 our father acquired a redundant box-shaped army signaller's caravan that was supported on concrete pillars. It became my bedroom and in due course that for John as well.

Holidays took on a typical pattern of mother being home for the Easter holiday in the early years and for the summer holidays, Christmas being in the Sudan (although one year I was with my Godfather).

1953-1957

In the autumn of 1953 I moved on to Marlborough College in Wiltshire. The following year rationing (begun during the War in 1940) finally ended!

Now that I was a little older Easter holidays were usually spent with my Aunt Sheila on the Norfolk coast. As she lived up a ladder in two rooms above the boathouse by the quayside she could not take us when we had been still too young. Also a rule of hers was that each day we must bring in free fuel and/or food. Firewood and well-washed coal were all collected from the tide line on Scolt Head Island. Free food included winkles, cockles, shrimps and flat fish. To catch the latter at low tide one walked steadily back and forth in large shallow sandy pools until one felt a fish under a foot. Instead of leaping back one pressed down firmly and then reached down and picked the fish up behind its gills. She also not only taught me to row and sail in tidal waters but she strongly encouraged my interest in natural history.

Aunt Sheila organized the annual regatta at Overy Staithe. I used to enter the rowing race as the tide was coming in fast past the quay. Having rowed the course many times I had got to know the quirks of the currents and back eddies and so usually did better for my age than some of the village lads. The last time I entered a loud-mouthed local youth boasted that no one had a chance against him. As the races started from anchor I shortened my rope to just a fraction more than the depth, with the result that with one jerk my anchor was up and I was well away while boaster was still hauling away, hand over hand, before he had recovered his anchor. The result was that I won! I was later to employ this incident in my long poem SECRET EDDIES (see chapter 10).

In addition to natural history, archaeology was increasingly engaging my interest. In the spring and autumn terms I regularly cycled off on free afternoons to the site of a Roman town of CVNETIO at Blackfields, Mildenhall and methodically walked up and down the furrows of the freshly ploughed field. I collected fragments of Roman pottery and glass, bits of bronze jewellery and ornaments, a spindle weight and a gaming counter. I was particularly pleased with more than a dozen coins including some of Galienus and Constantine and with one of the latter in almost mint condition. All the specimens were donated to the College's small museum. Stimulated by these finds in one holiday I took part as a volunteer in an excavation at the classic Roman site of Verulamium near St Albans.

EXCLUDED (CW)

When site of ancient Roman town
Is ploughed each year he works the field
With eager eye. Each furrow's scanned
In turn and slowly haul of shards,
Of coins, bits of brooches, nails
And bones are bagged. Indoors he scrubs
And cleans each piece with care and then
Displays his finds in ordered rows
On beds of cotton wool. His mind
Is host to legions marching forth
To quell the warring Scots or hordes
Of cattle thieves. He often dreams
In class of far off times, but lags
Behind in maths. But teachers fail
To understand it's through his strong
Obsession with the past he copes
With sense of being on his own.
Entrapped in private school, in which
His parents threw him as of old
The Christian martyrs found themselves
In circus faced with roaring beasts,
He's bullied by the bigger boys
At first; before he lashes out
Inflicting wound on worst of bunch.
So since, he's seen as loony crank
Who's left alone, outside the pack
Of circling wolves who rule the range.
Their single selves become submerged
In yes-man mien, while lonesome cat
Becomes a man with focussed aims.

Compulsory afternoons of games were part of the programme. With rugby football I got something of a reputation for aggressive energy. I usually played in the second row of the scrum. I think the aggressive component was an unspoken statement that I was not to be messed with! With regard to cricket it was another story. After exchanges such as "Why didn't you try to stop that ball?" and my response "Sorry, I was intrigued by a spider with her egg sac"; I was exempted from cricket and with another boy, who was too short sighted for cricket, we were allowed to cycle off in pursuit of natural history instead.

During the summer term of 1953 I excavated an old well at Panterwick near Marlborough. It had been filled in with rubbish during the 17th to early 19th Century. It yielded pottery and bottles (one labelled WM 1713), iron and other metal objects such as knives, pins, thimbles, hooks, buckles, etc. In particular it yielded a rich collection of the bowls and pieces of stem with maker's mark of clay tobacco pipes dating from about 1600 to early 19th Century (see Witheridge, A. G., 1956, Report of the Marlborough College Natural History Society for 1947-1955, : 96). In the summer holidays of 1953 and 1955 I was a volunteer in the excavation of Bronze Age barrows at Snail Down in Wiltshire.

In the Christmas holiday of 1954, in the Sudan, early in January I joined a trip organized from the Museum in Khartoum, to excavate the Coptic church and monastic buildings, dating from around 900 A.D., at Ghazali. Instead of following the River Nile where it sweeps in a great loop to the East we drove straight across in a straight line heading North to Merowe. We camped half way on folding camp beds open to the night sky. From the heat of the desert by day the temperature dropped many degrees to give a decidedly chilly night. However, never before or since have I experienced such a wonderful display of the stars, planets and meteors away from any light pollution on earth; as I later recollected in the following poem:

AWESOME NIGHT (RE)

Beneath a counterpane of stars
So clear and bright I feel both low
And lifted up as I recline
On folding bed in desert night.
The burning fires of midday sun
Are now replaced by chill so sharp
It brings recall of childhood's thrill
On winter's day when all was still
With frost, whose silent spell insists
We marvel at the magic scene.
Too soon the dawn awakes and noise
Begins to ripple through our camp
As bustle slow returns to drag
Us back to here and now. Perhaps
We need to glimpse a desert sky
At night to see ourselves aright,
As tiny specks within a vast
Expanse of universe. And yet
We're called to transmute awe and angst

To love that raises souls to realms
Beyond the reach of furthest stars,
As inner light defies both death
And sense we're all alone, bereft
Of hope. That tiny spark of grace
Within is worth entire embrace
Of all that's seen or just inferred
Of wondrous spread of time and space
And diverse creatures they have spawned,
Including selves who hear the call
To rise above our lowly births.

At Merowe we spent time in the wonderful, and too little known, Museum. It is dominated by the imposing polished black statue of Tirhaqa, the Sudanese pharaoh who ruled the entire length of the Nile. We also visited the Sanum Temple near Merowe, which was used by the Napatan kings. Both visits extended my appreciation of a culture related to, but differing from, the better known Egyptology. We then proceeded to Ghazali. The excavation got under way. When I removed the soil from a wall it revealed that it was covered in murals overlaid by a paper thin layer of later paint. I then found myself with the painstaking task of carefully using a pin to remove this overlay in order to reveal the earlier monastic paintings beneath. Regretfully I had to leave the team at it and was taken to Karina to catch the train back to Khartoum in order to prepare for the flight back to England and school.

Twice my father took me on walking and camping holidays on my own. He was, however (I realized in retrospect) trying to forge a closer relationship with me. The trip to the Black Mountains in South Wales to Llanthoni Priory in the Vale Ewyas, where, as a boy, he had been with his own father, was not a success. His endless talk of his warm relationship with his own father only served to highlight the contrast with our own cooler relationship. This was further indicated by the fact that I had brought a book on ferns with me, having read that the damp climate of Wales favoured these plants. Indeed I was eagerly ticking off species as we found them in the wild. However, instead of using a shared search for yet further species for my list of finds as a means of getting closer to me he seemed irritated by this 'diversion'!

A second trip was walking much of the Dorset coast. For me the attraction was the birds and the variety of fossils evident in the sequence of different rocks we encountered. The lack of reference to his father made for an easier atmosphere. It took time, over many years, for us to form a more relaxed relationship. Indeed it was following my marriage to Audrey that mutual acceptance of each other as being different in outlook and temperament was no barrier to mutual respect and affection.

During the holidays in Dorset my interest in Archaeology grew. I looked for artefacts wherever we went. For example I presented some flint implements, including a fine barbed and tanged flint arrow head of the Bronze

Age, to the Poole Museum (see 1956, Proceedings of the Dorset Natural History and Archaeological Society 76: 5).

During the summer term of 1955 I carried out an excavation at the western edge of the Mound in the middle of the college grounds. A brief report was published (1957, Report of the Marlborough College Natural History Society 97: 13-14). The oldest artefacts obtained were fragments of Norman pottery.

The teaching of physics and maths were not strong points at the college. There were two maths teachers who unnerved one for entirely different reasons. One was a first class mathematician but found it difficult to get down to the level of those not gifted mathematically. For example, he would be working through equations on the blackboard when suddenly the numbers all changed. When a boy asked how this had happened he replied that he had just turned the numbers into logs. When the boy responded 'but you didn't use the log tables' he replied that you don't need tables; one just converts the numbers in one's head! The other maths teacher when expounding algebra had the habit of dealing with one's errors by issuing a piece of graph paper whose area was related to the magnitude of one's perceived error. One's task was then to put a full stop in every small square on this sheet! I filled many such sheets. However, he was known to be rather fond of alcoholic refreshment. One day we got our own back when a boy rushed in just before class and reported that he had just spotted the approaching teacher who seemed to be slightly tipsy. So we set all the lights swinging in unison just as he was about to enter the classroom and we all swayed from side along with the lights. The teacher took one look at the swinging lights and boys. Muttering an oath, he declared he was not feeling well, told us to study a chapter in the textbook and then hastily retreated!

The physics teacher in the run up to physics GCE 'O' Level drilled us with definitions and passages to be learned by heart. His intent was clearly to prepare us for the exam. When we had an end of term exam I handed in the following postscript to my paper:

ELEMENTARY PHYSICS AT SCHOOL

I wish this subject wasn't dull;
I wish I wasn't quite so bored;
I wish this subject didn't lull
Me so. I snore and snore. A horde
Of formulae are milling round
And round inside my head;
If only Ohm had gone and drowned
Himself, his Joules and also Stead*.

*The author of our physics textbook.

To my surprise I received the following response from the master marking my script.

> The railway train, the I.C.E.,
> The pump that fills the swimming pool,
> The radio, and I.T.V..
> We owe them all to Watt and Joule,
> Volta, Faraday, and Ohm.
> These men, whose intellects have soared,
> Like Newton, Ampere, Coulomb, Boyle,
> Einstein, Thomson, Rutherford,
> Their lives devoted to the cause,
> By year on year of patient toil
> Revealed to us fair Nature's laws.
> They rest in heaven: their reward?
> They strove in vain, for D——'s bored!
> M.P.F

I was not only surprised to receive this, I was left wondering why we hadn't been taught about all these great people and how they came to their new insights.

I was even more surprised when I was summoned by my housemaster, who was brandishing my offending piece of doggerel in one hand and a cane in the other hand. He was proposing to thrash me for impudence. However, when I produced the above response I had received he was left nonplussed and handing it back to me, ordered me to get out! He had previously thrashed me for declining an invitation to tea with the House Matron. I had declined because I had already promised a friend I would operate the epidiascope for him when he was to give a talk to the Arts Society at the same time as the proposed tea. I did not understand why I had to be thrashed for this 'offence'. I had not realized that an invitation from the Matron was like a Royal Command that automatically took precedence over any prior commitment. I was not invited to tea with Matron again. My housemaster seemed to me to be primarily concerned with outward conformity to the conventions of behaviour expected of a Public School boy of the time. He seemed unaware that I, and several other boys, had been traumatized by our separation from our parents during the War.

CAST ASIDE (GK)

> A boy is left behind, when war
> Disrupts his parents' plans, along
> With sisters too – despite the fact
> That all are under six. It's thus
> The lonesome soul begins to grow;

Defying world in thought, in word
And deed. According to the shrinks
He should be up the wall, if not
Completely mad. But no, it's forged
Him man of steel who sets his eye
On goals ahead; who will not budge
From course he's set. Perhaps it's thus
Redemption worked its way. But why
Do some who suffered same neglect
End up delinquents lost to love
And joy? Perhaps a silent rage
Had kept him sane, or so it seemed.
Beneath the surface calm the flow
Of molten magma bided time.
A fickle faith had kept the lid
On boiling scene below until
The fluid slowly cooled to form
Enduring crystals in his rock
That glint and gleam when brought to light
Of day. The blinkered shrinks had missed
Their way when God was cast aside.
Their channelled views ignored the grace
At work through love of those who cared
About eccentric man that boy became.
For neither genes nor nurture rules
When Holy Spirit intervenes.

A school report from this time observed "if he devoted as much energy to his classroom work as he does to his spare time activities he might progress"!

1955: 8 GCE 'O' Levels (English Language, English Literature, French, Latin, Maths, English History, Chemistry, Physics with Chemistry).

I had started to learn the clarinet at the Dragon School and progressed to more advanced lessons at Marlborough. However, the teacher eventually advised me to give it up as it turned out I had poor auditory discrimination such that I could not tell whether a note was sharp or flat. When my hearing was further impaired by a couple of terrorist bombs (see chapter 2) the situation was made worse. It has been one of the regrets of my life that music did not mean more to me. This was emphasized when I married Audrey, who was an accomplished pianist and was always singing around the house. However, the English Literature teacher sparked an interest in poetry, which became the art that I took to with enthusiasm. He introduced us to the poems of Sorley, who is best remembered as one of the First World War poets, but as an old boy of Marlborough College had written poems about the Marlborough countryside.

It was these that, at the time, I relished. Furthermore they induced me to start writing poems myself.

ENCOUNTERING WILD CREATURES (MC)

Dampness drips from every frond. Gleaming wet.
The trunks and soggy earth so colourful
And so strangely wrapped in silence, despite
The loudly splashing rain. How pitiful
I feel beneath this drenching canopy
Of dank leafage. Rounding a prickly shrub
I stop still. There (beneath a tree) with back
To me – a squirrel digging near a stub
Of rotting wood. Soon it unearths a hoard
Of hazel nuts. I slightly shifted. Round
He whirls and stares at me. I hold his gaze
With mine – a timeless moment. With one bound
He reached the nearby trunk and, clinging fast
He looks me up and down – but I remain
Entranced. Impatiently he eyes me. Rain
Has dissolved his fear. And still there is rain.
Slowly it wanes. Trees give way to scrub. Clouds
Disperse as light leaks through. The turf and tall
Spiky thistle stems glisten as the shrouds
Are hauled from the sun. The rooks now call
And acrobat with jackdaws in the air.
A living restless calm is everywhere.
Between the tufts of wiry grass is seen
A way, a disused path no longer trod
By man. I knew that's where a way once ran,
It's only there the daisies (blessed by God)
Have grown. It's only they who use that track.
I pace along the verge with reverence
For such a sight. I stroll on. Facing back,
Some yards beyond, I pause – then climb the fence.
The daisies lost to view, I stand to stare
Across the open fields which now seem bare,
As the rolling downs sweep on before my eyes
While the springy turf is a boundless sea.
The breeze is chiding stray clouds across the skies.
Is that a speck I see above that tree?
That's a fact. Look! It quivers like a lark.
But no lark is as large. It slides, he slips
Towards the ground. Kestrel! No longer dark

Your rusty back and pointed wings whose tips
Are black, I see. He's up again with head
To wind. He hovers, soars, and glides. Again
He hovers – motionless. He drops, as dead
He falls. He's gone and only I remain:
Suddenly aware once more of myself
And the sombre, sad substance of my soul.
I am plunged earthwards into that intense
Personal world which seems, at times, the whole
Of reality, and yet seems to be
Fearfully separate from the fabric
Of the actual. This phenomenon
Of Homo sapiens. Weird cerebric
Energies welled forth from the womb of life.
The primordial protoplasmic mass
Aimlessly undulating o'er silent
Sea floors, with yearning beauties of a lass,
Or the terrifying powers of thought
As yet unleashed from this strange origin.
Magnificent, creative defiance
Of Time's erosion. Emerged from within
A great unfurling process. He's aware.
Became conscious. Has eaten of that fruit.
The fruit of the tree yielding knowledge. Good
And evil. This man free to prostitute
Or fulfil his destiny. My soul sways
Like a vast towering thing on a loose
Foundation. I turn from contemplation
Of natural creatures and I induce
Myself to behold huge buildings, huge schemes
And giant systems which crack and bring, upon
Their fashioners, disaster and wide wastes
Of disintegrating decay. I con
Insane, disorganized stupidity
Of persons who let themselves be told
What to do, what to think, by hypocrites.
But then I seem to see myself, when old
And sick with scurvy of the soul, the same.
Time smothering like an evil black fog,
As the autumnal blight of our hard won
Security settles. As we now jog
Along locked up in the sad psychoses
Of ourselves, prepared only for the grave.
Like mayfly swarms emerging from a stream
To allow internal drives to enslave;

As flying at the lamp, they drop with more
To lie there dead, or dying, on the floor.

When will we cease to follow our old trails?
Sadd'ning pressures to satisfy desire
For comfort, desire for significance,
For admiration and love. What foul mire
Clings to us? Why do pathological,
Hearty priests present the challenge of Christ
As a sugared pill – a do-it-yourself
Psychiatry? We have to be enticed
Today. To challenge is a sin today.
Where is that mythic mediaeval dame
I met in a book, I encountered in dreams?
Naïve she was. Simple. Slowly she came.
"O ancient woman with deep sunk eyes,
So filled with earnestness, beneath hair
So black that it seems moist and aflame
With the glow of the low red sun, where
Are you bound? And why the burning brand,
Why the pail of water in your hand?"
"I'm tired of seeing the Christ held up
Like a new product for washing souls,
By those who preach – without Him you will
Burn in brimstone lakes of white-hot coals,
Seething, fuming pitch and endless fire.
Hell with meaningless dark depths of dire
Dismay. Hell with no purpose – no aim.
Or else advertising heaven like
A holiday resort – dangling bait
Before our eyes – just waiting to strike
And count us in their catch. I intend,
Therefore, to quench every fire in hell
With my pail of water: with my torch
Of flame, I'll set alight and I'll fell
The walls of heaven. So God will then
Be sought – for Himself alone – by men."
I smile upon this large floppy woman.
She seems to dispel the stale fusty smell
Of inactive air. Release choking chains
Of restrictive morality. The swell
Of melancholy musings subsides.
I am coming up from a deep cavern
Underground, where there is nothing but dense
Darkness and moist stone; and a strange pattern

Of mental meanderings which rush forth
In torrents of complex conversation
When I am confronting somebody else.
Now only a calm, puzzling sensation.
I hear the lapwing's mocking mournful cry
Above my head. I halt. There at my feet
A caterpillar crawls along the ground.
His furry back and ginger flanks are neat
And clean – his skin is new. His back is crowned
With hairs, both long and grey, which catch the sun.
I pick him up and take him on my run.

The 'religious' element in this poem is clearly somewhat naïve but reflects my new embrace of the Gospel (see below) coupled with a distaste for simplistic, almost fundamentalist, elements in too many sermons (attendance at the College chapel being compulsory). The observations of nature are clearly the better component of this early, over long, poem! To some extent it sets the agenda for the eventual maturation of my faith as it is gradually stripped of second-hand accretions obscuring the gold of the Gospel. However it was to take the trauma of my experience in the army inducing a period of atheism merging into a stage of agnosticism as I gradually found my way back to an abiding faith in Christ (see chapters 2 and 3). Otherwise, my growing fascination with natural history was laying the foundation of a career as a professional naturalist. Thus this early poem is pointing to two primary obsessions of my life ahead. The essentially missing component (apart from hints such as "yearning beauties of a lass") is with regard to the discovery of life enhancing relationships with other people. However, this was the stage of my life when I was obliged to live in a male dominated boarding school in the run up to puberty. Such a situation tends to accentuate the normal stage of development when typically one prefers the company of members of one's own sex before one proceeds to an infatuation with the opposite sex. However, some find their homosexual phase not only prolonged but it becomes a permanent state; or else some end up in a perpetual oscillation between attractions to both sexes. It seems a frequent contributor to a failure to proceed to becoming a mature heterosexual adult can be such an artificial system of separation from one's home for much of the year. Furthermore, a curious culture prevalent in these single sex boarding communities was that it was regarded as inappropriate (indeed 'stupid') to let one's parents know that one was far from happy with this situation. While it is natural for a teenager to refrain from telling their parents about some of what they get up to (as they develop their own sense of independence), the culture of the school tended to progressively introduce a reticence with regard to what they would like to share with them.

In my case I experienced a brief stage when I was infatuated, at a distance, with a younger boy with a strangely beautiful face. This phase was almost abruptly terminated one night when a brazenly homosexual boy climbed into my bed and tried to indulge in intimate sexual relations. I was repelled. Incidentally, many years later I unexpectedly heard from him who had been that boy, who wanted to know if I would be interested in sharing a homosexual relationship with him. He was evidently disappointed to find I was happily married (I hope he eventually formed a partnership based on mutual affection, as he was essentially a kind hearted individual).

My switch to being fascinated by girls was essentially all in the mind as my shyness, induced by my experience in the War, persisted until much later (see chapters 2 and 3). Furthermore, the smutty jokes and pausing to ogle pictures of naked or scantily clad young women in magazines was a regular part of the everyday behaviour of the teenage boys at my school. I suspect that most, like myself, dare not admit that we found this all somewhat tiresome. Indeed in terms of leading on to a genuine relationship it was as a thirsty man pointing to a mirage ahead knowing it was not leading to a quenching of that thirst. The discovery of genuine loving relationships will normally lead to all such juvenilia being forgotten. I have, sadly, subsequently encountered a few for whom their immature, teenage perception of the opposite sex has persisted into their middle age or beyond.

The Final Two Years at School.

I carried out a project on snails in a stream on the water meadows by the river. This was a project for A Level Zoology. It was later published (Disney, R. H. L. 1958. Snails in the Marlborough Watermeadows. Report of the Marlborough College Natural History Society 98: 24-28 (1957)).

During one holiday when I was a sixth former, I attended a church in Poole where there was a relay of a Billy Graham rally. For the first time I began to grasp the unique significance of Christ's crucifixion and the overwhelming significance of Easter. I started to take Christianity seriously. However, both the befriender assigned to me and my parents assumed I had swallowed hook line and sinker the Billy Graham package. On the contrary, his repeated use of the phrase "the Bible says" struck me as stupid. He might as well have said "the library says"! When in 2013, as a long-time supporter of the Church Mission Society, I was subjected to an interview by e-mail and I was asked the question "How did you first encounter Jesus and what led you to follow him?" I referred to the Billy Graham rally and added my caveat regarding "the Bible says". I was amused to read the published version of this interview (Connect, CMS, Summer 2013 page 5) in which my caveat had been omitted!

My enthusiastic commitment to the Gospel sustained me through the difficult trauma of my National Service prior to the period of atheism it precipitated (see chapters 2 and 3). My recovery of faith was a prolonged struggle during my time as an undergraduate.

THE LEAP (RE)

As kids we climbed a sycamore
That strode above a tangled growth
Of rhododendrons dark and still.
With whoops of glee we launched ourselves,
From dizzy sunlit boughs, to land
In springy twigs that underlay
A coverlet of shiny leaves.

In youth a preacher ploughed my heart
When I had climbed a sycamore
Zacchaeus shared with me. And down
We plunged in eager joy to meet
Our Lord. A jungle growth of shrubs
And weeds arose from seeds that fell
Upon my empty earth that day.

Today I lean against that tree
With gleaming cutlass in my hand.
The rhododendrons all have gone.
The cherished hazels all are pruned.
I scan the bluebells round our feet.
I heed the light now leaping through
The springtime leaves where once I flew.

1957: GCE 'A' Levels (Zoology, Botany, Modern History). These secured
a place at Sidney Sussex College, Cambridge in order read Archaeology in
1959, following my National Service.

Having procured my ticket to university I have subsequently wondered
about how much had been at the expense of a true education. In later retrospect
my spare time interests proved to be more relevant to my career. My time in
the army (chapter 2) taught me more about getting on with all sorts of people
and about coping with adversity and the unforeseen.

EDUCATION (RE)

When boy he built himself a bike
From parts of older models left
To rot. It lacked that touch of style
Of those displayed in shops. To him
It was a thing of pride and joy;
And when he took it for its first

38

Of many rides he felt as free
As seagull soaring high above
A cliff as wind is thrust aloft
In great updraft that bird delights
In riding like a kite, before
It banks and glides to skim the waves,
Returning once again to base
Of rock to rise again at ease.
That bike became the means by which
He got away from troubled home
And bully louts at school. He sailed
For miles along the downs and lanes
Through woods and fields of corn or cows.
He taught himself the names of birds
And plants he found, by means of books
He bought from local Oxfam shop.
He kept a log of all his trips,
With lists of things he'd seen. Today,
When looking back on these escapes,
He claims they taught him more than all
The roller coaster chop and change
Of classroom work to make him what
He's now become – renowned in realms
Of scholarship across the globe.

CHAPTER 2

MILITARY SERVICE

1957-1959 National Service in the Royal Artillery

Naïve and still over shy, I had hardly left school when I received my call up papers. I was to report for basic training at Oswestry in Shropshire on the 15th of August. I was to be under orders for the next two years. Little did I imagine the diversity of experiences ahead and variety of people I was to encounter for good or ill. I was, unknowingly, embarking upon the most transforming phase of my education.

In terms of how we respond to people and events I believe we possess free will, despite clever, but unconvincing, denials by some philosophers. Being under orders for two years was a chastening experience but, despite unforeseen events, I endeavoured to remain true to my deepest convictions that included a belief that I possessed freedom as to how I respond to adverse events. At times I wondered if this conviction was a delusion, but only briefly when under stress. "We must believe in free will. We have no choice" Isaac Bashevis Singer (2014, quoted on TheBrowser.com)! Joking aside, Insofar as we exercise our free will we affirm our humanity.

FREE WILL (MC)

Our genes are recipes for selves
As long as oven's not too hot
And timing's right. Because our mums
And dads are learning on the job,
And other folk are dodgem cars
Beyond control, we find we reach
The day for leaving school as fudge
Of what we're meant to be, along
With load of foreign filth acquired
En route. But I can still employ
The paring knife, and still I'm free
To choose my future way within
Confines of circumstance. It's thus

The law can blame me if I go
Astray, or those above reward
Your triumphs with a prize; and Freud
Can pack his bag of phoney drives
He offers us as quack excuse.
I'm only human insofar
As will controls and love becomes
My goal. Authentic growth derives
From being true to inner light,
Plus honest confrontation's role
In chaining baser feelings so
They do no harm, but let me know
They're still alive. It's thus they serve
To keep my pride at bay. At least
It's thus I hope I may become,
Before my journey's done. Amen.

Basic training as a Technical Assistant Royal Artillery, Oswestry

We were all trained on 25 pounder guns and I was trained as a technical assistant (plotting targets, calculating angles of gun elevation, etc. – this being before the advent of pocket calculators, let alone portable computers, the Internet or SatNav). We were also required to be smart at all times and our beds made up in a precise way. Bullshit was the order of the day. Indeed it exceeded common sense when the annual brigadier's inspection was coming up.

HARVESTS (TL)

My sergeant made a garden grow
On piece of wasteland next the store
For weapons meant for war. But time
For yearly audit came. Before
That day, the paint and polish strove
To change the outward show of things.
The sergeant major cursed and swore
At men who raced around in rings.
He came to sergeant's patch of plants.
Disorder reigned! With pegs and twine
He made a grid. Condemned were vegs
He found to be away from line.
The favoured few survived in ranks.
In gardens God allows its weeds
Alone he casts aside. His blooms
Arise from freely scattered seeds.

41

It's thus we find each garden stands
Unique, embraced by loving hands.

Those of us with GCE 'O' levels or above were put in for Unit Selection Board for potential officers. If passed one would be sent to a War Office Selection Board prior to being sent to Officer Cadet School. The USB process involved interviews with officers, one's scores on one's trade tests, reports by one's NCOs and squad officer, and a final interview with the Commanding Officer. All seemed to be going well for me until the interview with the CO. He shuffled the papers in my file before he looked up and declared that I was just the sort of person the army did not want. When I chose to put my mind to things I did well, as indicated by my trade test scores, but my behaviour and bloody-minded attitude were intolerable. The idea of making me an NCO was laughable and as for an officer that was out of the question. I was taken aback! I said I did not know what he was talking about. So he started reading out excerpts from the report of the NCOs. I said that I did not recognize that as being applicable to me. He responded that my reply confirmed my bloody-mindedness. I weakly replied that I believed I had a right of appeal if I considered the report unfair and inaccurate. I thought he was going to explode. He angrily replied that he could not deny me such an appeal but assured me that he would ignore its findings. By appealing I merely confirmed my reported lack of respect for those in authority. In a state of shock I was then dismissed.

The CO's Dalmatian dog was called Tito!

I returned to my barrack and was assiduously polishing my boots when the Bombardier came in. "You look a bit down in the dumps. What's up?" I told him about my interview with the CO. "The Sergeant and I didn't write that for you. We wrote that for Bracey" he said. The two reports must have got transposed in error, with Bracey and Disney being the same length and both ending in 'ey'. He added that he would go and find the Sergeant and get this sorted out.

Bracey was a character, very funny at times but he regarded the army as a huge joke. He was the only member of the squad to acquire his own copy of Queen's Regulations, which he used to study in bed. He enjoyed seeing how close to the line he could go without crossing it. In addition he was a gifted all round sportsman. He relied on the latter gift to get himself on a sports fixture whenever we had a tough cross-country exercise or whatever. He was the bane of the NCOs.

The Bombardier returned sometime later to report that unfortunately the Sergeant had gone on leave two hours ago. He may need to wait till he returned.

A little later I was put before an Appeal Panel of three majors and grilled. Some days later I was called off the parade ground and told to report to the Squad Officer in the office. I knocked and entered. The officer was on the phone so I started to back out but he motioned to me to enter. On putting down the phone his first question was significant. "Who are you?" Now everyone knew Bracey! Anyway he told me that the Appeal Panel had recommended that

I be sent to WOSB. So I asked would the CO be agreeing with this recommendation. The gist of his reply was that he was due his assessment for promotion next week and did not wish to have to tell the CO that it seems he might have made a mistake when, having countersigned the NCOs reports, he had placed two in the incorrect files (with one being labelled BRACEY and one labelled DISNEY)! He assured me that the Appeal Panel's report was in my file so I was not to worry.

I was dispatched to Woolwich for a 'punishment posting' on active service in Cyprus. Bracey was sent to WOSB and rejected.

I went by troop ship to Cyprus. It was an irksome trip as I discovered I was unusually prone to sea-sickness, especially when traversing the Bay of Biscay.

With 39 Heavy Field Regiment
(acting as infantry) on active service in Cyprus.

On arrival in Cyprus I was summoned by the CO. He had my file in front of him and told me that if it was a correct assessment he did not want me in his regiment as unreliable soldiers were not acceptable when on active service. I explained what had happened. He said that he was inclined to believe me and would give me three months to live up to the sort of character I had given him of myself. He was as good as his word. In three months he ditched my file and promoted me to Lance Bombardier. However, I had been assigned to H Troop, which included the regiment's troublesome characters and a troop sergeant with a reputation for being well capable of handling such.

My mates were clearly intrigued by me as being a mixture of naivety but evidently educated, in terms of having GCE A Levels, to a higher standard than themselves. They took it upon themselves to 'educate' me in the ways of the **** world! My naivety caused them great amusement. For example they took me to a 'bar' one day and we sat at a table with our drinks. One by one my companions disappeared upstairs, returning some time later with satisfied looks on their faces. It slowly dawned on me that they were visiting prostitutes upstairs! Their merriment erupted when I declined the offer to ascend the stairs in my turn! On the other hand, when there were just two of us on guard duty or whatever at night, they would quietly confess they were ashamed of some of their behaviour when away from their families at home. Because I did not condemn them, but just listened, they felt at ease with me. Also they appreciated some of the things I did for them. For example I discovered that most were sending socks home to be darned when they developed holes in the heels. It was in the days when the socks were of wool and before the throw away instead of mend culture had arrived. I had brought with me one of those devices comprising a wooden mushroom surrounded by a set of warp and woof hooks that allowed one to weave a new heel over a hole in a sock. I soon had them sitting on their beds mending their socks for themselves! I also got them reading books by signing for a trunk of assorted books from the Education Corps. Some had never read a novel in their life before.

I was gradually accepted as another, albeit odd, mate. For my part I discovered that on active service the bonds forged with the most unlikely people were difficult to explain to those who had not experienced active service. We one and all would do anything for our mates if danger threatened or struck. For example some unexpected impediment in the road (placed there by the terrorists) caused an open top Land-Rover to flip upside down, trapping the men at the back. The smallest man, a lightweight amateur boxer, managed to wriggle clear. He then lifted the back end of the Land-Rover, thus allowing his mates to crawl out. He then collapsed, having torn muscles across his belly. He was in hospital some time. Once when we were at the coast on a brief Rest and Recuperation a sergeant, who was a strict but fair disciplinarian, was swimming when he drifted into a whirlpool and got into difficulties. He was astonished when his entire section dived in and pulled him clear.

When not at our base camp at Episkopi, my section or troop would be posted somewhere around the foothills of the Troodos Mountains or near the south coast West of Limassol. We regularly set up roadblocks, searching the vehicles and passengers, searching houses, patrolling dodgy villages and going on longer patrols along mountain tracks etc. Most of the time it was routine work but there were occasional moments of pure terror.

There were also occasions of traumatic tragedy. A fellow NCO, with a remarkable gift for making humorous remarks that eased the tension at critical moments, was at the rear of a patrol led by his fellow NCO. He failed to notice when a man dropped behind a tree to relieve himself. The patrol had moved past the tree when the NCO, hearing a rattle of stones behind him, swung around challenging and firing almost simultaneously at what, against the light, appeared to be a man with a rifle coming towards him. He was then horrified to discover he had killed his best mate. The NCO was a broken man.

Sometimes a mate could take no more and cracked up. Thus one member of our troop who was constantly doing spells in the clink for lapses of discipline or whatever, was under armed escort at the back of a Land-Rover on its way to the clink for another stint. He requested they stop so he could relieve himself. As he jumped from the Land-Rover he grabbed the submachine gun from one of the escorts and shot himself in the legs. After a spell in hospital followed by serving his sentence, he was returned to England as his injuries rendered him no longer fit for active service.

My section, comprising a sergeant, myself and a fellow lance bombardier and the men, was once billeted in a remote small camp, from which we were regularly patrolling mountain tracks. However, the sergeant was an awkward type not respected by the men. Furthermore one of the men was a wild Geordie. Indeed he had a short temper and was dangerous when roused. He had been put in the clink several times. Indeed he had already exceeded two years of his National Service, but time in the clink did not count as time served! Because of his belligerent temperament there was a standing order that he was not allowed to carry arms at any time. He was therefore banned from going on patrol with the rest of us. Consequently he was assigned as our cook, which he did well enough. Unfortunately, one day the sergeant arrived late for breakfast and complained that the fried eggs were cold and greasy. The cook leapt across the table and grabbed the sergeant by the throat. My fellow NCO and I managed to detach the cook and the sergeant stormed off to his billet. The cook however, shouted after him that as he was not a trained cook he was not going to cook another thing. The rest of the men responded by saying they refused to go on patrol if the cook refused to make up rations for them and would not be cooking for them on their return at the end of the day. On informing the sergeant of this situation he declared the men were guilty of mutiny and would be in deep trouble when the troop sergeant next came with the mail and rations. My fellow lance bombardier retired to his bed and read a novel! I went into the men's billet and sat on a bed. I quietly reviewed the situation for them. I pointed out that mutiny on active service was a serious offence. I also agreed that they had a legitimate complaint regarding the lack of a cook. I advised that they get back on duty and when the troop sergeant arrived to formally put their complaint to him. After a certain amount of discussion they agreed with my advice. I then informed the sergeant that the men would be ready for the day's patrol in half an hour. Spitting obscenities the sergeant declared they would not get away with this, but began to prepare himself for patrol. What he had overlooked is the regulation that a person in charge of a unit that mutinies automatically loses command of that unit. Consequently, the first priority for a person in charge of a unit that mutinies is to prevent knowledge of the mutiny reaching the next higher level of command. Quelling the mutiny is only his second concern. When the troop sergeant arrived on his next visit the men duly lodged their formal complaint. He realized what was going on and kept the truth from the Lieutenant. However, he persuaded him that it would be a good for the men's morale to vary the men's experience by reshuffling their assignments to the different sections. Furthermore, I was sent on a signals course and the sergeant on some other course before we were assigned to different sections on our return. Most mutinies in Cyprus never came to the attention of the officers. The NCOs made sure of that.

One night I was on a night duty with a fellow lance bombardier who had recently transferred from another regiment after an experience he quietly related to me in confidence. I subsequently summarized this tale in the following two poems:

SECRET WAR (CW)
(Based on a true incident)

As boy he dreamed of being great,
He'd conquer foes on every front.
His rules would be enforced without

Demur. At school he daily lived
In fiction world inside his head
Or gazed at passers-by instead.
He left without a pass in all
Exams he ever sat. And that
You might have thought was that. But no.
He joined the army for a job.
At first it nearly broke his will
As sergeant hounded him to hell.
But soon he's gained a stripe and starts
To learn a leader's not admired,
But feared or else despised. They think
Him fool for choosing extra load
For paltry pay. But now he sees
His sergeant through a different lens.
His heart is ice. He drives his men
From dawn till dusk. He plays the game
By ruthless rulebook's sacred words.
His rigid stance allows no lapse
In petty points of dress. In drill
Perfection must apply. Indeed
He works his men with mean contempt.
With triple stripes at last, he finds
Himself abroad in hunt for thugs
Engaged in terror raids against
The ruling cliques. But still his men
Are treated rough; but then he finds
The impish Ken, who's half his weight,
Is getting laughs at his expense.
In silent fury vengeance now
Erupts. He taunts the lad without
Restraint, beyond all reason's bounds.
At length our Ken retorts one day
'You wait I'll get you in due course'.
A month had passed when ambush fire
Engaged their truck. That day it's Ken
In charge of Bren. So as his mates
And sergeant dive for cover, in
A ditch beside the road, our Ken
Returns the fire of terror gang
And then in pause directs a burst
At sergeant's back before again
Engaging foe on slope above.
At base, inquiry found the brute
Had died from fire of foe, and so

46

Inform his mum he met his end
In line of duty. No one ranked
Above an N.C.O. had caught
A wisp of truth. When men are trained
To kill they'll use that skill as need
Dictates when tyrant goes too far.
Commissioned ranks are last to know.

BLACK AND WHITE LIES (CW)
(An incident on active service in Cyprus in 1958)

A sergeant Bill was friendless man whose soul had shrunk
From long neglect as child. In fact, as sadist warped
By hate and ill intent, he scorned the squad he led.
His bully ways had picked on Ken, a little man
With comic turn of phrase and jokes for every scene
Or small event. But Bill had crossed the bounds and tried
To crush the will of Ken without relent until
A day he went too far. "I'll get you yet" was Ken's
Response he'd hissed between his teeth. A month elapsed
When ambush struck and Ken was on the Bren that day.
As men had dived for ditch beside deceitful road.
Then Ken had seized his chance. A burst in back of beast
Curtailed his lashing tongue at last. When back at base
The men in turn professed the bloke was killed by foe.
The junior N.C.O. was left to last. The truth
He'd nearly grasped, but fell in line with lying mates.
One night his sleepless conscience stirred and out it poured
As we were on our own, on guard, in lull before
The dawn relieved our vigil's stint. "Perhaps it's best
To let Bill's mum believe he died a hero's death".

The fellow NCO who told me this was clearly still agonizing over whether he should own up and tell the authorities the truth. I pointed out that, apart from himself being disciplined for having not told the truth to the enquiry following the ambush and Bill's death, this would cause great upset to Bill's mother (who had been told her son had been killed by the terrorists), Ken would be court martialled and every member of his section would also be disciplined for having lied to the enquiry following the ambush and Bill's death. I suggested, perhaps wrongly, that I thought it better to let the verdict reached by the official enquiry to stand unchallenged. It remained so. Had my advice made me complicit in Bill's death?

On another occasion I had been conducting a roadblock and was returning to base camp in our one-ton truck when we rounded a bend and were confronted by a gruesome spectacle. A three-ton truck was slewed across the road on its side. A semicircle of wounded men lay on the road in front of us. To the side at the left was a surly group of Greek Cypriots gawping. By the overturned vehicle stood the driver with a submachine gun over his shoulder while he was trying to light a cigarette. I yelled at my section to tend the wounded while I did a flying leap at the driver and stopped him trying to light his cigarette lighter as fuel was spouting out of his overturned truck with a high risk of exploding in a ball of flame. I then returned to our vehicle and, although we had logged off the network we had been on earlier, I told our signaller, who operated a large vehicle mounted radio, to try to get into any services network he could while I worked out our grid reference. He managed to make contact with an RAF network and I gave him the grid reference and said to request ambulances soonest. I then surveyed the scene closely. My men were doing a good job making the wounded as comfortable as possible. The driver then told me that when they had rounded the sharp bend behind him he had been forced to brake hard as a large boulder had been placed in the middle of the road. Two ambulances arrived shortly after this. The paramedics dressed the wounds of the injured and lifted them on to stretchers. Then our major appeared on the scene. His signaller had picked up our message to the RAF. When I got back to base camp I was met by our lieutenant who seemed to be angry about something. It transpired that when briefing me before the operation he had forgotten to tell me that we were to drop off the large radio set at a camp before the scene of the ambush. However, as my signaller that day was known to be the most reliable in the regiment he had told him to tell me. He forgot! The only act of unreliability ever recorded against him! My reply to the Lieutenant was "Thank God he forgot". I later learned that had the ambulances not arrived as quickly as they did at least two of the casualties would have died.

I was often sent with my section to patrol a village that was divided by a stream running from the north to the south. To the east were Turkish Cypriots and to the west were Greek Cypriots. One night I was in the west half when we heard a rumpus coming from the coffee shop in the east side. I fixed my bayonet and then led my section east. I suddenly became aware that something was falling from above. As I thrust my bayonet upwards a man with an iron spike twisted violently in the air above me as he saw my bayonet. We both just missed each other, while he apologized saying he thought we were "Turks" from the east side coming to get them! Recovering my equanimity, and sheathing my bayonet, we crossed to the coffee shop fracas. It turned out two policemen had arrived on a motorbike to try to collect a fine from an old man. When asked why they did not come by day they said the old man was always up on the mountain tending his vines. I then received word that the "Greeks" were herding the women and children into the church and the men were mustering with pitchforks, etc. So I told the policemen to leave and to return in daylight. They refused. So I ordered my men to fix bayonets and to advance slowly towards the policemen, who then decided to leave. But they shouted back that they would report me to the authorities (who subsequently endorsed my action). I then returned with my section to the church and after certain lively exchanges persuaded them the "Turks" were not coming for them and would they all kindly return to their homes. We were fully alert for the rest of the night as we went from west to east and back again to reassure both sides. The next time I was patrolling the village by day people from both sides quietly came up and thanked me for defusing that situation.

Similar incidents were infrequent but sometimes gave rise to unintended tragedy:

MISCONSTRUED (TL)

An N.C.O. in charge of foot
Patrol is leading way towards
A rumpus noise across the stream
Dividing ethnic groups by night.
Their peaceful co-existence down
The years has cracked. Fanatics stir
The pot of history's dormant slights.
The Western tribe are restless now
As rumour raises fears. Do shouts
Denote attack is brewing? Soon
The soldiers reach the scene whence sounds
Originate. They quickly learn
The row is fired by feuding pair,
About some cash that's owed. To calm
The crowd the sergeant yells his call
For quiet and asks disputing men
To cease until the day returns.
With grudging nods they move apart
To join their mates. But one, with fist
Aloft, is hurling last abuse.
The sergeant intervenes at speed
And orders silence. Then he turns
Towards the stream on hearing shots.
One ricochets off church. He falls
With arms upraised in crucifix
Display, a bullet through the back
Of head. The ghouls disperse, the old
Departing first and then the young.
A woman weeps beside the corpse
As owl proclaims the sun has set.

With regard to the Cypriot Police, who we were in Cyprus to support as on their own they had been unable to cope with EOKA, we generally got on well

49

with the Turkish Cypriot police. However, with the Greek Cypriot police we were always somewhat on our guard as we were never sure as to where their loyalties ultimately lay.

When patrolling one village we discovered EOKA slogans painted on the side of the church. Our sergeant entered the church and tolled the bell. When the villagers appeared to see what was going on the sergeant told them we would be returning later that day and if the slogans were still there we would set fire to the church. They set to and scrubbed the wall clean. Our regiment had acquired the reputation for not making idle threats! Indeed we had a reputation for it being not a good idea to not treat us with respect. For example, one day we decided to look into a dodgy Greek Cypriot coffee shop. The first one of our mates to enter was the shortest man in the section, who was armed with a .303 rifle. A burly Cypriot with a chuckle asked my mate why he didn't get a weapon more suited to his size. My fellow NCO was a powerful man, indeed the strongest in the regiment. He grabbed the guy by his clothing and suspended him by the back of his coat from a hook on the wall, leaving him dangling. He was then told he would only be released when he had apologized unreservedly!

Several patrol reports relating to a village alluded to suspicious activities in the Greek quarter coffee shop. We were told we needed to produce hard evidence before an authorized search could be mounted. One day I was leading a patrol when we found a notice stuck on the pillar by the entrance to the coffee shop. It was plainly signed "E.O.K.A." at the bottom. I removed the notice and attached it to my patrol report on return to camp. My section were sure we had obtained the necessary evidence to allow a thorough investigation of the coffee shop. Imagine their anger and disgust when I told them that the lieutenant said he agreed it was the sort of hard evidence that was needed. However, he said he would let it pass this time as it would require authorization, if not actual command, by the major for a thorough investigation of the coffee shop. He said he didn't want the major turning up just then as his office was behind hand in assessing and filing the latest patrol reports and other matters he had let slip behindhand!

When my section was based in an old donkey stable attached to a remote rural police station we were visited by a captain who seemed something of a prig. He looked into our accommodation and became agitated. My men had brightened up the walls with photos of families and friends interspersed with pictures of pin-up girls. He said he would be back next day and expected to find all the 'lewd' pictures removed! When he returned all the 'offending' pictures had gone except for the most provocative of the lot. Enraged, he confronted my mate demanding why he had flagrantly disregarded his order. Keeping a completely straight face my mate replied that the picture was of his sister, who was in the fashion trade! As the captain beat a hasty retreat we were all convulsed in laughter. We never saw that captain again. My mates asked who my pin up might be. I responded that while awaiting my posting from Woolwich to Cyprus I had visited the British Museum and had been struck by

50

a beautiful and voluptuous statue of the Asian goddess Tara. Having just qualified as a TARA (Technical Assistant Royal Artillery) I had felt that she would be the appropriate choice for myself!

On another occasion the troop sergeant arrived with a colonel of an infantry regiment. We put on a ceremonial line for his inspection. He stopped at each one of us in turn and asked what we did in civilian life. When he came to me I replied 'potential research ecologist'. 'That's some sort of engineering is it not?' he replied. 'No Sir' I replied. He quickly moved on. Afterwards the troop sergeant congratulated me for deflating a pompous old ****ing colonel! However, I subsequently realized that back in 1958 the word ecologist was not familiar to the public in general, unlike today when it is misapplied by politicians without restraint! However, some weeks later I encountered the colonel again. He had evidently enquired about me after the episode and had been told I was a keen naturalist. Indeed I had acquired a reputation when I had installed a chameleon in my tent, by suspending a branch with a tin lid against a knot half way up the string to prevent escape. The chameleon lived on this horizontal branch and woe betide any fly entering the tent. My mates spent much time watching my pet until one day when we were out on patrol a drunken sergeant killed it. Anyway the colonel asked me as to what the most impressive natural history experience I had had in Cyprus. I pulled out my patrol leader's map and gave him the grid reference of a slope in the Troodos Mountains where I had crossed a ridge to be confronted with about ten acres of orchids. He was clearly sceptical. However, a month or so later I encountered him again and he told me he had attached himself to a patrol going that way and was surprised to find I had not been exaggerating! Indeed I had acquired a reputation for my map reading skills (acquired when a schoolboy pursuing my interests in archaeology and natural history). Furthermore, following my handling of the incident with the wounded men from the overturned one-ton truck (see above) and other events, I was promoted to the rank of a full bombardier. This along with my reputation for map reading, meant I was increasingly in charge of operations involving a single section. Thus on one occasion three patrols had been sent out into the lower slopes of the mountains for three days. A 2nd Lieutenant led one, a sergeant led one and I led the third. On return we made out our reports and handed them in at the battery office. As the leader with the lowest rank, I was the last in. When the officer and sergeant left the major told me to stay a moment. He told me the officer had got lost, the sergeant had got lost but had regained his route after some time, but I, a mere bombardier, had handed in the biggest correction to the map recorded so far! The latter had had me worried at the time. We had reached a ridge and I told my mates to rest while I checked our position with my prismatic compass. I was almost spot on as I had thought by dead reckoning. However, on looking into the valley below there was a village not on the map. I checked with the compass again. Puzzled, I told my mates we were going to divert to the village to find out why it was not on the map. We discovered that the village had been relocated after the original settlement had been destroyed by a flood. However, the new village pre-dated the last revision of the map! It transpired that the most recent revision of the map had been done from air photos only. A stray cloud had evidently obscured the village the day the photo was taken!

In view of my reputation for map reading I was later given an odd assignment. Intelligence had learned that a monastery was being used to store arms and explosives for EOKA. Two consecutive patrols had been sent to a ridge overlooking the valley road to the monastery, with instructions to log all traffic going to and from the monastery. Both patrols had gone to the allocated observation point but both reported that there was no monastery at the spot it was marked on the map! I was given the same orders as the two previous patrols but told that if I confirmed there was no monastery I was to descend to the location it was marked on the map and to search for it. We went there and then moved out in an expanding spiral course. We eventually found the monastery. It was two grid squares to the east. It was simply a draughtsman's error by the map maker!

When back at base camp for a spell I was given an unusual assignment relating to arms caches by EOKA. I was contacted by Intelligence who said they had learned of my interest in archaeology. They had obtained information that some ancient Roman temples and similar monuments were being used to store arms. On my rest days an armed escort would collect me and drop me off at such a site. I was to make intelligent conversation to the official guide for the monument while looking for 'keystone' situations. That is to say where there was dry stone walling look for a situation where a slab was supported at both ends so that a stone in the middle could be removed without the wall collapsing. This was all top secret. My mates had a field day speculating as to what I was up to when whisked away for an afternoon by armed military police. I was not allowed to tell them what I was doing. Unfortunately this assignment was cut short when I and my section were posted to an out station. I learned that the MPs had arrived to collect me the following Saturday to find I had gone. The intelligence officer had then stormed into my CO to complain. The CO had replied that if they were so ***** stupid as to have recruited me for this work without telling him then that was their problem. I was now engaged in my primary duty elsewhere and that was the end of the matter. Not for the first time I learned that Intelligence seemed to lack common sense!

One day at base camp I was relaxing in a tent, lying on my right side on a camp bed. Suddenly a bomb went off in the admin tent across from our tent. I sat up. Then a second bomb went off. In retrospect that was a mistake as the damage to my hearing was asymmetric (see chapter 9)! Luckily nobody was killed or seriously injured. The question was how had the explosives been smuggled in to the camp when all the civilian workers were thoroughly searched on entry. It was later learned that one had had a ball of string in his pocket, but this was not considered to be of any significance. He had then tied a stone to one end of the string and threw it through a culvert running under the rolls of barbed wire that surrounded the camp. An accomplice had untied the stone and replaced it with the explosives and fuses that had then been hauled back through the culvert.

When spending another spell at the base camp one of the meanest murders by EOKA took place. Opposite our camp was a compound of married quarters for the families of regular soldiers of another regiment. One day a van from a nearby village turned up at the gates with ice creams for sale. A sergeant bought ice creams for his two young daughters, who held their dad's hand with one hand while enjoying the ice cream with their other hands. Suddenly a man raced past on a motorbike, only slowing briefly to shoot the sergeant dead but leaving his daughters deeply distraught and traumatized. My mates were so angered by this outrage that they raced down to the armoury intending to collect their weapons and to inflict revenge on the village. The regimental police had the greatest difficulty in fending off my mates and eventually calming them down and making them return to their tents.

On another occasion my section was billeted on the edge of an RASC camp. This was not a good idea. It gave rise to some tensions in 'their' NAAFI bar at times. The REME officers increasingly became irked by some of the brawls. One evening I was walking along one side of the compound when a REME officer yelled out 'Corporal come here I want a word with you'. I, being a bombardier, took no notice, assuming he was calling one of his own NCOs. Enraged, the officer ran up to me and yelled at me 'Did you not hear me calling 'corporal'?' I replied 'Sir, the only Corporals in the Royal Artillery are some new missile system recently employed in Germany'. He was gratified when my section was posted to a new location!

When Barbara Castle visited Cyprus in 1958 she got wind of torture being carried out on EOKA suspects. Unfortunately she didn't keep quiet until she had obtained hard evidence. Consequently the military clammed up and she was subsequently successfully sued by a UK newspaper for defamation of our troops in Cyprus. However, she was correct. There was official torture in a facility on the edge of Limassol as well as unofficial torture. I had many disagreements with my mates on this topic. They argued that every time suspects had been tortured they had divulged the location of arms caches, etc. However, translations of parts of the captured Grivas diaries, periodically posted in Part 2 orders, indicated that this did not stop a planned operation but merely annoyed Grivas who had to use a different cache for the operation. I made a pact with my section. When under my orders they would not act contrary to Queen's Regulations. What they did under sergeant X or lieutenant Y was up to them. One day I found a rumpus going on in my section's tent. They were getting at one of my mates who had, apparently, been stealing behind my back from a bus we had been searching in a roadblock operation I had been leading that day. They were angry with the guy because he was breaking the pact and they didn't want trouble as they reckoned that I tried to treat them fairly. Indeed, they had been very grateful when on one occasion when patrolling a village the 'friendly' locals had offered my mates their locally produced whisky (these local brews were so strong that some served better as a fuel for cigarette lighters!). I suspected the friendliness was a ploy so I flatly refused to partake. The villagers were clearly annoyed by my refusal. As I realized my mates were getting tipsy rather rapidly I called a halt and we moved on. I had heard of a similar situation where all of a patrol had got drunk and had had their weapons stolen.

The biggest operation of the anti-terrorist campaign was Operation Kingfisher in 1958. Information from the criminal underworld had provided the location of the main hideout in the Troodos Mountains of Grivas, the leader of the EOKA campaign. Several regiments were involved when a cordon, of about three miles circumference, was put in place, arriving by helicopters and trucks from all directions. We were there for some weeks. By day our orders were to challenge anyone approaching three times (in English, Greek and Turkish) and to only fire if there was no response. At dusk a bugle was sounded and by night one shot on sight without challenging. Despite these orders one night a sergeant and I were lying down keeping watch on a slope ahead when we briefly recognized the silhouette of an officer coming towards us! Emitting an expletive the sergeant told me to cover him while he moved to a position behind a rock. When the officer came level with him the sergeant emitted a bloodcurdling yell as he sprang out with a bayonet fixed to his submachine gun. The officer had apparently come to see how we were doing! He was never seen after dark again! Tragically, a similar case occurred with a sister regiment when on another operation and the officer was killed by a burst of Bren fire. The court martial concluded the officer had been killed on his own orders. It seems there is no correlation between intelligence and common sense!

Anyway, back on Operation Kingfisher, a bugle at dawn returned us to daytime orders. My unit was often defending the rear of the Argyll and Sutherland Highlanders. On other occasions we were positioned facing into the cordoned area. There was much shooting at night, especially by the A & S and Cameroon Highlanders. This shooting was essentially at an owl or other cause of a noise in the dark. One morning one of the A & S Highlanders discovered a bullet hole through the overhang of his bonnet! The Brigadier was fed up with all this shooting and issued new orders. In future every round fired would have to be accounted for. The following night was very dark and also quiet as I lay in a shallow trench looking towards the rim of a drop into a ravine. I suddenly became aware of a pale shape seeping over the edge of the rim ahead. It was too dark to see the fore sight of my .303 riffle so I carefully aligned the faint line of its stock and squeezed the trigger. The pale shape subsided. In the morning an officer came bounding down towards my section and demanded to know who had fired a round in the night. I jumped up and said I had and I believe there was a corpse of something by the rim of the ravine. Indeed there was – a white cat with a black tail. It proved to be the pet of Grivas himself. The Brigadier issued an order for the day "would the infantry please note. They have wasted hundreds of rounds on this operation so far, with nothing to show for it. The Royal Artillery have fired one round and produced a corpse!" On the basis of this I was designated a first class shot without having passed the usual test! Subsequently it had one advantage when we were called out to deal with a riot. Three of us first class shots stood by the officer issuing orders through a megaphone while my mates armed with shields and pick handles were below us in two ranks. In turn one rank then the other battled with the mob. The procedure was that if the rioters failed to heed the repeated instruction to disperse the officer would instruct the first class shots to shoot a designated ringleader. Thankfully I was never called upon to do this. I merely watched my mates sweating it out below me.

With regard to Operation Kingfisher it was called off after locating and blowing up the hideout of Grivas. It was only later we learned (e.g. Doros Alastos, 1960, CYPRUS GUERRILLA, William Heinemann Ltd, London) that Grivas and his companions were in a panic as the cordon was being imposed from all directions when one observed to Grivas that the mountain hares were all running in one direction. 'Follow them' ordered Grivas 'they know what they are doing' and the hares along with Grivas and his men escaped through the last gap to be closed.

I subsequently encountered Grivas, but we did not realize this until after the event! We were guarding the large hospital at Dhekelia during its construction. The workers, and any visitors, were all searched on arrival each day. One morning an old women appeared with a basket of food for some of the workers. She and her basket were searched by a WRAC. We later learned that the 'old woman' was in fact Grivas in disguise! His mission had been to encourage the workers to continue their clandestine sabotage of the work. Their favourite game was to insert small explosive devices in the electrical fittings so that when later bulbs, etc., were added and the switches turned on the devices would explode. While this clearly posed a danger their main purpose was to delay completion of the contract and increase its cost.

One day, when my section was posted in a remote outpost in the foothills of the Troodos Mountains, the ration detail returned from base camp and told me there was a notice ordering me to proceed to Nicosia Airport for departure to England to attend a WOSB on a date in the near future. When I was given a copy of the order it stated that I was to proceed to Nicosia with all my kit which must not exceed a specified weight, which was far less than ALL my kit! When I asked the Troop Sergeant which part of the order I should obey he responded "Trust the **** army to issue a ***** stupid order. Well Bombardier you best take all your kit and sort it out at the airport." In the event I was relieved of half my kit at Nicosia, was given a receipt and told it would be sent on by sea. I never saw it again!

When on patrol one frequently had a heavy pack of tinned Compo rations, a supply of water, ammunition and often a radio (far larger than a 21st mobile phone). One needed to drink adequate water, regularly take the salt tablets supplied and when stopping for a rest break to seek the shade of a carob tree or whatever. Being fair skinned, I had since my days in the Sudan tried to keep out of the sun when relaxing.

SUNSHINE (TL)

Today the sun is painting scene
In wanton light, inducing sense
Of ease in colleagues bearing mugs
Of coffee onto lawn to bask
Beneath its warming rays. But not
For me such reckless disregard
Of risks to skin. I seek the shade
From where I relish routine views
Enhanced by welcome summer's day.
When walking northern hills I still
Prefer when skies are grey or else
There's broken cloud and shadows race
Across the fells all freshly lit
In wake of belt of rain that's cleansed
The air and scrubbed the pastures clean:
For even silly sheep are more
Alive on such a day, and grouse
Are less inclined to scold. But when
The sky's ablaze it feels as though
A spell's been cast and life has slowed.
It's only hover flies and bees
That then rejoice as we perspire.
I then recall the time abroad,
As youthful soldier on patrol.
I'd call a halt and sit in shade.
At first my men had basked in sun,
But one by one they'd join retreat
Beneath my tree. But Bill remained
Exposed until the day the heat
Had made him faint with stroke from loss
Of salt. There's always one who spurns
The wisdom handed down from past.
Perhaps he yearned to stand alone,
So far from home and sunshine girl.

It was also a good idea not to drink too much the evening before departure and leave with a hangover in the morning. One of my mates later told me that unfortunately the NCO who took over from me had not yet learned these simple survival rules:

CLOSE ENCOUNTER (RE)

At first a single shape that wheels
And banks in leisured lift as up
And up the rising thermal bears
Its weight. A further four now join
This ritual dance of vultures sprung
From air. By noon there's twenty three.
This saga launched when soldiers left
The beaten track. As mountain goats,
They'd strode in line aslant the slope
Of scrub and scattered rocks, alert
To any signs of gunman's lair.
Relentless sun the zenith claims.
They pause for rest while N. C. O.
Reviews his map. He finds it hard
To focus mind. A misty swirl
Engulfs both it and sight. The heat
Has struck him down. Excessive drink
The night before has wreaked revenge.
His men now ease him into shade
Of scrubby tree and make him down
A draft of cooling water, then
Await results. They slowly watch
Derangement overcome their mate.
It seems that none but he can read
The map or knows which hill they're on.
By now the day is nearly done.
Perhaps the cool of night will bring
Him round. But by the dawn they find
Him mumbling nonsense to himself.
So two are picked to head for sea,
In hazy distance glimpsed, in hope
Of reaching road and thumbing lift
For help. All day the rest just wait.
Another night of chill. By noon
They're growing weak as birds patrol
Above with patient stares. Before
Decease they plan to shoot those friends
Of doom, as dying gesture hurled
At heaven's gate. Their lives now pass
Before their minds as archive films.
They wish they'd learned to read a map.
They think of home and girls they'd hoped
To wed. At first they'd joked to keep
Their spirits up, but now all words
Are laid to rest. They listless lie.

And still those circling shapes encroach.
And then one lands, well out of reach.
With wary gaze it edges close.
Then distant shout ejects the brute,
As aid arrives. But many nights
Will pass before those wheeling forms
Will cease to haunt their dreams and lives.
That balding head and menace glare
Persists as threat consuming laughs
Employed to paper over fear.
They'd lost their youth in those two days.

It was a relief to return to England. However, I was given no counselling for Post-Traumatic Stress Disorder. Indeed I did not recognize for some time that I was suffering from PTSD, and would do so over the next few years. Indeed many years later I would have occasional throwback nightmares. The PTSD was augmented by a waning of my Christian faith as a result of my experience fighting terrorism initiated and sponsored by a church. To lose one's faith is both liberating and devastating. One is liberated from doctrines that obscured the truth of the Gospel, but to lose the guiding light of the Gospel tends to feed scepticism and despair. However, in finding oneself feeling sympathy for someone who has travelled further down the road of rejection one can begin to detect a glimmer of light suggesting the Gospel lives and, perhaps, it is only the atavistic doctrinal wrappings and hijacking of religion for political objectives that deserves to be shed.

IN ABEYANCE

By stealthy creeping drip by drip
Her youthful faith had leaked away.
Her frequent singing, cheerful smiles,
Had faded too. But yet her kind
And gentle nature, nurtured in
Her Christian home, remains as gift
To all who meet her still. But few
Beyond her closest circle glimpse
The parched and stony desert chill
Engulfing inner soul. There's not
A word that can revive her. On
Her own she fights her demons. Now
It's only music brings relief
For brief respites, before the bleak
Engulfing blackness once again
Demands attention, once again

Occludes the sun of former days.
We pray for warm refreshing rains
To wake her dormant seeds of hope,
Transform her inner landscape's bare
And scorching glare to spread of blooms
Of many hues embracing hum
Of life replenished full once more.
But only she can bring herself
To see beyond the mirage con
Of hope's defeat to vision faith
Renewed will bring to her and us.
I know from own encounters in
The past when peace returns at last
Then faith renewed is gold indeed.

It was only gradually during my student days at Cambridge that I gradually recovered my faith as a 'Lapsed atheist' (see chapter 3). I gradually dealt with the experience of Cyprus through a series of poems over many years. Here is a selection of these:

FAITH UNDER FIRE (MC)

(On active service in Cyprus in 1958, when terrorism was
sponsored by a church and a cat was mistaken for a man at night)

Behold these hills smothered with rich
Profusion of wild flowers, see
Spring's rainbow wash overwhelm
These stone-strewn slopes with gentle tide.
At dusk perceive the sinking sun
Suck colour from the anaemic
Land as, blood-gorged, it had begun
To disappear – while we lie lost
Within the circularity
Of ourselves and despair.
And now the moon descends while weird
Resounding calls of Scops owls give
Eerie overtones to the black
Depths of expectancy. Behold!
Revolving slowly by that dark
And silent stony gorge, whose sill
Is overhung by writhing stems
Which taunt our straining eyes with doubts,
Does Judas hang beneath that tree?
Are we the absent crowd who jeer
His end, disturb his anguished
Thoughts? Did he grasp Jesu's mission
As he died, while wind creaked the branch,
Flies walked his empty expression?
It's thus I muse until the crack
Of a rifle, or the jittery
Rattle of Bren-fire, brings us back
Intermittently to the now.

Grenades at tiny kids whose shrieks
Echo in vain – the homemade bombs -
Pierced bleeding guts of pregnant wives -
The booby-traps on corpse – No remorse
When performed for the cause. And we,
Despite our selfless comradeship,
With fierce festering fury sink -
Reaching bestial depths; irate,
Licentious soldiery who rape
Defenceless virgins; filch; torture
As ordered, or unauthorized.

For now a headline traps our gaze.
A complacent politician's
Paltry euphemisms now crawl
From the mourning black slabs of black,
Black type being fed by Fleet Street
To the indifferent and the damned.
My angry thoughts renew their quest
For reasons why poor Judas failed.
His corpse now slowly sways in mind,
Repugnant as some trendy priest
Who eschews the Way of the Cross
With talk of "call to freedom's fight
Which claims support from us at least."

A sudden gust hurls a strange cry
For mercy down the gorge of death.
A soft echo comes sighing back
"There, but for the grace of the Lord,
Goes each saint. Weep for Judas, weep.
With contrition water the land."
A soft pale shape seeped into view.
At once I'm straining every nerve.
Within me warred a deep desire
To kill, compassion, and a fear
That I would funk it when obliged
To shoot. All is opaque. The crack
Of the rifle in my hands brings back
My churning fears and thoughts to time;
To view a silent cat whose life
Is stopped, whose sudden death augments
The stream of blood with which a church
Astray impedes the love of Christ.
Again I ask – Did Judas find his peace?
And is the gilded cross above
Still lit by springtime's gentle sun?

I hear a silent shriek in my head.
I see the albatross past return
To the deep. The sky rends. Past is past,
And seems strangely detached, somewhere in which
I seem no more involved. Childlike
I now behold the world with new eyes
And find I'm exiled no longer
From mankind – despite a strangely sacred,

Sceptical vision. I recall
The splendour and scent of Cyprus
Blossoms in spring. I hear mountain
Streams whisper in my ears; sense Christ's
Love welling forth in the world.
Perceive Christ's love beneath the blood
And beauty. But as in a dream
Which one partly controls, I shrink
From an unholy church and all
Its accretions; I rebound, I
Contrive to circumnavigate
Its monstrous, twisted edifice.

Having left that building far
Behind, the cross on its burnished
Dome still casts upon living past
Its ever lengthening shadow.
On glancing back, there remains
Only the cross – haloed by Light.
And now I see the same ahead
As guiding star of faithful church.

HOPELESS CAUSES (TL)

Today we went to church to pause
With thanks for fallen dead in two
Engulfing wars and many times
Our service men, and women too,
Have put their lives on line in cause
Of bringing peace in distant lands.
There's fewer now with medals worn
That bear the head of George the King.
I wear a single silver disc,
With face of youthful Queen, to mark
The time I served in Cyprus when
A rookie lad. Those months had forged
Me into man before I knew
That what was seen as right back then
Had merely slowed the drift to mess
Of fractured land that foolish men
Had not foreseen when launching gang
Of bandits on the scene. Their aim
To force a favoured dream. We'd helped
To save some few from death for time,

But when we'd left for home the new
Regime had failed to keep the peace.
The flood of refugees across
The land, in counterflows, had split
Communities in two. I grieve
For them, as well as for my mates
Who died in hopeless cause. The use
Of death, as means to end, is not
A choice in eyes of Christ, who taught
A special care for those we hate.

DELUDING LIE (RE)

I'm immunised against desire
For war by active service in
My youth. And while I know I saved
Some lives, the larger problem still
Remained. And yet it's once a year
I wear my medal still, but not
With pride. I mourn the waste of life,
The injured children, seeds of hate
And fractured trust that still persists.
The use of force is seldom neat.
It tends to bring just brief reprieve
From fear and prejudice. The peace
We all desire cannot be bought
By use of arms, which just suppress
The flames of rage for while. Beneath
The surface glowing coals persist
Abiding time until we sleep.
But lesson's never learned, as when
With groans we witnessed once again
As Bush and Blair, with good intents,
Had blundered into swamp of feuds
Suppressed by Saddam's rule of bleak
Iraq, where blood is spilled without
Remorse as routine daily game.
Equating might with right has been
Deluding lie we still espouse,
Despite persistent cries of those
Who suffer still and urge a halt.
But atavistic Blair was deaf,
Along with Bush's gang of crooks.

DOUBLE STANDARDS (RE)

In youth I hunted terror gangs
In Cyprus, land of dreams that should
Have been a taste of paradise.
We exercised the greatest care
To not abuse our naked force,
Avoiding harm to mums and kids
And those attending vines, despite
The fact we couldn't tell the good
From bad amongst the men who sipped
Their tiny cups of coffee thick
With sludge of grounds. Our soldiers sent
To Ulster's troubled streets were same.
We fought the men who lived by gun
And death with cool restraint, despite
It meant our task was thus constrained.
We'd search each nook of suspect house,
While seething owners stood outside
Beneath the watchful gaze of dog
That's trained to kill; but kids we sat
Along a wall and gave them sweets!
Both Bush and Blair are not deterred
By risk of children's deaths. They launch
Their crudely aimed grenades and shells.
Iraqi mums and Afghan babes
Are zapped as part of cost, as words
Of easy 'deep regret' pollute
Our tele screens. The rubbled homes
Are stark reminder tactics used
Are not what we'd accept at home
As means to end that's justified.

I AM THE VINE (MC)

When youthful soldier in my prime
Patrolling sun drenched mountain slope,
Amongst some neatly ordered vines,
I passed a man whose weathered hands
Intently tended treasured stocks.
There's some that seemed as gnarled as he
Before inserted grafts restored
Their hope of harvest's gift. It's then
I heard afresh our Lord proclaim

'It's I who am the vine and you
Are called to be a branch designed
To bear the grapes for making wine.
It's you I call to share my cup'.
I also note that shoots that failed
To draw upon the sap of life
Were those that slowly withered, died,
And then were pruned with loving care
For what remained. My youthful cane
Had lain aside for while before
At last I'm firmly fixed and bound
To sturdy stock in place in sun.
Despite for long I'd lagged behind,
It's now I pause to hymn my thanks,
Along with all who've joined these ranks.
In lasting fellowship with all
Who share a common trunk, we find
The strength to bloom and bear our fruits,
By means of constant flow from roots,
Which being hid escapes the mind
Of mate who's yet to hear the call.

I have sometimes been asked whether my experience in Cyprus had made me a pacifist. My answer tends to be – only about 90% so. My reason for the qualified response is twofold. Firstly I know that on occasions my mates and I had prevented outrages against civilians. Secondly the EOKA terrorists took to lobbying hand grenades into playgrounds of children where the local community were judged to have been unsupportive of their cause. On one occasion a British soldier spotted a terrorist creeping along a wall to such a playground of children and he evidently had a grenade in one hand. Despite the range being nearly 1000 yards the soldier took careful aim with his rifle and shot the terrorist dead. I have met nobody who was willing to condemn this action of the soldier.

Woolwich and Officer Cadet School, Aldershot

I was based at Woolwich for a month before going to WOSB and for a month afterwards before proceeding to Mons Officer Cadet School at Aldershot.

At Woolwich the men were mostly straight after basic training and were in transit to Cyprus. A typical day involved a morning parade at which fatigue parties were allocated for the day. In addition two or three times a week we did night guard duties, there being several locations requiring an all-night guard. Being a bombardier back from active service I was often given charge of more

65

responsible tasks by day and more important posts by night. Thus by day I was often required to collect or deliver prisoners from the clink. One memorable occasion was when I was allocated a young lad as an escort and we dispatched by train to Liverpool to collect a prisoner who had gone Absent Without Leave (AWOL) from Salisbury Plain. My instructions required me to handcuff the prisoner to the escort and we must travel by taxi or military vehicle with him to the station and not take him handcuffed walking in the street. We were supplied with tickets and specific train times. I signed for the prisoner with the Military Police, having first handcuffed him to the escort. The first cause for merriment was to find the prisoner was a large man while the escort was a small man. If the former felt inclined he could easily lift the escort onto his back and run off with him. The MPs dropped us off at the railway station. I then discovered the clerk in Woolwich had looked up trains from Liverpool Street in London, not Liverpool on Merseyside! We would have two hours to wait. I then discovered the prisoner thought we were taking him to Salisbury. Furthermore his mother, who lived not far from the station, had been told the same. As the prisoner seemed cooperative I agreed we would use part of the wait to call on her and put her in the picture, on condition he behaved and we hid the handcuffs beneath a coat slung over his and the escort's wrists. When the mum opened the door she started screaming obscenities at me. But her son told her to stop it as I was doing him and her a favour. Whereupon she welcomed us in to a large one room slum dominated by a double bed, out of which three kids crawled to help her supply us with tea and cake. Refreshed, we returned to the station and boarded our train. By now I had got the measure of the prisoner and released the escort from the handcuffs and attached the freed end to a metal loop by the window. Gradually his story came out. A friend had written to say his girl partner in Liverpool was being unfaithful. He had asked for compassionate leave but had been refused. So he went AWOL. However, he had a row with the girl, who was living in a first floor flat, and she had thrown furniture down the stairs at him. He had then been picked up by the MPs. I duly delivered him to the clink in Woolwich and whenever I went to collect or deliver another prisoner he would give me a cheerful wave.

One day, however, I arrived to find the place in uproar. The only prisoner in evidence was my fellow from Liverpool. He came over and quietly told what had happened. They had been made to take the six foot folding tables from their cells to the yard and to give them a thorough scrub down. Having done so and having returned the tables to the cells an officious NCO had examined the tables and declared they were not clean enough and they must be done again. They had carried the tables back to the yard. When the NCO was called inside to answer the phone, the prisoners had quickly stacked the tables, one on top of the other, to form a ladder and had gone over the wall and away. When I asked my Scouse why he had not gone with them he said he was in enough trouble already without adding to it by going AWOL a second time!

When in charge of a guard before dispatch of each guard detachment to our various posts all the detachments had to parade in a line with a gap between each. The duty officer then inspected us before dismissal to our individual guard posts. One night the officer had halted in front of me and demanded to know why I was not wearing my best boots rather than scarred CWW (cold wet weather) boots. I replied they were in a kitbag on their way back from Cyprus by sea. Later he came to my post around midnight and I duly turned out the guard for inspection. They were fresh out of basic training. The procedure to dismiss them back to the guard room was to order "Slope Arms!" then "Dismiss!" The required response was to salute the officer, to left turn and then to walk back to the guard room. However, one guy saluted to his head instead of to his rifle butt. I immediately ordered "As you were" and told him off. The officer then confronted me and asked why I had not read out the orders for the guard post, including the drill for turning out the guard. I replied I had been unable to find any orders in the guard post. He stormed in and eventually had to admit there were none (I subsequently learned the guard on the previous night had been cold and had used the orders to light the fire!). A week later the same officer was on duty. I warned my detachment that he would be likely to turn out the guard and they had better perform the drill correctly. However, when he turned up later on he said there was no need to turn out the guard but he would welcome a cup of tea and a chat! He divulged that he had looked up my file and had discovered that I was awaiting my posting to Officer Cadet School!

ONE OF US (CW)

A mouse has learned to scrounge below
The board where scraps for birds are placed.
The crumbs that fall augment the meals
That nature gives, or else denies
When frost impedes its search or snows
Conceal its hopes. It brings us joy,
Despite the fact that if it came
In house, to seek a better life,
We'd set a trap to rid ourselves
Of guest we will not tolerate.
It seems that context rules the way
We view a modest creature. Just
The same applies to fellow men.
There's those who treat with mean contempt
A person from a 'lower' class,
As when an officer I knew
Had treated me before he learned
I'm soon to change my stripes for pips
Denoting subaltern – like him.
As, when cadet, a sergeant swore

And tore a strip or two from bloke
Who's fellow sprog, but soon to be
Of higher rank, when adjutant
Curtailed his spate of purple words
To whisper 'Don't you know that man's
A marquis from an ancient stock?'
The sergeant's face, more eloquent
Than all his former flow, was filled
With fleeting look of pure disgust
That's shared by all who overheard.

Another night a couple of civilian cars collided outside our guard post. I summoned an ambulance and sat an uninjured but shaken lady in the guard room and gave her tea while waiting for the ambulance. When they had all departed I wrote a summary of the incident in my guard commander's report. When the duty officer appeared later and asked if there was anything to report I handed him my written report. He was furious. I should have summoned him and not presumed to have dealt with it on my own. I quietly replied that I had dealt with far worse incidents on active service in Cyprus, but he didn't consider that was relevant!

Many days at Woolwich the duty allocated was completed by noon. Officially one was still on duty until five pm. As my parents were living in Putney at the time I would slope off home for the rest of the day. In order to seem to be on duty I had armed myself with a large brown envelope with "ON HER MAJESTY'S SERVICE" in bold along the top. I would then walk purposefully past the Regimental Policeman on duty as though I was heading across the public road to another part of the Woolwich complex. One day the RP challenged me to say what duty I was engaged in! I quickly perceived he was only a lance bombardier while I was a full bombardier. So I snapped at him to stand to attention when addressing a more senior rank and demanded to know why he was improperly dressed when on duty, with his beret askew and his top button undone. He spluttered a feeble response while I quickly moved off for a drink in the nearest pub to calm down before proceeding on my way! I was more cautious in future!

Shortly afterwards I was posted to Aldershot. In the Basic Wing we learned the essentials of being an officer interspersed with infantry drill and field exercises. We then moved to the main Artillery Wing and I was back on 25 pounder guns.

Each month there was a parade for those being commissioned as officers. For these a senior officer, usually retired and highly distinguished, took the parade. On one occasion it was Field Marshall Lord Montgomery. As Monty inspected the ranks he had just passed me when he turned back and confronted me. Indicating my GSM medal ribbon he demanded to know why I was not wearing my medal! I explained it was on its way back from Cyprus, having been dispatched there as I was posted back to England. It was evident that he had retained his eye for detail!

A major exercise was when we went to Sennybridge in South Wales to carry out gunnery practice with live ammunition. The farmers were warned in advance when they needed to remove their livestock from a planned target area. However, they sometimes claimed that the message had not been received. When a sheep or bullock was killed as a result they claimed compensation from the MOD. They also surreptitiously sold the carcass to a local butcher! We arrived with our guns one day to find the target area covered in sheep. So we calculated the range and added 200 yards and fired a shell. The sheep started racing down the slope towards us. So we dropped the range by 200 yards and fired another round. The sheep came to an abrupt halt and looked bewildered. We then fired a shell 200 yards to the left of the flock and they moved off to the right at a pace. We kept on firing rounds 200 yards to their rear as they fled to our right. We cleared the range without killing a single sheep! It had been the best piece of gunnery practice during this visit to Wales.

On another occasion I was involved in an unfortunate incident. Each cadet was in charge of a gun for an exercise. When the officer in charge shouts his orders the person in charge of a gun raises an arm vertically in the air to acknowledge each order, so that despite the racket of gun fire the officer knows his order has been received. On this particular occasion when the order 'Cease firing' had been given, due to my defective hearing (from the two bombs in the base camp in Cyprus) I failed to hear it and fired another round. At the ensuing enquiry the rest of my gun crew all testified that I had not raised my arm to acknowledge the order to cease firing. As a result it was the officer who was reprimanded for not noticing my failure to acknowledge his order.

IRKED (TL)

While being trained I found myself
In charge of gun and aiming shells
At distant slope of hill in Wales.
But when the captain loudly yells
His 'Cease firing!' I'd fail to hear
Above the thump and roar that masked
Command. I'd fired another round.
Inquiry then in turn had asked
Each member of the troop, and all
Declared I'd never raised my arm
To signal I had heard. It's thus
I'm cleared of blame. But captain's charm
Was quite expunged when board assigned
The guilt to him for being blind
To fact I'd not acknowledged loud

Command he'd thought enough. Behind
My back he marks me down as one
To watch until I give him cause
To reprimand for minor lapse.
Or else he gives me worst of chores
Whenever chance allows. He's guy
Whose spiky pride ensures he can't
Admit he's wrong in front of men
Assigned to his control. I shan't
Be miffed by irksome, petty sleights
By which he seeks revenge. Indeed
I feel for him, who's still as boy
Who won't confess to childish deed.

I received my commission as a Second Lieutenant shortly afterwards and was posted to Larkhill on Salisbury Plain (not far from Stonehenge).

With 192 Independent Survey Training Battery in U. K. – with rank of 2nd Lieutenant (to Lieutenant in Army Emergency Reserve after demob).

The battery was adjacent to the camp of a Medium Gun regiment and our officers shared their mess. I was junior subaltern, there being two regular subalterns who had been posted to the battery a little before me as their first posting after being commissioned, following their training at Sandhurst. The three of us were directly answerable to a major responsible for overseeing the training programme in artillery surveying.

I was made Fire Officer for the Battery and sent on a week's course with the Kent Fire Brigade. One day a grass fire started (probably caused by a discarded cigarette butt) at the edge of our camp. As the wind was blowing the fire away from our camp I gathered some of my men and got them to extinguish the flames. I was then reprimanded for not having sounded the fire alarm and summoned professional help! With regard to my responsibilities as fire officer I was obliged to regularly check all the firefighting extinguishers, and other equipment listed in my Fire Officers log. I would note deficiencies and send a memo to the Quartermaster. He, however, was of the old school of QMs who regarded his stores as being not for plundering. Issuing his precious stores went against the grain. My memos were just filed. However, the annual Brigadier's inspection was looming, so I sent the QM a memo pointing out that my Fire Officer's log would be inspected and that my previous memos had not elicited a response from him so that the column indicating the problem had been dealt with remained blank. The QM produced the replacement items, remarking that it seemed my time as an NCO had made me grasp better than he had supposed how the army worked!

As the Brigadier's inspection approached fresh paint appeared everywhere and all sorts of neglected tasks were completed. I witnessed one especially amusing incident. I was in the CO's office when the QM came in and said that in checking the stock of cordite he found there was a surplus of charge 3 bags. It seems that there had been a bout of firing on the ranges when only charge 1 and charge 2 bags had been used and the unused charge 3 bags had not been signed back in again on their return. Having surplus items was as much an offence as having items missing. A little later the QM appeared again and said we still had a one-ton truck that had been declared no longer worth maintaining and was supposed to have been delivered to a REME unit for decommissioning and thence to scrap. However, the CO (who had established a small market garden on some spare land at the edge of the camp) had delayed delivery as he had been using it for taking produce to sell in Salisbury. The CO picked up the phone and got on to the REME depot. He told them he was dispatching the truck forthwith, apologizing for the delay in its delivery. They replied that that was not on, as when they had found no record of having received the truck by the required date they had falsified their book entries to indicate that they had received the truck and that it had subsequently been scrapped! The scowling CO put the phone down and paused. He then brightened up and turning to the QM said the solution is simple. Put your two problems together out on the Plain, set a fuse, light it and get clear. There is a bowl shaped depression on Salisbury Plain to this day, which subsequently gave rise to the following poem:

PROBLEM SOLVING (CW)

A brace of scholars near Stonehenge
Were stood beside a hollow in
The lawn of turf debating who
Had made it long ago. The kin
Of Beaker Folk perhaps? Or else
Before? I started chuckling, not
Aloud, because I knew its date
For sure. Indeed it's not forgot.
I'd been in army at the time,
Along the road, when annual game
Of bullshit spin was well away,
So nothing would appear the same
On day the brigadier and team
Composed report on state of camp.
A week before, Q.M. had found
Some surplus cordite bearing stamp
Of 3, denoting guns had fired
A run with 1 and 2 alone;
But clown in charge had failed to log
Return of surplus 3s. The tone

Of gloomy quarter M was bleak
Indeed. Excess was just as bad
As loss. As C.O. pondered what
To do, the Q.M., looking sad
And more, returned to say a truck
Condemned as due for scrap had not
Been sent away by stated date.
The C.O. said he'd clean forgot!
He phoned the R.E.M.E. base to say
It's on its way. But they replied
That wouldn't do as when they'd failed
To find the truck confessed they'd lied
By fixing books to show it scrapped.
The C. O. swore and turned to face
The waiting quartermaster stood
By door. And then, without a trace
Of smile, he said 'There's simple way
To solve our pair of problems. Just
Combine the two on Salisbury Plain,
Ignite the fuse and run. I trust
That both will blow away'. Today
The only clue that's left is round
Depression near Stonehenge that set
In train our scholars' thoughts profound!

Another course I was sent on was a week at Warminster for Army Methods of Instruction. I learned more in one week of the essentials of effective instruction than on my subsequent Certificate of Education course (see chapter 6). Each of us was required to conduct a lesson on a subject of our choice, as long as it related to an aspect of army life. So we each chose topics as atypical as possible. Thus a WRAC told us how to choose and arrange flowers for a special event in the officer's mess! I chose a rescue excavation of a Bronze Age barrow threatened by tank training exercises. It was not the topic that mattered. The instructors and the whole class gave a point by point criticism of each presentation. This was humbling but extremely helpful.

Back at Larkhill my squad was taught the use of the theodolite by my sergeant (this was long before laser aiming devices let alone GPS navigation, etc.). I taught advanced map work both in the classroom and the field. The field exercises were sometimes memorable. One foggy morning I turned up for the parade before setting off and noticed the men all seemed rather pleased with life! I asked the sergeant why they are looking so cheerful. He replied the poor fools believe the exercise will be called off because of the fog! So I told to the men that I expected them to learn a lot today as the conditions mimic the situation when the enemy has put down a smoke screen! Their cheerful looks vanished! They did indeed learn a lot. To operate the theodolite with such a short range of vision one man of each pair advanced into the mist until his partner at the theodolite called halt as he started to lose sight of him. He then instructed him to move a ranging pole left or right until it was on the required bearing. He then moved the theodolite to the ranging pole and repeated the exercise until the set target came into view eventually. The fog slowly thinned during the rest of the day.

For another field exercise the men were required to survey in a wide circle from the courtyard of a pub, where the sergeant and I set up a computation centre, from one to another of a set of features on the map and back to the pub. The rules were that they had to close to within strict limits of accuracy horizontally and vertically. They one and all failed to close to these limits! So the sergeant and I went around with them. At first we also failed whether we went clockwise or anticlockwise. However when we checked the tolerances at each stage they were within the limits until the next target was a trig stone. When we left out the trig stone everything closed beautifully. So we knocked on the famer's door and said that according to our measurements the trig stone was not where it was indicated on the map. "Well you see" he drawled "it got in the way ploughing so I sort of shifted it to the edge of the field"! This taught the men to trust their theodolites and not assume that an object observed was necessarily where indicated on the map!

On another exercise I was pointing out distant features and asking for a precise grid reference as though it were a target for artillery fire. This entailed accurate map reading in conjunction with taking accurate bearings. In one case a distant object was on a straight ridge but the bearing went through a deep re-entrant in the ridge according to the contours on the map! We were perplexed. On return to camp I reported the dilemma to the major. He was delighted. We had discovered for ourselves a draftsman's error on the smaller scale map. He showed me that on the larger scale map there was indeed no re-entrant on the ridge in question. He was pleased that we were not fudging things but admitting anomalies. I got on well with my major as he, like me, had risen through the ranks before he had been commissioned. I also got on well with my sergeant major and my sergeant as well for the same reason and because I had been on active service.

With regard to the classroom exercises I would always end a session by saying that if anyone was still not clear about a topic to let me know and I would be happy to give a short extra session after hours, as I wanted all my squad to pass their trade test. One day two lads asked if I could give them such extra tuition. I told them I was just going to grab a cup of tea at the mess but to come to the office in twenty minutes. As I was drinking my cup of tea one of the regular subalterns accosted me and asked why I was still in uniform after the day's work seeing I was not orderly officer that evening. I explained that I was returning to the office in a few minutes to give a quarter of an hour's extra instruction to two of my squad. He exploded at me, saying that if the stupid idiots can't pass the trade test without out of hours extra tuition they don't deserve to pass. I begged to differ. In the event all my squad passed but several of his squad failed.

Subsequently I had a further confrontation from the subaltern and his mate. It had come to their notice that when off duty I had been going to the cinema in Salisbury with ordinary gunners. The background to this was that when my regiment had returned from Cyprus the mayor of Salisbury told the army authorities that if the 39th regiment returned to Salisbury Plain he would resign! It seems the regiment had a reputation for causing trouble in Salisbury on Saturday nights. So the regiment was posted to Carlisle. This not only gave rise to friction with the infantry regiment based there but the following incident went too far. A sergeant in my former troop had gone into a café for a drink, when the proprietor asked if his GSM medal ribbon was for having served in Cyprus. When the sergeant replied that it was, the proprietor responded that he was from Cyprus. As other customers left the café the proprietor disappeared and then returned with some fellow Cypriots. They then made to attack the sergeant. He extricated himself by pushing a table at them. On return to camp he went to the billet of my former section and recounted the episode. Adding that he was not suggesting anything but telling them the location of the café. Well, of course, the lads went there forthwith armed with a length of strong rope, as they knew the café roof was essentially supported by a central iron pillar. They marched in and while some confronted the proprietor the rest attached the rope to the pillar. Then as they left they heaved on the rope and dislodged the pillar half burying the proprietor in rubble from above. The authorities then decided to post the regulars of the 39th to Germany, but to redistribute the National Servicemen to other Royal Artillery regiments. It was thus some of my former mates ended up in the Medium Gun regiment adjacent to our camp.

I was delighted to link up with my former mates on Saturday evenings and to go out with them to the cinema in Salisbury, and to the pub afterwards before catching the last bus back to camp. However, the two subalterns were furious. I told them there was a bond between us as a result of having been on active service together. They were not members of our unit, I was off duty, in civilian clothes and was behaving within the law. What was their problem? They merely spluttered in reply. I continued to go out with my former mates. It was a matter for regret that, when relaxing in the Officer's Mess, I got on well with a National Service subaltern from the Medium Gun regiment but my relations remained cool with the two Regular subalterns of my own unit.

Two incidents stand out from these excursions to Salisbury. On one occasion the film we saw was Charlie Chaplin's film debunking Hitler (The Great Dictator). The film ends with a secular sermon from Chaplin arguing that you must treat even your enemy as a human being. Afterwards in the pub one of my former mates with whom I had argued about torture (see above) was very quiet as he downed his first pint. He then turned to me and quietly said Chaplin had made him at last understand when I had been arguing against the use of torture in Cyprus.

The other memorable incident I summarized in the following poem:

RETURN TO BARRACKS (CW)

Wedged in a window seat by a far from
Sober, expansive man (who reeked of staled
Beer and tobacco, who'd an unworried
Childlike, innocent air but who exhaled
With the wheezing of a tired consumptive
Old mongrel dog) I sat in the last bus
Back to camp: ensconced in wand'ring thought, more
Or less unaware of the eruptive
Bursts of laughter or the undercurrent
Of unmusical renderings of songs.
Sudden excruciating crescendo -
An explosive hubbub as of bored throngs
Of ignorant rioting malcontents,
Intrudes upon my private world. We'd stopped
At a desolate spot. The driver stood
In the black outside – smoking. Sentiments
Within were richly unrepeatable
And all totally uninformative!
Being not in uniform, I wriggled
And forced a way, through the lamentable
Mob to the rear. The conductor remarked
With amused resignation, that "old Jim
'E 'adn't driven on paynight before."
Not my will pushed me as I disembarked
To ask – what's up? "I'm not going a foot
Farther with that bloody lot of drunken
Slobs aboard. What with that row and with them
Ringing them bells and all, 't's enough to put
Any decent bloke up the wall". He paused
While he flicked ash from his cigarette. Me?
I offered to silence the lot! He peers
At me as though I'd, with a word, caused
The ground to gape wide open and swallow
His red double-decker – whole. He looked lost.
"Mate! If you do that I'll go. Any more
Bloody noise, mind you, and they can implore
Me how they bloody well like – I won't shift."
I apprehensively watch myself yell
"Listen everybody!" The din subsides.
"I'm an officer." A subdued soft swift

Hiss – timorous boos. The situation
Was briefly explained "…so calm down! Shut up!"
Reluctant engines sputter to life. Undertones
Of mutterings. Dreary barracks, lit up,
Loomed ahead. They filed out. Surly, sheepish
Looks. A man, I'd met once in a pub, placed
A light hand on my shoulder to murmur
Softly his thanks – and slipped with quiet haste
Into the dark. Did what I'd done deserve
Any commendation? Should I have leant
Upon my rank? Had I not now given
The shield of insignia my assent?
Pondering, still half in a dream, I went.

On two other occasions I was reprimanded for making snap decisions that seemingly exceeded my authority to do so. The first was when my sergeant phoned early one morning to say his young daughter had fallen sick in the night and he needed to take her to the doctor as his wife had an inescapable other commitment. I told him he had my permission to have the morning off, and I would cope without him.

The second occasion I was reprimanded was most bizarre. It was during the Easter break when I had drawn the short straw and remained at camp as the Duty Officer. In the night I was roused by the deputy mess steward to report that the guard for the officer's mess had gone on strike after encountering a ghost. I dressed and went down to the corridor by the kitchens, where the guard commander NCO was remonstrating with the guard. I asked the latter to start at the beginning and tell me what had happened. He said as he was walking the corridor checking everything was secure when he was confronted by the ghost of a headless man in a long cloak. The guard was clearly shaken, sweating and very pale. He flatly refused to continue on guard. I told him he was relieved and was to appear at the office in the morning straight after breakfast. I instructed the guard commander to rouse the man due to go on guard next and to order him to take over at once. At breakfast the next day everyone was talking about the incident when the mess steward returned from his break. He was astonished and said he had been reading some of the old mess logbooks and had read that a similar incident had occurred some years before! He went off to find the relevant logbook and after a bit of searching found the entry. The ghost had been seen at the same place and the ghost fitted the description the guard had given me in the night. When the guard appeared at the office after breakfast I told him that his refusal to continue on guard duty was a most serious offence. However, I had been persuaded he had not made up his story so I was not going to charge him, but I was going to let him off with a caution that any repetition would necessitate a charge and a full investigation. Later I was reprimanded for not referring the matter to higher authority!

There was little to occupy one on weekday evenings out on Salisbury Plain. I took to reading widely in the works of the atheist philosophers, works on religion, a translation of the Koran into English, etc. This was all part of my simplistic faith having been shattered by finding myself fighting terrorism initiated by Archbishop Makarios. This spell of atheism was reinforced by my then unrecognized Post Traumatic Stress Disorder (see above) which only became apparent gradually during my undergraduate days (see chapter 3). However, an amusing incident was when some gunners attended a fundamentalist preacher on Sundays. They were partly attracted by his preaching but partly puzzled by his rejection of advances of science such as evolution. One day a couple asked me to attend on a Sunday and to tell me what I thought of the preaching. Afterwards they asked me for my reaction. I said that his commending of living in accord with the Gospel values was entirely acceptable but his rejection of advances in scientific understanding was based on ignorance of the evidence and an idolatry of Scripture that was essentially stupid. It seems that the following Sunday they tried to engage with him in line with my observations, but without success. So they asked me to attend again on the following Sunday, which was just before my demob. They introduced me to the preacher and told him I was leaving the army next week. To my surprise he asked me to address the congregation but introduced me by saying that he disagreed with everything I was about to say! Afterwards the gunners thanked me for helping them to understand that by accepting the Gospel they were not required to reject advances in science and other areas of scholarship. Confronting an idolatry of Scripture was to become a recurring theme in my life (e.g. see chapter 8).

In August my education in the military ended and I returned home a different person from the day I had travelled to Oswestry for my basic training in the Royal Artillery. In retrospect my army service was the most important stage in my transformation from a shy and reticent boy lacking self-confidence, into an adult increasingly looking to the future with a growing optimism and hope. However, I only gradually became aware that I was to suffer Post Traumatic Stress Disorder as a result of my time in Cyprus (see chapter 3).

CHAPTER 3

UNDERGRADUATE STUDENT

1959-1962: student at Cambridge University
(Sidney Sussex College)

In 1957 I had obtained my place at Sidney Sussex College in order read Archaeology. However, during my National Service my primary interest in natural history reasserted itself. I decided to switch to the Natural Sciences Tripos. There was some concern at this as my GCE A levels in Zoology, Botany and Modern History were deemed to be not the normal combination expected. Indeed since then I would not have been accepted for Natural Sciences with this combination!

Returning to academic work after my military experience was not easy at first. However, it was great to be challenged and to join in extracurricular activities.

I joined the Cambridge Natural History Society (which was both Town and Gown); becoming secretary to the Entomology Section in my third year. In my second year I was invited to join the college Alchemists (which comprised six second year members and six final year members. The members of each six were required to represent six different branches of science). Each member gave a talk each year and a lively discussion followed the talks. Also in my second year I was invited to become a member of the University's Biological Tea Club for undergraduates and research students. Possible members were invited to a meeting. The strange rituals during the initial tea were not explained before a member gave a talk. At the next meeting the admission of the guest at the previous meeting would be put to the vote. Admission was based on evidence of genuine enthusiasm for biology PLUS a sense of humour! In my final year I was elected the convener. I also joined the William Temple Society, becoming its Treasurer in my final year.

In addition to these affiliations there was much informal discussion in fellow students' rooms, in pubs, cafés, etc.

A CAMBRIDGE CAFÉ (CW)

I sat, waiting in a friendly corner
Of a low-ceilinged café basement. Mine
Was a table for four. Idly toying
With a knife, I lose the dull, distant whine
Of traffic. The restless world was remote
Or non-existent. Drear, dazzling décor
Whose illusory mirrored space extends
To an illusion of nothing. I note
The squat, square, supporting pillar. The whorl
As each paper napkin sprouts from each glass.
Dendritic drainage patterns which wander
And meander through the dried sauce film on tall
Bottle necks, round whose bases cluster salt,
Vinegar and other odd additions.
The humming clatter to which there's no halt
The clicking cutlery and plates. The ring
Of the cash till drawer and chinking change.
Obstinate pepper refusing to sift.
Great mounds of chips. The varied, wide range
Of people. One guy's alone – I followed
His far-away gaze to a shimmering
Playing of light on a huddle of jugs,
On a shelf at the side. A hammering
Tread on the stairs, as a couple arrived.
He had a faintly intellectual air.
(It seems his dark-glasses were a device
For keeping his self out of sight!). Long hair
Encroached on his collar and ears. While she
Appears a glamorous asset of his.
(Perhaps he regards women as social
Adjunct and no more!). Her strange coiffure is
Seemingly supported by faith! He showed
Her to a seat. Her discarded glove lay
Like a dead man's hand in the dingy light,
On a neighbouring chair. Beside them flowed
An earnest interchange between a pair
Of aspiring Labour politicians,
Who, oblivious of the shades of grey,
Had assembled an odd horde of ideals
Analyses and cures in wild array.
Beyond – immaculate (waistcoats and all) -

79

Were three with looks of dogmatic contempt.
They seemed pitiably embedded. Matrix
Of oppressive monotony. Exempt
From the attraction of women! (Or else
Refugees from the irrational in
Themselves?). A disturbing distracting bray
Of laughter directed our eyes towards
A group dressed in well-styled jackets and ties,
Lacking ostentation – the young lady
In equivalent garb. (Did she surmise
That her audience were each so intent
On how to make an impression on her?).
To my right four fellows were discussing,
With much enthusiasm, the extent
To which it was likely some machine or
Other, would do something or other for
Which it was not built. Detailed descriptions
Of mechanical guts, and prescriptions
For how to achieve this or that. But one
Of them interposed interjections which
Were intended to imply vast knowledge.
Nearby, a lively debate between two
Who subsisted by metabolizing
Many books – so it seemed to me; to who
The satisfactions of controversy,
With no risks of expressing opinions
Of consequence to anybody, was
As some rare, white wine. But now companions
Had sat at my table. Jerseys and jeans;
Save for the Irish lass whose green-daubed nails
And red hair were a weird combination.
A semi-ritualized badinage screens
Our actual concerns, but reveals certain
Attitudes in common rejected. One
Positive bond existed – immersion
In humanity – yet we'd not begun
To be involved. (Did this desire to mix
With one's fellow men spring from residual
Psychological need? Or did it come
From a deep compassion?). Once more I fix
My gaze on that chap by himself – who sits
Enmeshed by his own reserve – but not through
Arrogant detachment, more from complete
Inability to enter a new
World not of his own choosing. (Yet don't we

Derive our abilities from the quite
Irrelevant contents of our childhood?
If Christ were incarnate right now, then might
We not find him here? Are we not today's
Lost sheep – blindly groping?). Our bills we paid.
In a lingering knot outside we stood.
Still frosty air and a faint misty haze.

A major preoccupation of my time as a student was gradually recovering my faith in Christ along with taming the Post Traumatic Stress Disorder, which had fuelled my spell of atheism as a subaltern. An amusing example of my PTSD was when I was walking up Sidney Street with Stephen Salter, with whom I shared rooms in my first year, when a student's old car backfired. At high speed I leapt into a shop front quivering with apprehension, while Stephen was engulfed in laughter on the pavement. It took me about a couple of years to stop reacting to unexpected loud bangs and the PTSD was only gradually recognized for what it was. Occasional nightmares relating to Cyprus occurred well into my sixties, but thankfully with increasing rarity. Occasionally Audrey had to shake me awake to ask at whom was my anger being directed.

Initially my slowly recovering faith was over intellectual. It wasn't until my 1995 collection that I published my more mature recollection of this pilgrimage. My approach was as touched on in the following poem:

HERE I STAND (GK)

The urge to reconcile beliefs
Derived from science unconstrained
With those espoused by church is not
A task for fools. My mind's restrained
By logic's nagging claims and need
To face the stubborn facts derived
From thorough observation, or
From careful trial that's well contrived
To test a guess. For me a claim
That's based on ancient texts alone
Can not be given weight, unless
It chimes with what I've learned from life
Itself. In past they might explain
The world in terms we can't espouse
Today. To cling to such is vain.
For us we need to re-assess
The legacies of old. We'll weave
Our own designs that reach beyond
Our minds to depths that won't deceive.

A key poem emerging from this process was the following:

AD FINEM AD INFINITUM (GK)

When reckless reason rode to hounds
On scent of dogmas dry as dust
It blooded youth with godless lust
For freedom from the faith of old
Unleashing energies sublime.

"Religion's all a pile of trash.
It's fed with fears and hollow dreams.
Despite its reams of wordy tomes
It can't survive the streams of sense.
It won't proceed from earthy facts."
It's thus their guru pours his views,
With reason's pebble-polished phrase,
With telling samples plucked with care
From diverse books and daily scene.

"But wait," a softly spoken voice
Replies. "What do you mean 'it won't
Proceed from earthy facts'? We start,
In all we seek to understand,
With mind. – (We need a mind to put
The case that mind is not the fact
From which all else must flow!). A cat
Observed is first inferred by mind
From clues retained by neural sieves."

"If cats, with other earthy facts,
Are first inferred from mental facts
Then what is source of other guests?
My mind is host to many things -
There's love, there's sense of right and truth,
There's sudden insights, purest joys,
There's hope and reach for lofty dreams.
Do these imply another realm
In which the Word and Love are King?"

"Since Buddha's bold despatch of God
A thousand lesser souls in vain
Have tried to stop Him creeping back.

82

Apart from those whose lack of faith
Is like a mirror's loss of light
When all is black, they're not content
To clear the ground. They feel compelled
To build anew. So Shelley tried,
And Russell too, and many men
Of lesser worth. They piled their stones
In ramparts high. All holy trash
And trappings burned to ash on pyre
Of church beyond the walls of New
Jerusalem. Their flag of love
Unfurled above. The children ask
'What word is this that flutters free
Against the fickle sky?' The men
Of learning search their tomes all day.
The clowns who govern scratch their heads
And ask commission for its views."

"The cleansing hose of change has sluiced
Our shippens clean. But time the sheen
Has dulled, while ordered boredom screams
For swifts ascending high aloft
To light, for pastures filled with sun,
For risk of rain, for hail, or snow,
For hope of seeing beauty robed
In truths beyond the whims of men."

A man of humble birth proclaims
"It's I who am the Word of Love
And God is gift of love to men."
The world grimaced and struck his face,
And proudly nailed him to a cross.
But still our hearts are stung with hope
As quietly love infects each soul.
And still commission's at a loss.
And still we rake the words of men
In vain, and dream of shippen's shade.

Ahead we glimpse a winding track
Amid the geometric maze
Of recent trails that slice across
The peneplains of bygone hills.
And yet that path, obscured by drift
Deposits dropped by snow and ice
That froze the souls of modern men,

Persists as intermittent link
To saints of old and light beyond
The edge of bowl in which we move
And build our piles of facts to help
Us peer across our crater's rim;
While poet steals the wings of bird,
Or else suggests he's angels heard,
And thus declares himself 'absurd'.
Today the poet's voice is faint.
The Eng. Lit. troops have dredged the past,
To free us from the choking form
To plunge us in a pond of doubts.
The image like a cancer spreads
Until all message now is dead;
Or else in jolly jingles jars
On admass cards by mammon's hacks.
So now a poet's left to cringe,
Or flee from those who want to know
The meaning hid within his words
That rise within his mind as stabs
Of light that shimmer bright, but fade
Before the thought is clear: or else
Refer the gasping reader back
To half a page of notes that please
The thesis chill, but saps the claim
That poetry speaks to normal folk.

The tool kit spilled upon the floor
Displays a choice not known before.
The rough-hewn planks in racks are stacked.
Their textures taunt the feasting eye.
The grain reveals a patterned song
That strains to be released at once.
But we, bewildered, dither long,
Or whittle wood away until
A heap of shavings masks the floor
And tells us more than what remains.

We fear that simple truths, that stand
Exposed, arouse suspicions black.
We feel that we must needs conceal
Our joys, our living lights, behind
The guise of worldly-wise; reveal
Our gold as girl who hides her charms
Behind her lovely clothes, that give

A tantalising peep to lure
Us on in hope that's not fulfilled.

Perhaps it's always so. Perhaps
We sit beside the sea, with sieve
In hand, to ladle leaking hopes.
Perhaps at death we find the phrase
For what we wish in words to say,
In songs to praise. Till then we bray,
Or stare in silence at the haze.
We seldom speak, we rarely pray,
Until the night has claimed our day.
Across the ocean's sweep we gaze,
Awaiting light of sun's first ray.

Our faded dreams defy the reams
Of reasoned prose that others strove
To lay before a world in need.
The wisdom won by many men;
A million words and many more
By those who felt compelled to write;
And yet the mind's a leaking pan
With little left to prove their point.
Our filtered views a lucky dip.
And less we claim our own, despite
Our constant search for meanings hid
Behind the masks of things and folk.

It's taken time to come to terms
With truths revealed by science free.
But now we see our minds are cleansed
From filth of atavistic fears
Which clothed the Gospel's truth, until
A crust of fiction hid its light.
But now, with Darwin's help, we see
That Paley's heartless artisan
Has shared all idols' fate and lies,
With image of a forceful God,
In fragments littered on the ground.
Our Lord did not the germ evoke.
The deadly sting was not designed
By He who shared with us the pain
Of life on earth, who hung on cross
Of shame. It's not for us to make
A cosy God whose 'providence'

Will steer our lives. He beckons us
To go with Him without a map -
Until we've done. For now it's blank.

Immaculate as freshly fallen snow
The paper glares at us, seeming now to fling
A challenge in our face to dare resist
Enticing call to be the first to mar
This glory spread like life anew for those
Who wish that time would run a rounded course,
That past could be erased and used again.
But no! Our marinaded selves are steeped
In joys and sorrows, triumphs, failures, hopes
In shreds, encounters in excess with folk,
With things, events and sheer routine until
The make-believe seems sole relief from time.
But now I find this sheet is fading fast.
A strange and holy glow reveals a form
Emerging slowly from a fog of doubt.
It stands and beckons slowly as he turns.
We follow, free at last from worldly cares.
We wend our way between some columns tall
That seem to rise aloft beyond our ken.
We find ourselves upon a plain that seems
To reach a boundless rim of endless sky.
And now it seems the ground has given way
To formless space that bears us up beyond
This spinning orb in whirling void of time
And place. And now it seems ourselves dissolve
And light is all and all around, and near
And far, before, behind, and racing rings
Within a vortex, rushing wind, and tongues
Of flame, gleaming glow of diamond sparks,
And colours pulsing from within a point
Of perfect peace and calm that lures us on
At breakneck speed towards a goal that seems
Is cased within a case within a case,
Like some celestial Chinese doll that we
Must take apart to find the secret hid
Within the secret hid within. At last
The centre's reached and we behold a pool
That like a glass now mirrors us, and He
Who holds our hands. His name is Christ. His face
Is love divine. His crown of thorns adorns
His brow and blood is clotted on his palms.

We turn to tend his wounds but find He's gone.
Instead there stands an empty cross that seems
To rear above a scene of rolling dice,
Above an endless stream of turning lights,
As God is playing ceaseless games of chance,
As time unfurls its seamless ribbon track,
As planets hatch and die and stars explode,
As speck of earth is born beside a sun
That spins within a minor rash of stars.
But then we see a ceaseless stream of love
Descend upon this tiny spinning grain.
We turn again towards the cross. It seems
Once more we're on our own as backward now
We fall towards the spinning orb of fire
Whose nights are black, whose winds have struck us chill.
And yet within we feel a warming glow.
And now we know why God allows the snow
To cover all his footsteps here, and why
He leaves the paper blank for us to fill.
And why His perfect spread of white is still
Unspoiled, save by the marks of children's feet.
Ad finem ad infinitum the call -
"Except you come as child we will not meet."

Or in summary –

LAPSED ATHEIST (GK)

I'd sloughed the careful choice of clothes
That others made with best intent.
They'd seemed to clash with inner self.
They'd made me refugee whose garb
Had come as parcelled aid from those
To whom I'm only abstract noun.

Instead I chose to cleanse my mind
In bracing bath of sceptic hue.
I'd stripped assumptions one by one,
Discarded views, unless sustained
By life's own reel of film or step
By step of reason's ruthless toil.

Oh God with honest doubts I'd turned
From Thee. I tried the godless creeds.

Alas the honest doubts remained.
I'd kneaded antiseptic dough,
Which lacked your loving grace. I'd baked
A bread of life devoid of yeast.

LOST AND FOUND (MC)

I can't return to childhood's praise
For nature's beauties. Since that dawn
I've come to know the darker side.
A silent song is now aroused
By novel facts unearthed by hard
And costly toil. The starker hues
Of rampant strife, the secret role
Of parasites, the dastard toll
From viruses in league with death,
All these are truths I can't deny.
And yet these constant wars bequeath
Us life in all its rich array
Of diverse forms and modes. With awe
I learned of wonders man can scarce
Conceive. Resourceful tricks, and slick
Solutions shaped from bum designs
Selection had no choice but hone,
I find abound. So now I feel
Profound respect, in place of thanks
I gave as child. I still perceive
Delight is right, but worship's praise
Is now reserved for God alone.
His grace accepts us as we are,
But summons us to rise above
The selfish beasts from which we've come.
We're called to walk the way of love
That renders death a passing phase,
That gives us hope beyond the grave.

EASTER'S SHOCK (GK)

It's not as explanation must
We conjure God to fill the gaps
In knowledge gained. It's not as cause
Before all others must our minds
Conceive a power beyond the rest.
Such may have lit the fuse to start

The monstrous bang beyond what thought
Can grasp. Perhaps it's only last
Of series since our universe
Restarted clock of time anew.
The psalmist erred in claiming God
As force that makes the grass to grow.
From what we know today such creeds
Conceal the lack of need for such
Hypotheses. Our search for God
Begins with hunt for aim of life
As we become aware of self
Within the wheeling scheme of things
And other folk. Perhaps it's all
A pointless game. But I have found
Beneath the clamour, hid within
The darkest depths, a yearning met
By silent voice who calls my name;
Inviting me to fan the glow
Of love into a flame that lifts
Emergent soul above this world
Of birth and death, of joy and pain.
Indeed that strangest man we call
The Christ proclaimed this truth in life,
And in his stranger death espoused
As act of trust the world is still
At loss to fully comprehend.
Incarnate love it seems is key
To his and our eternal hope
That life is more than ghastly joke,
As Easter's shock redeems our faith.

FACE THE FACT (RE)

Today agnostics choose to show
Us Jesus shorn of myth, as man
Who really lived; confronting those
Who ruled the Temple, pressing down
Upon the necks of common folk,
Whom man from Galilee preferred.
His challenge still disturbs the rich
And those who govern now. But when
It comes to Easter's morn our man
Of erudition passes by,
Despite the truth that Christ is known

Today because he rose from dead.
If, instead, he'd remained as corpse
In tomb, he'd long ago have shared
The fate of countless men who leave
No mark on history's page. So come
And face the fact that this event
Has turned the world of humankind
Upon its head. Since death is not
Our end the pilgrim's born. The love
Of God's become the light that calls
Us forth from dark abyss of time,
From which our monkey forebears came.
This lowly birth and lofty goal
Are linked in seamless whole by cross
And risen Lord who's gone before.
Allow this insight to transform
Our knowledge into grace of life
That's lived to full in way of Christ -
Until we meet upon another shore.

WHEN I WAS A CHILD
I THOUGHT LIKE A CHILD (CW)
(1 Corinthians 13: 11)

On peering back to when a child
It seems a stranger wears my face.
His mind is filled with fancies, plus
The wildest dreams. There's scarce a trace
Of what concerns my thoughts today.
But when the war had intervened
A lonely lot became my norm.
And only time had slowly weaned
That boy from sense of low esteem
And shyness like a dread disease.
The army turned my life adrift
As infant soul experienced freeze.
The thaw required a weary task
Rebuilding faith by slow degrees;
With bricks I'd gathered one by one,
And carefully laid to not displease
The mind and heart. But now I laugh
At those who preach that God is dead.
Their clever words are merely froth,
Denying life is more than head.

The Holy Spirit's not deceit,
But loving presence deep within
The to and fro of dialogue
That tries to keep me out of sin.
But greater far my soul imbibes
A sense of Kingdom Christ prescribes.

While I slowly recovered my faith it was shorn of much received, but outmoded, accretions from the past. Also there was disquiet at much still taught in the name of religion or worse done in the name of religion:

PALEY'S GHOST (GK)

Religion stains our weary world
From heights sublime, by way of joke,
To menace scarce the mind can grasp
In view of truth that love is heart
Of God and peace his will for all.
So how explain the man with bomb
Who thinks his way is blessed by God?
And what unholy man of cloth
Imparted such a lie? At times
An ordered church has seemed to me
Affront to freedom Christ proclaimed.
But when a faith is left to chance
Of local leader's whim I see
The point. Perhaps the price we need
To pay, for keeping hotheads off
Our backs, is atavistic junk
We're slow to dump, despite it's clear
Its sell-by-date has long expired.
So still I have to bite my tongue
As hymn denies the death of those
Who taught that beasts and blooms
Were made by God, while shunning facts
Revealed by microscope – the worm
That causes blindness, microbes hid
Within a tasty pie or brought
By flea or fly who seek our blood.
Or else we sing of virgin birth
Or earthy paradise in which
Our re-assembled bodies thrive.
At times I want to flee, to sing
Alone. But long ago I found

91

The inner light can lead astray
Unless constrained by shared attempts
To seek the will of God within
Our daily lives. It's thus I've learned
To curb my angry thoughts and seek
The way of love with those who hope,
Despite the mounds of dirt, the gold
Will settle out at base of pan:
And we will find we're part of plan.

SELECTIVE VISION (GK)

When Gilbert White declared the grand
Display of nature's joys proclaims
Benign intents of God, he wrote
Before the march of counter claims
Prevailed. When Wallace/Darwin ditched
Romantic Paley's tract the rage
Prepared the ground for Pasteur, Koch
And Lister's bomb, that microbes wage
A ceaseless war against ourselves
And creatures great and small. To add
To angst then Manson, Ross et al.
Had shown mosquitoes carry bad
Surprise as vector nurses worst
Of parasites require to thrive.
IF God had willed each creature found
On earth today then we arrive
At shocking truth – that fiction god
Is plain malign, a sadist sod.
But 'Lord of Love' was gospel taught
By Jesus who, by acts and thought,
Rejected illness, wolves and weeds.
He summons us to rise above
The jungle scene, embrace his love.
His grace, not nature, slakes our needs.

DUET (TL)

In ancient times this weird, benign
And fearsome world required a host
Of myths and earthbound gods to help
Ancestor humans make the most
Of lives perceived as all too short

And prone to hazards unforeseen.
Besides they wondered as to aim
Of spans so brief when each had been
A losing fight to stay alive.
But then the Jews had grasped that God
Is only one. Since then we've learned
That nature's dumb. We're on our tod,
But free to choose our way or heed
God's inner whispered Word. He'd set
The universe apart until
At length we humans formed duet
Allowing free response to call
To walk the road that moves beyond
Our self-concerns. By means of grace,
The Holy Spirit forms a bond
With parts of brain now free to choose.
Because our God enfolds us all
Within his boundless love our souls
Emerge from depths of primal thrall
To ancient drives. Then love becomes
A two-way flow from God to us
And we to those with whom we share
Our days. There's those who won't discuss
This truth that God is boundless love
And we are free to choose reply.
For them our science enterprise,
With all its gains, they just deny
Is not designed to teach us how
To love and get along with all
With whom we interact each day.
Until we each respond to call
To sanctify encounters made,
As though thereby we worship God,
We've not begun to make the grade.
We'll just remain inhuman clod
Devoid of grace. But when we learn
To see the glow of sacred fire
In other people then our lives
Begin to shed all base desire.
Then joy becomes our daily fare,
Whatever knocks befall. Today
I muddle through my life with hope
And trust I'm in the sacred Way.

EMERGENCE (RE)

Romantic poets may proclaim
That nature's all we need to feed
Our souls, or else there's Hopkins full
Of shining gems designed to turn
Such thoughts to God, but both deceive.
I will concede that beauty may
Uplift our eyes to heaven's gate,
But once one learns of nature's ways
One enters world of blood and pain,
Whose details render God insane
If you now claim He's artist who
Designed the lot. I believe he stayed
His hand when fuse was lit. He let
Explosion run its course until
A trillion worlds were spawned, until
On some at least some living forms
Emerged and then evolved. A few
Of these attained a mega-brain
Allowing knowledge of itself.
And thus appeared some beings fit
To exercise their freedom's choice.
It's these our Lord invites to be
A New Creation shaped by love,
As they imbibe his grace before
They meet Him face to face beyond
The grave, beyond the pain and blood.
Our souls emerge from lowly blooms
As long as they are free to grow
And strive towards the light of love
Without restraint, towards the sun
That shines above the dark in which
Our roots remain by fate of birth.
As souls are formed they're shed by plant.
Each spirit seed gives rise to new
And lovely child of God beyond
Confines of space and time. Amen.

FREEDOM'S COST? (CO)

A carping critic, missing sense
Of poem, failed to spot the clues
To whispered meanings; so instead
Imposed his own. They reeked of stale
Discounted Freud and other cons
Who offer theories built on sand.
They lose their cool when asked to test
Their flimsy claims against a haul
Of further facts obtained in trials
Designed with care, controlled and sieved
With statistician's skill. But who
Can teach a fool who lacks a sense
Stochastic realms impart too much
Of world in which we move, and thrive,
Despite the rolling dice? They shut
Their eyes to chance they feel is blind,
Despite emergent patterns seen
In Poisson curves and likes. They choose
Their anecdotes and fairy tales
Instead. They guard their secret rites
As voodoo priests when casting spells.
So when dissecting lines of verse,
Or deconstructing poems phrase
By phrase, they miss the tone and lose
The jokes that coyly lurk behind
A pun or hints of other realms.
Besides they fail to face the pain
That's wrought by nature on its own
Without the aid of men who serve
Their selfish ends alone. They're right
To ditch a devil used as stick-
-on-label that evades the need
To seek the truth. They're right to mourn
The thousand children dead when town
Was struck by earthquake shock at night
In distant land. They're right to damn
A god whom clever fools have taught
Is in control of all events.
The fact of Jesus on the cross
Exposes such a lie for good.
Our freedom matters more than all
The pain it must entail. Despite

It means that Herod's free to put
To sword those babes before they knew
The joys and sorrows life can bring.
Our Lord desires to summon forth
A diverse range of beings fit
To be the means incarnate love
May freely choose to open door.
His grace and force can never share
A common aim, for love requires
A grasp of self as free before
It may respond to God and seek
To join in Kingdom's joyful feast
Of justice, peace, eternal praise.
For now we're learning how to love.

Much of my recovery of faith was about shedding doctrines that advances in knowledge had rendered untenable. In addition it became ever clearer that it was how we lived our lives and how we related to other people that was what really needed to be our focus. As Peter said "I truly understand that God shows no partiality, but in every nation anyone who fears him and does what is right is acceptable to him" (Acts 10: 34-35). Too often subsequent church leaders, including Peter's subsequent popes, lost sight of this. Indeed, I have been told by some that Peter's declaration regarding Christ that "there is salvation in no other name under heaven given among mortals by which we must be saved" (Acts 4: 12) negates the above quotation from Peter's discourse! However, this would deny that many people act according to inner promptings to serve others, unaware that it is very likely that it is the Holy Spirit responsible for these promptings.

Furthermore Christ declared "whoever is not against us is for us" (Mark: 9: 40) and in his discourse about the sheep and the goats (Matthew 25: 34-40) he clearly indicates that salvation comes to those who serve the needs of others. Likewise Paul wrote "We have our hope set on the living God, who is the Saviour of all people, especially of those who believe" (1 Timothy 4: 10). To limit the activity of the Holy Spirit to those who explicitly acknowledge Christ is essentially to deny the universal offer of the gift of the Holy Spirit to anyone who freely responds to inner promptings to serve others, justice and/or peace. As I gradually became aware of the inner promptings of the Holy Spirit within myself I increasingly perceived evidence of the same in others – even in some who were professed atheists! Indeed some atheists I have met had rejected belief in God as consequence of narrow judgmental experiences aimed at them by some adherents of fundamentalist type Christians seemingly more concerned with assent to questionable doctrines than with living out the Gospel in their daily living and relationships. However, these atheists had not rejected the Gospel view that we are called to serve others and to work to make the world a better place. Apart from individual texts, an abiding theme of the

96

Gospels is the perception that the hallmark of God is a loving concern for all. Likewise the commonest phrase in the Koran refers to "Allah [i.e. God] the compassionate the merciful". Who are we to presume to set limits to God's all-embracing love for the wide variety of sinful human beings? We who admit to being believers are not better than others but are called to be the 'yeast' and the 'salt' in our daily interactions with others – a truly challenging vocation. Indeed the only judgment that should concern us should be aimed at ourselves and our limited success in embracing this vocation.

In my third year I met a girl I felt drawn to. She was a student of classics and daughter of a clergyman. We felt comfortable in each other's company without feeling ready to leap into bed like many of our fellow undergraduates. She came to meet my parents one vacation and there was an expectation that we were destined for a permanent relationship. However, there was a reticence in our relationship that was probably largely on my side. My persistent shyness when it came to sharing my feelings, aggravated by the lingering PTSD from my National Service, increasingly eased in her company. However, the thaw was incomplete by the time of our final year. I took her to the May Ball in June and we ended by punting up the river to Grantchester. When we said our farewells afterwards we did not say so but I think we both knew that it was not an au revoir.

In the following year my first (1963) collection of poems included the following.

TO SEDWELL (CW)

Sedwell – it has taken time to accept,
As reality, our realization
That we lack sufficient community
In our concerns; that we're nothing except
Strange friends to each other. To be as one
Was not for us. That curiosity
Concerning each other which we obeyed,
Half-willing, drew us together; but laid
Bare the dichotomy of interests
Beneath our common attitudes. Sedwell
I could not assimilate that – at first.
But now it seems so plain. We're only cursed
By surprised pitying words that imply
That we've failed. An ungerminated hope
For lifelong union – experimental
Exploration whose negative reply
Invalidates none of the richness gleaned
By us from our companionship – is seen
By the world as disaster where, instead,

I perceive an occasion of grace. Weaned
From my sense of isolation, by you,
No longer need I seek, or fear to form,
Relationships.

Once preoccupation
With things had ceased to satisfy, the storm
Of disillusionment pursued the wake
Of my endless "whys". A fresh awareness
Of people merely sickened, as I saw
My lopsided self tethered to the stake
Of my studies. To realize people were
More than environmental factors ate
Into my embittered being. At length
The gates gave way and released in full spate
Into my conscience mind – new self-knowledge;
Stabilized in the calm of our friendship.

Once more, with enthusiasm renewed,
I turn to the things that delight – pond snails,
Woodlice, birds or stones; but I acknowledge
Them no more as my gods, as my refuge
From human encounter. Does not the Lord
God redeem creative growth from friendships
Such as ours – despite short-sighted gossips?
Sedwell, we can still be friends – without fraud,
Though we're not entwined with a lover's cord.

1962 BA (Hons) Class 2(2) Natural Science Tripos (Part I in Zoology, Botany and Geology. Part II in Zoology). The BA subsequently matured to MA (for the required fee!) as a requirement for proceeding to my PhD (see chapter 8)!

I had enjoyed the Geology Part I option, especially the palaeontology and stratigraphy. I especially relished the vacation field courses on the Isle of Arran and the Pembrokeshire coast. However, within months of graduation papers initiating the Plate Tectonics revolution started appearing and quickly rendered obsolete much of what I had leaned for the exams! John Corner was streaks ahead of the other lecturers in Botany Part I, and, being a Fellow of my college, I greatly benefited from his Supervisions. He was a man of botanical genius but also (unknown to me at the time) a deeply flawed person as a human being (see John K. Corner, 2013, My Father in his Suitcase. Landmark Books, Singapore). He almost persuaded me to opt for Botany Part II, but I chose my primary interest in Zoology instead. However, one thing that stuck with me was his insistence that until one had experienced tropical rain forests one suffered from a distorted, temperate region, perspective on the world of the terrestrial biosphere. This undoubtedly contributed to my later decision to apply for the post in British Honduras (Belize) (see chapter 5). With regard to enjoyment, as well as benefit to my future career, I especially relished two vacation zoology field courses on the north Norfolk coast. For Part I we were based at Brancaster. The Part II class was small enough for us to be housed in The Hut on the west end of Scolt Head Island. In addition I spent a fortnight of my last Easter vacation at the Plymouth Marine Laboratory attending a course run by the staff of the Marine Biological Association. I especially benefited from opting for my project to concentrate on the marine isopods (relatives of our terrestrial woodlice). There was no identification manual for the species of British coastal waters then, only scattered papers on individual genera in various journals. However, when Mr. Spooner realized I was serious he spent considerable time looking out the relevant journal volumes and helping me tackle the identification of the many species we collected. It was challenging work, but it drove home my growing conviction that sound taxonomy was essential for ecological investigations to be of any value.

Before my finals exams I had landed a job, supported by testimony to my evident enthusiasm on the field courses, as the Deputy Warden of the Flatford Mill Field Centre with field zoology as my prime teaching responsibility. The boss of the Centre, Jim Bingley, was a remarkable character (see chapter 4) but something of an old fashioned snob. My appointment probably owed as much to the combination of me being public school and Cambridge University educated and having been an officer in the Royal Artillery as to any intrinsic merits I might have as a naturalist cum ecologist!

I did not take up post immediately after graduation as I was committed to being Co-leader of the Cambridge University Biological Tea Club Expedition to Corsica. This was a welcome pause after the ups and downs, confusions and gains in equanimity of three full years of student life.

BIOLOGICAL TEA CLUB CORSICAN EXPEDITION
(CW)

We'd pitched our tents on a flat terraced ledge
Perched above a fast-flowing mountain stream
Whose many-mooded pools were interspersed
By rolled, moulded boulders strewn, it did seem
Like vast worn pebbles hurled by some huge hand.
On both sides climbed slopes of scrub and parched grass
Which strove to envelop the mottled crags,
Dark clefts and cracks, or balanced blocks which stand
Exposed to the insistent sun, with screes
Of loose chunks of rocks still unclaimed by quiet
Mellowing lichen. Such a blend of lights

And shades, of greens, greys, and rich browns will please
For many a day my memory's eye.
We lived wildly withdrawn from the outside
World. The always-crawling ants shame us
With their endless industry while we lie
Lazing, like lizards, in luminous heat
Reflected from recumbent slabs of stone.
Slowly shadows shrank as each morning was
Consumed by scorching sun. We sat to eat
In the shade of some sapling figs beside
The ever-descending stream, whose softly,
Ceaselessly-sibilant, rumbling rhythm
Sings in our ears – an unheeded aside
To remind us of duration and time -
A time we otherwise measured in meals!
Like a passing drift of slow unhurried
Butterflies we'd near attained that sublime
State whereby it seemed no explanation,
To justify expenditure of hours,
Was required to calm consciences. And yet
We suffer so from indoctrination
By others' attitudes that we regard,
Unthinkingly, inactivity as
In some way shameful or distasteful. In
Order to exist we fear to discard
Our idol of doing. But I recline
In a water-sculpted bowl scoured and shaped
And hollowed by years upon years. I watch
Pond skaters skitter, slide and intertwine
Ephemeral paths in a cool, becalmed
Haven embraced by a purplish-green wall
Of stones spewed forth from ancient volcanic
Cones. Thus absorbed by trivial things – no call
To action rouses me, only a "why?"
Revolving in my metamorphosing
Mind as I idly diapause before
Emerging to creative acts once more.

CHAPTER 4

FIELD CENTRE STAFF

1962-1963 Assistant Warden of Flatford Mill Field Centre
(Field Studies Council)

Flatford Mill had been owned by the father of the painter John Constable. The Centre's buildings and the surrounding landscape featured in many of his paintings and much was still evident in the 20th Century as it had been in his day. Consequently it was a popular tourist destination. This meant one was apt to glance up when talking to students to see strangers peering at us through the window! Most day visitors posed no problem as long as they stayed outside the Centre's private access buildings and grounds. If they came to the office we were pleased to give them details of our courses. Only rarely did trespassers pose a security problem.

Jim, the boss ('the Warden') of the Field Centre, was a remarkable character. A boyhood accident had left him purblind in one eye and blind in the other eye (a situation I was to find myself in many years later – chapter 10). Despite this he had obtained a degree at Cambridge and was a competent botanist, often identifying plants by touch and smell as much as by sight. However he was an anachronism in terms of social attitudes, having come from a privileged background and been educated at Eton. He regarded Comprehensive Schools with suspicion and preferred to give priority to applicants for VI Form field courses to Grammar and Public school pupils. However, the rest of the Centre staff disagreed with him, believing places should be allocated on the basis of first come first served. Instead of arguing with him on this point, Audrey (the Centre Secretary) when reading out letters from applicants would give the name of the school but would miss out the word 'Grammar' or 'Comprehensive'! I had to suppress my chuckles when on the first day of a new course Jim would remark that he couldn't remember booking in this Comprehensive school!

My prime teaching commitment was field biology, with particular emphasis on zoology aspects and ecological principles. A tutor in botany complemented my zoological emphasis. For salt marsh days we tended to work together. Sometimes I would be required to conduct purely botanical days on my own when she or Jim (primarily a botanist but with wide ranging interests in all aspects of the environment) were otherwise committed. The habitats we used ranged from hedge banks, woodlands, succession from rough pasture to scrub and pioneer woodland, freshwater streams, mill ponds, river margins, brackish marsh and a short trip down stream to saltmarsh of the tidal estuary of the River Stour. We also made occasional excursions to seashore habitats near Harwich or to the intertidal zonation up the shore to sand dunes above high water mark at Shingle Street (beside the estuary of the River Ore) and its set of ponds of varying degrees of salinity. With adult courses we would make some trips further afield such as to a noted nature reserve or a reservoir good for water birds.

Sixth form biology students made up our largest student category. The next largest was adult courses, mainly during the summer holiday period. Bird courses were one of my most popular weeks. There were also university student groups and occasional professional groups, which required varying degrees of input by myself. With courses for trainee teachers I and my botanical colleague tended to conduct the entire course. I quickly acquired a wide knowledge of the varied faunas and floras encountered, with a particular emphasis on invertebrates.

From my early interest in freshwater snails, while at Flatford I made some observations on the larvae of a fly preying on water snails. This resulted in my first published note on a species of fly (Disney, R. H. L., 1964. A note on diet and habitats of the larva and an ichneumonid parasitoid of the pupa of Tetanocera ferruginea Fall. (Dipt., Sciomyzidae). Entomologist's Monthly Magazine 100: 88-90).

The winter of 1962-1963 was one of the coldest in the second half of the 20th Century. The River Stour was frozen over with ice extending into tidal waters. Water birds tended to visit the small patch of open water caused by the millrace of Flatford Mill (the main building of the Field Centre). Some would then settle for the night on the ice beside this patch of open water. Unfortunately the constant fine spray of water droplets then froze on them and they became stuck to the ice. So each morning I would walk carefully onto the ice with a bucket of warm water and release these immobilized ducks, moorhens or whatever. One day I rescued two very cold water rails and popped them in a cardboard carton and put them in the warm oven of the Agar stove in the Centre's kitchen but leaving the oven door ajar. The cook, however, closed the oven door without looking inside first! When I returned to check on the birds they were extremely perky! Fortunately they were unharmed and readily scampered off when I released them back to the wild. On a subsequent morning I strayed too near the edge of the ice and fell in. Shaking with cold I rushed back to the Mill and ran a lukewarm bath and lay in it gradually adding more hot water until I recovered from the threat of hypothermia.

In 1963 my first poetry collection was published – FINDING MYSELF (Outposts Publications, 20 pages).
The typescript was executed by Audrey while we were still at Flatford.
For me the most important occurrence at Flatford was my, sometimes somewhat awkwardly clumsy, courtship of Audrey White, the Field Centre's

secretary. She was the kindest person there and I fell head over heels in love with her. My delight when she agreed to my proposal of marriage cannot be measured. To convey something of her as a person and her background I give below some memories she was compiling for our grandchildren during her last years. I have added a few notes of my own to provide some additional background or clarifying comment.

AUDREY (22ⁿᵈ January 1928 to 1ˢᵗ March 2012)

Audrey's parents were Albert White, a first class French polisher, and Gertrude Cottle, who had gone straight from school into domestic service.

The most devastating event for the family was being buried alive, for seven hours. Audrey was squashed together with her two sisters, parents and some neighbours, in the dark in a Morrison shelter in the basement below the collapsed debris of the rest of the building, when Bath was bombed in April 1942. The account in the book by Niall Rothnie (THE BOMBING OF BATH. Folly Books, 2010) is largely accurate. However, her sister Muriel's reminiscences are marred by one omission. It was their Uncle Frank who directed the rescue workers as to where to dig. Muriel omitted this detail because she could not abide the extremely puritanical Frank!

Not only was the Admiralty moved to Bath during the War, the exiled Emperor of Ethiopia (Abyssinia) also moved to Bath, being housed in an apartment in the Royal Crescent. As an expert French polisher, Audrey's father was asked to restore some of the Emperor's scratched furniture. The empress asked Audrey's father if he knew a girl the same age as the princess, who was asking for someone to play with. As a result of Audrey visiting the princess in her Royal Crescent apartment, the princess took to joining Audrey at Brownies, along with Audrey's sister Jean!

Some Childhood Memories by Audrey

I was born on 22ⁿᵈ January in the Year of Our Lord 1928 at 67 Wells Road, Bath – the fourth child of Gertrude Mary White (née Cottle) and Albert Edward White. Their first child was Muriel Gertrude, born in 1919, then Cyril Edward, 1921, then Leslie Raymond in 1924, then me (Audrey Berrell) 1928, and lastly in 1930 my younger sister and their last child – Jean Louisa. I don't suppose that in those days many of us were 'wanted' children, but we never felt that to be the case. Life must have been quite hard for my parents. They had both left school at twelve. My father was a French polisher, and didn't earn very much, although he was very good at his job. At one stage he was asked to polish the furniture in one of the Northern Indian palaces of a maharajah, but Mum wasn't greatly enamoured with the prospect of being left with five children over a longish period. Of course, although Bank Holidays were compulsory, they were not paid – especially hard over the Christmas period.

My father was quite young. Every Sunday morning, we went to see his mother (just remembered as Grandma White) who lived just by the railway bridge at Twerton. She had a long garden and was a very good vegetable gardener. She kept her family fed and watered by taking in washing, and it was my Dad's job to fetch and deliver the washing in a wheel-barrow – sometimes quite long distances. For example, to and from the big Methodist Public School (Kingsdown) on Lansdown. His siblings were Mabel (who lived with Grandma White), Lilian, a brother called Fred, and I think there was another brother who married Alice, but I don't know his name. Alice lived a few doors away from us when we moved to Victoria Terrace after the blitz and Lilian lived with her family in the house opposite! Fred used to wind up the clock in the abbey, and I think other clocks in the city also. He had one son called Bob, whom I vaguely remember because at a time when there were very few scholarships to grammar school he got one of them.

My mother was also one of a large family – Ethel, Isabella, Louise, Elizabeth, Tom and William. Her father was a stonemason. My mother left school at twelve years of age, and went 'into service'. Her first job every morning was to get up at five thirty and empty the ashes from the fireplaces throughout a five storey house, and set the new fires ready for lighting.

I remember my grandfather (Grandpa Cottle) quite well, because our family and Ethel, Louise and Elizabeth and her family all lived within a few doors of each other at Wells Road. So there was never a problem with baby-sitting. Grandpa was always dressed in cream corduroy trousers. Quite often in the evenings, my sister Jean and I used to be with grandpa, Ethel and Bella and our occupation was to roll newspaper spills to light his pipe, and to gouge out the horrible black tar from the pipe stem! All the houses were four storeys high, so we had great times playing hide and seek. Aunt Lilian and Uncle Bob used to have wild parties on New Year's Eve. But if it was a Saturday, we always had to leave as the clock struck twelve, so as not to be making merry on the Sabbath!

Ethel and Bella later made horrible marriages. Ethel had an 'illegitimate' child. It died, but was not allowed to be buried in the consecrated ground at the cemetery (St. James's cemetery near the old Drill Hall) so my Mum and Aunt Ethel dug a grave just under the boundary hedge of the cemetery and buried the child in a little cardboard box. It was as near 'consecrated ground' as could be.

67 Wells Road was a large four storeyed house (the only one available to Mum and Dad when they married) and in a room on the top floor lived Mrs. Powell. She was a lovely old lady, and always had a big coal fire. We used to make toast on long toasting forks. Cyril and Les, who slept in the room next door to her, used to creep in and pinch her hot-water bottle – an old sort of stone one. Before the days of central heating, houses were freezing cold! I remember thinking the boys were terribly clever because they fixed up a tiny torch bulb on their ceiling which they operated on a proper switch by the door!

All this was before the days of electricity. The house was lit by gas. I remember my mother using an iron that you heated in the fire (she spat on it to test the temperature) then a charcoal iron, then, very posh – a gas iron! The living room had one of those iron stoves like you see in Museums – black, with a coal fire in the middle and oven either side. It was all terribly hard work for women – no washing machines, no dryers except mangles, and in the winter the fire was always surrounded with damp clothes. There were linoleum floors to polish. Certainly there were no ready-made meals, or packets of peas or beans! I don't really ever remember my mother sitting doing nothing, or reading a book. Before the days of manmade fibres, socks always got holes in the heels, and jumpers in the elbows. Darning was a constant chore. Woollen things frequently shrank or stretched in the wash.

Our house was the end one of a row of houses (now knocked down).The ground floor, with the living room, kitchen and scullery was at street level, with a door at street level, but there was also a flight of steps which went up to the first floor then into the parlour. Underneath this flight of steps was the coal house. We later had a similar one in the house at Victoria Terrace but larger than it.

The house was on the main road to the City of Wells, the lovely smallish cathedral city about twenty miles away, with a moat round the cathedral. (I recall that the cathedral had an amazing clock, and the verger rang a bell when it was time for the swans on the moat to be fed, and they all came swimming along so gracefully!). About two miles further on from the house, where there was later St. Martin's Hospital, there used to be the dreaded workhouse. A place of awful fear where men and women who'd been together for years were separated, and you only went there in total desperation.

Sometimes, when my Mum or Dad went to get the coal in the mornings from under the flight of steps, tramps would be sleeping there. They looked so wild. They were so poor, and unwashed, uncombed, and bearded and dressed in rags. They were on their way to the workhouse. It was an awful time if you were very poor. Of course, we children were scared of them, but we couldn't realise the total wretchedness of their situation. One day, I remember, Mum brought in a boy of about seven to give him some clothes Les had grown out of. Then as he was going, she gave him tuppence (two pence). He said, with wide eyes, "Can you spare it?"

Once, someone came rushing to the house to say that Cyril had fallen under a tram and his legs were cut off! Somehow my parents knew it wasn't true – he was often getting minor injuries, so nobody did anything and he turned up alright!

My elder sister Muriel was nearly ten years older than me, so she virtually looked after Jean and I. Jean and I shared a bed which was quite common then. Mur had been able to choose the colour of the room – it was deep blue paintwork with little blue-flowered wallpaper. Later on, as Jean and I shared a bed, we were endlessly making a line down the middle to separate our territories! One day we went up to bed and a big black spider was sat right in the middle of the quilt!

Our house had quite a long garden, and we all had a patch to ourselves. I can't really remember much except that my brother Leslie always had to have marigolds and cornflowers growing in his plot as well as tomatoes. I suppose none of us were very interested otherwise, and as an adult I don't think even Les' interest carried on. Dad was a good gardener and also had an allotment about a mile away. The garden had a wall running up the side, and ran alongside a little steep hill called Paradise Street. Fixed to the wall was a hand-rail, and on bonfire nights, a row of children stood on the rail to watch the fireworks, especially Catherine wheels in our garden. Compared to today's exhibitions, it was very unsophisticated, but I think, at least in retrospect, much more fun.

One rather mad thing I remember from Wells Road was when one of us was recovering from something – I think it was Cyril recovering from measles – and was sitting up in bed. Three of us knelt at the bottom of the bed – an iron bed with upright bars and brass knobs at the top. The three of us all had to kneel with our face between the bars and our mouths open. I think it was Les, me and Jean. Then Cyril had to roll marbles down his knees and try to get one into somebody's mouth! Luckily it didn't succeed!

Another day, during the Bath races (horses on Lansdown), some Irish men knocked on the door to see if they could have a bed for the night. My mum said yes, and gave them a meal upstairs in the front room (which used then to be called the parlour). She used her best plates for their meal. When she went to clear up, the men had gone, having left by going down the pit door front steps. She couldn't find the plates. She eventually found them broken in pieces on a ledge up the chimney!

Once we started school Jean and I were always dressed the same. We always had to wear hats and gloves on Sundays – some of the outfits were quite pretty. I remember our hats once were of a very fine pale pink sort of violet with little flowers all over, and wide brims. Shoes were always with an ankle strap, which I did not like! Once we got to secondary school, we were even in the same house, so both had blue Roxburgh house buttons! In the Brownies, I was in the Pixie six. I can't remember which Jean was in. I think Jean liked Guides, but I wasn't so keen. One of the boys, John Bessell, thought Jean was the most beautiful girl in our church. She was always very smart and efficient.

We all went to Oldfield Infants School about three hundred yards up the road, on the opposite side. We joined the nursery class at three years old. I remember, in the next stage, five – eight year olds, we had to stand on our chairs for prayers, and I always felt very giddy. One day, the inspector came, and it was very unfair. A boy aged seven, but big for his age, couldn't tell the time, so he was told off in front of the whole class. I doubt if any of us could have done any better. The girl who gave out the little bottles of milk (one-third of a pint!) each day was called Joy. Walking back home at the end of the day was terrifying because we always had to pass a woman who had been born with her feet on backwards!

We had a lovely ginger cat called Topsy. I remember recuperating from measles on a bed in the garden, with Topsy for company. I also remember Jean having whooping cough and my Dad walking her up and down the room for hours.

Sometimes, our cousin, Dennis, came to stay with us, because he just couldn't do anything right for his stepmother. His own mother had been my mother's sister, Louise (or Louisa, I'm not sure). She died of cancer. If my other cousin, Lionel, came to stay whilst his mother May (another sister of my mother) was ill, there were four boys, and that was really funny. We used to hear all sorts of stamping, and speeches full of saliva and schlschl's and Zeik Heils! One of them would be imitating Hitler whilst the others did saluting and the goose step. Then they would try to trail downstairs still doing this ridiculous step with their arms at the Nazi salute. Of course they always fell over. Sometimes one would be stuffed fat, like Mussolini. They were always reciting verses:

Hickamaliya Ha! Hickalmaliya Hee!
Boomalaka Boomalaka
Have you any doubt
We are, we are, the 4th Bath scouts!

Whistle while you work
Hitler is a twirp
He's half barmy
So's his army
Whistle while you work

Cyril used to recite:
Waste of muscle, waste of brain
Waste of patience, waste of pain
Waste of manhood, waste of health
Waste of beauty, waste of wealth:

That's as far as he ever got, but I've since discovered the rest:
Waste of blood and waste of tears
Waste of youth's precious years
Waste of ways the saints have trod
Waste of glory, waste of God

WAR! by Studdart Kennedy (a wartime chaplain known as Woodbine Willy from his habit of carrying Woodbine cigarettes everywhere).

Les was very strict about me knowing all the different cars, which were easy to distinguish then. I think Jean was too much younger. I remember cycling with him to Grandma White's in Twerton just after I'd learned to ride a bike; and he was so worried about me overtaking him on the inside. I remember that during the winter months, Les used to come home at dinner time crying with freezing cold fingers. He had to cycle from West Central School to Kingston Road and then back again.

A couple of frightening things happened when I was a child. At Wells Road, which was a fairly steep gradient, the brakes on a tram coming down the hill failed one day, and people were jumping over the top (all the trams were open-topped), and it crashed, and there were frightful injuries. Later when I was at Junior School (St. Mark's) we had to walk over a wooden bridge which was about twice as long as the garden at Cambridge (about sixty metres). It was called the 'Tuppenny Bridge' (two-penny), because there had at one stage been a toll. It was quite high, just behind the station at Bath, and one winter's day it collapsed. I suppose the wood was rotten. Many people drowned. The water must have been freezing. Another collapse I remember people talking about was of a sort of swing-type ski-lift over the Bristol Channel to Newport. No wonder I became such a nervous wreck!

This rather pleasant existence at Wells Road ended when May, my Mum's sister died (she had cancer and one of the treatments then was to eat raw liver to keep up iron content in the blood!). My mum decided that we would move to Kingston Road to look after Uncle Frank (May's husband) and his son Lionel. My dad was against the move as it was a much smaller house, there was very little garden, and he was concerned as to what would happen to Mrs. Powell. In addition Uncle Frank was very 'religious'. But in the end, we moved because I think my mother was just too glad to move away from cleaning four flights of stairs, etc.

I was very sad to leave Wells Road, but we all settled into 2 Kingston Road right in the middle of town, and it was also time to change to Junior school – St. Mark's. Jean was still at Oldfield Infants, if I remember right. I don't remember much about it, except that the vaguely enforced uniform was brown and orange, and I remember on Friday afternoons when we had stories, we had to knit. I just sat and cried because I couldn't turn the heel on a doll's sock! I certainly still can't! The school was very keen on quick mental arithmetic and tables, which I've been glad about ever since! I remember there was one quite posh boy, John Dancy, who went on a skiing holiday. None of us had ever heard of it, so he had to give a little talk when he came back. I suppose it must have been quite difficult for him without any gadgets such as projectors! Because it was a Church school, we had to go to church on the first Wednesday in every month. If you forgot your hat, you couldn't go, but had extra work to do instead.

Cyril was a brainy boy and was awarded the Mayor's scholarship at the 11+ exam. This was awarded to the top boy and the top girl. The boy went to King Edward's and the girl to the Girls' High school. He used to come home after the rugby match on Saturday with always the same plea "It matters not..." (whether you won or lost, but how you played the game)! He was really interested in history, and used to cycle everywhere probing about in old churches and long barrows and knew all about market crosses for miles around.

Life at Kingston Road was dominated by Uncle Frank who had had a sudden religious conversion when he was young, and was totally dedicated. He was brilliant at metal work, and made beautiful things, but the only real obsessions in his life were his son Lionel, who was actually good fun, and Manvers Street Baptist Church. On Sundays, we could only sing hymns; we weren't allowed to play games, or even cut things out in paper because we should be "cutting the eyes of Jesus"! However, School, Brownies and the local church filled our lives and we children were quite happy. Looking back, I can't see how my parents could have borne it. Uncle Frank sang hymns all the time, but I don't think it would ever have occurred to him to wash-up or help in any way in the house. That was woman's work! Imagine washing, cleaning, ironing, cooking for nine very day! My Dad must have been almost out of his senses, especially with the lack of a garden and never really in charge of his own household.

Lionel was quite artistic, and once for the Scout concert, painted a whole beautiful backdrop of silver birch trees. Just before we left Wells Road, when I was seven I joined Brownies at Manvers Street Baptist Church. It was wonderful. It was a very well organised and lively Pack and I loved it. I remember Mur teaching me to knit for my Knitter's Badge. She was very patient. We knitted quite a good pink doll's pram blanket. It had to contain both plain and stocking stitch. Les, I remember, was called 'Sugema' in the Cubs. He was the smallest cub. Their pack had a very imaginative 'Akela', Leslie Moore. The 'sixers' had names like Blue Smoke, Grey Brother and White Fang. I also remember reading my first whole book at Wells Road, 'Froggy's Little Brother'.

Every evening at Kingston Road, the gas-lighter came around with his long stick to light the street lamps.

In those days it was the fashion to learn lots of things off by heart. Sunday Schools were big, with about 150 kids at ours, divided into four departments. One Sunday, in the Juniors (8-11) Miss Ainsworth said "Wouldn't it be lovely if we all knew where to find our places in the Bible? Anyone who could say the books of the Old Testament would have a prize". So, of course, I learned them, (the only one!) and got a little Conway Stewart fountain pen. So she said, "Well, let's see if we can ALL do a bit better with the New Testament". So, next week, again I was the only one who'd bothered, but then she said, "Oh well, you can't have a prize. You had one last week"!

Mur and Cyril were in the Guides and Scouts. At Church Parade the two organisations had to sit on opposite galleries in a not very wide church, but were not to look at each other! One day, Miss Blandford, the very strict Guide Captain, called at our house. "Did my mother know that Muriel (aged about fourteen) was walking home with John Seaman?"

"Oh yes, because she's going to tea with him!" Well, that was quite a rumpus. Mr. Bush, the Scout Leader, was also very strict. He was also superintendent of the Intermediate Department at Sunday School (11-14). One day, he saw one of the boys chewing. He stood and made a little cone out of a bit of paper, walked up to John Bessell, and simply said "Spit"! But both he and Miss Blandford took the scouts and guides to glorious camp sites in Cornwall and Devon, which Mur and Cyril both spoke of with great memories. Mur, I think, must have been really fed up with me and Jean, having to trail us round with her when she was in her teens!

Mur for the first time had her own bedroom at Kingston Road, so she sat in glory with all her books. She was devoted to Sunday School teaching. She was also very determined, and gained the Licentiate Piano Diploma of the London College of Music without any teaching other than that she'd had as a young child. She saved up and bought her own piano. She should have had a great education, and was a born leader.

In 1939 I started Secondary School and that was the year that war was declared. Nobody knew what to expect. I think all the adults expected bombing straight away, but nothing happened, so we all went to bed normally after a week or so. Anderson Shelters were built in the roads, and Morrison shelters distributed around the houses. The 'blackout' at night was quite scary. Windows had to have light-proof curtains, and strips of sticky paper stuck all over them, so that if a bomb dropped nearby, the splintered glass would hopefully not be quite as dangerous. Quite often at night, you would hear a deep voice shouting "Put that light out"! This was the Air Raid Warden making sure that no light showed around your curtains. Quite a little light could be picked up by an enemy aeroplane. There were simply no lights, and buses had metal screens across their lights with little slits in, so that they were virtually useless. Going out in the evening was quite scary. Air-raid Wardens were very strict about the tiniest bit of light, not only coming through curtains, but also no smoking in the streets. Once I remember hearing that a bus had mown down some sailor cadets by the station, so, thinking they were at the platform, they stepped out into space and fell into the river.

Men came round to the houses collecting anything made of iron, gates for example for heavy artillery, and aluminium saucepans for planes. At senior school we also knitted. At first this was a disaster, as four girls knitting a khaki jumper ended up with pieces of all different sizes! Eventually we were organized into groups who knitted with more or less the same tension, so the problem was remedied. We tried to help the war effort by collecting stinging nettles for soup. They were dried and dispatched in sacks for processing. Sometimes at school we had to collect rosehips for syrup, rich in Vitamin C.

Cars were not very common, because of lack of petrol. For example, outside our church with a congregation of about 4 – 500, there were only ever four cars! We presumed they were of officials such as air-raid wardens.

At Kingston Road, I remember Les going for his first (and only) job interview. There was he and another boy. The other boy was really poor, so Les came home hoping that this boy had got the job, but he didn't. So Les was installed at the Guildhall.

During the war we listened to the news every evening. It always began with the first four notes of Beethoven's Fifth symphony, because in the Morse code, they signified "V" ..._. It was broadcast everywhere. Of course, we didn't know this at the time, but it apparently upset the German orchestras, as they felt it would be disloyal to play this tune adopted by the opposite side although it was by such a famous German composer! Every Sunday evening the BBC broadcast the national anthems of all the allied countries, despite most of them already being overrun!

Cyril was conscripted to join the navy as a signaller. He was enrolled on 'The Duke of York', a big battleship whose duty it was, amongst other things, to escort convoys across the Atlantic. At least once it escorted Churchill on a visit to President Roosevelt, so Cyril had a few days in The States. He brought back tins of crushed pineapple, which we thought was very odd, because we only remembered pineapple rings or chunks. Later he was on convoys to Mermansk. They were all issued with one-piece woollen garments, including covering the arms and legs. But they had been made without taking the oil out of the wool, for warmth I imagine, and were so tickly that nobody could wear them. So Mum, Mur and Mary washed them to get the lanolin out, and then Mary and Mur unpicked them, and then knitted them up into jumpers. Once we heard that 'The Duke of York' was on the news at the cinema. Mum had never been to the cinema, so at first was scared at having to be shown to our seats in the dark. Then she didn't know to turn her seat down, so was quite a lot higher than everyone else. Then when the news actually came she couldn't bear it because the sea looked so rough, so her one and only trip to the cinema lasted five minutes!

Later Les was conscripted into the navy, also as a signaller. He had to go to Skegness and sent home for a mouse trap! Later he was sent to Sierra Leone in West Africa. Whilst he was in Africa he was nominated to have two minutes in 'The Forces' programme. So on the designated Sunday morning we all gathered in the back room at Victoria Terrace waiting for this broadcast from our wireless, replete with its big glass batteries newly charged at the local garage! And there he was "Hullo Mum and Dad and Uncle Frank (and everyone else he could think of) I am well and hope that you are too." It was over, but Mum especially was so thrilled to hear him. He and the other men from West Africa all came home very yellow! The anti-malarial drug then was quinacrine, which was fairly effective, but left you with jaundiced skin for some while. I try to imagine what it was like for Mum, Mur and Mary never knowing whether the boys had been torpedoed and sunk or killed.

Jean and I had sometimes to go and sleep two doors away with a neighbour, Mrs Coates. She was in a very nervous state because her husband was a navigator (aeroplane crew), and she never knew whether he was in one of the planes flying over to the continent with the bombers. He was eventually posted 'missing presumed dead'.

Just a little scrap of paper
In a yellow envelope
And the whole world is in ruin

Even hope.
(Another little verse from Studdart Kennedy)

Once on my birthday at Victoria Terrace, Jack (Muriel's future husband)
was home on leave, so he said I could have a party. He made lots of cakes, from
what I can't think, because rations were very limited, but the interesting thing
was that he boiled up some parsnips, mixed them with banana essence, so we
all enjoyed banana sandwiches! (My nephew Andrew copied this at a
subsequent family jamboree at Saffron Walden).

At St. Mark's school we were taken for swimming lessons once a week.
We were very lucky in Bath because there was one very old bath simply called
'The round bath'. It was run off the hot springs, and was normally lovely and
warm to learn in. But sometimes, the mixture of hot and cold water must have
gone wrong, because it was just too hot to get in! Jean and I also joined the
Bath Dolphins Swimming Club. Once when about four of us were larking about
by the river at Cambridge a man came along exposing himself. We all ran away,
but I left my gloves behind. So that night, I couldn't go to swimming club for
being so careless! We didn't dare tell why I had lost the gloves! We wandered
for miles, at quite a young age, but if you ever go to Bath, take the bus to the
Isolation Hospital on Combe Down. Drop down through two fields on to the
Aquaduct (where the canal crosses over the river) cross over and go across the
field diagonally towards a tiny wishing well at Conkwell. Turn left into a little
wood covered in early purple orchids in Spring, cross the big field called
Warleigh Manor (brilliant for black-berrying) and up on to the hill at
Batheaston, which is sometimes called the Pepper Pot, sometimes Brown's
Folly. It's a glorious walk, with deep springy turf at the end. All the walks
around Bath are wonderful. One bit I loved was coming down through a small
path through the wheat fields from Lansdown to Weston when the corn was
golden ripe. After the War another favourite was walking down Widcombe Hill
at night with the Abbey floodlit and all the lights in this huge valley. Our (Jean
and me) usual Saturday pastime was to go and cook sausages at Hampton
Rocks. This is a stony sort of area on one of the hills around Bath with lovely
grassy rocks and caves (a source of stone for Bath Abbey), and there's a lovely
little path leading from this place down to the canal. The stones for the Abbey
were trundled down this path, and then put on barges in the canal into the town.
My mother remembered paying tuppence (two pence) at the entrance of one of
the caves to see where somebody was murdered!

One of the highlights of our year was Good Friday when a goodly number
of the congregation of our church walked to a nearby village called Dunkerton.
We followed the old railway line with a stream running alongside, and it was
quite beautiful, with early Spring flowers and pussy willow trees (we used to
call it palm) all in furry bud. Then we all had tea in a hall and a service with a
congregation which packed the tiny church. It was such a good memory. There
was no problem with age groups (a modern thing, and in any case the word

'teenager' hadn't been invented!). Later it was in this church hall that we slept after the blitz.

Another walk I enjoyed was going along the canal with Dad. Before the sides were straightened for sightseeing boats, the walk was wonderful especially beyond that along to Bathampton. There were always moorhen nests and swimming snakes. When I was about twelve, I went for a cycle ride with Mur and her friend Joyce King. We were supposed to cycle along the canal path to Bradford on Avon, but the canal was so marvellous with dragon flies flitting everywhere that we just sat and watched them for a couple of hours. Later Joyce was killed in the Bath blitz. Many years later, pushing Adrian in his pram along the canal by Bathampton Bridge, we stopped to watch a snake. Quick as lightning, the swan, nesting on the opposite side, came zooming across. It must have thought we were going to hurt its young.

In 1939, when the war started, I began secondary school at the City of Bath Girl's School. In our class we had four Jewish girls who had trekked across Europe avoiding the Nazi persecutions, and had lost their parents on the way. So for the first term or so they were really disorientated, and didn't speak English, but eventually were all adopted into caring families. Because they were mostly going to synagogue on Saturdays they talked about religion a lot, so it became a hot topic of conversation for us all. One of us, Dorothy Solway, was of the Plymouth Brethren tradition and was never allowed to come to the pantomime at Christmas (the Admiralty was evacuated from London to Bath, they organized events for all the schoolchildren every Christmas). Barbara was staunch Anglo-Catholic and was obsessed with the 'Apostolic Succession' (whether all the bishops and clergy had been blessed by bishops right back to St. Peter, because Christ had said to Peter "you are the rock, and upon this rock I will build my church"). My best friend Pauline, belonged to the Christian Scientists, and I remember my Mum saying "well, they can't be very strong ones; her mother's got quite bad feet"!

One of the Jewish boys at Sunday school, Verner Schwarz, was adopted into a fairly elderly family of a sister and two brothers, Irene, Theophilus and Edward Willway. They made sure that he always went to synagogue on Saturdays and I think he came to Sunday school voluntarily on Sundays. Eventually he went to be a chef in a big London hotel. His wedding was very posh, and Miss Willway and her brothers were given the seats of honour. They were so thrilled and proud beyond measure. They had done a really brilliant thing very humbly.

I enjoyed secondary school. It was strange having to change classrooms and teachers for every lesson, but we soon got used to it. I remember at register we had to answer "present, yes, yes'. The first yes if we had changed into indoor shoes, and the second if we had remembered our gas masks! If we'd forgotten them we had to go home and get them, and then get extra homework. We had to carry them everywhere, school, shopping, Brownies, Guides.

At the end of the first year thirty girls were put into the Latin division, so I was quite lucky as I enjoyed Latin, apart from Caesar's Gallic Wars Book V!

Our teacher was Miss Beeston and was brilliant. Our English teacher, Miss Brooks was lovely and always wore patterned sort of muslin dresses over deep coloured petticoats. I don't think we ever had any discussions about anything to do with 'real life'. It was all school subjects for School Certificate. In music we just sang songs, carols, etc. but never studied the 'great composers', and likewise in art classes. But our music teacher was very tall and lovely. Miss Duge, the art teacher was the opposite. I hated art classes. We always had to draw with charcoal, so that we couldn't rub out, and mine was always a terrible mess. There were lots of quite wealthy girls from Admiralty families who normally would have gone to major Public Schools, but because of the war they were sent to day schools. They were all very articulate. One was the grandchild of Elspeth Huxley, who wrote 'The Flame Trees of Thika'. Another, Elizabeth Richardson, was brilliant at essays and her father was the President of the Free Church Union. She later joined the British Council in Russia. Pat Frisby was billeted near the top of Entry Hill with a pair of elderly sisters (Spears of Spears sausages) who had a tennis court, so that was quite fun, and we had a little Saturday morning group for a couple of violinists and a cellist. I was the piano accompaniment. Sadly, the girl who organised us, Pamela Jefferson, had a very bad breakdown later in life.

I didn't like games much. A strange thing was our hockey field being on top of Combe Down, a hill about three miles from school. We were taken by bus, but had to get home independently. It was a lovely spot, with a lovely walk down through two fields with a stream and a little pond leading down to Entry Hill. But none of the girls who liked games could ever walk! Usually I walked home by myself or with one other. We played hockey and netball in the winter, and tennis in the summer, plus swimming once a week.

When I was about fourteen my school friend developed a real interest in old tombs, long barrows, etc. so on Saturdays we used to cycle all over the countryside looking for such things, but there were no signposts! These had all been removed to muddle the Germans! Somehow we always arrived home despite our not very brilliant map reading!

I don't remember any bullying at school. I think it was a very ordered existence. We had quite a few inter-house competitions, featuring singing, drama, etc. In the autumn term we had the option of either playing hockey or collecting blackberries for school dinners, as wartime rations were bleak. Indeed, at school assembly the headmistress lectured us about merchant seamen losing their lives to feed us. During the summer holiday in the fifth year we went away for a week potato picking and haymaking. If children did this now it would bring so many immigrant children into feeling part of the place. Some kids now don't know that peas grow in pods, or that potatoes are dug up from under the ground!

Looking back, it amazes me now how quickly a country can get organised in a crisis. Suddenly, not long after war was declared, there were metal dustbins at the end of each road – Pig Bins – where we all put our potato peelings, cabbage leaves, etc. and then they were taken off each day, and processed to feed pigs. Lawns in gardens and parks suddenly became vegetable plots, metal railings disappeared from everywhere for use in making weapons and even aluminium saucepans were collected for making planes. It's hard now to imagine a world without even plastic bags or nylon or ball pens; let alone computers and mobile phones! Once during the war, at Christmas, Jack was on leave, and sent me to buy some silk stockings for Mur. They were very precious.

Rationing increasingly impacted on our meals. For example mixing ridiculously small bits of butter with a horrible hard margarine which never seemed to soften even in the summer! Powdered egg omelettes were good. I'm sure that many mothers went hungry trying to spread the rations around the family. Carrots were used quite a lot for sweetening. Bread was all simply 'wartime bread'; not brown or white.

Likewise at school, before we could have a new 'rough note book' the old one had to be examined by our form mistress to make sure that every scrap of paper was well used: no margins; no lines between paragraphs, and both covers (inside and out) covered with notes. The paper was quite rough with sort of wood chips in it, almost like the fashionable banana paper you buy for presents now! Nobody wanted sailors at extra risk bringing in unnecessary wood for paper.

Clothing was also rationed by means of coupons, and people became very clever at 'MAKE DO AND MEND'. The husband of our next-door neighbour was quite keen on golf, and had some sort of plaid plus-fours. He was then 'called-up' so after about two years, his lovely 'plus-fours' became a skirt, and then a couple of years later, some shorts for their little boy! Everywhere people grew vegetables, even on top of their Anderson shelters. 'DIG FOR VICTORY' was a government slogan.

Towards the end of the war the roads were always full of khaki coloured convoys sometimes open with soldiers, but more often covered. Soldiers, sailors and airmen were everywhere, and we got quite proficient at recognizing what they did by their various badges and stripes. For some of us, it was the first time we had ever seen a black person, men in the US army. It was very strange with American soldiers all over the town. Sometimes the men were invited into homes. One Afro-American came to tea one day, and Jean asked him, "Will you go white if you stay here long enough"! He replied by asking her what happened when our mother burned a cake in the oven!

After the blitz, first of all we lived for a bit in a house near Twerton Roundhill, yet another of the hills around Bath. The family from the house had moved into the countryside because of the blitz. After a few months or so they came back, so we just had two rooms in Shaftesbury Avenue. We eventually moved to a house at 12 Victoria Terrace. I had to go to violin lessons the other side of the river. It was really scary coming home in total blackness over a bridge where no traffic could go, and then along a road sort of through the gas works area. The lesson was a total waste of money because I could think of nothing but walking home in this blackness, so never got anywhere with the violin. Much to my regret later.

Most of the school years were dominated by war news, yet the strange thing was, that on D Day, which began only about fifty miles south as the crow flies, we just went to school as though everything was totally normal. Now, looking back, I can't believe that that was possible, but it shows also that propaganda worked. Everywhere were notices like 'walls have ears', 'dig for victory', 'coughs and sneezes spread diseases, trap the germs in your handkerchief'. School assemblies and church were quite emotional as everyone knew someone in the forces. Where I went to church there were loads of young men away. At Sunday school whenever we sang 'Land of our birth' the superintendent, Mr. Bush, always said to remember that for some of us (the continental Jews) this meant territories that were then enemy countries, and with 'Eternal Father strong to save' hymn, to remember that there were many enemy sailors also at risk at sea. The worst thing was someone being just reported 'missing'.

It was such a totally different world, but somehow, apart from the killings, I'm really glad to have lived in it.

At school in other ways as well as war, we were used to death. Classmates died of TB, diphtheria, infantile paralysis. It was subsequently amazing to witness what progress had been made in medicine in just half a century. For people working overseas, it was simply normal to go by boat. Air travel was terribly special, for which you really dressed up. I remember going to watch planes take off and land at Heathrow when it was just a long strip with a glassed-over viewing platform! I also remember, but much later, when I was sharing a flat in London with a girl called Caitlin, that we ran up to the top of a block of flats nearby to watch the first 'Sputnik' going over! Crowds of people were on the roof.

After the war, Mur and Jack and Mary and Cyril got married. For Mur our dresses were green, but I can't remember what they were for Mary. Men came home from the forces, and whereas we'd become used to the men in the back row at church all sitting in khaki, they now sat in the suits issued at demobilisation – all in brown! There was quite a bit of discontent amongst women, having to stop working. It was a strange attitude and one that is rightly gone. At the end of my first year at secondary school, our French teacher, Miss Cleek, got married, so had to leave! I can't remember ever having been taught by a man or married woman.

How hard it must have been for grown-ups to settle into a completely different life. The husband of one lady at Church, Mrs. Williams, had a really tough time. Her husband had gone to the war a perfectly lovely lively man. After three years in a Japanese prisoner of war camp, all he could say in a very stuttery way was "Have you seen the Southern Cross" over and over again. I don't suppose he was even registered as disabled.

Altogether, by today's standards I suppose our childhood was very limited, but looking back, it seems to me to have been mostly happy and full. Holidays just didn't happen and my Mum's only time away was for three days on her honeymoon! In many ways, for mothers especially, the physical labour of maintaining a home and family were terrible. There were no washing machines, just a mangle for squeezing out the water, lino floors to polish, no prepared foods, coal fires, no Hoovers; and Dad sitting outside, three storeys up cleaning the windows. On the other hand, I don't really remember ever going out with my Mum just for a walk, for example, and she never worried about coming to 'Parents' Evening'! There weren't today's demands in other ways and we could just go everywhere by ourselves, swimming club, brownies, parks, etc. and with bigger families, someone was always doing something such as working for a badge, going to camp, going hiking, etc. I don't remember ever being terribly bored!

After school, we all thought we ought to be medical missionaries, but as I couldn't stand the thought of nursing I decided to do dispensing. Two girls in our gang were brainy enough to be doctors, and some became teachers. In those years, dispensing was quite fun. My Monday morning job was cocaine lollipops for an elderly woman in the Royal Crescent who couldn't face going to the dentist! Everything was individual. One person was on valerian pills, but couldn't stand the thought of handling something so smelly, so they were very expensively coated with gold leaf! (Les hated the smell of valerian and wouldn't sit next to me at the table when he was home!). Handling gold leaf was quite a difficult job as the leaf was so fine it flew away at the slightest breath. It was also terribly expensive. (I'd actually seen my dad use gold leaf on fine tables, and when we came to Cambridge, I found a whole 'booklet' of real gold leaf in the shed; the previous occupant having been a carpenter). I gave this find to Georita, a former lodger who became a notable botanical illustrator. She used the gold leaf in some of her pictures for special events. Another lady always wanted her face powder without Orrisroot. It was quite hard work before the days of liquidisers. All the medicines were made with chloroform water (144 minims, i.e. about two teaspoons) to a Winchester quart bottle as a sweetener and preservative. You had to shake like mad for ages to get the chloroform evenly distributed. All the common indigestion mixtures had to be mixed in a huge mortar which was really heavy. It was quite exhausting. The measures were difficult to get the hang of at first. Apothecary ounces were divided into 480 grains weight or 480 minims liquid, whereas the avoirdupois (our everyday ounces) liquid measure was the same, but weight was only 437.5 grains to the ounce. How all these things come about, I never learned. Another job I liked was making camphorated oil. It took ages, but the smell was so lovely.

Sometimes suddenly a doctor across the road might ring up for carbon-dioxide snow to burn someone's wart off. It came in a little cylindrical shaped pencil from a large carbon dioxide cylinder. Liquorice flavoured nearly all the cough medicines. Penicillin was very precious but for a long time not particularly stable, so for external use was kept as a powder, then dissolved in sterile water and mixed in a fine skin cream for early use. The newest person's job was to make sure the 'still' was kept topped up for distilled water. There

seemed to be loads of sulpha drug tablets, such as sulphonamide, then sulpha-diazine, dimidine, guanidine, mezathine, merazine, nilamide, pyridine, suxidine, thalazole, and phthalylsuthalazole, and quite a few more. Barbiturates were handed out willy-nilly as well as amphetamines. I remember going down to the gas works for coal tar, to make zinc and coal tar ointment, and also zinc and cantharides ointment – crumbled up Spanish beetles! I think the idea was that it hurt so much that the pain was transferred from the original site to wherever you put the ointment! For ringworm and other head creatures you got in a terrible mess making Castellani's paint – bright red, or Gentian Violet pant. One interesting thing was that so many ingredients used were plant extracts, most of which you could see around Bath but one of them, henbane (Hyoscyamus niger) although it grew in this country, wasn't rare, but wasn't common either. Then one day, years later, going across the water-meadows at Dedham Vale in Suffolk, I saw it in a hedge. Just the one and no others about.
    Audrey.

These recollections by Audrey only hint at what a lovely, caring, person she was. When dispensing, Audrey, despite being the shortest member of the team, often had to lift a heavy drum of liquid. One day when so doing she strained herself, and her heart in particular. Her doctor advised her to cease lifting these heavy drums. So she answered an advertisement for a governess for a young British boy in Kerala, India. She was there two years and her charge went on to become a jumbo jet pilot! She was greatly appreciated by the family and they kept in touch ever afterwards. On her return she enrolled on a secretarial course in London and supported herself by dispensing at the University College Hospital in the evenings. She then became secretary to the boss of a popular national newspaper, but they parted company when the boss told her to go out and choose a present for his wife's birthday. Audrey replied that a husband should choose presents for his wife himself! So Audrey then became the secretary at the Flatford Mill Field Centre on the Suffolk-Essex border.
    At the Field Centre in the 1960s the staff were obliged to live in. There was only married accommodation for the Warden. We would therefore have to leave Flatford in order to marry. Jim was not keen on this prospect. He particularly didn't want to lose an excellent secretary. He was also reluctant to lose me, I was later told, as I had introduced some innovations in the teaching and worked well as his Deputy. In addition he and his wife thought the age difference between Audrey and myself meant our relationship would not last and us leaving would all be for nothing. So, as I was about to leave on a weekend break, Jim decided to give me notice of dismissal. I replied that I would give him my response when I returned next week! On my return I said to Jim that we were going for a walk during which I would explain why I was unable to accept his notice of dismissal! It was a long walk, but the notice was withdrawn and Audrey and I stayed on until October. Before we left Flatford Audrey had invited a friend to stay one weekend. She was an experienced nurse

who had worked with the ophthalmologist at the hospital where Audrey had dispensed in the evenings while training as a secretary in London (see above). She examined the scarred cornea of Jim's purblind eye and told him that advances since his boyhood accident meant he could have a corneal graft to restore vision to the eye. Jim was understandably hesitant, with it being the only eye of any use to him. However, he agreed to consult his own ophthalmologist. The latter agreed with the nurse's assessment and Jim subsequently had the operation. When some years later I crossed London with Jim I was hard put to keep up with him as he dashed across roads dodging the traffic or wove his way past pedestrians on crowded pavements. Back in 1963 when I had last crossed London with him I had been obliged to steer him by holding him by an elbow!

Incidentally, when I was a student at Bristol University for my Certificate of Education (see chapter 6) I was contacted by Jim with a request that I take charge of the Field Centre for a week. He had forgotten he had given his then deputy leave for that week when he had subsequently booked himself to be away the same week! This request by Jim was, I felt, far better than a formal testimonial with regard to what he really thought of me as confirmed when he subsequently strongly supported my application for the wardenship of the Malham Tarn Field Centre (chapter 8)! Anyway I much enjoyed that week back at Flatford Mill and returned refreshed to educational theory, etc. at Bristol University.

David Lewis, then working at the Natural History Museum in London but supported by the Medical research Council, had been the Medical Entomologist in the Sudan when I was a boy. I had been out with him when he was trying to reduce the mass emergences of non-biting midges that caused allergic reactions to some people in Khartoum, and which had forced them to move well away from the waters of the Niles. David persuaded me to apply for the post of entomologist at the Dermal Leishmaniasis Research Unit in British Honduras (Belize) funded by the Ministry of Overseas Development. Despite all the other short listed candidates having a PhD I was offered the post. When I later asked Dr Lewthwaite from the Ministry why me rather than one of the better qualified candidates he replied that it was as much based on my military experience as my academic credentials. He thought I would cope better with the conditions (physical, bureaucratic and political) in B.H.

If the NCO's reports for Bracey and myself had not been transposed during my basic training in the army (see chapter 2) I doubt that I would have ever ended up in academia!

Jim would not allow his permanent staff to live out. Subsequently they were allowed to live out; only the seasonal domestic assistants being required to be resident (and provided with their board and keep). Indeed the warden himself ended up living out. If Jim had allowed Audrey and I to live out when we got married we would not have left, and the following chapters would have been very different! Perhaps, after a few years, we would have moved to Malham Tarn in Yorkshire. On the other hand my eventual appointment as the warden of Malham Tarn Field Centre owed much to my experience in research as a medical entomologist, as a part of my remit (see chapter 8) was to revive the tradition of Research that had been a feature of the Field Centre in the past.

From the above list of unforeseen events that preceded Audrey and I meeting and falling in love and our subsequent life together, it seemed indeed that 'a planned life is a closed life' (to quote a saying from the film THE INN OF THE SIXTH HAPPINESS)!

CHAPTER 5

CENTRAL AMERICA

Audrey and I were married in Manvers Street Baptist Church in Bath on 23rd November 1963. The service was conducted by John Clarke, the husband of Audrey's sister Jean. This was the day after the assassination of President Kennedy. We had booked our honeymoon in County Cork, Ireland. We crossed to Ireland in a ferry and arrived to find the country closed down and flags everywhere at half-mast.

Our destination was a small holiday bungalow (belonging to a friend of my parents) in the south of County Cork. We arrived by bus hungry, having had little to eat at our reception in Bath, as everyone wanted to have a chat! We were expecting to buy food when we left the bus only to find all the shops and even the pub shut down because of Kennedy's death. However, neighbours kindly helped out until the community slowly came back to life again the next day. Until then we soon got the peat fire going and began to recover from the journey and relax as newlyweds in love.

FIRST VIEW (RE)

The cuckoo's call is sign for spring
To come to drive the winter chills
Away. It lifts the dormant joys
My spirit craves. But when I first
Beheld the actual bird in tree
It lit a thrill of thanks and praise,
Until surpassed by awesome time
I first beheld the naked form
Of she I've loved for forty years.
Its beauties seldom seen that live
In mind and not those on display
Without restraint and every day.

After the honeymoon and before departure for Central America, I learned about the parasites and staining techniques at the London School of Hygiene and Tropical Medicine and about Neotropical biting sandflies, etc., at the Natural History Museum in London.

We crossed the Atlantic in a commercial banana boat. These ships had a shallow draft to allow access up relatively shallow creeks in the Caribbean in order to load bananas. Consequently these ships rolled a lot in even moderately calm weather. I spent much of my time reliving the seasickness I had experienced on the troop ship to Cyprus, while Audrey lived it up on the captain's table at meal times! From Miami we flew on to Belize City. We then travelled west by road to Central Farm not far from the border with Guatemala.

1963-1966 Entomologist at the Dermal Leishmaniasis Research Unit in British Honduras (Belize) (Ministry of Overseas Development)

Central Farm was a government agriculture research station with a hostel for small farmers attending short courses on new methods. Our medical research unit was located beside the main road next to a small post office serving Central Farm as whole. There was a general store nearby selling a range of basics. San Ignacio to the west offered a wider choice for shopping, had the nearest government offices and a GP practice.

Because my predecessor had published almost nothing, despite having amassed many data, Dr Lewthaite had given me one very specific instruction – Whatever you do publish. If you bang your head against a wall for six months without results for goodness sake publish that so others don't bang their heads against the same blank wall!

He got me into the habit of publishing even the smallest contribution to knowledge, be it a positive gain or the negation of an attractive hypothesis. Indeed going up blind alleys is all part of research. Many years later I was surprised, therefore, when a correspondent reprimanded me for publication of the refutation of a hypothesis I had published some years before, as to do so would not help me to progress in my career! I had replied that I reserved the right, possessed by a bacterium, to modify my behaviour in the light of experience. I later penned the following poem.

ADVANCING KNOWLEDGE (GK)

For days on end I'm poacher just
Intent on putting ferrets down
Each hole that's not been blocked to flush
The rabbits into sack. At night
My thoughts and dreams engage in task
Until at last the problem's cracked.
I'm then a puppy's tail employed
In dance of joy. The setbacks, slogs
Without results, are then forgot,

As sense of triumph overwhelms
With pure delight. The toil and sweat
Are pruned from formal script I send
To journal read by colleagues left
In dark regarding many blanks
I'd first explored, before the truth
Was cornered once for all, beyond
Dispute. An iceberg's tip is what
They see of hours I wrestled long
Beyond the second wind when hope
Was getting dim, as tempting thoughts
Proposed it's time to take my ease.
But critic comments on the fact
I've dumped an early view of mine.
It's only sense to do just that
When novel data undermine
One's former guess. He'd sure be right
To pour his scorn if I'd adhered
To dodo view, like fools who stick
With Genesis in place of light
That Darwin shed across the board.

My remit from the Ministry in London was to research the ecology of the parasite responsible for Dermal Leishmaniasis. The parasite, Leishmania mexicana, belongs to the trypanosome family. A related species in this genus causes Intestinal Leishmaniasis that could be fatal if not diagnosed early enough. While it was commoner in the Old World, cases had been reported in the Yucatan Peninsular. The Trypanosomidae include a number of genera that vary in the number of forms they undergo during their life cycles and whether they are restricted to invertebrates. Thus Trypanosoma species undergo four stages – trypanosome, leptomonad, crithidia and Leishman-Donovan body, the last being the final stage in a vertebrate host. Leishmania has a leptomonad stage in the insect vector and an L-D stage in the mammal host. Leptomonas has the leptomonad stage in insects but no vertebrate host. In the 1960s we lacked the later developed immunological tests and even later molecular ('barcode') tests to distinguish the genera and species. So if we found leptomonads in an insect we inoculated a blood agar culture and a hamster to see if we produced other insect stages or L-D bodies in the hamster. Because of the risk the leptomonads might be from the intestinal Leishmaniasis species we had been banned from inoculating human volunteers.

There had been at least ten years of research by a team in Mexico as well as the work in our Unit, being continued by Paul, its then current director, on the three principal man-biting sandflies (Phlebotominae) without having identified the vector, apart from my predecessor having successfully inoculated a hamster with a 'soup' of ground up wild caught sandflies comprising a mixture of species. So I decided to base my research by confirming and extending the list of mammals that are the normal hosts of the parasite of our concern and investigating what bloodsucking insects, especially sandflies, were biting these hosts. To undertake this I live-trapped and screened a larger range of mammals for the presence of the parasite and I set about trying to design a trap for blood-sucking flies attracted to a live bait animal. I not only employed three types of mammal trap, but also used mist nests for bats and put a notice by the post office offering money for mammals brought in by hunters and small boys. When the latter brought me vampire bats I would carefully transfer them to a cage and then ask if they knew what sort of bat it was. When they were told they were vampire bats they disbelieved me as, like fishermen describing the fish that got away, their parents exaggerated the size of vampires, which occasionally struck them at night. Usually they attacked cattle, or a horse on a ranch nearby was frequently attacked. A risk with vampire bats, as well as the large Didelphis opossums, was rabies. So I and my assistants were inoculated against this fearful infection. However, in those days it was hit or miss as to whether this had worked, so a few weeks later we were tested to see if we had developed the antibodies. Only I and one assistant had done so. A few months later he moved on to another job, leaving me as the only member of the Unit known to be protected. Consequently I was often called upon to handle any suspect mammal!

One day a patient turned up at the GP in San Ignacio having been bitten by a dog with foam around its mouth. The GP shot the dog and buried it, but was then reprimanded and told the dog's brain should have been removed and sent to Belize City to be tested for rabies. I was called upon to take the dog's brain in a jar of physiological saline down to Belize City. I sat next to the driver with the jar on my lap. The lid of the jar was a ground glass stopper. When the Land-Rover hit a bad pothole or a badly corrugated stretch of the road the saline tended to slop and leak onto my lap and my hands clasping the jar. At the central hospital they were not pleased at this leakage and made me strip off and they then swabbed me down with phenol! The dog's brain was flown to Guatemala City where it was tested and found to be positive for rabies.

My notice offering money for live mammals brought to the lab had two columns. The first was headed UNINJURED and had a price depending on the rarity of the mammal species that ranged from 50BH$ to 5$. The second column was headed INJURED and had a fixed price of 50 cents. A 50$ species was the beautiful, honey eating tree opossum. One day a specimen was brought in but it had been badly tied by one leg and had consequently sustained a dislocation. I gave the man 50 cents. He was furious, but I took him round to the notice and pointed out that his specimen was covered by the price in the second column. Grumbling he went away. However, the word got around that my good prices only applied to uninjured animals.

The rarest mammal which was brought to the lab was a species of bat I had not seen before. The fellow who looked after the hostel for farmers coming on short courses at Central Farm was rather fond of the local rum. One morning, evidently suffering from a hangover, he arrived with a cereal box with a bat inside. He said he had seen two bats flying towards him (I suspect there was only one bat and he had been seeing it double due to his drunken state!) and he had made a grab and had got this one in the box. After screening it for parasites I preserved it and sent the specimen to the Royal Ontario Museum in Canada for identification. They were greatly excited by it. It was only the second specimen ever caught. Furthermore it was of the opposite sex to that of the original specimen. They had tried to catch further specimens during a recent expedition but had failed. They asked me 'how does one catch this species?' I replied that the only known method was to 'get drunk on the local rum and have an empty cereal box handy'! We never got a further specimen.

The largest catch ever on one day was an entire colony of a species of bat, obtained in the following manner. Nearby the Salvation Army ran an institution for bad boys (for example, one had tried to lead his mother into a canal in Belize City), nowadays political correctness says we must call them 'maladjusted'! As keeping the boys occupied was a full time task they asked if I would talk to them about our Unit. I had observed that in the large hall in which we were assembled there were many resting bats between the rafters. After my talk I asked the Sally Ann officer if he had any objection to sending the boys up onto the beams supporting the roof to collect the bats. He agreed straight away as he thought it would be a memorable adventure for them (no safety regulations impeded such initiatives in those days!). So I announced 50 cents a bat. In no time at all they brought me more than 50 bats. All were of the same species and in the lab they were screened for parasites.

My largest series of specimens of a species of mammal was for black rats (Rattus rattus), with the largest sample being from a Mayan village deep in the rainforest. I set live traps on the beams of the people's houses, as when I had initially set the traps on the floors I tended to catch their baby chickens as well. The villagers were very cooperative as they welcomed me reducing these pests (even if only temporarily). Back in my lab all the rats were screened for their parasites. A bright young boy was intrigued by my rat catching and when I arrived in the village in the Land-Rover each morning would run up and tell me which houses had traps with rats in them. In view of his helpfulness and interest we invited him to stay some weekends with us at Central Farm and on one occasion took him to Belize City for his first visit. When asked what he would like as a souvenir present he immediately opted for a pair of shoes, his first ever as all the children and most of the adults in his village went barefoot. However, we never saw him wearing the shoes. Instead he tied the laces together and wore them around his neck! One weekend when he stayed with us he was suddenly sick and unwell for half a day. When we returned to his village on the Monday to our surprise his mother was sitting by a boulder some distance well before the village. As I came to a halt she rushed up to the Land-Rover and her first words to her son were 'What was wrong with you on Saturday?'! She seemed surprised when I asked how she knew he had been unwell! In effect, her reply was because she loved her son!

However, I had to discontinue this rat-trapping project in that village for an unforeseen occurrence. A lady kept on at me to cure her of her ailment. I kept repeating that I was not a medical doctor but I dealt with non-human mammals, parasites and biting insects. In the end in exasperation I asked her what was her ailment. She responded by exposing one breast that clearly displayed an unpleasant lesion. I told her I did not know the cause but advised her to attend the local clinic in the nearest town. She told me she had done so and they had given her injections. So I then advised that she should attend the main hospital in Belize City. She said she had done so with the same result. So I told her there was an excellent clinic just across the border in Guatemala. She had attended it with the same result. So I said that while I did not know the primary cause of her affliction it was evident to me that there was at least a 'secondary' infection by a fungus and I would bring her a medicine to deal with that. Accordingly next day I took her a large beer bottle of potassium permanganate solution and told her to wash the lesion first thing in the morning and last thing at night and then apply the medicine. I warned her it might sting a little, but that would show her it was doing some good. To my astonishment it completely cured her! It seemed the fungus infection had in fact been the primary cause of her nasty lesion. The villagers then disbelieved me when I still denied being a medical doctor and they urged me to cure all their ailments! Consequently I had to cease trapping black rats in that village.

Many of the black rats we caught were pregnant. This was useful as we could wait for them to give birth and the offspring were weaned. We knew we then had rats free of the parasites we were interested in and could use them for laboratory inoculations from our parasite cultures. One day I found an assistant had inadvertently allowed a rat to escape. After requesting that more care be taken in the future, I thought no more about it. However, the next problem in my lab was that the mounted needles I used for dissecting the sandflies kept vanishing and each day I was obliged to make new ones. In the end it was getting beyond being an irritation. All my assistants denied having taken them. Exasperated I replied then they must still be in the lab so please search every nook and cranny while I go and attend to something else. A little later I was called back to lab. In a corner behind a cupboard they had recovered the escaped rat and discovered it had constructed a spherical nest built entirely of mounted needles with all the needles pointing outwards!

I was sending skins and skulls of mammals to four museums for identification (The Natural History Museum in London, the Canadian Museum referred to above and two museums in the USA). The rodents were invariably identified to the subspecies level. I began to realize that the subspecies seemed to be a function of the museum not the specimen! To test this I set traps in the Pine Ridge Savannah habitat that was dominated by the cotton rat (Sigmodon hispidus). I split the catch into those caught in odd numbered traps as opposed to those caught in even numbered traps and sent them to two different museums. Sure enough they were assigned to two different subspecies! I then circulated the four museums with my evidence that the subspecies seemed to be a function of the specialist not the specimen. Two responded that it was long overdue that someone demonstrated this to them. One said they had not got time to look into the matter. The fourth declared that where there was disagreement he was right and the rest were mistaken! I then decided to ignore the subspecies identifications and to stick with the species names only.

Another surprise identification was when I had kept the offspring of a pregnant climbing rat (Ototylomys phyllotis – the prime natural host of Leishmania mexicana in Yucatan) we had trapped. These offspring were used for inoculation experiments. They were still juvenile when I prepared their skins and skulls and these were sent with their mother's skin and skull to a museum. Despite my data labels indicating that the juveniles were the offspring of the mother (with its code number linking it to its offspring in the list sent with the specimens), they were identified as a different species – Ototylomis brevirostris! Their shorter snouts were merely because they were juveniles. Consequently O. brevirostris became a synonym of O. phyllotis. This set me thinking back to when I had lost one of my upper incisor teeth in a childhood accident and my overcrowded teeth slowly shifted to close the gap. The fact is that the teeth of humans (and to a lesser extent those of their closest relatives) tend to be crowded because as adults we have retained the shortened rostrum (snout) of their juvenile stages. This seems to be a result of our relatively large heads (to accommodate our enlarged brains) characteristic of our newly born baby stage being retained in the adult stage, but at the cost of also retaining our shortened juvenile proboscis, with a consequential crowding of our second set of adult teeth. This is why many youngsters have to wear braces for a time to straighten their teeth that have become misaligned due to this overcrowding! This is a good example of how an evolutionary advance may give rise to a poorly adapted adverse secondary consequence for another feature due to development constraint unavoidably linking the two features. See, for comparison the example of the giraffe's neck cited in the poem UNINTELLIGENT DESIGN (in chapter 10).

One day a hunter shot a peccary and then found two newly born piglets, with umbilical cords still dangling. These he brought to the lab. Our animal house assistant tried to care for one, but it died a few days later. I took the other home. Audrey fed it with a medicine dropper pipette every few hours until it took to solid food. I had a fly trap baited with a live mammal across the adjacent pasture in the nearest rainforest. I used to visit this trap before breakfast each morning. The peccary came with me. Indeed he became imprinted on me. While I was tending my trap he would go off foraging. When he discovered I had moved on he came frantically looking for me. The children of our neighbour used to tease him. But as he grew up his tusks developed. Indeed, sometimes when he followed me to the lab to fetch something he came with me and increasingly people drew back because peccaries have a reputation for attacking people. Fearing that he might attack our neighbour's children I reluctantly gave him away to an American.

Twice I had my lines of traps in the forest interfered with. The first time it was by people from the nearby village. They were astounded when I went on the national radio and named them as impeding medical research! This not only elicited an apology from the villagers but also alerted others to the fact that it was not a good idea to interfere with my traps! However, the second time my traps were disturbed was when a tapir had seemingly lost its temper with them. From the confusion of its footprints it seemed that a medium sized opossum (Philander opossum) that was in the first trap must have uttered its vociferous calls combining alarm with threats (which my Mayan assistant likened to the sound of the airbrakes on a large lorry being suddenly applied). This must have made the tapir lose its temper!

Ants, of every sort and size, were frequently a cause for pausing to watch them at work. One day we were having breakfast on the verandah overlooking the garden (the house being on stilts as a device for reducing invasions by unwelcome creatures) when we realized every rose bush had been stripped of its leaves. When I went to investigate I was able to follow a trail with dropped leaf fragments across a cattle pasture into the forest beyond where the trail ended at a vast underground nest of leaf cutter ants. These ants cull leaf fragments and use them to culture special fungi that they feed to their larvae. Many years later I was to publish much on the scuttle flies that parasitize these ants (see chapter 10).

Working daily in the rainforest I was constantly delighted by creatures new to me, some of which remained long in my memory:

SENSE OF AWE (GK)

A rubber frog with staring eyes
Appears on kitchen table's top
Behind the marmalade. It must
Have leapt from cornflakes box as sop
Designed to make a child demand
We purchase more. Its baleful look,
Without a blink, begins to crush
My sense of ease. And yet in crook
Of twisted limb of jungle tree
I once surprised its living clone.
It gifted sense of joy at chance
Encounter. Then I'd felt alone
As sudden leap deleted sight
Of breathing beast that brought delight.
As child I'd learned that God had made
Us both. But soon beliefs abrade,
As Darwin's insights take their place,
Until today my pleasure comes

From knowledge gained by patient toil.
Revealing secret truths becomes
A source of rapture clothed in sense
Of awe at diverse forms and ways
Of life, despite their constant wars.
So still I hum my songs of praise.

On another occasion before breakfast I had a different encounter in the rainforest. This subsequently featured in the following poem:

TRANQUIL PLACE? (GK)

Today our garden's glowing green
With daubs of colour, strokes of sun,
And not a breath of breeze. The birds
Are busy searching, searching, while
The bumble bees are early hard
At work before the hover flies
Awake. But closer to, I watch
A chalcid wasp at hunting hosts,
And ladybird who's chomping prey
Of aphids, while a spider eats
Her mate whose duty's done. I'm pleased
I'm distanced by my scale from world
Of constant raids by marching packs
Of ants, the ambush webs, the probes
Of parasitic flies whose eggs
Become devouring grubs within.
But I recall the years I worked
In jungle day by day. For most
Of many hours I spent the blight
Was blood imbibed by leeches, gnats
And biting flies, or fleas and ticks,
Or else a brush with toxic hairs
Of caterpillar I'd not seen
Or else a poison tree, or all
Those fiendish thorns like fishing hooks.
At times a snake, too close for ease,
Has caused me pause. One dawn I dropped
To ground from tree, in which I'd fixed
A trap for vectors of disease,
And froze with dread. A puma walked
In line ahead that aimed for me.
It checked, and so did I. We stared

A ceaseless age, in game of fear
As far as I'm concerned. It seems
Its hunt that night had been in vain.
To break the spell I must not turn.
With thumping heart I walked towards
Those eyes, engaging mine, with gaze
Returned with feigned contempt. My pace
Was slow but firm. Its will began
To wane as my advance became
A threat it didn't understand.
And so it slowly yawned before
It swiftly turned and strolled away,
As silent as a shaft of sun
That clearly lit retreating spoor.
It's now I can recall its grace
And poise and marvel at its strength
And self-control. I'm glad we met,
But gladder still it went away:
And I am here today to view
Our ordered lawn and scene that seems
A peaceful place devoid of strife -
Despite its constant secret wars.

On another occasion I was leading my team through the forest when I found myself leaping backwards before I had consciously registered the nature of the threat. As I landed a jumping fer-de-lance just missed my knee as I was taking off for a second backwards leap. The bite of this snake is not only highly poisonous, but the species was the most aggressive we ever encountered. The snake remained staring at me slowly swaying back and forth. I knew that if one ceased to stare back it would seemingly vanish as it repositioned itself for a second attempt. So I called back to my Mayan assistant to cut a frond from a cohune palm, to strip its leaflets and then pass me the remaining midrib. The latter is long, strong and highly flexible. With it I whacked the snake and then ran forwards and beheaded it with my cutlass (the local term for a machete). Back home I skinned the corpse and rubbed the inside of the skin with salt before pinning it out on a board. Years later our son Adrian displayed the skin on the wall of his bedroom in Yorkshire and he developed an intense interest in snakes! Indeed he obtained a pet snake and acquired a wide ranging knowledge of snakes such that if he had entered the T.V. Mastermind competition and his special subject were to be snakes he would have had a faultless round!

On another occasion I spotted a trail leading into the forest from the edge of the road and decided to investigate it as a possible site for laying a line of mammal traps. It proved to be suitable so next day we laid the traps. The following day we found we had caught a number of cotton rats. Back in the lab when we carried out post-mortems to screen them for parasites I was astonished to find they all had multiple nodules that looked like cancer. Next day we decided to investigate where the trail went to beyond our line of traps. To our surprise the forest suddenly opened up to a bowl shaped depression planted up with drug producing crops. Furthermore at the edge of the forest beyond was a colony of howler monkeys, who started vocalizing threats. When we approached the vocalizations grew more intense and we had to be careful. If we wandered beneath them they tried to bomb us with faeces. If out of range for this tactic they plucked some fruits with hard stones, beneath the flesh, that were like small cricket balls. These they would hurl at us. On returning to the road we encountered some surly men who demanded to know what we were doing. We said we were leaving and as we did so we lifted our line of traps and left. We inferred that the men farming drugs in this hidden clearing had chosen it precisely because the howler monkey colony was a superb early warning system for alerting them to the approach of unwanted intruders. I also inferred that they were using a cocktail of insecticides to protect their illicit crop, and these insecticides were the cause of the cancerous nodules in the cotton rats. One was left wondering what insecticide residues remained in the extracted drugs that were eventually sold to drug addicts and with what consequences for them.

Apart from the hazards of working in the rainforest there were frustrations due to corruption and bureaucratic nonsense. For example, according to my contract my salary was to be paid through the Medical Department in Belize City, but the overseas allowance would be paid via the Finance Department headed by the Prime Minister of British Honduras. However I was not receiving the overseas allowance each month as prescribed in my contract. Having tried to get an explanation from both Departments, without success, I copied the correspondence to the Ministry in London. The result was a reprimand from London to the Prime Minister of B. H., resulting in me suddenly receiving six months' worth of the overseas allowance outstanding. It transpired that the B.H. Prime Minister was investing my allowance with the intention of paying it at the end of the year but putting the interest earned into his party's funds!

An example of bureaucratic nonsense was when an official turned up unannounced to check the inventory, when Paul was away in Panama and I was acting head of the Unit. I told the official that I was busy so one of my assistants would help him with his task. The assistant kept coming to me to tell me that the fellow was crazy as he was trying to count the coverslips for slide mounts for the microscope, etc. So I went to him and pointed out that consumables and non-consumables should be treated differently and he should concentrate on the latter. After some discussion he grudgingly accepted this distinction and released me to get on with my work. After several other such cases, my assistant then came and said there were a dozen slide boxes (for holding slide mounts of sandflies, stained blood smears with parasites, etc.) missing. I told him to tell the fellow that they were in my house and that they were full of specimens for the Natural History Museum in London and the London School of Hygiene and Tropical Medicine and the boxes, therefore, were consumables. My assistant returned to say he would not accept that. So I went to explain to the fellow that the slide boxes would not be returning empty from London, hence they should clearly be classified as consumables. He continued to disagree. In the end I grabbed a pen and against the entry on his form for slide boxes I wrote "12 boxes stolen by Disney". He objected, but I replied that unless he accepted that the boxes were consumables then that was the appropriate entry! Eventually he left and I heard no more about the slide boxes!

Other problems were caused by corruption. For example I drove a Diesel Land-Rover but the Unit also had a petrol Land-Rover. Our vehicles were repaired and serviced by the adjacent Agriculture Department garage of their experimental farm. On one occasion they seemed to taking a long time to repair both vehicles, so I dropped in a memo asking when my vehicle would be ready. At first I received an evasive reply. I sent a second memo saying I needed an answer in order to plan ahead. The reply I received was that, because of delays in receiving new parts on order, they had been obliged to cannibalize parts of the engine of my Land-Rover to repair the other one. I replied that, although not an expert mechanic, I did not understand how parts of a Diesel engine would fit a petrol engine. I got no reply! So I copied the exchange of memos into the inventory file that was being subjected to its annual inspection shortly. The boss of the garage was furious when the central administration asked him to explain his responses to my memos. He wriggled out of it with them by saying he had confused two Land-Rovers! He didn't try to play tricks with me again.

Other unexpected callers to the lab we were only too glad to be able to help. For example a rancher came in and said two of his best cows were suddenly poorly. An assistant went off with him to see the animals and took some blood samples, which our excellent Research Assistant, Bob, examined and reported that if they had been from a human he would have diagnosed metal poisoning. So I sent my Spanish speaking Mayan assistant to question the rancher's cow handler. It transpired that the handler had decided to tackle an infestation of ticks by swabbing the cows with a copper sulphate solution, which the cows had then been licking off as they groomed themselves! Being a small community everyone knew each other and one learned who was expert at what and whose expertise might be limited! For example when half a herd of cattle on the government agriculture research station suddenly dropped dead on the same day, the young, recently arrived Welsh vet new to tropical situations, decided this was caused by a parasitic infection he had been reading about. The fellow responsible for the cows decided to ask our lab for a second opinion. We said we didn't go along with the vet's diagnosis as to suddenly lose so many animals without a gradual build up, the case was more consistent with a sudden access to something toxic. When we looked into it we found that some fence posts at the edge of the pasture had been freshly painted with wood preservative to prevent attacks by termites. Furthermore a farm assistant reported seeing the cows licking these posts as though they were a salt lick. When we examined the cans that had contained the preservative the labels revealed that the principal toxic ingredient was arsenic!

The development of a flytrap that would procure biting insects, especially sandflies, attracted to a living mammal host bait took some time. I started with a trap that had been developed in Trinidad for catching mosquitoes. An assistant and I went through a number of designs before I eventually produced a trap that caught a range of biting flies, and plenty of sandflies in particular. A suspended cage, beneath a metal sheet roof to keep out the rain, with the bait animal was surrounded by a metal tray with a film of castor oil. Most of the flies were caught on entry, rather than after taking a blood meal from the bait animal. I would lift off the flies with a mounted needle and briefly rinse them in physiological saline plus a drop of detergent (to get rid of the castor oil) before transferring them to a tube of saline alone and the tube being placed in a thermos. Back in the lab the flies were dissected under a low power stereo microscope to look for parasites. Any possible Leishmania parasites were then procured with a hypodermic needle and a blood agar culture inoculated and the tube given a code number. The dissected fly was then mounted on a slide labelled with the same code number, for subsequent identification under a compound microscope. If the parasites multiplied in the culture tube we would then inoculate a hamster to see if it was the species of parasite we were after. The trap (Disney, R. H. L., 1966. A trap for Phlebotomine sandflies attracted to rats. Bulletin of Entomological Research 56: 445-451) subsequently became effectively used in South America in studies of a related parasite and became known as the 'Disney trap'.

Sometimes I raised a trap well clear of the ground by means of an improvised pulley system. Across from our house I used strips of scrap lumber nailed to the trunks of two trees standing close together to make a ladder. An odd consequence was that when I was up attending to this trap humming birds would sometimes buzz around my head as though I was an exotic flower! On one occasion I had a surprise when I dropped to the ground after attending to the trap (see the poem TRANQUIL PLACE? above).

Many of my studies were in 'medium bush' as the locals termed mature secondary rainforest. I decided to lay a line of traps in really mature rainforest for comparison. So we set off for a suitable site and spent the morning creating a trail with our cutlasses extending about one kilometre from the road. To our surprise we reached an outcrop of limestone with an entrance to a cave. However there was quite a drop to its floor below. So we returned with ropes and torches next day. We gained access to a passage that showed signs of human activity but was now inhabited by whip-spiders, scorpions and their prey of crickets. The passage ended where descending stalactites had encountered ascending stalagmites and fused. However, peering through the gaps we saw a chamber with earthenware pots arranged across the floor. We had clearly stumbled upon an ancient Mayan site. Fearing news of this would leak out and hunters for ancient jade artefacts would wreck the archaeology, I swore my assistants to secrecy and informed the Government archaeologist in Belize City. A week or two later he appeared and we invited him to our house. Over a drink he waxed eloquent about his experience of working in the bush. We then set off and Audrey came along too. As I was leading the party along our freshly cut trail a rather attractive snake crossed our path. The archaeologist started looking nervous and asked if there many snakes. I replied that there were not that many, only one every 200 to 300 metres or so! When we reached the cave he was somewhat nervous about the drop to its floor, however remaining alone with the snakes was seemingly more daunting. So we all entered the cave. Audrey was a bit nervous with regard to the whip-spiders, having long had a phobia with regard to arachnids (indeed her major problem with regard to the local wildlife was that as she hung out washing on the line she had to keep a nervous eye on the tarantulas sitting in the entrances of their nearby burrows), but she was more relaxed than the archaeologist. When he saw the pots he was quite excited and dated them as about 900 A.D. He said the arrangement of the pots and seeming absence of other artefacts suggested it was an example of a Mayan practice of regarding water obtained from the drippings from stalactites as being especially pure and thus very suitable for certain religious rituals. He was clearly relieved when we returned to the road! Back at our house for cool beers he said he would return shortly to carry out an excavation. Weeks passed and nobody appeared and rumours were going around that we had found a Mayan treasure! I then encountered an American archaeologist from a university in the States and took him to the cave. He organized a professional excavation. I took one Mayan bowl as a souvenir, which eventually we passed to Trudia as a memento of the country where she was born.

8th February 1965 – Our daughter Trudia born.

With the greater part of the road to Belize City being corrugated and riddled with potholes, when it was getting near the time for the birth of our first child I installed Audrey in a hotel in Belize City near a small private hospital run by a Christian sect but whose excellent doctor was not a member of the sect. I would join Audrey at the weekends. Meanwhile an elderly couple from Canada arrived at the same hotel. He had served in Europe during the First World War. They were engaged in a long and thoroughly planned adventure driving from home to South America. At that time the only part that could not be undertaken by road was from British Honduras to Honduras. They had booked in advance for a place on the ferry that bridged this gap. However, on arrival in Belize City they discovered the ferry was in dry dock having its hull scraped clean of the barnacles, etc., and being repainted. They struck up a friendship with Audrey. When I arrived the following weekend there was obvious consternation. The Canadians' large, well equipped, car had been broken into and much equipment, tools, etc. had been stolen. Unless most was recovered or replaced they would have to cancel the rest of their trip. The police didn't hold out much hope of recovering the items. However, I got chatting with an ex-policeman. With him I went out at dusk and we hid in the shadows and observed thieves checking vehicles. The ex-policeman then went off and returned later to report that he may have contacted the leader of the gang who had robbed the Canadians' car. He introduced me to the guy, who denied that he was responsible for the theft but said he thought he knew who was! If I got a list of what had been stolen he would endeavour to recover the items in exchange for a cash payment on completion of the deliveries. The Canadians consented to the arrangement and gave me a list and I returned to an agreed meeting point. The gang leader said the items were stashed away at a number of locations in the city. Over the rest of the night I would park the Land-Rover at an agreed point and retreat while a shadowy figure deposited some of the loot in the back of the Land-Rover. Chatting to the gang leader it transpired that he was on the run from the Chicago Police, so had organized a local gang to continue his business! There was a crisis at one point when the Land-Rover was stopped by the police enquiring what I was up to. I said I was recovering the goods stolen from the Canadians, provided they kept out of my way. They said I would need to give them a full statement afterwards. I agreed as long as they did not interfere before I had completed my mission. This encounter had been observed from the shadows by the gang leader. He now approached me in an agitated state. What had I told the police? I said I had told them to keep out of my way. He replied that he had a good mind to dump me in the nearest canal, where the huge vicious catfish would soon consume every last scrap of my flesh! With false bravado I retorted that they would then have the police in full force after them. He then demanded to know how come I was driving a government vehicle after dark when it was against standing orders without a special permit. I replied, truthfully, that because of my special work for the government I had a permit to drive at night at any time. I did not explain that my 'special work' involved studying insects and mammals active at night! He calmed down although clearly puzzled as to who I was. He agreed to carry on. There were humorous moments. I was offered a portable toilet but that was not on the Canadians' list. He insisted it was part of the loot. When I returned with it to the hotel the Canadians agreed it was theirs but had felt too embarrassed to list it! The next surprise was to be offered a box of 'bombs' not on the list! I said that there was no way the elderly couple would have a box of bombs. They insisted it was bombs as there was a picture on the box of one exploding. It turned out they were rescue flares! The next argument was over a pair of binoculars that meant a lot to the old man, as they were those he had worn in the trenches in France during the First World War. The gang leader said they could get a lot of money for them in the market. I told him straight that would be foolish as they were the only pair of binoculars like that in the country and the police would quickly track down who had sold them to the buyer. Anyway I got them back. We were getting on fine. There was only one more consignment to recover, the valuable tool kit. I parked the Land-Rover and retreated to the shadows when a police vehicle arrived at the Land-Rover. The man approaching with the tools ran off. The police asked me how I was doing. I replied all was going well until they had now messed things up. They said to remember I had undertaken to give them a statement about the gang when it was all over. I replied that my undertaking had been conditional on them keeping out of my way. Furthermore, most of the gang came from Hattieville to the west of the City. It was the remnant of the refugee camp from Hurricane Hattie that had devastated Belize City in the 1950s. I had to drive through Hattieville on my way back home the next day and I didn't fancy being attacked in revenge for me not having completed the deal by handing over the agreed money from the Canadians. In the event I picked up one of my assistants who had spent the weekend in Belize City. He kept a sharp lookout while I drove at high speed through Hattieville.

As the Canadians were still stuck in Belize City when I had attended the birth of our beautiful daughter, we invited them to come to stay at Central Farm, along with their superbly trained old sheep dog. We were greatly amused when the dog rounded up our neighbour's chickens. Apparently when training the dog they had started it with chickens before moving it on to sheep.

The name Trudia was derived from two names. Audrey's mother was Gertrude, which however was regarded as being too Victorian for the 20th Century. Ria was one of the liveliest Dutch girls on the domestic staff during our time at Flatford Mill. She readily agreed to be godmother to Trudy. In the event when Ria got married communication with her dwindled and we eventually lost touch with her. We used to wonder what had happened to her.

After the Canadians had left to continue their adventure, we were surprised when the ex-policeman called in at Central Farm, saying he'd come on a truck and was staying nearby. After giving refreshment and chatting amiably he left, but it struck me his mood had shifted from being initially cheerful to a look of discomfort. The next day I learned he had been for a walk by the river but returned in a state, having been menaced by a snake in a mass of creeper beside the path. The snake was of a sort that local superstition associated with a disaster in the offing. He committed suicide later that day. Audrey never did learn that it was not the snake that was the principal event that precipitated the suicide. I never liked to tell her the real reason. He had evidently mistaken Audrey's warm friendly disposition towards him for her fancying him. His visit to us at Central Farm and witnessing Audrey and I being even more in love as we delighted in caring for our lovely new daughter made him realize he had been deluding himself. The following poem was prompted by this event, but the context (not to mention the sex of the baby!) have been changed:

UNAWARE (TL)

A lass arrived from far to stay
In hostel near the clinic where

Her nearly-term expected babe
Would enter world. It's there
She met a man called Bill, but failed
To see he'd fallen for her charms.
When caring husband called each day
It sounded no alarms.
He thought he'd made his mark with girl
Whose guileless, friendly smiles were just
Her natural way with all she met.
It's thus his burning lust
Was blind to facts that others saw.
The couple truly shone with joy
At birth of son at end of week.
They doted on their boy,
When three returned to country home,
With bonds of love renewed by gift
Of child for whom they'd waited long.
But Bill believed a rift
Was cause of smiling looks the girl
Conferred on him, so bold as brass
He soon appeared and asked to stay
A night or two, with farce
Of tale of how he came to be
Their way. It wasn't long before
He grasped he'd made mistake. They found
Him hung from sycamore.

For Audrey and myself it was the wonder and delight in our daughter that
enriched our loves beyond our expectations:

PENDULUM YEARS (TL)

As pendulum on clock
She sits in swing
And I propel her high
To keep the thrill
In proper time. She comes,
She goes, she's near
She's far away at end
Of upward sweep.
Too soon she learns the skill,
Declines our aid.
In future years I fear
We'll be the same

As ties are loosed and love
Matures, restrains
Its open hand to let
The child transform
To adult free to be
Herself apart
From us who gave her birth
And watched her grow.
Will she return again
With child of own
To bring us joy when age
Has blurred our minds,
Recalling years when we
And mum were young?
Will we then take her girl
To park for swing,
Before advancing years
Subside to halt?

We would invite neighbours in for a drink or a meal, while others were apt to drop in unexpectedly for a drink after work. Some were more welcome than others! On one occasion we had invited two young primary school teachers when an agronomist with a reputation for hard drinking dropped in. As the beer caused his anecdotes and language to deteriorate, to the evident embarrassment of the local lasses we had invited, I spotted a scorpion under his chair. I pointed this out and added that it was covered in baby scorpions some of which kept falling off their mother. The agronomist leapt up, made his excuses and left as we fell about laughing. I then swept the scorpions into a dustpan and deposited them outside.

Other frequent visitors were a family also with a young daughter. The father was of African ancestry and the mother Canadian of European ancestry. The father was a first rate member of the Department of Agriculture but his promotion had been blocked by a superior who was a time server and prejudiced against his subordinate's mixed marriage. Consequently the father was increasingly frequently the worse for excessive drinking. His wife was getting desperate and kept urging that they move to Canada where he could start afresh. One day they arrived and the father was clearly inebriated. After discussing the situation with his wife we offered her cash so she could order plane tickets to Canada for herself and their daughter. They then left to pack things up for departure. Meanwhile we locked the father in the kitchen until he was sober and with a certain amount of shouting at each other convinced him to resign his post, buy his own plane ticket and re-join his family. We were delighted that in Canada he then became a great worker for the interests of the native American 'Indians' until his untimely death from prostate cancer diagnosed too late for treatment, unlike my own case many years later (see

138

chapter 10). When we were in Cambridge his daughter came over from Canada and stayed with us for six months.

The Professor of Medical Entomology, Professor Bertram, from the London School of Hygiene and Tropical Medicine came to visit our lab to do some work on day-biting mosquitoes and I helped him in the field. When I subsequently returned to England he tried to persuade me to register for a PhD with him and to take on some teaching for a member of his department who was on sabbatical. I said I would like to think about it first. So we lunched together at the School a week later. I thanked him for the offer but had decided to turn it down for two reasons. First he had asked me because he thought I knew how to set about doing research from what he had learned of my work in Belize, and a prime function of a PhD is to certify that one knew how to engage in worthwhile research. Secondly, I did not fancy focussing down on a single topic, under someone else's supervision, after my experience of tackling a number of different topics in parallel to the benefit of the larger project as a whole. I did wonder for some years if I had made the right decision. In the event it was right (see 1971 in chapter 8).

In January 1965 a party led by Dr Beltran came with some postgraduate students from Professor Biagi's Department in the University of Mexico City, primarily to see Paul, the Head of our Unit. Paul mentioned that I was collecting data that I was claiming cast doubt on the assumption that the vector would prove to be one of the three principal man-biting species of sandfly. Although Paul said he remained unconvinced, he suggested that Dr Beltran and his party should have a session with me. Initially Dr Beltran was somewhat condescending. However, as I presented the data from my fly traps baited with the normal rodent hosts of Leishmania mexicana and other observations he became engaged and asked if I minded if he took notes. I replied that I had no objection and that I was still trying to convince Paul as regards the implications of my data. I subsequently learned that, on his return to Mexico, when he showed his notes to Professor Biagi he had dismissed them as being the product of a young man in a hurry! However, Biagi began to wonder about my data, while remaining convinced that the vector must be one of the three principal man biting species of sandfly. Meanwhile, in October 1965, I proved my fourth species (see below) was acting as a vector to the normal rodent hosts of the parasite. I sent a telegram to Dr Lewthwaite in London telling of this achievement. Biagi, however, was unaware of this when in December 1965 he set up an expedition to the Yucatan Peninsular to prove me wrong. To his surprise, by isolating the parasites from different species of sandfly and inoculating hamsters as well as feeding known species of sandfly on human 'volunteers' he found I was right about my fourth species! On his return to Mexico City he found a letter from me requesting copies of some of his recent papers and I had added that I had now proved my fourth species of sandfly was acting as a vector to the rodent hosts. Unwittingly this precipitated a chain of events culminating a few years later in a controversy with consequences. This story continues when I had moved to Cameroon (see chapter 7). An interesting discovery in the 21st Century was that in Peru the principal man-biting species of sandflies were acting as vectors of Leishmaniasis to man. This reflected the very different ecosystems and an entirely different set of mammalian hosts. Thus the main rodent host in Central America (Ototylomis phyllotis) does not occur in Peru. I likewise found that a blackfly species known to be a vector of river blindness in East Africa was not biting people in Cameroon (see chapter 7).

I had decided not to sign on for a second two year term. The reason was partly that, having nailed the vector species, I had achieved the primary objective of my initial appointment. The second reason was that Paul, although essentially kind-hearted, was not a good director. There were a number of occasions when his behaviour caused problems with regard to the smooth running of the Unit. His defects mainly related to his alcohol problem and to him being a homosexual bachelor. With regard to the latter he tried to bribe assistants into having sexual relations with him. I had had a session with him over this matter in which I said his private inclinations were his own business, but when they impacted on the relations with our assistants and on discipline then it was no longer a private matter. However, the last straw was when Paul had inoculated a hamster with parasites isolated from one of the common man biting species of sandfly shortly before he was due to go on leave to England. Because the lesion, if there were to be a positive result, would develop while he was away he asked me to witness the inoculation of a 'volunteered' assistant and to report the results in both the hamster and the assistant. I refused, reminding him of the risk of intestinal Leishmaniasis and the ban imposed by London on inoculations of extracted parasites into human volunteers. A few days later I learned that while I was away in Belize City one day he had gone ahead with the inoculation of the assistant. As soon as Paul had departed for England I informed the Chief Medical Officer of the situation and he ordered our Research Assistant to carry out a number of tests. Mercifully, not only were the tests for intestinal Leishmaniasis negative but, in the event, neither the hamster nor the assistant developed a dermal Leishmaniasis lesion.

I learned later that Paul was puzzled by my higher frequency of the vector species biting man than he had found to be the case in his extensive studies. He suggested to my assistants that I had 'exaggerated' my results. They hotly denied it. The difference was due to our methods. His extensive records of the species biting man were based on the human baits being static, sitting on a log, mainly in the evenings. My counts were based on my observation that the human cases of Dermal Leishmaniasis were dominated by forest workers (mahogany hunters and chicle collectors) active in the forest in the mornings. So I made it a rule that when we were active in the forest attending mammal and fly traps in the mornings that if we felt a sandfly biting, the nearest person was to trap it in a tube and note the time. So Paul tested this by repeating his standard catches but with the modification that one pair was accompanied by a third person leaning on a stick; but with second pair the man with the stick walking slowly in circles around them stirring the leaf litter on the forest floor.

The numbers of the vector species biting the bait person in the second case reflected the figures I had reported.

When packing up in preparation for our departure to England I decided to visit a lumber mill by the Guatemalan border. I purchased some slabs of mahogany which I then got made up into our packing cases that would be going as freight by ship. If imported to the UK as timber, one had to pay duty, but packing cases were exempt. The cases were somewhat heavier than if they had been made from the usual pine planks. In due course much of this mahogany was made into bookcases by a craftsman. They adorned our home ever since. Audrey's Dad had French polished many old pieces of mahogany furniture in the past and would have greatly appreciated our bookcases.

When we flew to Miami we stopped off for a few days before catching our flight to Heathrow. On arrival I declared the cultures of the Leishmania mexicana and presented a letter from Professor Sir Cyril Garnham in London explaining their purpose and importance. The official declared he didn't accept documentation from London and said the cultures were a threat to the U.S.A. and would have to be incinerated! After an altercation I said I had been told there was a mosquito official for the airport. He agreed and he was summoned. Thankfully he persuaded the official that my cultures were not a risk to the U.S.A. as they lacked the necessary insect vectors. However, it was agreed to lock the cultures in a security box for the duration of our visit and this was guarded by a rota of large policemen bearing two pistols protruding from their belts. When our flight was ready Audrey, myself, Trudy and my cultures were marched to the plane first before the other passengers boarded! At Heathrow our reception was quite different. A public announcement told us that once we had cleared customs there was a minicab awaiting us at a particular exit. Professor Garnham had arranged this in order to get the cultures delivered safely!

A few days later I went to see Professor Garnham, at the London School of Hygiene and Tropical Medicine. On learning of the data I had accumulated and the results I had obtained he telephoned Dr Lewthwaite at the Ministry of Overseas Development. Dr Lewthwaite immediately agreed to extend my contract by six months to allow me to write up my results for publication.

My sister Halcyon was completing her medical studies in Cambridge prior to moving to the Middlesex Hospital in London for the next stage of her training. She had secured the rental of a flat near the base of the Post Office Tower as her base for this stage. So we occupied it before she was due to move in. For access to relevant libraries and reference collections it was convenient for the London School of Hygiene and Tropical Medicine and a straightforward trip on the Underground to South Kensington for the Natural History Museum.

CHAPTER 6

POSTGRADUATE STUDENT

1966-1967 – Postgraduate Student at Department of Education, Bristol University.

We rented a ground floor flat in Batheaston and I went by bus to Bristol each day.

Early in the course I had a short placement in a large comprehensive school on the edge of Bristol. I took some lessons and observed others. Being a 'mature' student I observed some classes taken by a teacher younger than myself! One such class was a practical; examining samples of soil and carrying out simple analyses of structure and aspects of chemistry. The class was pure chaos. Small pebbles from the samples were being flicked across the room, soil was being put down the neck of a fellow student, etc. At the end I said to the teacher that I would not have tolerated such ill-discipline as it was frustrating the aim of helping to get her charges through their exams. She was furious and riposted that it was not ill-discipline I had observed but 'high spirits'! Back in the staff room she complained to colleagues about my observation. So they decided to assign me to take a bottom stream class with a reputation for being troublesome. Sure enough a boy at the back started interrupting with remarks causing others at the back to dissolve into giggles. So I strode to the back and confronted the trouble maker. I said "You are clearly not interested in what I am trying to tell you. What are you interested in?" With a sneer he replied "Fishing and football". I replied "Fish is biology. Get up to the front of the class and tell us about fish!" Astonished, and grinning from ear to ear, he sauntered to the front. He then delivered an excellent account of the different coarse fish he encountered when he went fishing, giving detailed accounts of the habits of the different species. The class listened with rapt attention. I thanked him for his interesting talk and asked him to return to his seat. I added a few comments of my own about fish and then returned to my original script. The class gave no further trouble. Back in the staff room I was asked how I had got on. I said X had tried to be disruptive but I told them what I had done. There was a mixture of suppressed chuckles and astonishment tinged with disappointment that I had coped when they had expected me to have been totally frustrated! What shook me most was that his teachers had wrongly written off X as 'stupid' when it was clear that when something engaged his interest he applied himself with a critical intelligence.

The course itself comprised a series of modules delivered as lectures and discussions in tutorial groups. At the conclusion of each module we were assessed by a series of questions being posted on a notice board. We selected one of these and wrote an essay of a given minimum length to be handed in by a specified deadline. We were free to use the library in composing our essay. I preferred this continuous assessment to final exams. However, I ran into a problem with the psychology module. The two lecturers belonged to totally different schools of psychology. One was a Neo-Freudian while the other was into experimental assessments of intelligence with white rats and pre-literate children. As part of the reading following the lectures I read some of Freud's writings as well as authors like Skinner. Despite their very different insights it seemed to me both were flawed. Freud clearly too often went beyond the evidence, as in his case of Little Hans who had a fear of horses (he had been involved in an accident when a shaft broke and the passengers fell alongside a wildly thrashing horse, and when he had offered a horse a titbit and his hand was bitten. Freud, however, decided the horse represented the father of Hans, who had a complex relating to his father). Skinner, by contrast, ignored what was not readily subjected to experimental analysis. When it came to the essay assessment for the psychology module it was obvious which question had been set by which lecturer. I selected one set by the Neo-Freudian but answered in terms of the other lecturer. My motive was to understand how one assessed an essay when the rival schools of psychology were almost completely at odds. The system of assessment was that the lecturer who had set the question marked it, assigning the mark S if satisfactory, S- if not or S+ if more than satisfactory. If it was S- or S+ then it had to be assessed by the other lecturer to confirm or refute the assessment. In the event the Neo-Freudian assigned my essay S- but the other lecturer assigned an S+! The result was almost comical. A special faculty meeting was held to try to resolve the situation, but without success. I was then informed by my tutor that it had been decided not to include the assessment for the psychology module in my final assessment!

FREUDIAN FANTASIES (CO)

My dreams are sometimes very odd;
But always I discern a link,
However thin, to some event,
Impression or remark from day
That's passed. At first these fleeting bits
Are merely dumped in pending tray.
At night they're filed. For some the mind
Is left in doubt, and tries first here
Then there before decision's reached.

It seems each byte must slot in place
That fits with rest already stored.
But if the body feels the cramp
Is creeping up with silent step,
Or need to go to loo persists,
The mind assists in waking me
By making tale requiring leap
From bed or warning yell to move
The fantasy ahead. It's then
I wake with lingering end of yarn
Escaping from my grasp. But Freud
Would have us think these ploys reveal
Events of childhood's past. For some
The future they foretell. But both
Are using claims to rule our lives
By stirring dormant fears or hopes
With cunning lies. But I despise
These modern tyrants in disguise.
Their unctuous concern conceals
Control they exercise, as once
Those Jewish priests that Jesus chose
To castigate. For their desire
To purify all thoughts and acts
Had stifled joys. My mental romps
When half awake at night amuse,
Or serve to make me search for clues
To grotesque scenes my mind constructs
From random litter dropped by chance.
My brain prefers to hoard the scraps
That don't make sense, in case they can
Be used another day. Indeed
Its attic's full of junk in hope
Of finding use in future plays.
It's only those who wipe their disks
At end of day who feel desire
To wish the same for saner folk
Whose folders house computer games,
And old e-mails, forgotten scraps
Of half conceived reports and drafts
Of papers meant to shake the world,
Or lists of names and shopping lists.
I know my mind's a rubbish tip,
But then my dreams are much more fun
Than those who worship tidy desks.
Perhaps in act of writing this

I'm strutting peacock fanning tail -
And Freud had really missed the point
In thinking dreams were key to truth
About an infant's sexual drives,
Whose fruits are really adult's art
Displayed to world as potent signs.

The most useful part of the course was a full term's teaching, which I did in the Bath Technical College. Periodically my tutor sat in on the class and gave me constructive criticism. I took G.C.E. 'O' and 'A' level classes as well as extras such as teaching natural history to nursery nurse students. My 'A' level class included Indians who had decided to get out of Uganda as a result of the troubles between the Baganda and Obote (before those that followed later under Idi Amin). They were highly motivated but had mostly learned by rote. When I innovated some field work and some experiments in the lab on populations of freshwater shrimps from the canal in Bath they kept asking what the correct answer was. When I replied I did not know until we had analysed their data they were initially perplexed!

11 December 1966: Adrian born.
Adrian was delivered at home by a formidable midwife.

1967 Certificate of Education

1967 Guinness Award for Science Teachers in Training. This was awarded for an essay I wrote on 'field studies and the secondary school child' that my tutor had entered for the award scheme.

For much of 1967 the Field Studies Council had been negotiating for a new field centre in Monmouthshire. A large house and associated outbuildings were set in a substantial park, all owned by the local council. I was seen as a potential first warden for this centre. The local council wanted to hand over the entire management of the park to the FSC. However, this would not allow the FSC to balance the books for the proposed field centre. While the negotiations dragged on I worked in a market garden in Bath in order to support the family. One morning the boss told me to spray a bed of chrysanthemums with an insecticide. I read the instructions on the can. These clearly stated that one must not spray within forty-eight hours of the flowers being picked. As I knew the girls who culled the flowers for the local florists were due to harvest these chrysanthemums later that afternoon I drew the attention of the boss to this statement on the can. He replied that he didn't bother with such nonsense! So I asked for my cards and left.

I then signed on as a mason's mate. It was the era of Wilson's crazy Selective Employment Tax. So I was not employed but was subcontracted as a device whereby the builder avoided his obligations to employees under the new law. To save money, he laid us off between jobs without pay. I mainly mixed the mortar, wheeled barrow loads of building materials and so on for the mason, Bill, who was very skilled. We built a bungalow in re-constituted Bath stone. After that we worked on Executive houses in Bristol that were part finished. A team had done all the easy bits and then walked out, leaving Bill and myself to tackle all the tricky bits, such as fancy stone chimney stacks.

IN ONE'S PLACE (CW)

I watch a mason choosing stones,
From pile of random shattered blocks,
To build a fancy chimney stack.
His mate admires uncanny eye
Appraising gap before he lifts
The only one that fits the space.
And where design requires an arch,
Above the hearth inside, he needs
To clout and trim some rocks to shape
Until he reaches top and slots
The keystone into place to hold
It firm and true. Is this the way
Our quirky selves are meant to be
Assembled in community?
Or is our lot as useless heap
Of rubble dumped beside a road
As infill laid below the bed
Of graded gravel packed beneath
A carriageway of gleaming tar?
And are we merely part of road
For those to come or are we now
Intended for an edifice
Displaying each as chosen for
A part in all embracing whole?

One day an inspector appeared and noticed the roofers were installing joists measuring 2x2 inches when the regulations required 2x3 joists. The roofers said they knew but the boss had told them to use 2x2s. They added that the boss would be calling in for his daily inspection shortly. When the boss arrived he suggested to the inspector that they go and discuss the problem over a drink. Half an hour later the boss returned and told the roofers to carry on as before!

We were then laid off for a fortnight. Audrey put the money for rent, rates, electricity, etc. in envelopes in a locked cupboard in the kitchen. We then went for a holiday with Aunt Sheila in Norfolk. When we returned we found burglars had sawn round the Yale locks on the inner and outer front doors. They had broken into the cupboard in the kitchen and taken all the money. They also smashed a piggy bank that Trudia had, taking the silver but leaving the copper coins on the carpet! We were confronted with pending bills and very little money left, the grant for the course at Bristol being exhausted. So I got out the Sunday papers and found the Medical Research Council wanted an entomologist to work on the vectors of River Blindness (Onchocerciasis) in Cameroon. So I applied. Although I was the only short-listed candidate without a PhD I was offered the job on the basis of what I had done in British Honduras. The MRC supported me for a few weeks in the UK while I familiarized myself with Afrotropical biting blackflies (Simuliidae) at the Natural History Museum in London and made a visit to Durham University where novel techniques were revealing cryptic sibling species of blackflies in Britain.

CHAPTER 7

WEST AFRICA

1967-1971 – Entomologist at the Helminthiasis Research
Unit at Kumba in West Cameroon
(Overseas Staff, Medical Research Council – Technical
Aid to Cameroon Government).

When our sea borne freight eventually arrived at Kumba it caused some astonishment as it included a large box containing Audrey's piano. My assistants contemplated the problem as to how to unload it from the truck without dropping it with the risk of the impact causing damage. With a gathering audience of curious onlookers they solved the problem by laying down a carpet of old vehicle tyres onto which the box landed with a slight bounce and the sound of twanging wires sounding forth. The piano was soon installed and Audrey back to playing her beloved music and simple tunes for the children to sing to.

I was assigned a good team of nine assistants headed by Mr Oguama, a Nigerian Ibo, who had worked his way up to his position of responsibility. The rest included a Muslim from north Cameroon who frequently had us all laughing, and a local man who was illiterate but was a first class man to have in tropical rainforest. He could survive indefinitely in the forest. When thirsty he knew which creeper to cut with his machete below an internode and then to cut below the next higher internode. He then upended the detached section and drank the fluid that emerged. Likewise he knew which fruits, leaves, etc. were edible along with flying stage termites and other creatures. We worked well together as a team. They clearly appreciated the fact that I worked with them in the field. Indeed I was to discover that my nickname in Pidgin English, that was their common language, was 'whiteman done work'! The Unit's excellent Research Assistant, Peter, was nicknamed 'Government spy' as he was always right up to date with the latest gossip!

When giving Mr Oguama the programme for the day and the times involved I often had to tell him to emphasise to the team that when I said a particular time for setting off, or whatever, that I meant real time not African time! So what were the tasks we undertook together?

River blindness (Onchocerciasis) is caused by a parasitic nematode worm – Onchocerca volvulus. Its infective larval stage is transmitted by biting blackflies (Simuliidae), whose larvae live in fast flowing clean waters. A World Health Organisation (WHO) Scientific Working Group had produced a review of Onchocerciasis research and suggested future lines of investigation. Brian Duke, the boss of the Research Unit, asked me which of these I proposed to take up. I replied that is what others would no doubt be pursuing and as I had some different ideas I was going to try them first! However, I had one definite remit from MRC. It had been established by the Unit that there was another blackfly species, apart from the known major vector, acting as a secondary vector of River Blindness in the Forest Zone. Brian had sent specimens of the females caught biting people to the Natural History Museum in London. They were identified as Simulium aureosimile, with a caveat that they seemed a little atypical. Brian had just published a paper on this as a secondary vector when it was concluded by the NHM that it was a distinct species, but they needed males and/or pupae to determine whether the species was indeed a new, undescribed, species. I therefore searched a wide range of rivers and streams for larvae and pupae that appeared to be previously unrecorded. We turned up four species new to science (one of which added to the list of species named after Audrey! See Appendix E) but still no sign of Brian's species. In East Africa two groups of so called 'phoretic' species had been reported, including a vector of Onchocerciasis. Phoretic species have larvae that are not attached to stones or trailing vegetation in a river but instead attach to some specific invertebrate host, which in East Africa was either river crabs or mayfly larvae. The species whose larvae attach to crabs in East Africa is a vector of river blindness. My predecessor had reported an absence of phoretic species in Cameroon. But I gathered his search had been somewhat perfunctory. So I organized my assistants into collecting crabs and mayfly larvae. We quickly obtained blackfly larvae on river crabs and on four species on mayfly nymphs, of which two were new to science with one of the mayfly species being new to science also. But we still had not found Brian's mystery species. So I said to my team that it must be phoretic on some other river invertebrate. So it proved. I found the larvae of Brian's species in the gill chambers of a river prawn (family Atyidae) and the pupae at the base of the antennae. In addition there was second species new to science whose larvae attached to the antennae of the same prawns. Brian's species was subsequently named Simulium dukei. Prior to that David Lewis suggested I submit a note to Nature on the discovery that the larvae and pupae of the secondary vector of River Blindness were phoretic on these prawns. David pointed out that the first reports of mayfly and crab phoretic species had been reported in Nature. However, the Editor ruled that such a note was "too specialised for the general readership of Nature"! So I resubmitted my note to the Transactions of the Royal Society of Tropical Medicine and Hygiene. Its editor's response was quite the reverse. He replied that he hoped I didn't object but he had corrected the proofs himself as he was keen to get it into the next issue! I followed up these discoveries with a series of papers on these phoretic species. Thus the novel associations with river prawns culminated in a detailed account (Disney, R. H. L., 1971. Association between blackflies (Simuliidae) and prawns (Atyidae), with a discussion of the phoretic habit in Simuliids. Journal of Animal Ecology 40: 83-92). Two of the four species new to science whose pre-adult stages we had caught free living in the rivers, before turning our attention to phoretic species, were represented by only two specimens and a single specimen. We never found further specimens among thousands of non phoretic larvae and pupae collected subsequently. I strongly suspect that both these rare species were in fact normally phoretic. If so then one of my unsolved problems was what were their hosts? Might they be another group of aquatic insects or even a fish?

A problem reported by studies in East Africa with the species whose larvae they found attached to the sides of river crabs was they never found the smallest, first stage, larvae and were puzzled as to how they arrived on their hosts. I found that the first stage larvae were present, but attached to the eye stalks of the crabs. Furthermore I carried out experiments with crabs of the same species but obtained from a crater lake, where blackfly larvae, who require running water, could not live. These 'clean' crabs we put in cages which we then placed in a river known to harbour the crab phoretic species. This experiment indicated that the larvae arrived on their hosts one at a time by chance encounter. It was of interest to note that our crab phoretic blackfly was the same species as the species in East Africa. However, we never recorded it biting people. A further case of different patterns of ecological relations in different widely separated regions, as found with the main man biting species of sandfly that were not acting as vectors of Leishmania in Belize in contrast to the situation in Peru (see chapter 5).

One of our methods for catching crabs was the use of local basket traps designed to catch fish. They also caught snakes, some of which were poisonous. However, my assistants shared out the fish and snakes for consumption at home. With the poisonous snakes they deftly removed the heads with a machete and saved the rest for eating at home.

When my friend from my student days, 'Sally' (Sarah) Corbet (with whom I later co-founded and co-edited the Naturalists' Handbooks series – see Appendix G), and her colleagues came out for a few weeks to study the fish, especially those of our local crater lakes, I let them look over our catches in the rivers before giving the rest to my assistants. It turned out that two of the fish in my regular working sites were new to science (the ugliest, with poisonous tips to sharp spines in their fins was the one named after me by Dr Trewavas, the fish taxonomist with the party! – see Appendix F). I had made this group of fish experts, official guests of our Unit in order to minimize problems with officialdom. I told them, however, that near the end of their stay we would need to spend a whole day in Douala filling in and rubber stamping forms in order to export their fish specimens in two batches – preserved specimens and live fish destined for aquaria in the U.K. Having completed the necessary forms we proceeded with the cargo to the airport. There the official was intrigued by the unusual cargo and asked if he might see some of the preserved specimens. Unfortunately after viewing a few different fish he unwrapped the one non-fish in the collection. This was the mammal Potamogale, a feeder on fish and river crabs. It is hairy but with a large flattened scaly tail it uses for swimming after its prey. The official commented that it seemed to be a rather funny looking fish. The professor replied that it wasn't a fish. So I hastily tapped him on his foot. He started up again, but Sally realizing something was up, tapped more sharply on his other foot. So the professor, realizing he needed to correct himself, told the official that it was a very odd fish as the scales on most on its body resembled hairs. The official was satisfied and rewrapped the specimen. Afterwards the professor demanded to know what had been the problem. I told him that mammals required an entirely different set of forms to be signed by an entirely different set of officials – so I hope he didn't mind but I had reclassified his beautiful Potamogale as a fish!

An unexpected result of the visit of the fish biologists was to lead to the averting of a conservation disaster for the large number of endemic species of our local crater lake Barombi Mbo. In West Cameroon there were many Voluntary Service Overseas young people and also American Peace Corps volunteers. Most were based in rural communities or smaller towns than Kumba. They regularly travelled to Kumba in order to replenish their stocks of food and other necessities. We kept open house for them to drop in for a light lunch before returning to their bases. These included some Peace Corps volunteers engaged in damning small streams to produce fish ponds for introduced hybrid fish to provide an extra source of protein for the less well off. One day they said they were planning to introduce these fast growing larger hybrid fish to Barombi Mbo Lake. We pointed out that the unique endemic species were not only the livelihood of a village but the introduced species would be likely to out compete the native species and drive many towards extinction. They replied that their orders were from the local Peace Corps office in Yaounde. So I said I would report the matter to Dr Trewavas, the leading taxonomist of African freshwater fish at the Natural History Museum in London. She got onto federal government environmentalists in Washington who then got onto the head of the Peace Corps. He in turn told their office in Yaounde to back off as he was in real trouble over the project. Next time the fish project Peace Corps volunteers dropped in for lunch they gave me the good news – "we guessed Dr Trewavas would blow her top but we didn't think she would blow it that high!" To which I replied "why did you think I approached her rather than the Peace Corps office in Yaonde?" I told them that I did so because I knew her to be a formidable lady who would go to the top if she knew her beloved rare fish were under threat. Incidentally, the villagers from the fishing village at Barombi Mbo used to pass our house on their way to sell fish in Kumba market. They would stop by and Audrey would buy fresh fish from them. Those endemic species were delicious!

Anne was a V.S.O. volunteer we got to know well. She was assigned to the Teacher Training College in Kumba. She married Mambo, a farmer in a local tribe, who was more go ahead than his fellow farmers. He not only went on an agriculture course in England, but he diversified so that if the price for cocoa was good one year but poor for coffee he would still make a profit. A new crop he had started was rubber and the trees were getting mature enough to start tapping. So Audrey and I gave them the cups for collecting the latex as our most unusual wedding present! We kept in touch after we left Kumba but tragedy was to overtake the family later (see chapter 8).

With regard to my investigations of the prime vector I decided to tackle some basic questions about its fundamental natural history. It had been established that the peak numbers of nulliparous females (i.e. those seeking their first blood meal prior to producing their first batch of eggs) of the main vector biting man was in the afternoon. By contrast the peak numbers of older (parours) flies was around midday. A nullipar when coming for its first blood meal has its first opportunity to acquire the larvae (microfilaria stages) of the parasite. Thus only a parous female can inoculate a person with the infective larval stages. Dissection of flies caught biting people had also established that nullipars had already taken a sugar meal (required for the energy to power their flight) and had mated (as evidenced by the contents of the sperm storage sac). There were two hypotheses as to why the younger females mainly sought a blood meal later in the day than the older females. One inferred that they were too busy hatching from their pupae and then seeking a sugar meal (nectar or honeydew) and mating. The second hypothesis was that old and young flies responded differently to the prevailing environmental conditions (temperature, humidity, etc.). So I investigated the timing of hatching from the pupae and the timing of the first blood meal following this. It turned out that the first blood meal is taken the day after hatching from the river.

Another problem was that the mass of data for the village of Bolo, where the Unit did much of its field work, had shown that the ratio of parous to nulliparous flies biting people varied with the time of year. When, drawing heavily on data from our Unit, in 1969 Mills (in Scotland) had published an attempted computer model of the epidemiology of Onchocerciasis where he had laid out his assumptions. These included the proposition that the distance between the breeding site of the flies and the village was presumed to be a constant. When I remarked to Brian that I thought that was an untenable assumption he seemed surprised. To disprove it involved the largest effort of all my investigations. I made monthly collections of blackfly pupae from eleven sites of the river system embracing Bolo. To carry out such a survey we suspended palm fronds from ropes so that the frond was suspended in a fast run of water. Initially we encountered a problem of the theft of our ropes. After talking to the local village headmen the thefts abated but did not cease altogether. In exasperation I asked my chief assistant what we should try next. His prompt reply was "why not try juju?" I asked what the most effective juju was for the purpose. His answer was "dried human heads tied to near the upstream ends of the ropes"! So my next question was to ask what the second most effective juju was. The answer was monkey heads instead. So we procured these from the local market where monkey meat was regularly sold. We tied the heads to the upper ends of the ropes and added the additional deterrent of whitened strips of bamboo with 'HRU 13" painted on them, HRU being the initials of our research unit. To test the efficacy of these jujus we tied some ropes rather conspicuously to the rails of a bridge and then hid ourselves in the rainforest nearby and waited to see what happened. It wasn't long before a car drew up and the occupant went over to the ropes. However, on peering over the rail he almost jumped back, raced back to his car and drove off at speed. We never had any further thefts of our ropes. A curious postscript to this solution was when I stopped off in Liberia, on the way back on leave, to visit a German lab working on river blindness. When discussing my studies in Cameroon I mentioned the problem I had encountered when trying to obtain comparative quantitative samples of larvae and pupae in the rivers. I was told they had also tried trailing ropes with replicated units for the larvae to colonize but had given up because of repeated thefts of the ropes. So I told them how we had solved this problem. I was urged to put this in a paper when I wrote up my methods. This I did but the editor queried this. So I recounted our experience and accordingly the recipe for an effective juju was included (Disney, R. H. L., 1972. Observations on sampling pre-imaginal populations of blackflies (Dipt. Simuliidae) in West Cameroon. Bulletin of Entomological Research 61: 485-503)! My visit to Liberia resulted in a joint paper with my host in which the first of the species to be named after Audrey was published (Garms, R. & Disney, R. H. L., 1974. Eine neue Simulium-Art aus Kamerun (S. audreyae n. sp., Simuliidae, Diptera). Zeitschrift für Tropenmedizin und Parasitologie 25: 128-133).

On leave in Bath we enjoyed renewing acquaintance with our families and the children enjoyed new experiences, such as the play facilities for children in the city's parks. One fine sunny day we put a tub of water in the back garden and the children splashed about in it with much enjoyment. A neighbour, however, was shocked by their nakedness! Next day she had a fence erected to screen such a lowering of the standards of the neighbourhood! Worse was to come when I embarked on my investigations of dog dung and flies (see chapter 9). We were making our way up the hill to the house when we spotted a neighbour dash into our front garden to see what the bottles on the window sill were about. On seeing their contents to be dog dung she recoiled in disgust and retreated fast! Another neighbour, however, was intrigued and did not regard us as lowering the standard of the neighbourhood!

Back in Cameroon, with the sampling method for pre-adult blackflies sorted, we embarked on the massive survey of the breeding sites that might be supplying biting blackflies to the village of Bolo. The sites represented the main river Mungo, major tributaries and minor tributaries that only flowed at the height of the season of the greatest rainfall. I identified the pupae to species and counted 187, 235 pupae obtained in my samples. What I found was that the peak numbers, for the main vector species varied from site to site, but in broad terms most breeding was in the main tributaries but a single generation emerged from the minor tributaries when the rainfall was sufficient to provide sufficient flow and breeding occurred in the main river especially at times of low flow in the rest of the system. Elsewhere in West Africa it had been reported that well away from rivers people were bitten dominantly by nulliparous flies and that parous flies were primarily biting close to the breeding sites. My data therefore suggested that the fluctuation in the parous rate was probably at least in part due to the seasonal changes in the breeding sites supplying biting flies to Bolo. When I eventually published the results of this mammoth survey (Disney, R. H. L., 1976. A survey of blackfly populations (Dipt. Simuliidae) in West Cameroon. Entomologist's Monthly Magazine 111: 211-227 (1975)) I received a letter from WHO in Geneva expressing the opinion that it was the most important paper on blackfly population ecology published that year. However the letter added that it probably would not be appreciated as such. This proved to be too right a prediction as evidenced by a major book on the natural history of biting blackflies published in 1990. It cited all my papers on my work in Cameroon, with the notable omission of this 1976 paper! The key fact that lies behind my findings compared with many papers on blackfly populations in temperate regions is the difference in the durations of development. In Cameroon from egg to adult took about three weeks. In England it takes many months. Hence in England the breeding sites are more or less fixed with regard to the flies biting hosts nearby. With a short duration for development different breeding sites supply biting flies to a village like Bolo according to the patterns of rainfall in space and time. It would have been good to follow up this study by marking and releasing flies from a major tributary some distance from Bolo and seeing if my prediction that some would be recovered biting man at Bolo would prove to be correct. Unfortunately I was running out of time as I was not signing on for a third tour because of my problems with Malaria (see below).

Previous studies had established that in the savannah a higher percentage of the flies biting man were parous than in the forest zone. I decided to make a trip to the north in East Cameroon, towards Lake Chad, to carry out some comparative studies. To organize such a trip was not easy because of security problems and corruption. One needed a pass to work in any district other than the one in which one was resident. With most Government officials a dash (i.e. a bribe) would facilitate the procurement of the required document. However, it was officially against the law to dash a Government official. The permit I required to travel (with three Land-Rovers, our Research Assistant and most of my assistants) to the northern region of East Cameroon had to be obtained from the Security Police. If one tried to dash them they got you for breaking the law. After being told three times to come back the next week I decided enough was enough. When told yet again to come back next week I replied that I needed the permit right now. I could see no reason why they couldn't produce the permit there and then. I got an evasive response. So I replied that I bet them 1000 Cameroon francs that they couldn't produce the permit there and then if they tried. My bet was accepted and I lost, but I had the required permit! It eased our way through a couple of roadblocks where our papers were checked.

An amusing incident on our way north was when I spotted a chameleon on the road. I stopped the Land-Rover and picked up the splendid creature and placed it on the trunk of a roadside thorn tree and photographed it. My African assistants regarded a chameleon as an agent of an adverse juju. For the next hour they debated as to when I was likely to be struck down! When nothing happened they then debated as to why not. They concluded that the juju was only effective against Africans and that I as a European was protected! Anyway we arrived safely by a small river amongst dry savanna with scattered thorn scrub and pitched our tents. Other creatures were associated with jujus. For example the large cylindrical millipedes. My assistants were astonished when I regularly picked these up and examined them, which I did after noticing small flies running about on their backs. I preserved the flies, which I only set about identifying years later when I realized that one species comprised assemblies of the males of a scuttle fly, which became the second species I named after Audrey (Disney, R. H. L., 1978. A new species of Afrotropical Megaselia (Diptera: Phoridae), with a re-evaluation of the genus Plastophora. Zeitschrift für angewandte Zoologie 65: 313-319). This was my first publication on an African species of the huge genus Megaselia. The African species were to pose a particular challenge (see chapter 9).

During our studies of the timing of emergence of adult blackflies from the river, we stumbled upon resting blackflies choosing the underside of the guy ropes of our tents to avoid the sun. Furthermore it was evident that many females had their abdomens swollen by a recent blood meal. So I put the assistants to collecting these and I then expelled the blood meal onto a filter paper kept in a sealed container to avoid ants and other unwanted intruders. Each sample was numbered and the rest of the fly was preserved in alcohol with the same code number. Back in Kumba I identified the flies. The dried blood meals I sent to the Nuffield Institute of Comparative Medicine at London Zoo, where they were reconstituted in physiological saline and using an immunological technique (it being before the days of later molecular techniques) the source of the blood meal was identified. The results showed that not all the blood meals were from primates (Patas monkeys and men) but some were from birds (Disney, R. H. L. & Boreham, P. F. L., 1969. Blood gorged resting blackflies in Cameroon and evidence of zoophily in Simulium damnosum. Transactions of the Royal Society of Tropical Medicine and Hygiene 63: 286-287). Perhaps the parous rate varied according to the availability of preferred vertebrate hosts. So back at Bolo I set up a comparison of the catches coming to bite a man and those coming to bite a chicken. The chicken was tethered to a stake with a supply of food but suspended from a beam above it was a screened cage with an open bottom. This end of the beam comprised one end of a see saw. The other end was on the ground held down by a boulder. At intervals the boulder was rolled away and the cage enveloped the chicken beneath. As the flies left the chicken they were collected by means of a sleeve in the side of the cage. Sure enough the parous rate of flies biting man and the chicken were different, with a lower percentage of parous flies caught at the chicken (Disney, R. H. L., 1972. Observations on chicken-biting blackflies in Cameroon with a discussion of parous rates of Simulium damnosum. Annals of Tropical Medicine and Parasitology 66: 149-158). It seemed the older flies tended to prefer biting man.

In all my studies we had to improvise apparatus. The see saw arrangement just described being an example. The Unit employed a carpenter who was skilled but not entirely honest, but was still a useful member of the team. However, a visitor was appalled when we turned a blind eye to some of his deceits. For example we needed timbers for building some apparatus. If I went to market, where there were no fixed prices but one haggled with the stall minder, I could only beat the seller down to 1000 Cameroon francs. By contrast our carpenter came back with a receipt for 800 francs. We knew that in fact he had beaten the man minding the stall for his boss down to 600 francs by persuading him to make out the receipt for 800 and splitting the 200 difference between himself and our carpenter. Our visitor could not endorse our view that by turning a blind eye to this ruse we had saved the government 200 francs! Incidentally our Research Assistant, Peter, when on leave in England but forgetting he was not in Cameroon, having asked a shop assistant the price of an item replied by saying he would give her half that amount and no more! The assistant went into a fit of giggles!

More blatant cheating was dealt with appropriately. For example the assistant, Simbo, responsible for purchasing food for our experimental animals would drive to nearby villages for this purpose as it was cheaper than buying the same products in Kumba market. One day, when on my way to a river where I was carrying out studies, we passed a palm wine establishment with Simbo's Land-Rover parked outside. Several hours later when returning to Kumba we observed Simbo's vehicle still outside the palm wine establishment! Accordingly I instructed the Unit clerk to cancel Simbo's overtime claim for that week. A few days later Simbo was unloading a stem of plantains when a snake stuck its head out and bit him. We told him to go straight away to the hospital next door to get injected with anti-venom. He responded by declaring there was no point as clearly someone had put a bad juju on him, as first he had lost his overtime payment for the week and now the snake had got him! So I ordered four assistants to grab Simbo by his arms and legs and to carry him, despite his protests, to the hospital, where he duly received the anti-venom shot. Apart from a sore arm for a few days he fully recovered.

The senior technician at the hospital had been trained by our Unit. Furthermore he was a keen naturalist and would draw my attention to interesting creatures. One day he summoned me to see a pair of burrowing vipers he had caught and had in his lab. When I went over to see them it turned out he had put them in a large container with a ground glass stopper in the lid – but he had omitted to put the stopper in place! As he cursed himself the junior technicians absented themselves at great speed! We eventually found the vipers behind some medical books on a shelf and got them securely back in the container with the stopper firmly in place so we could observe without danger.

On another occasion I was summoned to the hospital because a ward of patients were in state of terror because a 'stick' almost 30 cm in length on the insect screening of the window had suddenly flashed orange wings! They were astonished when I picked up the 'bad juju' and thanked them for directing me to the largest stick insect that I had ever seen!

With timber purchased by our carpenter, he built traps I designed and which we then placed in rivers to catch emerging flies. Likewise we constructed two artificial streams from giant bamboo stems converted into open gutters. The one in the lab was supplied with untreated tap water gravity fed from the Barombi Mbo crater lake (at home the water was boiled and filtered for human consumption). The outflow of this stream discharged into a circular flow of water in half a large vehicle tyre that had been sawn into two. The flow in the half tyre was created by welding paddles (half circles cut from large metal cans) to both ends of a metal bar, with one end in the tyre and the other in the waterfall discharge from the bamboo gutter stream, which then rotated the metal bar. The second stream was built from an extended line of similar bamboo gutters that diverted part of a stream to an open sided hut built by our carpenter. To record the durations of development of the pupal stages of the blackflies at different temperatures posed the problem as to how to regulate the temperature when we only had an unreliable intermittent electricity supply. We solved this with two kerosene operated fridges, one of which no longer worked but was a well-insulated container. With the working fridge we manufactured ice. With the dud fridge we installed flasks of pupae on the bottom shelf beside a thermometer. We placed a tray of ice on the shelf above or the top shelf. At regular intervals a new tray of ice replaced the previous tray and the temperature was recorded. Once we had worked out the interval required between changing the ice trays in order to maintain a nearly constant temperature we obtained some excellent results. The assistants were pleased because they earned overtime when they came in out of hours to change the ice trays and record the temperatures!

When we returned to England it took time to readjust to a culture that relied on off the shelf purchases and disposal, rather than repair, when it went wrong. In Cameroon almost anything could be fixed. Ibo tinkers were especially good improvisers. Give them a sketch of a piece of kit one desired and they would produce what one wanted.

DISPOSABLE (RE)

When I was boy the gypsies came
To peddle wooden pegs to pin
Our dripping clothes on line to dry.
Today they're made of plastic, in
A gaudy range of colours. But,
The sun destroys them, bit by bit,

Until the hinge becomes too weak
To hold. It can't be past the wit
Of man to make enduring peg.
Today the greed for profit rules
That products not be made to last
For years. They count on craven fools
Who don't complain or else ignore
Them when they do. The same applies
To microwave that's dead for want
Of part that no one now supplies,
Or so they claim. But when abroad,
In 'undeveloped' land, they used
Their nous, and odds and ends, to fix
And mend a range of goods abused
By years of wear and tear. The same
Applies to youths who've gone astray.
We write them off without attempts
To guide them back to narrow way.

If one needed more sophisticated apparatus that needed to be imported one had to allow at least six months for its delivery. In addition there were often bureaucratic impediments. For example I was notified that a box of mainly personal imports had arrived at Douala in East Cameroon. When I went down to clear it the official declared I would need to pay duty. I produced a copy, in French and English, of the Technical Aid agreement between the U.K. and Cameroon governments under which U.K. Technical Aid personnel were exempt from Cameroon import duty. The official looked aggrieved but then suddenly brightened up and declared that he required a written statement from the head of my Cameroon Government department stating that I was covered by the agreement. Our Unit was in fact the smallest Government Department and Brian, the boss, was then on a visit to Geneva leaving me as Acting Head. Accordingly I requested use of his typewriter to enable me to produce the requested document (for such contingencies I always carried a small suitcase with a supply of the Unit's headed notepaper and rubber stamps under the driver's seat of the Land-Rover). The official objected! After a tedious altercation he said he would arrange for the box to be shipped across to Victoria in West Cameroon and I could clear it with the customs official there. A week later I went south from Kumba to Victoria. On arrival at the customs office I said to the official that I had come to clear the box that was visible in the shed opposite that had DISNEY in big letters painted on it. He responded by saying he first needed to check the manifest of the lighter from Douala. He then revealed that my box had not been ticked to indicate that it had arrived! When I objected that obviously it had arrived, as it was visible in the shed opposite. He responded by showing me the manifest. He was correct that there was no tick against Disney. However I noticed that a Disley had had a box on the same lighter so I suggested to the official that there had obviously been a simple error that had caused the two boxes to be confused. He would not accept this explanation! So I went to the Land-Rover and told my assistants to load the box while I continued arguing with the official, and to signal to me when they had accomplished this. On receiving the signal I cut short the discussion in mid-sentence and told the official that the problem was solved. As we drove off with the box clearly visible in the back of the Land-Rover he yelled out that I would be in real trouble! Indeed a few weeks later the Unit clerk came into my lab to inform that there was a letter from Yaounde to say I would be deported if I did not get the box properly cleared by a certain date! I told the clerk not to worry. We then loaded the box into the Land-Rover. However, instead of going back to Victoria we headed west for the Nigerian border. Having located the office of a remote customs post we found no official. Fortunately the village schoolteacher informed us the official was sleeping off a huge alcohol-induced hangover. With the teacher's help I found all the right forms and rubber stamps in the customs office. Three copies were duly made out, rubber stamped and signed by the teacher on behalf of the official. We left a completed copy for the files of the customs official and a copy for him to send to Yaounde, and I took a copy for the Unit's files. We never heard anything more from Yaounde – the correct headed notepaper with the correct rubber stamp had done the trick! Indeed on another occasion when we went to obtain a box of imported equipment the official would not release it because the document we had been sent in advance lacked a rubber stamp! So I went into the local market and got an Ibo tinker to make a rubber stamp with a suitable design. I then used it to embellish the document with a couple of rubber stamps. On returning to the official the document instantly allowed the release of the box!

Apart from problems with officialdom there was a serious security risk. One river I sampled was on the boundary between West and East Cameroon where the local tribe was in rebellion against the President (who came from the northern part of East Cameroon). Here we had to have our foreman of our daily paid assistants stand guard with a shotgun in case of trouble.

Because of this security problem the East Cameroon military occasionally descended on Kumba to carry out checks. One day, when Brian was away in Geneva, I arrived at the lab to find only our office clerk. When I asked where everyone else had got to he said the military had rounded up people the other side of town. So I told him to jump in the Land-Rover and we would investigate. The military had thousands of people assembled on a football field and seemingly just one clerk slowly checking each person's details. So I accosted a soldier and asked who was in charge and eventually was directed to an officer. I informed him that I had come to collect the Unit's employees, for whom I could vouch for, and I would be obliged if he helped me to locate them and release them into my custody. When he objected I said I would return to the Unit and phone Yaounde to inform them that he personally was impeding vital medical research (our clerk had copied his details displayed on his uniform!). He relented and released our men. We later learned that by dusk

159

they had not checked all the men so had locked the rest in a church for the night but had sent the women and children back to their homes. No arrests of suspects were reported. Furthermore, having turned everyone out of the market some soldiers had then helped themselves from whatever had taken their fancy of the goods left abandoned on the stalls! So we concluded that the main security risk had been from the soldiers!

Our lab received a number of visiting scientists, usually backed by W.H.O., but sometimes by foundations backing research on primates or other vertebrates. Most were a pleasure to meet, but a few were all talk and no substance:

SPOOF (GK)

When Rob invaded lab for month,
With funds to study little known
Elusive creature found in crowns
Of largest trees in forest clad
And rain drenched peaks that climb above
The jungle far beneath, he took to beer,
Not bought by self, and talked at length
About himself as gift to field
He'd make his own. But when we led
Him, preened in freshly purchased boots,
Designer clothes and flaunting hat,
To recce feet of slopes and cut
Some trails for future work, it soon
Became as clear as day the bloke
Was petrified by snakes, afraid
Of sudden squawks and spiders near
At hand on thorny trunks of trees
Festooned with creepers that conceal
A lurking threat in mind at least.
His nerves revived at base when beer
Began to flow, along with boasts
Of past achievements none could check.
He then began to ask about
The local hunters, loggers, such
Who might recount their knowledge gained
Of beast he'd come to claim as own.
A plan was hatched. A planter, Bill,
Who lived for drink, was offered meal
And freely flowing beer and shorts
For telling fairy tales, as tall
As fancy free embraced without

160

A flicker smile, of creature's way
Of life. Our trusting clot imbibed
The lot, including wildly weird
Invented courtship dance performed
At night when moon is full. His notes
Record each purple phrase that Bill
Expounds as drink released a mix
Of myths he'd heard as child, of facts
He'd read in magazines
And nonsense gleaned from novels swift
Forgot as soon as read. The strain
Of keeping laughter well in check
Was hard indeed. Our thirsty friend
Had scarcely climbed his peaks for more
Than dozen times before his month
Was up. He claimed the heat and rains
Curtailed his plan of work. He drank
And talked instead. A year elapsed
Before a copy, nicely bound,
Of thesis came with note of thanks.
Within were Bill's delightful tales,
Disguised in ghastly jargon prose,
Arranged in neatly packaged chunks.
No wonder later came report
That Rob was dropped from funder's list
When paper by another gave
Account of creature's ways that lacked
The wild excess that Bill's conveyed.
It's shame! We'd oft repeat his tales,
Embellished here and there each time,
Until we half believed in beast
That lived within the myths he'd spun.
But was his spoof a joke too far?

A local visitor was a student from the Teacher Training College in Kumba. They had been set the task of making a collection of two dozen different sorts of insect to be divided into beneficial and non-beneficial insects. The student decided that with an entomologist being in our Unit to bring his collection to me. He was somewhat surprised when I sorted his collection into three groups, the third being both beneficial and non-beneficial! For example one of his specimens that I classified as both was a sweat bee. These could be extremely annoying by landing on one to imbibe one's sweat, commonly preferring one's head. He said that surely it was non-beneficial. So I told him to come and look at some coffee shrubs growing nearby and in full flower. Now, I said "what are the dominant insects visiting and pollinating the flowers?" He was astonished to report that it was sweat bees! His tutor quibbled about his three categories instead of two! I think the student should have been commended for having used his initiative to visit the only professional entomologist in Kumba. I later learned that my visitor became the headmaster of a rural primary school.

Many locals found it odd that I was interested in insects in general. Like the student teacher's instructor, insects were either 'good' (like honey bees or some beetle larvae and flying termites which they ate) or 'bad' (like mosquitoes or caterpillars that ate their crops). However, sooner or later even the most worldly might be spotted pausing to watch ants doing something striking. In our house the dining table had its legs in tins of kerosene in order to prevent ants swarming all over the table top. However, one of the smallest ant species outwitted us. They climbed the wall, walked across the ceiling until over the table and then dropped onto it. When they had fed on anything they discovered they then went to the edge of the table and dropped to the floor. I presume one ant had accidentally dropped onto the table and found good feeding and had then dropped off the edge. As foraging ants tend to leave a scent trail of minute droplets other ants from its colony had presumably then followed the trail, successfully foraged and reinforced the scent trail.

1 April 1968: Rachel born

Two Very Special Blessings by Audrey

I was sitting on the grass patch in the hospital compound in Kumba, West Cameroon, with a couple of hundred African mothers to be at the local ante-natal clinic. I had just arrived in the country, and was seven months pregnant with our third child. Having recently arrived, I couldn't stop saying "What a glorious day" to all and sundry! They, of course, must have thought me quite batty, but were very polite, and longsuffering with such a strange announcement! The mid-morning sun was high in the sky, and the conversation and laughter of the African women was so relaxed after the sometimes awkward silences or rather forced greetings of an English surgery's waiting room. The clinic was held in the grounds of the hospital. The organisation of the clinic seemed to be that the mothers gradually moved towards the top of the mound to a small palm-roofed space where two nursing sisters sat at the head of a table. Four women moved along on benches on either side of the table, and after questioning by the Sisters were either able to go home or were required to wait for further examination.

After a time, of course, it became obvious to me that my sentiments about the 'lovely day' had been a bit premature! As the day grew hotter and hotter, so I gradually wilted. Fortunately for me, the women spotted my discomfort and generously, amidst much laughter, allowed me to skip the queue, so that I arrived quite quickly at the 'top table'. (I think for many of them the day at the clinic was a welcome rest from chores!).

Once under the 'tent', however, my apprehension reached a point of alarm, as I listened to the questions the Sisters asked the pregnant women.

The first question was "Na wa tribe you?" (Which tribe are you?)

Followed by "Na wa name" (Now, what name?)

The next questions, however, were the ones that really unnerved me!

"Na, when for the piccin come?" (When is the baby due?).

"For de second moon, Sistah", or, "For the rain commencement, Sistah" came replies from women well versed in the intimacies of nature. Good heavens! What was the state of the moon likely to be in early April? Could I imagine rain in such a place? How little of anything really important had I learned in my life!

The questions continued:

"Na, how many piccin you?"

"I hab tree piccin Sistah".

Again "Na, how many piccin you?"

"I hab tree piccin Sistah".

"Na, you no hab tree piccin. You tell me true. How many piccin die?"

'No piccin die, Sistah".

Again "Na, how many piccin die, Dey bahn (born) good, dey die for belly?" Sister persisted with relentless determination. Eventually the mother would admit that she had had six or seven children, but four had died (not an unusual situation at that time when only half the children reached school age, but of this I was ignorant at the time). In the calm light of reason afterwards, of course, I realised that Sister needed to know whether the birth was likely to be difficult, or whether the cause of death in the case of some of the children had been due to one of many fevers, but I thought with little clarity during these interrogations.

Gradually my line of answers formed in my mind. The time of birth, early April, was easy to calculate in weeks. Perhaps I could fend off the number of children? I was thirty-nine. At my age I must have had at least six or seven children so my reply was obviously to be "six; t're die fever, – England bery bad place!"

I reached the top position next to Sister on my side of the bench and the questioning began again "Na wa tribe you?"

"English"

"Na, wa name?"

"Audrey Disney"

"Oh, Mrs. Disney", answered Sister in a perfect Oxford accent. "My sister asked me to look out for you!" My look of amazement made everyone burst into prolonged laughter. I didn't yet really know any Africans; how could I possibly know her sister? She (Sister Morra) then explained that I had apparently given her sister's child some boiled water during a long delay at Paris airport! Small incident for such ample divine intervention! After that, I was able to allay all my fears. Both Sister Morra and Sister Ndiba were brilliant and hugely experienced nurses and midwives, trained at the Hammersmith Hospital and would have excelled anywhere in the world.

After a couple of months, I appeared at the hospital to give birth to Rachel. Henry, had been unable to take me because he had gone into a cerebral malaria coma two days before (see below) and was still very weak. His boss, Brian, kindly drove me to the hospital.

I was very grandly put in solitary isolation in the operating theatre on the very narrow operating bed. After about half-an-hour, the Greek doctor came through, took my pulse, and with a cheerful "Oh, you're quite strong" passed on his more urgent and extremely busy way. Sister Morra popped in and out to keep an eye on my progress, but was very busy with other mums in labour in the next room. I would hear "Sistah, Sistah, de head done come" and off she would rush. After another half-hour, Sister decided that I should have an injection, and although I demurred, knowing that the birth was imminent, she perhaps thought, that being white, I would expect it. She duly gave me the injection announcing that I should now have a nice sleep for a couple of hours! Fifteen minutes later Rachel made her appearance against my enormous struggle not to fall asleep fearing that she might fall off the narrow bed. Soon, however, Sister Morra reappeared, and placed Rachel safely in her pram. A couple of hours later, the doctor came through again, took my pulse, not even noticing that the bulge was gone! "Actually", I said "the baby's born". "Oh congratulations, well done", said he, and once again sped on his way to treat the ills of patients drawn from a region of an area the size of an English county.

I was moved to a little room with three beds. The occupant of one of them was a woman suffering from prolonged and heavy nose-bleeds, but I never found out what troubled the other. It was about 11 o'clock in the morning.

During the afternoon, streams of people came through to look at the first white baby to be born in that hospital. I struggled to keep awake against the morning's injection, fearing lest someone might remove the little mosquito net from the pram. There were large plump African women in exotic prints and glorious head dresses intrigued at the size of Rachel (9lbs 15ozs – usually their babies seemed to be much smaller, around 5lbs average, but all walking much sooner than white babies). There were young men in smart Western suits giving the Western "Congrats", but the two visitors who intrigued me most were two small, thin, elderly women who stood in the corner of the room, too humble to come forward. They were dressed in what looked like old sacking. One carried a cooking pot, and the other had a hole where a nose should be and just stubs left for fingers. When everyone else had gone, they still stayed, so I asked them if they would like to see the baby. Gently, and very competently, the able-bodied one lifted Rachel from her pram, handed her to the lady lacking a nose, who held her and kissed her and said simply in a very strange high-squeaky voice "Welcome to this world". Smiling, she gently handed Rachel back to her friend, who put Rachel back in the pram, covered her, and they were gone. A Very Special Blessing, for I later learned that she had suffered from leprosy. Such an extraordinary blessing from the very, very poor.

The day wore on. I slept for a couple of hours. The woman in the next bed was quite chatty, but kept on insisting that I change the baby. Since the hospital was without running water, and Sister had said not to get out of bed, I didn't.

At about seven o'clock in the evening, a young French Canadian doctor came on the evening rounds. First of all, he told me in broken English that I should have made sure that Henry had taken his malaria prophylactic (which in any case he was most meticulous about doing) and then, because he seemed to be a bit tongue-tied, I asked, just for conversation, and because it was April 1st, if they celebrated April Fool's Day in Canada. He looked puzzled, so I proceeded to relate various childish pranks to illustrate the English custom. Immediately I could see medical wheels turning behind his eyes! Obviously this woman was quite delirious, and so for the second time that day I received an undeserved injection!

The day ended in laughter, though. The morning injection had worn off. Because there were no cooking facilities within the hospital (relations of patients either brought food or stayed with them and cooked it outside) my two neighbours, and Killian who was looking after our other two children, all brought me supper! It wasn't really a problem to dispose of two of them.

Next morning, a second Very Special Blessing took place. A humble domestic/ward-maid, (in a rather dreary brown dress) entirely of her own initiative and far beyond any call of duty, gathered some wood, made a fire, and brought me a bowl of warm water for a wash. She also scrubbed the lavatory floor (just a hole in the ground), and I was able to spend a penny at last, and change Rachel's nappy. The woman's humanity was so precious and strong and the memory is treasured as a great gift.

Later in the day, Henry was fit enough to drive down, bringing Trudy and Adrian with him, Trudy in just a pair of orange knickers, but no dress. My room-mate, of course, told him what a dreadful mother I was, not having changed the infant for so long, and how he should have dressed the girl. Confident Tru, aged three years and two months, spoke up, "It's alright, Mummy's got me and Adrian already, and she knows what to do!" All argument ceased! Finally, we were all safely in the Land-Rover, the engine starting up, when we heard voices calling "Madam, Madam". A nurse, surrounded by laughing Africans was bringing us the placenta on a banana leaf, to place under a rose bush! What a dreadful waste here in the West not to do something so eco-friendly here. It was quite a drippy ride home though!

This was all a long time ago, but often in our modern grabbing society with its emphasis on rights and compensation, I look back on those three ladies who had absolutely nothing material in life. Two of them welcomed a little foreign baby into this world with such simplicity and beauty; the other prepared a jug of warm water. They loom like shining beacons in an often hard and self-seeking world.

Audrey

A small postscript to this joyous birth of Rachel to complete our family is an incident the day after I had gone into the coma. Sometime before these events we had acquired as a pet a tree hyrax (Dendrohyrax dorsalis) that we had been brought by a local person who had been hunting in the forest. It was very entertaining and Trudy and Adrian were very fond of this unusual creature. However, it developed a respiratory infection and sadly died the day after my collapse. Audrey solemnly dug a little grave for it and with the help of the children buried it. They then gently placed flowers over the little mound of earth. Trudy, as practical as ever, then asked Audrey "If Daddy dies will we do the same for him?"!

Apart from the hyrax we also kept chickens in a pen at the back of the house. The children enjoyed looking to see if there were eggs in the box tipped on its side that the hens retreated into to lay their eggs. We then acquired a baby goat that was the under-sized, runt of a litter. Its owner had been going to dispose of it as he thought it was the result of a bad juju. So we took it on instead and put it in the hen pen. It began to think itself as a chicken and every now and then it would sit in the box intended for egg laying, until a hen gave it a good scolding when she wished to enter the box for its legitimate purpose.

I was able to return to work with my studies of blackflies and river blindness. Apart from my set piece investigations (sketched above) I continued to make unexpected natural history observations. For example, the larvae of the miniature caddis flies of the family Hydroptilidae were, according to the textbooks, feeders on algal filaments by piercing the cells and sucking out the contents. However, I discovered that species in Cameroon were piercing and sucking out the contents of the eggs and pupae on the blackfly vectors of river blindness (Disney, R. H. L., 1973. Larval Hydroptilidae (Trichoptera) that prey upon Simuliidae (Diptera) in Cameroon. Entomologist's Monthly Magazine 108: 84-85 (1972). Likewise, I discovered that a species group of Drosophila 'fruit flies' had larvae that were aquatic predators of the eggs and youngest blackfly larvae (Tsacas, L. & Disney, R. H. L., 1974. Two new African species of Drosophila (Diptera, Drosophilidae) whose larvae feed on Simulium larvae (Dipt., Simuliidae). Zeitschrift für Tropenmedizin und Parasitologie 25: 360-377. Disney, R. H. L., 1975. Drosophila gibbinsi larvae also eat Simulium. Transactions of the Royal Society of Tropical Medicine and Hygiene 69: 365-366). The case of D. gibbinsi was amusing. Subsequent to the description of the species their larvae and pupae had been reported from under water but this observation had been explained away by surmising that the river must have risen due to heavy rainfall. When I borrowed some of the preserved larvae from the Natural History Museum in London and dissected them I found their guts full of early stage larvae of blackflies and non-biting midges (Chironomidae). This discovery of predatory aquatic larvae in the genus Drosophila gave rise to considerable surprise in the Drosophila 'industry'. Further examples of predatory aquatic Drosophila larvae were subsequently reported from East Africa. Incidentally, years later Dr Smart (who had taught me at Cambridge) pointed out that when Aubertin described D. gibbinsi in 1937 he had not realized Gibbins was a woman and he had given her a male ending when naming the fly after her, instead of with the appropriate female ending – gibbinsae! Years later I nearly made the same mistake when I named some scuttle flies after my Estonian and Benin co-authors (Disney, R. H. L., Kurina, O., Tedersoo, L & Cakpo, Y., 2013. Scuttle flies (Diptera: Phoridae) reared from fungi in Benin. African Invertebrates 54: 357-371), Dr Kurina had the first name Olavi, which I had erroneously assumed was a woman's name!

One day Audrey decided to hold a Scottish dancing party at our house. This amazed our African employees, with one commenting "I didn't know the British did tribal dancing"! They were even more amazed when we were invited to a fancy dress party at a large commercial cocoa estate and Audrey and I went dressed as each other! Another case of gender confusion!

In 1968 I unexpectedly received a letter and documents twice. First from Professor Biagi and a day or two later from Professor Garnham at the London School of Hygiene and Tropical Medicine. These related to my work in British Honduras. They informed me that Biagi had been sacked on the grounds that he was a plagiarist of my work and he had been obliged to take refuge in Geneva with the World Health Organisation. I only later learned that it was some of the medical establishment in Mexico City who had put the charge to the university's authorities. I carefully read the papers and noted that a key document was the following report of an exhibit made on my behalf by Dr David Lewis: – Disney, R. H. L., 1967. A rat-baited trap for sandflies (report of laboratory exhibit). Transactions of the Royal Society of Tropical Medicine and Hygiene 61: 456-457. In this I reported that by means of my fly-trap data I had demonstrated that the sandfly Lutzomyia flaviscutellata was a significant vector of Leishmania mexicana in British Honduras and cited my paper 'Observations on a Zoonosis: Leishmaniasis in British Honduras. In press.' In this report of the exhibit a key sentence is as follows: 'Biagi et al. (1965) were also stimulated by the fly-trap data amassed in British Honduras and were able to demonstrate independently, a month or two later, that L. flaviscutellata is an important vector in Quintana Roo, Mexico.' I concluded that the charge was incorrect, as Biagi had not known I had demonstrated L. flaviscutellata was the vector until he had returned from his expedition to Quintana Roo in December 1965. I therefore wrote a letter for the correspondence section of the Transactions of the Royal Society of Tropical Medicine and Hygiene, but I sent it to Professor Garnham to submit if he approved of my summary of the facts. He did approve and submitted it forthwith: – Disney, R. H. L., 1968. The discovery of the vector of Leishmania mexicana. Transactions of the Royal Society of Tropical Medicine and Hygiene 62: 457 (letter).

The response was extraordinary. In such situations dates are critical. One leading researcher in the field concluded the paper by Biagi and his colleagues was fiction as their photographs of the lesions in the hamsters were several weeks old but the hamsters had only been inoculated in December 1965 and yet were reported in a paper dated 1965! However, it turned out that Biagi had managed to get their paper slipped into the issue of the journal INTENDED for publication in December 1965 but in reality was only actually published well into 1966. Furthermore my paper cited as 'in press' had been intended for publication in 1967 but was delayed and became the first paper in the journal's issue for 1968 instead: Disney, R. H. L., 1968. Observations on a zoonosis: Leishmaniasis in British Honduras. Journal of Applied Ecology 5: 1-59. A copy of this 1968 paper had been sent to Biagi. However, in his letter from Geneva he took issue with this paper saying I hadn't demonstrated the parasites from the flies were those of Leishmania mexicana! Somewhat baffled I replied that I realized English was not his first language, but if he referred to certain figures, and tables detailing inoculations of hamsters, etc., in my paper, he would see that his claim was unfounded. I had successfully isolated three strains from the vector sandfly species and inoculated hamsters to demonstrate they were the correct parasite species. I had no response. When I returned to England I went to see Professor Garnham and showed him Biagi's letter and a carbon copy of my response. Garnham assured me that I had acted entirely properly. He subsequently, on a visit to Geneva, accosted Biagi and told him that by not acknowledging that it had been my data that had caused him to set up his expedition to Quintana Roo he had laid himself open to the charges made against him. Furthermore by trying to challenge my own achievements he was only adding fuel to the fire. Biagi never got back into academia but ended his career in private medical practice. I felt sorry for him. It seemed that pride prevented him acknowledging that a young man, then without a reputation, had made the breakthrough by focusing on the wild animal hosts instead of the incidental human host. If he had presented his Quintana Roo results as confirmation and reinforcement of my contribution he would never have been sacked.

To all of us in the know with regard to the world of research on the various forms of Leishmaniasis this whole affair was widely commented on in 1968 and 1969. It was put into perspective for me two decades later when among books I was asked to review for Natural History Book Reviews was THE CAMBRIDGE ENCYCLOPEDIA (1990, Edited by David Crystal, Cambridge University Press). To exhaustively review such wide ranging works requires a polymath. My approach was to review entries for topics for which I possessed firsthand knowledge. It was thus a humbling, but amusing, experience to learn that Leishmaniasis is restricted to 'the Mediterranean shores, Africa and S. Asia'! All the studies in Central and South America had evidently not registered with the writer of that entry!

When returning on leave and we were flying across the Sahara we hit a highly turbulent patch of thermals that caused the plane alternately to suddenly drop and then suddenly rise again. Most of the passengers anxiously became silent as they felt decidedly queasy and grabbed their vomit bags in case needed. Adrian was quite unconcerned as he gazed at the waves of desert dunes below. He then turned around and announced in a high squeaky voice "there's all this sand but not a single camel!" This instantly relieved the tension as a wave of laughter engulfed the passengers!

One of the increasingly troublesome concerns of our time in Cameroon was the outbreak of the civil war in Biafra, just across the border in Nigeria. As the conflict progressed reports of growing numbers of orphaned, undernourished children increased. The concern grew in Kumba to do something to help. A plan was made to receive these desperate children into the local R.C. Teacher Training College after sending its students on vacation a week early. The refugees would then be assessed and then allocated to families who volunteered to adopt a child. We put our names on the list of potential adopters. At the last minute the whole scheme was cancelled. It turned out that de Gaulle, who had been openly backing the cause of the Biafrans, had persuaded the President of Cameroon (a Muslim from the N. E. of Cameroon) to block the scheme in order to prevent the Biafran problem spilling over into West Cameroon. It turned out that de Gaulle was not really interested in the fate of the Biafrans. His concern was for favourable access to the rich oil reserves in Biafra.

Two of our assistants were from Biafra, with my chief assistant, Mr Oguama, being from the large Ibo tribe. In addition he was an active member of the local Jehovah's Witness meeting. This had the advantage that he was absolutely honest. The disadvantage was he clammed up whenever I mentioned evolution or the antiquity of some of the rocks!

Then another problem arose for Mr Oguama. There was an 'election' for the President of Cameroon. It was announced beforehand that a record would be made of those who did not vote. In the event the election was a farce as there was no other candidate! At the polling station the voter was handed a piece of paper with the President's name and party symbol and envelope and told to put the 'ballot' paper in the envelope and then into the box. The alternative choice was to put it in the waste paper bin next to a gendarme holding a weapon with its bayonet attached! The prediction was a 100% vote for the President! In the event it was just over 90% and the largest group of non-voters were found to have been the Jehovah's Witnesses, as it was against their principles to take part in a secular election. A few days later it was just after six a.m. that I heard on the radio that henceforth public meetings by the Jehovah's Witnesses were banned and their publications such as the Watchtower were also banned. So I leapt into the Land-Rover and drove to Mr Oguama's house. He had also heard the announcement and was in a state of panic. I told him to calm down and to gather up his 'subversive' literature and pile into the back of the Land-Rover. We then put all this into boxes in a store at the back of our house with top dressing of papers on helminthiasis. Two days later Mr Oguama rushed into the lab late saying he had been raided at dawn, his house searched and told he was to be interrogated for two days, but they had released him briefly in order to come to tell me the situation. He was very agitated as he feared deportation back to Nigeria and loss of his pension. He had worked for the Unit from before Cameroon independence, when the Unit was transferred to the Cameroon

Government from the former West African Council for Medical Research. I told him to calm down. I said that he should not attempt to explain the reason the Jehovah's Witnesses decline to vote in secular elections. I told him to just keep repeating that he admired the President but, as a Nigerian national, he was not entitled to vote in a Cameroon election. It worked and he was released. We later moved all his Jehovah's Witnesses literature from our house to a derelict hut at the back of the village of Bolo.

We encountered another problem relating to our Nigerian nationals. The Nigerian Government suddenly announced that all current Nigerian passports were declared to be invalid and were being replaced by a new issue version. However, the supply of new version passports at the Nigerian Consulate in Buea (in the south of West Cameroon) was inadequate for two reasons. The Nigerian Consul was a northern Nigerian unsympathetic to southern tribes such as the Ibo. In addition he was corrupt. We later learned he had given a large stock of the new passports to a Cameroonian friend in exchange for a substantial sum of money and the Cameroonian was then offering these for sale at inflated prices. Secondly the Cameroonian Government (the President being from the North of Cameroon) announced that there would be checks that Nigerian nationals had one of the new passports and, if by a certain date, they had not they would be sent back to Nigeria. So when I went to Buea I dropped off an assistant at the consulate. After completing my business I returned to pick up the assistant. Twice he had failed to procure a new passport. On my third trip when I returned to collect the assistant there was the same result. So I went in and told the receptionist that I wished to speak to the Consul. She replied that I needed to fill in a form in order to book an appointment. I filled in the form and in the box requiring one to state when would be suitable dates for the applicant I entered 'now'. The receptionist said that was not allowed. I replied that never-the-less I wished to see the Consul 'now' and was not leaving until my request was fulfilled. After an altercation she ascended the stairs to the office of the Consul. I could hear muffled exchanges before the receptionist reappeared and said the Consul had agreed to make an exception, despite I had not booked an appointment beforehand. He kept me standing in front of his desk, like a small boy in front of the headmaster, and delivered a tirade culminating with him saying he was inclined to call the police and have me charged! So I sat down with a bump in the chair behind me and told him I was intrigued and looked forward to knowing under what Cameroonian law the police would bring a charge for asking him for passports for Nigerians for whom I had a responsibility. He was so taken aback by my reaction to his threat that he was momentarily speechless. He then said that his stock of the new passports was depleted. I explained that the police were calling on Nigerians and if their documents were not in order they were being deported. For that reason I had applied to him, because I had understood that he was the person appointed to look after the interests of Nigerians living in West Cameroon. After a certain amount of discussion he produced a document for each employee, on headed notepaper that was duly rubber stamped and signed with a flamboyant signature, stating that a new passport had been applied for and this was to cover the named person in the interim. A week later the local police called at the homes of two of our Nigerians to check their passports and were saved by these documents.

However, a matter of concern to ourselves was the prevalence of malaria in Cameroon. I was strictly disciplined in taking two prophylactics every day. However, after I had spent a strenuous day in the rain forest with my assistants surveying a series of streams for the presence of the main blackfly vector of river blindness. I relaxed in a bath afterwards but when I had stood up and stepped out I had collapsed in a coma on the floor. When Audrey had got no response and couldn't open the door she had gone round to the back of the house and peered through the window to see me motionless on the floor and blocking the door. She thrust Adrian into the arms of the astonished night watchman (for the Unit's garage repair shop and the diesel generator for our house) and rushed across to Dr Duke, who lived across the way. He managed to extract me from the bathroom and get me to the hospital. We strongly suspected that this frantic rushing about for help precipitated the birth pangs that preceded the birth of Rachel (see Audrey's account above).

Modern drugs failed to revive me. Fortunately injected liquid Quinine from our lab (the hospital only having tablets) brought me back to life.

'ALL CREATURES GREAT AND SMALL' (MC)

Emerging from a coma's night,
Arising from malaria's blight,
I lay with line of facile hymn -
'All creatures great and small' – as grim
Repeating joke afflicting mind.
It seems the Church remains purblind
To facts revealed by science freed
From the romantic poet's creed
No peasant ever shared. Besides,
While I'll concede no king presides
Whose raiment is as fine as blooms
Of humble weeds, that finest looms
Can not produce designs to match
The parasites that chose to hatch
From haemocytes that keep alive;
However hard or long you strive
You'll not convince me God prefers
These creatures small – and thus confers
On them a living glory high
While leaving single me to die.

Instead I thank the quinine's gift
Allowing me another shift.
I'll sing my thanks to God above,
A God whose hallmark is his love
For us to whom his Spirit came
To call us children in Christ's name.

My assistants had been wondering if I had been got at by a bad juju until I recovered! Their belief in juju affliction or protection was entirely compatible with our scientific explanations of causation. Thus our Unit was treating a couple of crater lakes where the snails harboured the larval stages of schistosomes (bilharzia) parasites before the stages infective to man were shed into the water. We supplied wellington boots and rubber gloves but some of our assistants ignored them and waded into the infected waters. When we asked them whether they disbelieved the science they replied, in effect, that the science only explained the mechanism of transmission. Whether one got infected or not depended on whether one was protected by a good juju or was got at by a bad juju! We had to treat several assistants for the disease. This is perhaps not unlike an Old Testament view that some agent must be to blame for natural disasters and afflictions; and that among such some were the result of the wrath of God. A view that lingers in the minds of even intelligent, well informed people as recalled in the following poem:

A RESPONSE TO SIR JOHN BETJEMAN

Our dear Sir John your "honest doubt" makes clear
Your patron prophet's Job. His tiresome quest
For answers true remains the burden borne
By all who now embrace the sceptic West.

The proper question we must ask, when "good
Men die in dreadful pain", is "Where's Our Lord?"
The cross proclaimed He shares our anguished wounds –
While atavists still claim He guides the sword.

FREE TO CHOOSE (GK)

When life has dealt a blow by chance
All talk of God seems hollow joke,
Perhaps because as kids they told
Us He is in control. His love
Requires another scene. As we
Are free to choose His way or go
Alone, then He must needs restrain

His urge to shield us from the fall
Of bomb or warn of floods to come.
We are not toys in hands of Lord
Who pulls the strings to make us dance
To tune of His desire. The choice
Is always ours. When random hurts
Afflict He shares our tears, His grace
Sustains resolve to pick ourselves
From floor of rage and pity used
To quench our will to carry on.
Remember Christ in pain on cross.
From that vile deed arose our hope
Of life beyond our bleak despairs.
So come, rejoice, our choice remains -
We'll howl along with gales of fate
Or steer by light of Gospel's glow.

When I got cerebral malaria again, but without going into a coma this time, it came as a surprise as I had been taking two prophylactics in double dose since the previous attack. Again it was quinine rather than the more modern drugs that provided an effective cure. However, it initiated a lengthy correspondence among the medics. Was I the first case of Chloroquine resistance for West Africa? Eventually a professor in London concluded that it was not so, but that I had an over efficient liver that was rapidly breaking down the prophylactics and I was then excreting them in my urine. Estimates as to the dosage I would need to take to overcome this raised questions as to the likely side effects. Meanwhile, Audrey wrote to the Medical Research Council expressing her concern. A long handwritten reply from a senior MRC person reduced to its essence said that if I died MRC would pay for the transport of my coffin back to England! This was not what Audrey wanted to read! Indeed we both felt the response, coupled with increasing awareness of the risk to the children from malaria, enteritis and other diseases that afflicted so many of the local children. Added to this was my reluctance to send the children to boarding school if we signed up for a third tour. So we decided to return to the UK at the end of the tour. My British colleagues and MRC found this reluctance with regard to the children going to boarding school in England puzzling, especially as MRC offered financial assistance for school fees. My own experience did not endorse their perceptions! While private boarding schools ('Public Schools') have many positive features, their usual requirement to first attend a Prep School meant separation from parents for too much of the year at too early an age. At least that was a view that had not only been shaped by my own experience (albeit more extreme because of the preceding War time separation from my parents – see chapter 1), but by observing the emotional effect on many children, despite an outward air of greater independence. By contrast, it seems that it is as teenagers that children can benefit from spells of independence away from home for part of the year. Indeed this was to prove to be the case for Trudia and Adrian (see chapter 9).

As the Biafran war continued my chief assistant, Mr Oguama, was increasingly concerned about the fate of his relatives in Nigeria. Knowing I was leaving at the end of my tour, and that I was working hard to complete a number of projects, he asked if he could save up his leave and take a large block when I left so he could spend time in Nigeria finding out about the situation there. I was happy to endorse this proposal as it would benefit us both. For the result of his visit after we had left Cameroon see the next chapter.

By now my faith was firm, my enjoyment of nature undiminished but freed from sentimental reverence incompatible with both the Neo-Darwinian paradigm and the other great biological theory of the 19th Century, the microbial theory of infectious disease (Pasteur, Koch, Lister et. al.) and its 1877 supplement, the theory of the necessity for the development and transmission of many parasites of an intermediate invertebrate vector (Manson, Theobald Smith, Ross, et al.).

AWE (CW)
(= reverential fear or wonder)

In youth delight in nature's range
Of scenes and creatures, varied way
Beyond what human minds conceive,
Was such I felt I must convey
In stumbling verse a sense of thanks.
But as I read how poets down
The years have said it better, when
I learned, concealed beneath the gown
Of many hues, that nature's ways
Are endless strife and pain, it's then
I laid my pen aside. But now I once
Again attempt, what better men
Than I have tried, to paint in words
My felt response to beauty seen
At every turn. Despite the blood
And ceaseless wars that surely mean
The darker side is not ignored,
I must confess to pleasure pure
And unalloyed at beauties seen
And savoured. Now you can be sure
No taint of Paley, nor a hint
Of Mrs Alexander's hymn,
With sentiment will mar or stain
The sense of awe I feel. The grim
And bloody truths ensure I view
The scene as expert strokes the blade
Of finely crafted sword without
Denying role for which it's made.

EVOLUTION (RE)

The tooth and claw, the probe and sting,
The snare, the web, the cunning trap,
The serpent's strike, the swoop of hawk
Embroider life with diverse forms.
The beauty seen in perfect pounce
Redeems the fearsome flow of blood.
It seems the birth of love in man
Has sprung from brain designed to kill.
But now his need for flesh is tamed
He turns to hunting self instead -

Or else denies his brother's right
To run his race another way.
He slowly nails him to a cross,
Or else he slams the door on maid
Who seeks a place to cradle Christ,
Whose word of peace dethrones our past,
Whose grasp of truth will pluck us clean.

Apart from my problem with Malaria, the ever-present risks in the tropical forest zone were a cause for concern with regard to the children. Severe enteritis and strange viruses were prevalent. In addition there were dangers from some of the local wildlife. Of snakes in the garden a few were poisonous, but rarely posed a danger as they were usually more concerned with avoiding people or else the young lad who kept the grass short around the house and Unit's vehicle workshop dispatched a dangerous snake with a blow from a machete. One day he killed a snake hunting in the rafters of the house. It proved to be not a poisonous species. It had a bulge from a recent meal, so Audrey opened it up with the children to expose a rat. So the snake was actually beneficial! By contrast one day I arrived home for lunch when Audrey announced that she and the children had caught a glow-worm. Alarmed, I replied that they were not known from around here! When I saw the captured creature I warned them to keep clear of it and I will show them something. I fetched the book on West African snakes. The species they had caught was poisonous and the author commented that it was the only snake he had not discovered how to pick up safely, as it always managed to get you with at least one fang. He added that was how he had been bitten on the tip of one finger, which consequently went necrotic so that he had to have the tip of the finger amputated! Thank goodness nobody had been bitten by this 'glow-worm'. We had had another nasty scare a short time before. We had constructed a small paddling pool in the garden for the children, which they and their African friends enjoyed splashing about in. One day they announced that one of their friends was lying face down on the bottom and wouldn't move! Luckily Audrey managed to rescue the child and restore his breathing.

While our children enjoyed playing with their African friends a minor hazard was that ours used to occasionally catch ringworm fungus from them. Accordingly an essential inclusion in our first aid cupboard was potassium permanganate crystals. Dissolved in water and the solution painted on the infected part worked wonders (see chapter 5 for a striking example of its effectiveness). The purple patches on their skin looked rather conspicuous on their pale skins compared with on their African playmates. Years later in Cambridge, potassium permanganate was suddenly put on the list of restricted chemicals. When I asked our excellent Safety Officer the reason for this he said he had been told it was because it could be used for making homemade explosives! I asked him whether, on the same basis, he thought they would be adding sugar and flour to the list next! He laughingly agreed that the authorities seemed to be getting ever more paranoid.

Audrey had been teaching the children, with the help of a correspondence course and her own creative imagination. However, it was clear that Trudy at least was ready for school. It was time to return to England. So I applied for, and in absentia but with strong backing from Jim our former boss at Flatford Mill (see chapter 4), was appointed as the Warden of the Malham Tarn Field Centre and Nature Reserve in Yorkshire.

I will forever remain amazed at the way Audrey calmly accepted the risks and unexpected challenges experienced in the years following our marriage before we returned to England with the blessing of our three children. Her support throughout allowed me to cope. So many of the bachelor British we encountered increasingly turned to alcohol as their means of coping with daily risks, prevalent corruption, inefficiencies and the stupidity of officials more concerned with their status than with service.

One regret was having to leave Audrey's piano, as the freight costs were prohibitive. However, it was gratefully received by some Baptist missionary friends as a parting gift.

CHAPTER 8

YORKSHIRE

1971-1984: Warden and Director of Studies of Malham
Tarn Field Centre. (Field Studies Council)
and Manager of the Malham Tarn Estate Nature Reserve
(subsequently declared a National Nature Reserve)
(FSC and National Trust).

To move from the tropical forest zone of Cameroon to living above 300 metres (1300 feet) altitude in the Pennines early in the year was quite a shock to the system. Indeed our daughter Rachel felt it most as she had been born in Cameroon and only briefly been in England when on leave in Bath. She went all puffy looking, but it very gradually adjusted with time. We all had to accommodate to a very different climate and landscape.

One thing was missing. Audrey had no piano. So one day I announced that we were going to Bradford where there was one of the largest piano shops in the country. We then chose a superb modern piano, which Audrey loved but declared to be too expensive. It was indeed the most expensive present I ever bought her, but she played it with gusto and pleasure for the rest of her life.

The winters were more prolonged than in the southern lowlands. As the Centre was half a mile from the public road we had a small snowplough that attached to brackets on a Land-Rover. However, when its weight started to crack the chassis, a second-hand tractor was purchased and the brackets transferred to it instead. We would clear the private estate road and await the council's plough clearing the public road.

Our children went to the primary school in Malhamdale and later to secondary school in Skipton. Usually Audrey would drive them down to Malhamdale, and when at school in Skipton to the bus stop in Malhamdale. Sometimes we could not get down because of the snow, especially when it had drifted in high winds. We would phone the school to say we could not get down because of the snow to be asked 'what snow?' The headmaster would then look out the window and report that he could see a snowline at around the 1000 ft. contour.

On one occasion while I was attending a committee meeting in London a blizzard struck Malham Moor. I stayed overnight with my sister Halcyon at Kingston-upon-Thames before catching the train back to Yorkshire in the morning. When I arrived back in Malham village the previous day's blizzard had ceased. So I set off walking up onto the Moor by following the tops of the drystone walls beside the road blocked by snow. When I reached the top my route was then only marked by the telephone line. However, the wind got up and lifted flurries of the previous day's snow so that visibility dropped to a few yards only. Although nearer home than the village I was forced to retrace my steps to regain the line of the walls bounding the blocked road. I then struggled back down to the village and stayed the night with a farmer friend. Next day I got home safely. Survival on the Pennine hills depended on always knowing where one was, even if it meant going by a longer route. For another example, I was once on the top of Fountain's Fell when cloud suddenly spilled over its top and I was suddenly only able to see a few yards ahead. Accordingly, instead of following the ill-defined footpath I latched onto a drystone wall and followed it round three sides of the rectangle of the pasture it bounded as by this means I knew where I was all the time.

In severe cold spells the Tarn froze over and we would sometimes get cut off by the snow for days, the longest being for 10 days when the council's snowplough kept finding the part recently cleared was filling up with the next blizzard before they had finished the task. We bought small plastic skis for the children and they enjoyed whizzing down a slope, usually accompanied by some ducks and one of our cats enjoying a ride on the back of a ski. On one occasion, when no tourists or walkers of the Pennine Way were able to get up onto Malham Moor and beyond, we went across to the long gentle slope of the lower part of Pen-y-Ghent, which we had to ourselves alone. The children went down on little toboggans while Audrey and I made do with old plastic fertilizer sacks.

At times the Tarn froze over. In one prolonged cold spell the ice was thick enough to support the weight of the estateman's Land-Rover. When frozen over a problem was keeping the neighbours' sheep from getting onto the main reserve. One farmer would put his dog on a chain where the fence ended at the edge of the Tarn. The dog was supplied with an upturned barrel for a kennel and fed periodically. Another farmer, who regarded the nature reserve as a waste of good agricultural land, was uncooperative when asked to round them up and remove them. We got fed up with having to do the job for him and, having warned that we would not be bothering to do so one day, let them roam. The result was they headed for the only green they saw protruding above the deep snow. However these were the tops of yew trees, whose foliage is highly poisonous to sheep and other livestock. The farmer then grudgingly rounded up his flock, but not before several had died.

Late snowfalls were a real problem when they coincided with lambing. Our handyman Arnold (later to take over from Harry as estateman), had a beautifully trained brown and white spaniel called Bess. When ewes sheltered against a drystone wall when a blizzard struck at lambing time they would then get buried in the snow, but air reached them between the stones of the wall. Bess was the best dog for miles at locating these buried sheep and their lambs and so farmers would ring up requesting Arnold to come with Bess. Bess, however, would only get to work when the farmer's sheep dog was got out of the way! One year Bess located and saved the most expensive tup (as Yorkshire folk call a ram) on the moor.

One year a late blizzard caught the lambing yews below the peak of Fountains Fell and the farmer was running out of feed for abandoned lambs. A man struggled up from Malhamdale with two sacks of powdered sheep milk tied to two ends of a rope, which was draped over his shoulders. He arrived exhausted at our house and I took over. When I got onto the exposed road heading north it was alternately bare stretches and then huge wave like drifts of snow. After I had been blown over twice by the howling wind it was evident I wasn't going to make it. So I struggled back home. The next morning I got through. The farmer was greatly relieved as he was down to less than half a sack of dried sheep's milk. The next day the weather allowed a helicopter drop of more supplies.

When some ewes on a neighbour's farm dropped their lambs into a late snowfall and abandoned them we put the lambs into a hastily erected pen by the Field Centre. We had a primary school from the south of England on a course at the time. With their accompanying teacher's enthusiastic consent, we put the children onto bottle feeding the lambs. The teacher reported back later that it had been the best field course ever and the children kept telling all their friends and relations how great it had been. One's carefully prepared exercises were sometimes trumped by unexpected events!

Gradually we grew much attached to the varied landscape of Malham Moor and its even more variable weather. To our children it was the central landscape of their childhood.

CHRISTMAS EVE ON MALHAM MOOR, YORKSHIRE
(MC)

The Gordale Beck by Mastiles Bridge
Is where the Pennine lure is hid.
It's here the boulders choke the stream
That thundered forth from melting ice.
It's here the ancient shales still hold
In greying palms the waters cold,
Above the thirsty limestone gorge
That gurgles down the frequent rains.
The sheep-walked interlocking spurs,
The drystone wall of garnered blocks,
The dipper darting up the dell,
The Roman marching fort to tell
Of human strife of old, the cry
Of redshanks on the wing, the mew
Of lapwings overhead, all these
And many other sights and sounds
Will scour the cares of frantic times.
They let our spirits gather speed,
As flowing free in dancing rhymes
To joy alone we give our heed.
But also when our skies are black
And storms have filled our beck to brim,
And cascades leaping through the Scar
Are sweeping peace away with wild
Forbidding force. The angry snarl
Of water, swirling flecks of foam,
Will mock us till our gloom dissolves,
And self-regard is washed away,
As wonder floods our mind and soul
In face of such a naked will
That brooks no staying of its play.
Perhaps we need a cleansing stream
To clear the junk of mounded trash
That clogs our thoughts and chokes our hearts.
But life is doomed as racing brook
That cannot choose its own clear way;
We're called to ride the fleeting wave
That moves against the fretful flow
Upon the living surge emerged
From spinning wheels of chance. We find
The wind of love upon our backs.

We freely climb the ancient hill
On which the star of truth still shines
Beyond this laughing, teasing rill.
We seek, in mind, a peaceful Tarn.
The air is chill. The snow has dressed
The trees in breathless white, while puffs
Of flurried flakes now fly across
The silenced life of restless lake.
The mournful, skidding coot regain
The shrinking rim of ice-ringed pool,
Where concentrate a hundred birds
In frenzied search for last remains
Of hope. It's thus we cling to life.
It's thus we search for light within
The fading glow of falling night.
Oh soon, oh soon, we dare not doubt,
Our springtime shall arise again.
But now the day is dark and wild.
The wind is piling foam on rocks.
The pochard flocks are huddled close
Beneath the peat, as tireless rain
Descends in curtained sheets that taunt
The racing waves and scudding spray
From water whipped to furied rage.
Yet will impatience soon assuage.
The skies will clear with time. The air
Will hum with summer sounds, and flies
Will skim and dance above a glass
Of mirrored blue. The trout will rise
To rings of rippling light that spread
Beyond the shores of time and dread:
Beyond the lapping water's scorn,
The flotsam hopes of slipping years,
The seething swirl of spiral thought,
The boiling cauldron's spitting fears.
Beneath the fickle surface dance
We hear the living waters sing.
Beyond the charm of loveless lake's
Inverted view of worldly lies
The sinking sun, with angels' fire,
Descends with pentecostal flame.
We join the humble folk who seek
The hidden place where joy is born
We learn of camel trains that bring
Their precious gifts of lasting worth.

We marvel at the melting morn,
Released from Tarn's mirage of death.
We watch the breaking ice disperse.
We celebrate a secret birth.
We raise our carols high aloft.
We praise our Lord in rhyme and verse.

HIGHFOLDS, MALHAM TARN, YORKSHIRE (GK)

The climb through woods is steep.
The path is rough where stones
Protrude, and after rain
One's boots may slip and slide.
Emerging from the trees,
With limestone clints and grykes
Displayed behind the edge
Of scarp, I sit to stare
At landscape laid below
As distant map that holds
My gaze, as though I'm in
A trance. There's silent lake
And winding fen beside
An acid bog. There's sheep
On slopes they've mown to lawn
Of patterned carpet spread
Across the rising fell,
Whose darker top is capped
With wispy cloud like smoke.
In mind I travel back
To time when ice had gripped
This awesome scene and shaped
Its contours, scouring parts
And leaving drifts beyond.
I feel I'm like this land.
Upon genetic bones
My self was shaped by odd
Events, both good and bad,
That scarred and smoothed the rough
Design I had at birth.

As the children made friends at school Audrey and our friend Heather decided to start a Brownies plus Cub pack in the church hall of Kirkby Malham church. This became a great success and certainly helped us 'off-comers' to be more quickly accepted by the local Dales folk. The regional Brownie and Cub authorities were somewhat alarmed at some of the unusual activities Audrey and Heather included, but most of their concern seemed to derive from the formation of this joint Brownie-Cub pack. Audrey, however, had been a Brownie in Bath and was thoroughly versed in what she had enjoyed as a child (see Chapter 4).

I received a letter from my former chief assistant, Mr Oguama, after his return from Nigeria to find out how his relatives had fared in the Biafra conflict (see chapter 7). Sadly about half of his relatives had not survived. Of more immediate concern was his report that on crossing back to Cameroon he had been strip-searched and a Jehovah's Witnesses calendar had been found concealed under his clothing. He was summoned to appear in court on a certain date. Again Mr Oguama feared he would be deported back to Nigeria and with the loss of his pension due from the Cameroon Government. It so happened we had a cocoa estate's manager from Cameroon visiting us during his leave and he was a drinking companion of the police chief of the district where Mr Oguama was due to appear before the magistrate. He wrote a chatty letter to the police chief and added that Mr Oguama's case was arousing interest in the U.K. 'at the highest level'! When the case came to court there was a whispered conversation between the magistrate and the police chief and the magistrate then slowly scrutinized the file of papers before looking up and declaring that he was dismissing the case on the grounds of 'insufficient evidence'! It seemed a corrupt system could sometimes serve the cause of justice!

I was appointed to the post at Malham Tarn in charge of both the Field Centre and the Nature Reserve. My remit was to deliver high quality courses at the Field Centre, to review the management practices and policy for the Nature Reserve and to revive the tradition of Research that had been a feature of the Field Centre in the past.

With regard to the Nature Reserve, parts of which were a Grade 1 Site of Special Scientific Interest, I realized I had much to learn but that some of the management practices were clearly inappropriate. I therefore put together a preliminary review of what seemed to be appropriate practices and submitted this to the FSC Executive Committee with the proposal that an Advisory Committee be established representing the National Trust, the FSC and relevant scientific expertise. This was accepted. My draft review was then taken apart, modified and revised again until approved by all and I was instructed to submit it for publication: – Disney, R. H. L., 1975. Review of management policy for the Malham Tarn Estate. Field studies 4: 223-242.

Subsequently, in the early 1980s, this was about 90% endorsed when the Government re-notified the owners and managers of Sites of Special Scientific Interest as to what were the appropriate conservation measures for their own particular SSSI. Unfortunately, when routine responsibility for the management of the Nature Reserve was transferred from the Field Centre to the National Trust in 1985 there became a tendency for National Trust employees to carry out changes without reference to the agreed policy. For example, the Tarn Close between the lawn of Tarn House and the north shore of the Tarn was ungrazed limestone grassland on a south facing slope and largely protected from cold northerly winds on three sides. Its tussock community supported a different vegetation to the large tracts of grazed limestone grassland on the adjacent farms. Furthermore the enhanced humidity within the tussocks allowed a rich invertebrate fauna (of small snails, millipedes, woodlice, beetles and numerous other insects). Indeed it was a rare ecosystem to find in England above 300m altitude. The Trust, however, decided to restore the old Victorian paddock on Tarn Close and periodically stocked it with cattle. The result has been a regrettable loss of an interesting and uncommon ecosystem. A similar preference for tidiness triumphing over the interests of conservation took place in Cambridge many years later (see chapter 10).

A problem that cropped up now and then was poaching. This was mainly of pheasants and grouse, but also young of birds of prey such as sparrow hawks for which there was a lucrative trade to those who trained the birds for hunting game overseas. In addition there was illicit trapping of fish from the Tarn, as evidenced one day when we found perch and trout being sold in Settle market with a notice proclaiming they were fresh from Malham Tarn!

One Sunday my estateman summoned me to come quick as poachers were loose on the Nature Reserve. We raced to the far, south side of the Tarn and wrote down the details of the car of the poachers. We then ran after the poachers who raced to their car and set off north in the direction of Arncliffe. We let them go but went back and phoned the police, who arrested them at the lower end of the dale running south from Arncliffe. There were freshly shot grouse and pheasants in the car. They were charged with illegally taking game out of season, and on a Sunday, and with the possession of an unlicensed shotgun. The magistrate imposed substantial fines.

On another occasion some youths broke into one of our boathouses and took out one of the boats we hired out to anglers. They made slow headway as it was a windy day. Once again we went and procured the details of their car before making after the culprits. They beached the boat and ran to their car. It turned out one of the youths was son of a police chief! When he phoned I said as long as we received money to cover the cost of the damage done to the boathouse I would not take the matter further. I bet his son got more than just a mild reprimand!

The absentee farmer who hired a manager to run his farm on the moor (see below) resented the fact that the water, mineral and shooting rights for his land had been sold separately early in the 20th Century and were subsequently part of what was given to the National Trust, who then included these rights in the lease to the Field Centre. The farmer couldn't accept this situation and phoned me to say that I should get my solicitor and he would get his and he would then shoot a grouse in front of the assembled company and we could see which solicitor won! I declined the invitation pointing out that I had a copy of the lease in the Centre office and its meaning was clear. I informed the Trust's Regional Director of the situation who told the farmer to back off or else!

I sublet the shooting rights for grouse to two old soldiers, one to the northern part covering the lower slopes of Pen-y-Ghent and the other to Fountains Fell. Both were very careful to operate with the interests of the two tenant farmers taken fully into account. I could have charged more to a syndicate but they had a reputation for tending to ride roughshod over a farmer's concerns. These shooting tenants used to deliver a brace of grouse every now and then as token of appreciation. We never liked to say that Audrey did not cook them in the traditional way, after they had been hung in the garage for a spell. Instead she prepared suitable vegetables and cooked them with the grouse in a pressure cooker. We reckoned they were not only tenderer but they tasted better. The shooting fraternity, however, regarded the way the Victorians cooked grouse was beyond being challenged – it was the 'proper' way and that was the end of the matter!

Soon after arriving in Yorkshire I received a communication from the Inland Revenue leading to a correspondence of bureaucratic stupidity one associated with countries like Belize and Cameroon. The 'problem' was that I was owed three months' salary, covering leave I was owed, by the Medical Research Council. The result was that I was in receipt of two salaries for the first three months of my employment by the Field Studies Council. When I informed the Inland Revenue that the MRC salary was not subject to UK tax as I had been a member of their Overseas Staff they requested documentary evidence to support this. Accordingly I sent a copy of my contract with MRC. After some weeks I received a letter requesting evidence that I had paid tax to the Cameroon Government. I then sent a copy of the Technical Aid agreement between the UK Government and the Cameroon Government under which Technical Aid personnel were exempt from Cameroon tax (this being a perk given us in compensation for having to deal with the problems of working in a country like Cameroon with its risks to health, political nonsense and corruption). The Inland Revenue would not accept that my MRC salary was exempted from all tax! In the end I copied the correspondence to the Chancellor of the Exchequer, who duly told the Inland Revenue to stop being stupid.

Another exchange with Inland Revenue occurred following our agreement to help with the reception of people who needed to escape fast from the troubles in Northern Ireland. A network of Christians (Quakers, Roman Catholics, Anglicans, etc.) formed a network, out of the public eye, for this purpose. One young man from the Republican community but with relatives in the Unionist community was under a threat as a rumour was going around that he had reported some Republican IRA militants to the police. One day he was photographed by two youths on the Pennine Way as he came out of the main Field Centre building. The two youths then ran off fast. Our escapee was terrified, rightly inferring (it turned out) that his whereabouts in England had been discovered. So we sent him to meet a Roman Catholic priest on Leeds Railway station who accommodated him elsewhere for a month; until it was learned that he was no longer under threat as he had been eliminated as a suspect by those who had been after him. When he returned we employed him at the Field Centre for a while until he found a job in Settle. As it happened, although we were obliged by the FSC to live on the job at Malham Tarn, we had recently taken out a mortgage on a bungalow in Settle. A condition of the mortgage was that we could not rent the property. However, we let our Ulster lad move in rent free, but he paid the rates and utility bills and kept the bungalow in a good condition. Sometime later I received a letter from the Inland Revenue stating that 'they had reason to believe' that I had failed to declare rent received in my income tax return. This would incur a penalty unless I remedied this omission by a certain date. When I asked what the 'reason' was that led them to this conclusion, seeing that the occupant of our bungalow did not pay rent, they became somewhat evasive until our occupant confirmed that he did not pay rent!

In 1970 Dr Ken Joysey, who had supervised me as an undergraduate for the final year vertebrate palaeontology option and on the Scolt Head Island field course, wrote saying I seemed to be publishing quite a lot. Did I realize that under the Special Regulations after being graduated eight years I could submit published papers for examination for a PhD. So I duly submitted my 1960s papers. There was a long pause. The Biagi scandal (see chapter 7) seemed to pose a problem. In the event it was realized that the one person who understood the entire picture regarding that scandal was Professor Sir Cyril Garnham, Head of Parasitology at the London School of Hygiene and Tropical Medicine. So he was appointed the external examiner. During the Oral Examination Garnham three times asked me why I had written X and not Y. I had replied that I had written Y but the editor required me to change it to X. So he turned to the internal examiner and said that I had clearly passed so let us waste no more time and take the candidate to lunch at his college – Darwin College!

1971: PhD (Awarded by University of Cambridge for 1960s publications).

Most of our teaching of school children was for Sixth Form students studying for GCE, A Level exams. It was constantly gratifying to witness the subject coming alive as they encountered living creatures that up until then had been merely figures in a textbook (usually with no indication of the scale!). We also ran courses for younger children. Their uninhibited enthusiasm and delight was a real pleasure to witness and to support.

FELLOW CREATURES (MC)

With fresh delight the children peer
At bowl of creatures net has hauled
From depths of murky pond. As I
Expound the names of each, and tell
Of ways they hunt and eat, their cries
Of glee and shining eyes renew
The awe I felt as kid when first
I viewed a caddis larva's head
Protruding from its case or else
A nymphal dragonfly who stalked
Its prey with cunning stealth of lions.
We learned that wars in pool, if raised
To scale that put ourselves at risk
Would make us prey. It's then I shed
Romantic view of nature seen
As all benign. Design of frog,
Or diving beetle's streamlined shape,
I still revere, but now I know
It's ruthless strife, not God, which made
Them so. And I am shaped by same;
But I can rise above the scene
To contemplate these awesome beasts
And wonder what my life is for.
I'm free to soar above the raw
And bloody game by which I came
To be. I'm free to think, admire,
To wonder at, but not to praise,
Our fellow creatures on this earth.
But daughter's child is more than worth
Of thousand species in a lake.

One task I had to tackle was the problem that during dry spells the springs supplying the reservoir at 1500 feet on the lower slopes of Fountains Fell were inadequate to supply the needs of the Field Centre and two farms. Furthermore the water was fed to the reservoir by open gutters. For the Field Centre the water descended from the reservoir by gravity to the Pennine Way valley and then rose the other side to a point where it could then descend again by gravity to our various buildings. During dry spells there was not enough head of water in the reservoir to achieve this. So I used to have to cease supplying water to the baths from this supply and to switch over to pumping water from the Tarn, by means of a pump in the East Boathouse, to a separate tank for feeding to the baths only. This water was clearly not for drinking, as evidenced by the odd creature or two that would emerge from the cold taps! My predecessors and I had repeatedly requested the FSC Executive Committee to allocate the funds to remedy this state of affairs, but to no avail. One day when the Chairman came on a visit during one of these dry spells he was taken by my estateman, Harry, onto the fell to the reservoir. He was surprised and concerned to see a dead sheep lying across the gutter from the springs. Later when I was chatting to the Chairman in the Staff Tea Room Harry came in and reported that the pump had broken down and it might take a while to repair. He requested that I announce to the staff and students that bathing was cancelled until further notice. The Chairman was clearly taken aback at this turn of events. Shortly after he had departed the next day Harry announced that the pump was fixed. He was somewhat evasive when asked what had been the problem with the pump! Likewise when I asked where the dead sheep had come from! Anyway the outcome was the Executive Committee allocated the funds to sort the system out.

Having assessed the possible solutions it was decided to tap springs just below the top of Fountains Fell and gravity feed the water by means of a mile and half long buried polythene pipe to the reservoir, with one break tank part way as the fall of 500 ft. would otherwise create too much force by the time it reached the reservoir. The man from the local council took samples for testing the waters from the high springs we proposed to tap and advised we install a porcelain filter candle unit to purify the water at a position just before the entry of the new pipeline to the reservoir. That was the plan. The proposed pipeline would cross three farms, the last being where the reservoir was based, but the reservoir itself was owned by the National Trust and was leased to the Field Centre. The first two farmers were pleased to approve the scheme. The third famer, however, lived elsewhere and hired a manager to run the farm. Even his manager told me his boss was an awkward man to deal with (see above with reference to shooting rights). So I wrote to the owner and informed him that that the last 100 yards of the proposed pipeline would be on his land. He got his solicitor to request that I supply him with the precise route of this last bit of the pipeline. I sent him a set of twelve figure grid references. The solicitor replied requesting me to send the information as a line on a copy of the relevant section of the OS one inch to the mile map. I did so but pointed out that the thickness of the pencilled line rendered this a less precise indication! The owner then wrote to say the FSC would have to pay him way leave. I responded that would be fine but then the FSC would have to charge him for supplying his cattle troughs from the reservoir, which up to then we had supplied at no cost. The FSC did not pay the way leave!

We implemented the scheme but within hours encountered a problem. The filter candles were completely blocked by a brown, gravy like, deposit. I called up the man from the council who took samples away for analysis. When he reported back he said the problem was iron compounds. I asked how that had not been apparent in the analyses carried out before the scheme had gone ahead. He said they were not expecting iron compounds so had not tested for them –

despite one could see the iron staining in some of the strata at the springhead! So we had to dump the filter candle system and devise an alternative treatment. This time we decided to devise our own scheme with the help of the excellent local contractor who had installed the new pipeline for us. At the Field Centre's building situated highest up the hill behind the Centre's main building was a large header tank from which the water was then gravity fed to the other buildings. On top of this we added a smaller tank into which we directed the inflow pipe with a chlorine drip feed unit discharging into it. The inflow pipe was fitted with a tap after the point where branch line led to cattle troughs. Furthermore we installed a float with vertical rod on its top in the main tank. As the water level ascended in this main tank the vertical rod, whose top was attached to tap controlling the chlorine drip slowly turned the tap off. We thus only treated water destined for human use. The final piece of kit was a meter recording residual chlorine placed next to the boiler for hot water in the main Centre below. Thus the handyman or estateman when checking the boiler also checked this dial each day, as well as once a week refilling the container for the chlorine drip.

Some years later there was a further problem with the old pipeline from the reservoir. The original 18th Century pipeline from the reservoir had been replaced with high quality iron pipes in the 19th Century. However, when a fellow from the local council using a metal detector tried to discover how the pipe connected to the reservoir he was surprised to find the head of the iron pipe had been cut off and sealed and did not connect to the reservoir! A later metal pipe was found to be joined into the iron pipe a bit lower down but the metal detector failed to trace its connection to the reservoir! Accordingly I paid a water diviner to find the connection, which he did in no time at all! I then received a query from Head Office as to why I was paying for a water diviner. To which I replied that I had done so because he was superior to modern technology!

I have sketched this saga briefly because it was to prove an excellent illustration for the courses comprising one of my innovations for the Field Centre. This was getting the London School of Hygiene and Tropical Medicine postgraduate Diploma course in Medical Entomology and Parasitology to do their field course at the Centre. This was followed by the same for the Liverpool School and related courses from Leeds University and Leeds Metropolitan University. The courses embraced water supply, microbes in the supply and treatment. Our new private system tapping springs on Fountains Fell was an ideal model for systems found in the developing world. Otherwise my input to these courses was mainly on the entomological side but I would also get them to find the larvae of parasitic flukes and worms in their water snail hosts. On one occasion the lecturer from the London School introduced me to two doctors from Peru who worked on Leishmaniasis. He added that I had worked on a related species in Belize where I had developed the 'Disney trap' for sandflies (see chapter 5). They were taken aback saying they thought I must be dead seeing I was in their textbooks!

Another innovation was being in at the start of the Field Studies Council providing the summer schools for the Open University's new Ecology Option. They were probably the most motivated students we ever taught. At the same time they were challenging because some were professionals in some related field (e.g. a laboratory technician in a university biology department) while the next might be a gardener responsible for the public flowerbeds in a town's roundabouts. One had to steer the better informed onto tackling more difficult identifications (such as water mites or midge larvae) while easing a novice into identifying dragonflies or ladybirds.

Another new initiative involved all my staff when we ran a course on the environment for senior managers from large industries (BP, Shell, ICI, etc.). Journalists learning about this course requested they be allowed to attend. Having previously been misrepresented by journalists too often I declined and signed up a freelance reporter instead, on the understanding that I vetted his copy before he offered it to a paper. However, a journalist from a national newspaper gate-crashed the course when we were in Skipton, a large enough town, but not too large, which I had selected as a means of examining problems relating to the urban environment ranging from the historic centre familiar to tourists, a major livestock market, the accretion of industry at its edges and the scruffy parts at the end of the ginnels (a Yorkshire term for narrow alleys) running away from the historical centre. When the journalist asked why we were bothering with this run down part of town I replied that we wanted to consider all aspects of the town's environment and quipped "because it is like a baby with a clean face and a dirty behind". This appeared in the headline of the report in the paper! As a consequence the town council launched a clean-up campaign!

Among our courses for adult amateurs I personally ran an annual week's course on flies, midges and gnats (Diptera) that greatly extended our knowledge of the species present on the nature reserve by augmenting the Yorkshire Naturalists Union survey from 1954-1958 of the insects of the Malham Tarn region (published in 1962, see below with reference to Phoridae). I was particularly gratified to add two non-biting midges whose larvae had unusual habits. One was a leaf miner of a pond weed and the larvae of other one are phoretic on the stream dwelling larvae of the mayfly Ephemera danica (Disney, R. H. L., 1976. Two interesting additions to the list of Chironomidae (Dipt.) for the Malham Tarn area of Yorkshire. Entomologist's Monthly Magazine 111: 173 (1975)). My extensive work on phoretic blackfly larvae in Cameroon (see chapter 7) had made me aware of such associations. Some participants on my annual course became regulars and lasting friendships were formed. Indeed Zak went on to do a six-year postdoc with me in Cambridge (see chapter 9). There was often a student from overseas. Indeed the distinguished entomologist from the university in Kuwait arrived one year with boxes of specimens from her country. This posed something of a challenge! However, I owned many volumes of the monographs (edited by E. Lindner) of Die Fliegen der palaearktischen Region. With the help of a German dictionary we named a surprising number of her specimens. Another year a student asked me to check her identification of a beautiful fly of the family Dryomyzidae and asked me what was known about the habits of its larva. I said I thought its habits were known but I would need to search the literature for the answer. This was in the days before one could look things up on the internet. The next day I was able to give her the answer – a fellow called Disney published a note some years ago (Disney, R. H. L., 1974. Diptera and Lepidoptera reared from dead shrews in Yorkshire. Naturalist, Hull 927: 136. (1973))! The student looked at me as though I was evidently getting past my sell-by-date! I later referred to this episode in the poem EVENING YEARS (see chapter 10). This made me realize I must compile a list of my own growing list of publications as I was beginning to forget what I had published!

OBSESSION (GK)

They've come from far and wide to learn
From me about the way to name
The many kinds of fly, which most
Despise. This job's beyond the days
Allowed. Indeed towards the end
Of life, devoted most of time
Researching tiny flies, I feel
I'm only just beginning now
To know these fascinating beasts.
Each course I run I sense I learn
At least as much as those who come.
I'm still a child who's overawed
By creatures unaware of how
I mark their beauty, learn their strange
And almost fiction ways. To me
They pose an endless quest to wrest
Their secrets from their wayward lives.
Perhaps the only thing I have
To give, to those who come to share
The feast, is childlike joy at great
Display of diverse forms and lives.
If I infect a few with zeal
To want to carry on the task
Of learning all we may about
These wondrous creatures then, perhaps,
I've given all I can. There's risk
I may have handed on a drug
That gets them hooked and thus impairs
Their former easy days with spouse!

When sowing seeds we can't predict
The ones that will succeed or those
That grow to be a rampant weed.
When handed piece of gleaming steel,
It seems each person has a choice
To forge a ploughshare or a spear.

"YOU STUDY FLIES! – BUT WHY?" (RE)

I do. To me a fly's a gem
Beyond one's wildest fancy's flight
When viewed beneath a microscope.
As seen beneath an S. E. M.,   [S. E. M. = scanning electron
Discerning critic's eye is held   microscope]
Entranced. One's entered world beyond
Imagination's furthest reach.
Yet that alone will not suffice
To justify long obsession
With these much scorned flying marvels
Of design. There's also the lift
Derived from unearthing secrets
Of elusive lives and patient
Piecing together of a new,
Unexpected, picture's surprise.
And if fallout has benefits,
Beyond my most simple delight,
Then that's a bonus prompting thanks.
But that's not all. To unearth facts,
Exposing them to light of day,
Is not an easy task. They seem
To hide in unsuspected ways.
They refuse the call to arise
With hands above their heads.
They are wild gangsters on the run.
They set booby traps and false trails.
They vanish into space. A mirage
Is favoured trick. They're very slick.
All this long game of hide and seek
Is not for those who crave a life
Of ease or cannot stand a tease.
For those who stay the course a new
Humility is found as awe
Replaces youthful certainties once
Considered inviolate. So come

Employ the microscope's sharp eye
To learn the hidden truths of self
When its pale naked ignorance
Is exposed to view and joy prevails.
And learn in retrospect to see
How blind one was before the truth
Emerged. It's just as now I see
In quiet recall what part-time dad
I was to my three kids – too late.
Perhaps that's why some folks delude
Themselves with dreams of being born
Anew for second go. But no –
Unless we came with wisdom from
Initial round it would be vain.
We journey to a better goal.

Anne (the VSO volunteer), Mambo (her Cameroon farmer husband) (see chapter 7) and their first child came to stay with us at Malham Tarn when they were on leave mainly to visit Anne's family in Scotland. We were not to know that this was to be the last time we were to see Mambo and their first son. They had more children and Anne became principal of a teacher training college and Mambo's farm prospered. It was a great shock, therefore, when many years later we were horrified to learn that Anne had fled to Scotland after Mambo, their eldest son and Mambo's sister had been poisoned by a small group in the tribe who resented the fact that their tribe's best farm was to be inherited by half Scottish children. They put it about that a bad juju had killed them. But why had Mambo's sister been killed? It seemed she had got on too well with Anne. Some years later, when we had paid off our mortgage, Audrey and I decided to make a significant donation to the maternity unit in Kumba hospital where Audrey had given birth to Rachel and Anne had also received excellent care from the dedicated maternity unit nurses. We dare not risk sending the money as it would be 'diverted' by some official for personal use. Nor would it be safe for someone to take the money and hand it over to someone in charge. In the end we sent the money to Anne for one of her surviving sons going on a visit to Kumba to take with him. He then consulted the maternity unit nurses as to what equipment they would like to help with their excellent work with limited equipment and very basic facilities. He then purchased the equipment and gave it to the nurses direct. The murderers of his father, elder brother and aunt were never apprehended. My one regret was that Audrey died before this mission had been accomplished.

A major component of all my teaching was concern for conservation and the environment. I was also asked to speak to audiences away from the Field Centre. This sometimes resulted in published records of my talks (e.g. Disney, R. H. L., 1973. The environmentalist's concern. Environment 43: 12. Disney, R. H. L., 1975. Environment and Creation. The 1975 Charles Coulson Lecture.

Chester House Publications, London. 36pp. Disney, R. H. L., 1976. 'Malham Tarn principal on Dales Park myths'. Craven Herald and Pioneer February 13th. Disney, R. H. L., 1976. The environmentalist's concern. Environmental Education Journal of the Cumbria Association for Environmental Education 1975/1976: 8-16. Disney, R. H. L., 1979. Field studies and the conservation, safeguarding and improvement of our natural environment. Journal of the Royal Society of Arts 127 (5273): 266-267. Disney, R. H. L., 1981. Field Centres. Chapter 5: 87-95. In Seaward, M. R. D. (Editor) A Handbook for Naturalists. A Constable Guide, Constable, London. Disney, R. H. L., 1981. Conservation Sites (correspondence). Nature, London 290 (58050): 432. Disney, H., 1981, editor of chapter II (Technology of Living Things) and chapter VI (God in a Changing World) in Edgar Boyes, editor-in-chief Shaping Tomorrow. Home Mission Division of the Methodist Church. Disney, R. H. L., 1984. Malham Tarn Field Centre – A focus for conservation. Yorkshire Dales Review 6: 8 – 9). This was essentially me musing in public about my concerns. Initially I wondered why I was taken seriously. It seemed that my refusal to align myself with the more strident environmentalists was behind this willingness to listen to me. My unsentimental outlook was partly grounded in my experience as a medical entomologist and partly my association with neighbours endeavouring to make a living from a challenging landscape.

COUNTERPRODUCTIVE (RE)

An econut is ranting wild,
With heart that's sound but head that's not.
Indeed simplistic views of child
Are mixed with fair amount of rot.
His problem plain for all to see -
Conclusions pre-select his facts.
It's thus he seems the apogee
Of loony cultist pushing tracts.
His just concerns are lost to view
Beneath a muddled spate of words.
Until he's willing to pursue
The truth, he's cat to flock of birds.

THREE FARMERS (RE)

(Originally circulated at a Seminar on Environmental Education at the Royal Society of Arts on 15 November 1978)

To Hubert every living thing
Was sacred as a royal smile
Or Holy Writ. He wouldn't swat
A fly or kill an ant. He grew
A faddist's fill of fancy foods
At prices only few can find.
His banners cried concern for all
Who strive to save our threatened beasts;
But asked to save the body louse
Refused to offer self as house.

Our farmer Fred professed belief
In progress, modern methods, fat
Returns on funds invested, cash
In bank, and most efficient use
Of land t'achieve that end for all
To see. And so he ripped each hedge
And ploughed the lot, and filled his barns
With grain galore. Alas the wind
His topsoil took. His profits fell.
He cursed the Min. of Ag. to hell.

But Joe he worked as hard as Fred.
He picked and chose amongst the new
And latest things. He kept each hedge.
He left a spinney here and there.
He loved his land. He liked the birds,
But culled the pigeons off his crops
And ate them in a pie. He sprayed
His pests and weeds but left alone
The verges round his fields. His views
He ne'er proclaimed. They made no news.

DAY EXCURSION THROUGH THE PENNINES (RE)

With juddered climb in grumbling gear
We crawl behind a tripper's car
Unsure of walled-in, blinkered ways
With startled sheep to test his brakes.

The town reduced to ordered spread
Of lifeless model far below,
Is now embalmed within our minds -
Which seek the tree-shorn fells for ease.

We shed the claims of tasks and talk
Devouring time, impeding peace.
These naked hills embrace with calm
And wider views. We feel afresh.

No shepherd's free to map these moors
With contours drawn from urban whims.
No weather-chastened man survived
By moulding truth to suit his dreams.

HILL FARMER (MC)
(First published in May 1983 in The Dalesman 45(2): 109)

The wind is clawing through his hair,
While sheep are scratching snow in search
For dregs of summer days, and sun
Disdains the scene with distant stare.
With smoking breath and muttered curse
He hurls his dog behind his flock.
Both they and he are locked in grip
Of need to show these savage fells
That life and death will weave their dance,
Despite the frozen grin that marks the rim
Of hope below the scar. Despite
The lure of ease in ordered dale
These hills and he in silent rage
Engage in feud, that time has forged,
Until respect their hate has purged -
Until each task is sanctified.

As a consequence of my views and perceptions being in the public domain I was invited to join a moderate campaigning body:
1972-1975: Member of the Yorkshire Council for the Environment.
This in turn lay behind me becoming a member of the local planning authority:
1975-1981: Ministerial Appointee on Yorkshire Dales National Park Committee of North Yorkshire County Council.
My remit from the Secretary of State was to represent in particular conservation and the educational use of the countryside.
I learned much about politics in practice. Most members were trying to do what they thought was for the best.

YORKSHIRE DALES (CO)

When I recall the years I served
As one of planners placed to care
For National Park, I know I failed
To please as many folk as those
Who cheered our stands against the greed
Of moneyed men for whom the Dales
Were profits on a tree they wished
To pluck before they fell to waste,
Or went for free to local lads.
In several bids by rival schemes
There never seemed to be a way
To reconcile the claims that weighed
The same. A role of dice was just
As fair as long debate or vote
On compromise that angered both.
Behind our pompous words we knew
That much was merely muddle in
Disguise. We were not wise. We shared
A common love for landscape, ways
Of life, that man had shaped and time
Had mellowed down the years. It seems
We often felt that change was not
To be desired, despite the fact
That what we cherish only came
To be the way it is because
Of those who felled the trees and built
The drystone walls, and thus transformed
These hills and dales to what today
We praise. Indeed the wealth from wool,
From mining lead, allowed the use
Of quarried stone to build in way

We now admire. A modern man
Who wished to sink a mine would not
Receive consent, not even if
His plans included careful screens
Of trees and spoil disposal scheme.
The houses most admired by those
Who relish Dales were built without
An architect, and yet endure
In harmony with nature's scene.

RESOLVE RENEWED (TL)

As wind is racing wild across
The fen, the bog beyond is dance
Of cotton grass and skulking grouse,
The menace skies are dark, the sheep
In distance huddle close in lee
Of drystone wall that claws its way
To top of distant fell. A sense
Of doom, or evil spell, precedes
The flash of lightning; followed by
Resounding thunder's roll as storm
Erupts. Relentless rain descends.
But far from fear, I'm filled with calm
And sense of drama lifting gloom
That dogged my angry thoughts that grew
From dirty trick a rogue contrived
On me last week. But now my mind
Is clear as summer's day, resolve
Is drawing strength from this wild scene.
As I behold bedraggled fox
That's slipping silent past a copse,
I see a way to right the wrong.
I know that patient wait for time
To strike is all I need. And now
The clouds begin to break, a chink
Of light begins to peep afresh
On newly laundered peaceful scene.

Concern for the conservation and the environment had been a concern of
many for years. But it was only after I had moved to Cambridge (Chapter 9)
that it became a topic frequently engaging the talk, at least, of our politicians
and the press.

TALKING GREEN (GK)

Our politicians now, at last,
Are talking green. Where have they been?
It's more than forty years I wrote
And spoke of these concerns. The scene
Was nothing new when I began
To teach my students what I knew.
Today computer models try
To scare us witless as they spew
Predictions that assume the worst
Is true. As carbon correlates
With climate change the causal links
Become more clear. But trite debates
Ignore the other facts involved.
The party line is carved in stone.
Excess of people drives decline.
But atavistic popes intone
That birth control is sin, despite
It's poor who suffer most from such
A dry-rot dogma taught by priests
Denied the dance of sex. Too much
They've clung to rancid views for long
Renounced since science shone its torch
Exposing paradigms now dead.
As deserts spread the sun will scorch
Remaining crops, and goats will starve
Along with children left alone
When parents die of AIDS. It's time
To harvest funds, and facts now known,
To lift the poor from hopeless plight.
Instead our stupid wars negate
Our good intents, consuming cash
And leaving rest of world irate.
And as for leaving fate to faith
In rampant market place they must
Be out of mind. It's reckless plan
Reducing planet earth to dust.

4th March 1974: Aunt Sheila died in a care home in Winchester.

Sadly she had become very mentally confused towards the end of her life and had been put in the care home by her elder brother (my uncle Pat). This was a great change from her home on her cherished Norfolk coast. When Audrey had visited her in this care home she thought she was some other member of the family. A year or two earlier when she had come to stay with us at Malham Tarn she was still mentally alert and had much enjoyed walking beside the lapping waters of the Tarn.

Her legacy allowed my study of scuttle flies to take off as indicated in the preface to my most cited publication (of 1994, see chapter 9) on this extraordinary family of small flies – 'A late aunt, Sheila Disney, encouraged my interest in natural history when I was a boy, and her legacy enabled me to buy my dream compound microscope. Without this good microscope I would never have been in a position to tackle the taxonomy of such small insects as the scuttle flies. With it I have been able to produce many detailed descriptions and hundreds of drawings used to illustrate both papers in scientific journals and the identification keys I have published. While a less sophisticated microscope is adequate for the identification of phorids, one needs a superior instrument to produce detailed drawings and descriptions'.

In the early 1970s I was intrigued by the elegant larvae of the meniscus midges that I encountered with students in ponds, the sedge beds of the Tarn and in streams. I set out to rear the species through to the adults so we could name the species of the different larvae. I slide mounted larvae and cast larval skins and those of pupae for examination under a compound microscope. I decided to slide mount the adults as well, despite these midges being traditionally pinned. In Belize I had always slide mounted the sandflies and likewise the blackflies in Cameroon. This project ended up as a standard key work, illustrated with drawings by Joan Worthington (Disney, R. H. L., 1975. A Key to the Larvae, Pupae and Adults of the British Dixidae (Diptera) the Meniscus Midges. Freshwater Biological Association, Scientific Publications 31: 1-78. SBN 900386 23 1). Working with Joan was an interesting experience. She was an excellent biological illustrator. However, she drew what she saw! For example I would give her a slide mount of a larva and ask her to draw the tail end. I would then comment on the drawing suggesting small amendments. One time such a drawing was marred by a pair of asymmetrically placed 'rugby footballs'! I pencilled a note 'what are these? Please remove them.' Joan was a bit taken aback. When I looked at the slide I saw these were faecal pellets, which I had therefore mentally taken out! I thus learned that a successful entomological drawing involves selection of what is significant with respect to recognition. I learned a lot from Joan, but ever since I did my own drawings even though not as aesthetically pleasing as those by Joan. Having completed this work on British Dixidae I split the collection into four and deposited these in Cambridge, the Natural History Museum in London, the Manchester Museum and the Keighley Museum in Yorkshire. My motive was simple. A number of important collections of insects have been destroyed in wars, fires and other mishaps. It seemed to me sensible not to deposit the entire collection in one place.

Many years later I was asked to undertake a second edition as the first edition had sold out. Furthermore in 1992 I had published an additional species for the British List. I decided to add the trickle midges, whose larvae had also intrigued me, apart from the fact that the larvae of these two families of midges are very sensitive to surfactant pollutants such as detergents and their presence are good indicators of the absence or minimal levels of these pollutants. For the additional meniscus midge and the trickle midges I undertook the drawings myself (Disney, R. H. L., 1999. British Dixidae (Meniscus Midges) and Thaumaleidae (Trickle Midges): Keys with Ecological Notes. Freshwater Biological Association, Scientific Publications 56: 1-129). In this second edition I also reproduced the cladogram for the British Dixidae that I had given as a worked example in my A SNOPSIS OF THE TAXONOMISTS TASKS that I published in 1983 at the request of teachers (see below).

Following the first edition of the key to Dixidae I became intrigued by scuttle flies (Diptera, Phoridae). This was partly because they had been omitted by the Entomological Section of the Yorkshire Naturalists Union survey, 1954-1958, of the insects of the Nature Reserve (1962, The Insects of the Malham Tarn Area. Proceedings of the Leeds Philosophical and Literary Society, Scientific Section IX part II: 15-91), because of the taxonomic challenge they posed, and yet were clearly abundant and diverse on Malham Moor. Also they were clearly more frequent flower visitors (e.g. Disney, R. H. L., 1980. Records of flower visiting by scuttle flies (Diptera: Phoridae) in the British Isles. Naturalist, Hull 105 (953): 45-50) than the literature suggested. I suspected that this was because they are quick to depart when a collector attempts to catch the insects visiting flowers. I found that generally one needed to go for the phorids first and then go for the larger species of fly. Indeed many of the larger flies could be identified and recorded without capture. In addition I had reared two species from larvae that contradicted the textbook statements about the habits of larval phorids (see chapter 9) (Disney, R. H. L., 1976. A further case of a nematoceran fly (Diptera: Sciaridae) parasitized by a species of scuttle fly (Diptera: Phoridae). Entomologist's Gazette 27: 91-98. Disney, R. H. L., 1977. A further case of a scuttle fly (Dipt., Phoridae) whose larvae attack slug eggs. Entomologist's Monthly Magazine 112: 174 (1976)). The first of these notes spawned the following poem:

THE FALL (MC)

Beneath the microscope is revealed
A small marvel of intricate design.
Tiny parasitic arthropod
Heralding thoughts of God. There's no art
Produced exquisite detail so fine.
When I contemplate this fly, entombed
Upon its slide, I recall a sense
Of elation at the stumbling chance
Revelation – the hidden secrets
Of its maggot life. And yet I feel
The awesome, gruesome fate of its host.
That ill-fortuned larval midge consumed
By a monstrous intruder within,
Who postpones inevitable death –
Who devours the minor organs first.
But before the final coup de grace
It accepts its victim's parting gift –
A finely spun cocoon to purloin.
What ingenious exploitation!
What perfect synchrony! What selfless
Sacrifice by larval midge! Oh fly
What devilish designs spawned your form!
I can conceive your beauty sings of God.
But Oh I cannot believe your ways
Were willed by the God whom Christ revealed
As love. As I wonder at the shapes
And patterns of your being I see
In my mind the whirling, flashing sword
Of he who prevents Adam and Eve
Entering Eden again – prevents
Us meeting God face to face in this
Vale of tears. Within the ancient myth
I hear the mighty wind of Our Lord
Issue forth like a thunderbolt hurled
Into the void. With a painful wrench
He averts His gaze. He must release
His loving grip. This vortex of light
Foreshadows the Cross. It must be so.
Only so will chance unleash, in time,
A being truly free to respond
With love to His own fathomless love.
We search the cosmos in vain for God.

203

He is not there. Only fingerprints
Of beauty – left on the thunderbolt
Of genesis – permeates the all.
We search in vain for God along life's
Way. He withdrew Himself by the act
Of creation. And yet we perceived
He could not be far away. We scoured
The universe. We strove to find Him
In a thousand concoctions of our
Groping minds. Oh fly we never thought
To look within each other until
Christ embraced His errant thunderbolt
Upon the Cross. Oh Lord embrace me –
Let me encounter Thee in other folk.

The identification of the scuttle flies (Phoridae) was indeed a challenge, especially as the leading specialists in the 20th Century (Wood, Brues, Malloch, Schmitz, Borgmeier, and others) all insisted that the primary collection should be specimens mounted on micropins or card stages mounted on larger pins. As these flies range in size from 1 to 6 mm in length, with most 2 to 3 mm, this meant that too much emphasis was being given to small differences in the wing veins. When I tried identifying the species of the genus Metopina, which are at the lower end of the size range, I became very frustrated. So I decided to abandon pins and switched to slide mounting instead, as I had done with the meniscus midges (see above). The result was my first significant revision of a genus of scuttle flies (Disney, R. H. L., 1979. The British Metopina (Diptera: Phoridae) with description of a new species. Zoological Journal of the Linnean Society 67: 97-113). This added two species to the British List, including the one new to science, and established two new synonyms. Ever since I have routinely slide mounted scuttle flies for examination of details under the compound microscope at higher magnifications than those employed for observing pinned specimens under a dissecting (stereo) microscope. Furthermore, having developed a procedure for remounting pinned specimens on slides, I frequently found specimens borrowed from museums had been misidentified (e.g. Disney, R. H. L., 1983. The type series of Megaselia collini (Wood) (Dipt., Phoridae) has four included species. Entomologist's Monthly Magazine 119: 245-24).

The move to slide mounting allowed steady improvement in my drawings of critical features. The drawing attachment for the microscope allowed me to mark the key points in pencil and then complete the drawing by eye alone. I then converted it to black ink and added a scale bar. I was surprised, however, when I was asked to exhibit my drawings and I suggested better examples in classic texts, but was told they were already included! They said they also wanted drawings by a living entomologist who did his own drawings! (Disney, R. H. L., 1980. Exhibit of entomological drawings. Measures, D. & Cartwright,

P., Handbook for "The Artist Naturalist in Britain", Yorkshire Museum and York Festival Exhibition. 28 pp: p. 26).

The above sketch of my known research was part of the process of restoring the tradition of research at the Centre. I also welcomed many projects from others. Their results frequently produced papers in the FSC's journal Field Studies, which required contributions to be written so as to be accessible to a wide audience. Other papers were published in other more specialist journals. Jenny Baker, the FSC Research Director, was very supportive of the revival of the tradition of research at Malham Tarn.

In 1976, the year of the greatest drought in the second half of the 20th Century, we went for our family holiday to Inishbofin off the west coast of Ireland, staying in an old fisherman's bungalow. Instead of the normally to be expected frequent rain we had the most glorious weather. We made friends with a local man who let the children ride his donkey when he went to fetch a load of peat. We all look back on it as the holiday by which all subsequent holidays were to be compared! For Audrey and myself it recalled our honeymoon in Ireland! I set my normal insect traps (that work around the clock while I am relaxing with the family during the day) extracting the scuttle flies early each morning and preserving them in tubes of ethanol for subsequent study back in Yorkshire (Disney, R. H. L., 1977. Scuttle flies (Diptera: Phoridae) from Inishbofin, Co. Galway. Irish Naturalists' Journal 19: 57-61).

In 1978 I was asked to advise the Sri Lanka Ministry of Education on their field centre programme. They had asked the British Council to recruit someone with both field centre experience and tropical ecology experience. When they had listed separately possible advisers under the two heads I was the only one on both lists! I ran courses for teachers at Peradeniya (near Kandy) and in the far northeast, as well as advising on a suitable site for a field centre in the extreme south. I also incidentally collected some new scuttle flies, including one reared from a species whose larvae lived in the waters of a pitcher plant (Disney, R. H. L., 1982. A new species of Megaselia (Diptera: Phoridae) that breeds in pitchers of Nepenthes in Sri Lanka. Ceylon Journal of Science (Biological Sciences) 14: 89-101) and proved to be the same species, initially only tentatively identified, as a parasite of a young Japanese girl who had excreted mature larvae in her urine (Disney, R. H. L. & Kurahashi, H., 1978. A case of urogenital myiasis caused by a species of Megaselia (Diptera: Phoridae). Journal of Medical Entomology 14: 717. Disney, R. H. L., 1991. The aquatic Phoridae (Diptera). Entomologica scandinavica 22: 171-191)

A result of this visit was that I had had to familiarize myself with the literature on Oriental scuttle flies. This proved useful when I later took part in Project Wallace in Indonesia and when Audrey and I visited China (see chapter 9).

Another result of this visit was the following poem:

THE WINDING TRAIL (RE)

I. A West African Sacred Tree

The tree was gaunt against the sky.
Alone it stood, a crippled giant.
A lightning strike had split its heart,
But still it bore its fruit and leaves
Defying fire, and shading those who sit
Within its care to flee the sun
That seared the burning, hostile land.
Admired by men its wounded pride
Had saved it from the axe that cleared
Its kin and laid the bush to waste.
As now revealed it seemed a god
To symbolize the furies foiled.
The thunderbolts of hell had failed
To fell its mighty soul to death.
Eternal sap restored its hope
For years to come. It looms alone
Against the dying sun, its form
Is etched in black and twisting bones
The ripped-off veils of forest flung
Aside had left exposed to view.
It's little wonder men revere
This deathless tree and worship here.

II. A Mayan Pyramid in the Yucatan Jungle

We climbed the panting steps and pause
To view the scene. The snaking forms
In frieze of rock embrace a face
Of proud and haughty Mayan priest.
At length we reach the top to see
The lapping bush encroaching once
Again towards the ancient stones
That failed t'appease the thirsty gods,
Who drank the blood of maidens slain
On dates, at times, foretold by stars
And calculations fine. When crops
Had failed then hunger gnawed the faith
In priests who ruled the minds of men
Who feared the unseen shapes in dreams
That haunt the lives of toiling folk

Who know not how or why or whence
Our lives are sprung, our course is set.
Such piles of stone will time forget.

III. A Modern Statue of Buddha in Sri Lanka

A monster Buddha in repose
Did dwarf the people bringing gifts
Of fragrant flowers, bowing heads
T'appease whatever powers might
Avenge neglect. The lotus pond,
Below the monstrous feet of he
Who chose to spurn such atavist
Deflection from the path of true
Desire to shed the shackled ways
Of fear of unknown gods, proclaimed
A sacred peace for pure delight
Of perfect blooms. And yet that face
Of cheaply crude and idol art
Reflection thrust upon the eye;
And mocked the man whose words did seem
In vain, whose dethroned gods now laugh
To see him placed in high esteem
His own enthronement can't redeem.

IV. The Old Covenant

The Jews once stumbled in the dark
But slowly see a glow of light.
Their many fears and many gods
Retreat before the dawn of one –
The only Lord. They grope their way
From sacrifice to righteous law
To lay before their wrathful God.
They dimly feel a warmer fire.
They claim a special place with Him
Who made us free. They bind themselves
With rules and rites. They bicker, fight,
Repent, and lapse again. They glimpse
A greater light to come. They quench
It when it's here. They fail to see
It flame anew from empty tomb.
They sing our God has chosen them
Alone. Proclaim themselves a right
To pride of place. Oh Jews we love

Thy human follies, stubborn faith,
And courage tried by fire and woe
Beyond the lot of mortal man.
Your role has passed. The destined plan
Has run its course. The tides of time
Have cleansed thy gold for Christ's own rhyme.

V. Islam

When Christ destroyed in fires of love
The chains of priest and law his sheep
Did frolic free at last. But soon
They fell to bleating loud, and ran
Amok as each believed he'd found
A better patch. At length a man
Arose who strove to form the flock
Anew. He fenced them in with rule
And rite and simple, austere faith.
The Prophet spake as man to child.
His voice was stern and clear. He bade
The faithful tread his road to save
Them from the fearful doubts of those
Who fly in songs of love, from He
Who stays his hand to see if you
Can stand alone and follow free.

VI. Jesus

A wheezing episcope had cast
A coloured blur upon our wall.
The slowly focussed lens a form
Now dimly brings to life until
We start to guess the shape of things
To come. The children see a ship,
A beast, a monster thing from space,
In scudding clouds. It's thus we thought
We knew our Lord emerging on
The screen ahead. We're at a loss.
The light reveals an empty cross.
It holds our gaze as songs of praise
Now guide us slowly through the haze.
Laplace had searched the heavens through
His sums and found no God, he had
No need of Him t'expound the sweep
Of endless stars, the cosmic sphere

Of countless lights. And he was right.
But when we turn to look at Christ
The gospel cry 'Who is this man?'
Still hounds our hearts, disturbs our minds,
And echoes in our dreams. No fraud
Was He it's plain. His claims still throw
Us reeling back. Was He a crazed,
Deluded man? We flee this way
T'escape His blinding light. We hear
Our queries curving back upon
Ourselves, as tripping flat upon
The floor we find it's we who now
Have balance lost; while He, whose love
And calm still sloughs all labels stuck
Upon Himself or on his cross,
Still reaches hand to raise us up.

We cannot run from Thee, oh Christ.
But as we bind ourselves to Thee,
Oh Lord, the more you set us free.

17th January 1979: my mother died (in hospital following an accident a few days before when the car skidded on ice and hit a wall). My sisters and I kept vigil for several days while she was unable to speak but seemed to grasp that we had informed our brother John (on the Queen Charlotte Islands off the West coast of Canada). When we said we had a message that he was on his way to England she seemed to relax and shortly afterwards died. I was then dispatched in advance of my sisters to tell our father who, having been only slightly injured, had been taken to a different hospital. That night I got up and wrote down the following poem almost as though it had been dictated, and left it on the table downstairs for my sisters to discover in the morning. It is the one poem that I have never changed a word since!

BEREAVEMENT (MC)
(for my father at the time of my mother's death)

We move through the darkest deep with aching heart
We soar above the peaks borne aloft by love
We meet our Lord walking on our sea of grief
Our choking tears now flow – cleansed to joyful wine
Endless vigil of our night eclipsed ourselves
We heard the inner impulse now – calling clear
It was thus our self-regard was swept away
It was thus that God could weave his healing shroud

209

It was thus forgiveness wrapped His cloak of light
We now accept each other's burdens with delight
We now perceive the sun emerging from the cloud
With awe we watch our hope renewed enhancing life.

Later in the night I had a strange experience. As I lay awake I had a vision (quite different from a dream. More like a sudden and unexpected interruption in the flow of one's thoughts) of my mother sitting in a tall throne-like chair, her face was as when she was much younger and she had her right arm around a small girl standing by her right knee. As I lay pondering this I was gradually made aware that the girl was my brother's daughter Vanessa, who had died of whooping cough with complications when still an infant. I had never met her. It would be just like my mother's soul to seek out Vanessa's soul as a priority after relinquishing her physical body. Why was it I who had received this vision? I concluded that it was most likely because I was probably the most sceptical member of the family, hence my testimony would be the more convincing.

Following my mother's death my father's anecdotes, which had long been dominated by reminiscences of his years in the Sudan, started going back to his boyhood days. He would vividly conjure up some incident from the past; for example when he was a schoolboy cycling near Marlborough.

PROGRESS? (CW)

A swirling, coughing cloud of powdered chalk.
A cursing man who stumbles into view
With snorting team of horses, harnessed two
Abreast with two behind, and straining wheels
Which groan beneath a creaking wagon's load.
A measured drawl of ancient's youthful tale
Upwells from mists of distant past where now
His mind would dwell. The diesel fumes
And ceaseless crawl of cars ascend the hill
Where once he pushed his bike towards that form,
Whose sturdy frame and steady pace, whose oaths
And glinting eyes, had reeked of ordered lives
And people in their place. But now a haze
Ahead conceals a world advancing fast
Towards an abstract-artist's shattered view
Of simple things. Dismembered corpse of hope
Is cold upon the slab of time, as death
Is looming through a fog his hearse pursues.
I doubt a lorry driver's horn could raise
A carter's ghost to marvel at our race

Of insulated comfort borne along
A way his weary walk had worn the wind
And rain, the flicking flies and fickle sun.

17th August 1979: my father died.
My father had suffered from Leukaemia for some time before my mother died, and had assumed he would die before her. He'd arranged his affairs on that assumption. He rearranged things and then died 7 months later. He was stoical to the end and didn't want any fuss.

Some months after his death I received a letter from an American specialist on the ecology of Central American mammals. He said he had been meaning to write for some time but then had been told I had recently died. Someone had seen a notice of my dad's death rather than of mine! Referring to my 1968 paper (cited in chapter 7) on my work in British Honduras, he said that he always took my paper with him when traveling to engage in further fieldwork as I had documented so many new data and had linked my observations to much information already in the somewhat scattered literature.

As I published ever more small papers adding species to the British List, describing species reared from previously unrecorded hosts or situations, etcetera, I began to be approached by ecologists with large samples they wished to be processed. Although a formidable prospect I decided that if I was going to really get to grips with the huge genus Megaselia then I needed to accept this challenge. The result was two substantial ecological papers in which I undertook the identifications of the few thousand specimens involved:

Disney, R. H. L., Coulson, J. C. & Butterfield, J., 1981. A survey of the scuttle flies (Diptera: Phoridae) of upland habitats in Northern England. Naturalist, Hull 106 (957): 53-66. Disney, R. H. L., Henderson, I. F., Perry, J. N. & Clements, R. O., 1981. Phoridae (Diptera) from English pasture soils. Pedobiologia 22: 366-378. One thing these studies brought home to me was that some published comparisons of the surveys of different sites were often difficult to evaluate because different methods give different results. Thus in the above surveys the upland one employed pitfall traps and the lowland pastures survey employed traps set to catch flies emerging from the soil. After listening to a talk in London when the speaker compared his results using flight interception traps with someone's data from another site that had employed pitfall traps, I had observed that the differences told me more about the differences between the collecting methods than about the differences in the insect faunas between the sites. I was surprised by the ensuing debate, as I thought my observation would have been taken for granted! Accordingly I assembled at Malham Tarn some of the regulars on my fly courses and a member of my staff (Alison Woods) and we spent a week carrying out a series of simultaneous collections employing different methods. The resulting paper at least served to silence those who had objected to my observation at the London meeting (Disney, R. H. L., Erzinclioglu, Y. Z., Henshaw, D. J. de C., Howse, D., Unwin, D. M., Withers, P. & Woods, A., 1982. Collecting methods and the adequacy of attempted fauna surveys, with reference to the Diptera. Field Studies 5(4): 607- 621).

In 1979 Dr Sarah A. Corbet, known to her friends and colleagues as Sally, and myself persuaded Cambridge University Press to produce a new series of Naturalists' Handbooks to be co-edited by ourselves. Sally and I had been students together at Cambridge. We continued as co-editors, despite a number of changes of publishers, for the first thirty-one titles of this to be acclaimed series (see appendix G).

In the same year John Hillaby called in at the Field Centre in connection with some piece he was involved with for the media. Exasperated by his fellow programme makers quibbling over irrelevant details, he left them to it and asked me to go for a stroll. We were some time. When we returned his accomplices got back to business quickly as by then time was pressing and a thunder storm was getting closer! However, as a result of our conversation John published a (somewhat hyped!) piece about me (Forum, Out and About, Thunder Fell. New Scientist 21 June 1979: 1022)!

Less welcome to Malham Moor were increasingly frequent incidents of low flying military jets flouting their restriction for this part of the landscape to flying above 250 feet altitude. One day a jet dive bombed over the Tarn before abruptly turning skywards at the last moment. It nearly swamped some anglers in one of the boats we hired out. Then another flew so low that it had to rise a little to avoid hitting the drystone walls and when it encountered a wall my estateman, Harry, was repairing it blew his hat off! I therefore lodged a formal complaint with the Ministry of Defence. They replied that they had interviewed the pilots and they denied that they had flown below 250 feet altitude. I replied that I was prepared to get the Yorkshire Council for the Environment to bring a legal case against them. A provost sergeant appeared at the Centre in response and proceed to tell me that it was a highly technical job assessing the altitude of a plane. I replied that I knew that, having been trained as a Technical Assistant in the Royal Artillery. Apart from that I could produce witnesses who with myself had observed jets flying BELOW us! He apologized and reported back that I could produce a case that would stand up in court! The nuisance abated for the next six months. In the meantime I submitted a motion for the National Park Committee as the nuisance extended well beyond Malham Moor. This resulted in a lesson in politics. I was phoned a little later by a Tory councillor to enquire if I would be able to attend the next meeting of the Committee. I replied that regretfully I had a prior teaching commitment but would be attending the meeting on the following month. My resolution was then tabled at the meeting when I was absent! At the following meeting the Chairman asked if there were any amendments to the minutes of the last meeting. I said that the motion I had submitted had two parts but according to the minutes only one had been debated. I was assured that the minute was accurate. Furthermore, according to the rules of procedure an individual member's motion could not be reintroduced for at least a year. Some ex-military Tory members had emasculated my motion and ensured it was tabled when they knew I was not going to be at the meeting. Although strictly not in breach of the rules it was not defensible to have denied me the opportunity to present my own motion.

As I got wise to the tricks some members played I began to prepare a fall-back position if I thought a vote might go against what I thought to be desirable. I was prepared, therefore, when an outrageous submission came before the Committee. The applicant wanted to create a caravan park for 60 tourist caravans in the middle of a site of outstanding conservation importance that had been well documented by the Yorkshire Naturalists Union since the 19th Century. Unfortunately the submission by the Nature Conservancy Council was by a well-meaning but limited individual who failed to consult the Yorkshire Naturalists Union or the literature on the site. Instead he did a quick survey of the ground flora and declared it not to be especially worthy of note. The YNU would have agreed with him, but the whole interest of the site was that it had one of the richest moss and lichen assemblages in the north of England as well as one of the most outstanding lists of species of land snails in the country. On the basis of the NCC submission the National Park Officer had recommended acceptance of the proposal. At the meeting of the Committee I objected and supported my objection by declaring the NCC report to be fundamentally mistaken. I requested a site meeting before the Committee voted on the proposal. This was carried. At the site meeting the National Park Officer admitted he had been misled by the NCC report. I replied that he should go over the head of the author of the report and get his boss in Newcastle to replace it with a competent report. He said he could not do that as an officer serving the Committee. So I wrote instead. Meanwhile I learned on the grapevine that the applicant in fact wanted a facility for 120 caravans, but had been advised to go for 60 and when the fuss had died down to put in an application for a further 60! When the application came back to the committee political games were in evidence. I was asked to open the debate. Then a motion was put that each member could only speak once, but before that vote was taken my supporters amended this by adding that I could speak twice! After I had closed the debate, the opposition to the proposed caravan facility just lost the vote, a previous supporter had switched sides. A fellow Ministerial Appointee whispered to me that the councillor had been seen in a pub with the agent of the applicant and the latter had passed a brown envelope to him under the table! The opposition to the application having been defeated, the Chairman called for the next item. I interjected and requested that we put some conditions on the application just allowed. I proposed that the caravan site be properly fenced off from the rest of the wood, that no further applications for additional caravans be accepted, that an area equivalent to that being given over to the caravans be fenced off at the edge of the wood and planted up with trees of species approved by the NCC. The Committee agreed. In the event the applicant found these conditions upset his calculations for the profit expected from his project, so he leased the site (with its planning consent) to a holiday caravan organization. The latter decided they wanted an ablutions block and applied to the Committee for planning permission. I proposed acceptance on condition that the maximum number of caravans allowed at any one time be reduced to 45. The Committee agreed. The result was the project was abandoned as the sums did not add up!

An even more bizarre example of political nonsense was experienced on another occasion. The County Council started overturning decisions of the National Park Committee. Some fellow Ministerial Appointees tabled a motion of objection on the grounds that the Countryside Commission, when appraised of this situation, had replied that by the delegation of powers to the Committee the County Council was then obliged to accept the Committee's decisions. The Chairman, turned to the young legal advisor to the Committee (who had evidently been briefed beforehand by some Tory County Councillors) for his advice. He ruled that the power to debate the delegation of powers had not been delegated to the Committee! A fellow Appointee next to me muttered in exasperation that the Minister in London should be told of the situation. I replied "why not? Let us meet at my Field Centre and work out a plan of action to put into effect your suggestion". We met and put together a document listing unacceptable actions of the County Council with respect to the Committee since the beginning of the Local Government reorganization some years before. We then got a sympathetic environmental lawyer from Leeds to scrutinize the draft document and to suggest changes. We then sent this to the Minister. We were then summoned as a delegation to meet the Minister in London. He was 100% sympathetic and said that as long as we kept it out of the press he would sort things out. In due course a delegation to Westminster from North Yorkshire County Council was summoned to the Department for the Environment where the Minister for Local Government reprimanded them in no uncertain terms. On their return to Yorkshire the County Council rescinded their decisions that had overturned decisions of the National Park Committee.

Around this time I obtained and read Hennig's classic Phylogenetic Systematics, which was the key publication leading to the cladistics revolution in biology. I read it through twice with growing excitement. It answered the question that my degree course had failed to answer to my satisfaction. How do you work out the evolutionary (phylogenetic) relations of present day species? As I increasingly referred to this in my teaching at the Field Centre visiting teachers urged me to write a simple introduction to what taxonomy was all about. The result was a paper in Field Studies (Disney, R. H. L., 1983. A synopsis of the taxonomist's tasks, with particular attention to phylogenetic cladism. Field Studies 5(5): 841-865). It was well received at the time, but today the section on the contribution of molecular data would require considerable expansion. In this paper, having outlined the principles of cladistics, I then gave an example of its application by presenting a data tabulation and cladogram derived from it for the British meniscus midges (Dixidae). I subsequently reproduced the cladogram in the second edition of my key to the British Dixidae (see above).

BREAKTHROUGH (CW)

It's rare indeed to read a book
That has one hooked, one can't put down
Until the final page is turned.
It's rarer still when cover's brown
And unadorned in any way,
And subject's quite arcane. But such
Was Hennig's book of '66.
As student I had learned how much
The Neo-Darwin paradigm
Explained, but felt I'd not been told
The truth entire about the means
To judge the warring camps who hold
Contending views about the links
Between 'related' species. Here,
In closely reasoned text, at last
We had a key. His scheme is clear,
Despite Teutonic prose so dense
In parts one needs to read a page
At least three times to grasp its gist.
In places mind does not engage
With over tidy views that try
To cover more than logic can
Sustain. But central theme donates
A lasting light, a master plan.
But since we've learned how virus rogues
Inserted novel genes inside
The boughs of branching tree. Result
Is tangled growth's no longer guide
To simple picture showing how
My forebears fathered present me.
These novel gifts to ancient limbs,
Allowed a faster growth of tree.
Indeed without these virus rogues
We humans never would be here
To tell the tale. But cost was high,
As first invaders got so near
To genocide of early stock
Before it tamed invading tribes
To form alliance good for both.
This tale that recent work describes
In part confounds, in part augments
The scheme that Hennig gave before

These novel facts were shown the light
Of day. A settled truth is bore.
The same applies to boom and bust
Resulting from the weird belief
That money markets uncontrolled
Will trickle down to give relief
To those on lowest rungs. Unless
Controls are put in place then greeds
Will bring about a crash before
They're made to serve society's needs
For enterprise and fair rewards
For all. It's like our virus gains.
It's only when the money made
Is tamed that justice then pertains.

It is perhaps worth recalling that Darwin's great book (On the Origin of Species by Means of Natural Selection) was flawed by his espousal of blending inheritance (pangenesis), which was subsequently discredited by the work of Mendel and what followed on from his work.

DESPITE IT'S FLAWED (GK)

When Darwin launched his greatest book,
In eighteen fifty nine, he changed
The way we understand the world,
Ourselves and much besides. He'd ranged
Across a spread of diverse facts
To show us how they fall in place.
He altered sense of what we thought
We knew. But soon his critics' mace
Had tried to smash his scheme because,
Without the gene, it falls apart;
As Fleming Jenkin showed beyond
Dispute. But now we know the heart
Of Darwin's tome was right. It's since
We've understood the genes and role
Of DNA his book became
The key to how we view the whole
Of life on earth and more besides.
The fact his theory failed in part,
At time proposed, is lot of all
Who break the mould and thus depart
From what we thought we knew before.
We only grasp a part of truth

216

As much remains concealed. In time
Another eager, dogged youth
Will open eyes to knowledge long
Disguised by prior modes of thought
Impeding search by wasting years
In cul-de-sacs that we'd been taught
Were fruitful routes to new delights.
But then a piece of luck, or work
By rebel, unimpressed by tale
In textbook's dodgy claims, will jerk
Us free from dogma long assumed,
But based on guess alone. The same
Applies in daily life when people talk
Of other folk in gossip's game.
From tiny facts a person's name
Is made to seem as lacking white,
Until we learn the portrait formed
In mind is far from being right.
However skilled we claim our art,
We only ever know in part.

STILL LEARNING (CW)

Today the cult of youth exceeds
All sense. But as a kid, whose life
Was not much fun, I longed to be
A grownup free to do my thing
Without constraints that seemed to box
Me in at every turn. As boy
I wished to go my way instead
Of endless grind ingesting facts
For pointless tests, exams I do
In slow pursuit of subjects learned
For sake of mix required to get
A place to study more when school
Is left behind at last. It's not
Until I could pursue my own desires,
And teach myself as I proceed,
That I became a man at last.
It's only then I felt I'm free.

As scientist of some renown,
I'm really child again amongst
Array of novel toys I'm left

Alone to relish at my ease.
But since the crawl of time had ceased
To drag, I've found it leaks away
At breathless speed I can't restrain.
I wish I could reuse the waste
Of hours I spent in childhood's days.
Or did the feed of futile facts
Create desire to seek the holes
In spread of what was known and make
Me have a go at filling some?
And this I've done, but still the lure
Of next prevents me feeling fed.
As long as day persists the hunt
For clues remains my restless quest,
As is our ceaseless search for God,
Who summons us to stay the course.

After a severe storm when about 100 trees on the nature reserve were toppled over, some had blocked the estate road between our home and the Centre. One was across the telephone line. I was on a ladder trying to free it, when it suddenly sprung clear but then whipped back and caught the top of the ladder causing me to fall. I was somewhat bruised and hobbled a bit for a few days. Sometime later my left eye seemed foggy in the middle. My GP sent me to Airedale Hospital for investigation. They diagnosed Central Retinal Vasculitis, and thought it might be a delayed reaction from the fall. An amusing incident occurred one night. Having been the only patient in the ward who had declined the offer of sleeping tablets I was sound asleep when a confused old man had climbed into my bed beside me. I never stirred as the nurses carefully extracted him. I only learned about the incident in the morning!

My former colleague from Cameroon, who had previously worked at Moorfields Eye Hospital in London, arranged for his former colleague there to do a thorough examination, which confirmed that the flow of an artery supplying blood to the middle of the retina had become blocked so that the adjacent capillaries had taken over the flow and become swollen as a result. I still had a sound right eye so was little inconvenienced by this impediment until 2012 (see chapter 10).

I had employed a local disabled lass, Marion, to help part time with washing up and other duties. When the opportunity arose I reorganized the allocation of duties and appointed her caterer cum bookkeeper, as being the two sitting down components of the posts of cook-caterer and housekeeper plus bookkeeper. Furthermore I allowed her to stay living in Settle as my remit was that as long as the catering was accomplished and the books balanced it did not require her to live in. Furthermore if a blizzard prevented her car getting up onto the Moor then she could work at home until the weather improved. I got a query from Head Office in London enquiring as to why I had not allocated jobs according to standard FSC practice? Anyway she was appointed to a salaried post for the first time in her life, became a very loyal member of the staff until retirement with a pension. When it was her 70th birthday the family invited Audrey and myself to a special celebration in a grand Yorkshire restaurant cum pub. The family kept expressing their gratitude that we had employed Marion in a 'proper' salaried job.

On a later occasion the then Director decided to circulate all staff at all the FSC Field Centres with a questionnaire requiring a breakdown in percentages of the time they spent on their various duties. In principle I could see this would provide him with useful information. In a preliminary trial he selected a representative of each staff category. I was the Field Centre Warden chosen for this. I pointed out that his list of duties did not allow for an activity scoring twice, which explained why my percentage figures added up to a figure over 100%! Thus some of my research activities became incorporated in my teaching. For example my research comparing collecting methods for insects became part of my teaching programme on University courses. In the final 'comments' section I pointed out that, unlike other staff, the contracts for Wardens explicitly stated that they did not have fixed hours of work. Instead there was a list of their responsibilities. When spending time, for example on my National Park Planning Authority obligations, that were not part of my FSC responsibilities, that was not hours 'lost' to the FSC. I concluded that the exercise was therefore not appropriate for Wardens.

A previous Director had been somewhat taken aback by my response to a confidential memo sent to the Wardens of all the Field Centres. In the 1970s economic cutbacks caused some Local Education Authorities to cease funding students going on field courses. This was causing serious problems for the financial viability of the FSC. The Director's memo required me to list the order in which I would lay off staff if it came to the crunch. I put myself as the first to be laid off, as this would save the greatest amount of money. I put the cook last to be laid off. The Director phoned me and asked me "what would happen if the Acting Head, my Deputy, was unable to cope with an unexpected problem?" I replied that he would contact him for the answer, as that was why the Director was paid more than the rest of us. I added that I did not wish to lose my job. My suggestion was an honest response to what I considered would be in the best interests of the Centre.

As a manager myself I was, of course, learning all the time. When there seemed to be an unfortunate gulf between my academic staff and the rest (cooks, catering, domestic, administrative, handyman and estateman) I used a small grant for my research to employ one of the domestic staff (Alison Woods) part time as a tutor teaching some of my days on courses for Sixth Form students. She in fact became a co-author of the paper comparing collecting methods for insects (see above). Later there was a bit of a problem when the long serving estateman Harry had retired. I had transferred the handyman, Arnold, to being the estateman. Arnold was literally a poacher turned gamekeeper! He had a deep understanding of the countryside and was an excellent worker. He carried out the tasks I allocated to him to my entire satisfaction. However, there was no way he was going to keep regular hours! If he had overslept after a night at the village pub next day he would be working late into the evening instead. Some of my staff complained to me about his irregular hours. They seemed puzzled by my response that as long as he did the work I had assigned him then I was going to let him carry on his somewhat irregular routine. Clearly the teaching staff, cooks, etc. were obliged to keep regular hours. Besides there was no dissent with regard to the irregular remit I had given the disabled Marion, despite my allocation of tasks to her having been questioned by Head Office (see above).

Fortunately only a few times, was I obliged to sack a member of staff. For one I had no choice as he, a seasonal domestic assistant from Germany, had broken into the office and stolen his wages to pay for his, unknown to us, drug habit. He was deported by the court. The others were unfortunate and upsetting for me as well as them. The first was a young man whose behaviour became increasingly unacceptable. The final unforgivable act was when late one evening he laid a minefield of drawing pins, points up, from a student bedroom to the toilet. An office worker had to go when we discovered that she had lied about having dealt with some correspondence and had then been discovered to have had a boyfriend to stay surreptitiously not only without permission but thereby avoiding having to pay the basic fee charged for staff guests (to cover meals, etc.). It seems her priority was to her boyfriend and her obligations to her job and the Centre took second place. Two Swedish seasonal domestic assistants complained to me that they objected to the overzealous supervision by my excellent housekeeper. So I asked the latter to give me her side of the story. She said they needed close supervision because when, for example, they pushed open the door of a toilet to sweep the floor they neglected to look behind the door where rubbish remained! When I recalled the two assistants and said the level of supervision would relax when they showed it was no longer needed they reacted by resigning. They moved to a hotel in the south of England, but a few weeks later pleaded to be rehired. They found the supervision at the hotel made us look relaxed by comparison! We, however, did not re-employ them as we had in the meantime taken on replacements. Having to sack people was an aspect of management that I found upsetting. A cook became a problem when he regularly failed to return after his days off and appeared later with a doctor's certificate saying he had needed to take a rest. I contacted his doctor, who was as clearly fed up with our cook as we were. So I gave the cook the option of either stopping this nonsense or resigning on the grounds of ill health. He resigned. Apart from these unfortunate losses of staff, I was forever grateful that most of my staff were loyal, agreeable and carried out their duties satisfactorily.

I became a churchwarden and got to know local farmers and others better than before. Also my faith was growing until I gradually began to feel a sense of vocation. After discussion with the vicar I was seen by the Diocesan Director of Ordinands prior to an interview with the Bishop of Bradford. In due course

I attended a selection conference. I evidently split the selectors into two camps. At least one considered me too 'heretical'! The result was a recommendation to my bishop to not put me forward for training for the priesthood. I felt perplexed by this decision, as I had been sure I had been prompted by an inner compulsion to put myself forward. The Bishop, however, evidently reckoned my sense of having experienced a vocation to a special calling to be a 'minister' within the church had been genuine. His unexpected response was to recommend me to the then Advisory Council for the Church's Ministry as one of his pastoral selectors for candidates for ordination! He thus led me to experience and ponder deeply what a special calling entailed. I gradually came to understand that the bishop realized that I was too 'liberal' in my rejection of much of the cultural and historical baggage in the Bible that tended to obscure the pure gold of the Gospel. Many in the Church of England were not ready for this. The bishop, however, reckoned that as a selector I would perhaps contribute to the C of E gradually adjusting to a more mature understanding of what being a Christian in the 20th Century entailed. The idolatry of Scripture still persists amongst a minority of priests in the 21st Century.

As regards my own sense of having felt I was being called to a 'special' service, I gradually came to realize that a call to service is the universal call to all followers of Christ. Ordination is just one particular option that selectors are called upon to evaluate. Indeed, as my reputation as a scientist grew I came to the realization that scientists (especially biologists) of my generation who were Christians and who openly perceived no conflict between their faith and their science were uncommon. Was I, perhaps, being called upon to witness in my person that there was no conflict between contemporary science and being a follower of Christ? Furthermore the increasing requests to use my ever growing expertise to help others became the driving force of my science.

HOLY ORDERS? (CO)

To spend a life researching flies
Is odd at least; but even I
Am called to enter Kingdom's feast.
In past I've felt a nagging call
To serve my Lord in overt role.
But no, it seems my way is meant
To be the use of arcane skills,
At sorting tiny scuttle flies,
To transform even this strange game
By letting grace employ my time
As means of service unforeseen
And out of sight. Indeed the thought
I might be led to help police
In solving crimes, or farmers far

Away with pest control, had not
Been in my mind when I embarked
On first attempts to name some flies
I'd caught on Pennine hills. But soon
Requests to do the same for those
Researching problems far and wide
Became a constant theme until
It seems I'm now an expert world
Renowned. In fact I'm still a boy
Intrigued by tiny creatures found
Beyond the scale of daily round.
Their secret lives reveal a scene
Of wars and symbiotic themes
I'd never dreamed were taking place
Beneath my lawn. I'd never thought
I'd see myself assisting those
In lands I had to find on map
Or those in nations scorned by press
For 'backward' ways, or evil rule,
Or strange beliefs. But now I know
My knowledge slowly gained is used
As means of reaching helping hand
Across the walls of creed and race:
And often putting name beside
My own, on papers sent for print,
Has lifted self-esteem of those
Who feel they're second best because
They're not in famous lab in West.
By saying yes to each request
To help these folk I've lost the hours
I'd meant to give to projects planned.
But sense of gain now far exceeds
The hopes I'd entertained for schemes
I now perceive will never be.
It seems that even monkish life,
Of self-indulgent search for truth,
Can be transformed to means of grace.
Despite the endless doubts of self,
About my way of spending time.
Perhaps I'm priest in this small field.
Perhaps we're only called to share
Our humble skills as sacred gifts.

With regard to assessing candidates for ordination there were those whose potential was clearly evident but 'not yet' was our decision. In such cases we tried to recommend a course of action before they re-apply. For example:

CALL ON HOLD (GK)

He's shaped by best of private schools
And then by Oxford, as his dad
Before. Without intent and not
Aware, he acts as though he's glad
He's not as other folk. He's shunned
By some who think he's haughty snob.
He just assumes they're shy. He feels
A call to be a priest as job
In which he'll serve and lead. But when
Selectors put him through their sieve
They come to common view. He needs
To learn about the way to live
With poor, who lack the things he takes
For granted in his life. It's thus
He finds himself at work abroad
In city slum. When stirring fuss,
With those who rule, he's shown the door.
Apart from sponsor's funds, he's on
His own, with mission's monk, to try
Their best to rectify the non
Existent hopes of those they seek
To serve. Their resignation galls;
But slowly, step by step, he finds
Himself the same, as vision palls.
A gloom engulfs his soul, as bit
By bit his drive for action wilts.
But now compassion starts to grow.
As love enfolds his spirit lilts.

One of the most unexpected occurrences was when my Deputy came to me one day and said she could no longer teach the age of the carboniferous rocks as given in the textbooks. This was most unexpected as I regarded her as a fine geologist and a gifted teacher. It turned out that a medical doctor from Leeds who was a fundamentalist had got at her and convinced her that science had got it all wrong! I told her that she must continue to teach the ages of the rocks as given in the textbooks as that is what the GCE 'A' level syllabus required. If she did not agree then it was up to her to hand in her resignation. It was impossible to reason with her. For example she told me Moses wrote the first

223

five books of the Bible. I replied that he couldn't have done as it describes his death in the fifth. Her response was that she didn't know how to explain that but she knew in heart that she was right. I replied that I knew in my heart that she was mistaken, but I preferred to discuss evidence not feelings of the heart. I got a friend of hers (from another FSC Field Centre), who was a fine geographer but had been brought up as a fundamentalist, to try to make her see sense, but no avail. Likewise the FSC Director was equally baffled. It seemed to us that by her espousal of fundamentalism she had ousted her former critical appraisal of evidence and it had been replaced by an irrational treatment of the Bible that ignored the contradictions between books composed at different times and with different understandings of God and our relation to Him. An idolatry of 'Scripture' (be it books of the Bible or the Koran) is the essential error of fundamentalism.

CONTRADICTIONS (GK)

Despite the prophets crying out
Against who burden poor with rules,
They mine the Pentateuch for clues
Along with rest of Jewish texts
Of old. They won't admit they're not
A seamless whole, their authors all
Anon by name, that parts are lost
For good, that contradictions reign.
The view of God as tyrant king
Requiring sacrifice to calm
His rage is cartoon lie. This book
Of many books does not convey
Coherent view. Indeed relief
Is felt as tribal texts are left
Behind and Gospels give us blaze
Of light awash with love of Christ,
Who claimed his soul at one with God.
Let scholars probe the lists of rules
Impeding gift of grace that's free
From nagging sense of guilt induced.
For most the call to join the ranks
Of learner saints is all we need
To follow way that Jesus taught.
It works for justice, peace and world
That's free of greed and need to win
Success at other's cost. It dreams
Of everyone fulfilled by time
Of death, our gate to ceaseless bliss.

For her degree my deputy had learned of the geological evidence for evolution and she had been teaching our students for years about the antiquity of the rocks of the landscape of Malham Moor. Her rejection of evolution was total, unlike a theologian I encountered later who accepted evolution but regarded natural selection as secondary to God's 'guiding' of the process!

CHOICES (GK)

She won't accept our science means
That random throws of dice provide
The grist for evolution's mill.
She feels there must be secret guide
To urge the process forward till
We humans first appeared on scene.
In symbiosis, selfless acts,
She sees a driving purpose keen
To gain award of conscious thought.
But such a fairy tale is blind
To teeming bands of parasites
And warring beasts, all far from kind.
The odd and even numbers on
The dice had equal chance of win
At every hopeful roll. In time,
A run of luck began to spin
And weave a better brain until
It freed itself from robot rules
As choice prevailed. At first it's case
Of making many useful tools
To ease our lot in life. But soon
We came to wonder what we're all
About, and whether conscious thought
Is means by which we hear the call
To reach for God by way of love,
Enhanced by Holy Spirit's grace.
Indeed the Gospel tells us straight
We humans are a chosen race.

My deputy eventually realized she would have to hand in her resignation if unwilling to abide by my instruction to teach the textbook version of the age of the rocks on which the Field Centre was standing. We tried to keep in touch but after a time the American funded sect she had joined forbade her to communicate with us. I was particularly condemned because I was a churchwarden and yet I published on evolution (e.g. see above my 'A synopsis of the taxonomist's tasks, with particular attention to phylogenetic cladism', which we sold in Field Centre's office)! My army service (chapter 2) and commitment to my science had helped to free me from the obsolete cultural perceptions of many authors of books of the Bible that tended to obscure the Gospel of Christ. It is evident to most readers that much of the Old Testament is marred by what today we would designate as spin. Thus when the Jews won a battle it was because God had favoured their side. When they lost it was because they had displeased God and thereby invoked his wrath. It is unfortunate that New Testament writers too often found it difficult to jettison this anachronistic and atavistic notion of God's wrath, despite the Gospel teaching that God is the ultimate in terms of love, mercy, compassion, etc. Fundamentalists who threaten one with God's wrath if one doesn't espouse their perverted version of the Gospel are not only to be pitied but their threats are to be strongly condemned. Their condemnation of myself recalled my experiences with the problem of belief in jujus in Cameroon. In particular when I nearly died of cerebral malaria and I had concluded that the attribution of my coma to a juju was perhaps not unlike an Old Testament view that some agent must be to blame for natural disasters and afflictions; and that among such some were the result of the wrath of God. A view that lingers in the minds of even some intelligent people in Britain (see chapter 7). My military service had immunized me against a theology divorced from the realities of living in a complex world. My science ensured that beliefs I espoused were intellectually defensible and open to reappraisal if new data were to indicate a need for revision. Much in the Bible records mistaken interpretations of events before the liberating impact of the Gospel, and the unfortunate persistence of these misconceptions in some of the New Testament writings.

FUNDAMENTALLY MISTAKEN? (GK)

He claims his trust in Pentateuch
As telling truths beyond dispute
Entails belief that much that's taught
By science must be wrong. To shoot
Him down with naked facts will not
Suffice to change his mind. He cites
The sightings, people tell the press,
Of mystery, slowly moving, lights
Observed by watchers seeking signs
Of visits made to earth by folk
From other worlds a trillion miles,
Or more, away. He doesn't joke.
When pointed out that most reports
Are soon resolved as mundane things,
His swift retort is some remain

To be explained. It's thus he clings
To fact that science still remains
In dark about a range of strange
Accounts. From this he then proceeds
To claim, because enormous range
Remains to be explored, we must
Ignore the knowledge gained to date.
Unless we build on what we know
We'll find ourselves in mental state
When black is white, the moon is made
Of cheese and sea is marmalade.

Biologists and others who dismiss all religion can be equally entrenched, despite the fact that science as science can neither prove nor disprove the existence of God. Indeed fundamentalist atheism can be as indefensible as fundamentalist religion (see my comments on Richard Dawkins in chapter 10). In America the so-called 'creationists' are deeply entrenched, as discussed in a timely article (Marsden, G. M., 1983, Creation versus evolution: no middle way. Nature 305 (5935): 571-574) published just after another fundamentalist had condemned my claim to be Christian as heresy because of my simultaneous acceptance of evolution! However, I was now resigned to the fact that communication with such closed minds is a waste of time. One can but pray for them.

SON OF MAN (CW)

When earnest youth, whose faith is dose
Of tidy dogmas lacking depth,
Declared that I'm a heretic,
A humanist whose claim to be
A Christian will not wash, I caught
A whiff of burning at the stake
If I had lived in former times.
He cannot grasp, when Jesus claimed
To be the Son of Man, He wished
To lift our human selves from mire
Of sterile rites and phoney faiths.
He longed to hitch our daily lives
To God's desires by placing love
Upon the throne of our concerns.
He's humanist before all else,
But knows that truly human means
We need to rise above the beasts,
From whence we came, and feed on bread

Of grace divine, and so transcend
Our merely human lives until
We find emergent soul has won
Eternal crown beyond the grave.

Those critics quick to accuse me of heresy were recent converts of evangelists from America. These American preachers seemed to be characterized by a profound ignorance of science along with an idolatry of Scripture with a capital 'S'.

FUNDAMENTAL FAITHS (GK)

A tiresome man from Bible Belt
Condemns all faiths but his alone.
He thus commits a sin against
The Holy Ghost by setting bounds
To love of God without so much
As by His leave. Another man,
Psychiatrist by trade, condemns
Religion's claims as myths espoused
To fill the voids derived from lack
Of self-esteem: and yet when asked
To give the grounds for his beliefs,
In flimsy theories built on sand,
He loses cool and splutters like
A faulty safety valve atop
An angered pressure cooker. Both
These fools are dug so deep within
Their private pits they cannot see
The landscape as a whole. For both
Are deaf to other points of view,
And make such puerile dins they drown
The voice of Holy Spirit's Word.
They're blind to grace that shapes the lives
Of humble folk that God, who's known
By many names, confers without
Concern for strange beliefs they hold.
As Christ confirmed, the House of God
Has many rooms. His mercy knows
No bounds. His love is ocean wide,
Extending far beyond our reach,
Beyond what human minds can grasp.

RESPONSE (GK)

A preacher's lost for words when Bill
Proclaims his sermon's load of crap.
"It's plain to all but fools that God
Declines to pull the strings. Indeed
If God were in control of world
And universe, which gave it birth
Within created straits of time,
We'd feel secure. We'd lose our fears.
But would we then be free to learn
To love or hate, to worship self
Or seek to serve, to relish joys
And suffer grief until we found
Eternal home with Christ? He went
To cross in place of forcing us
To enter Kingdom's gift. Unless
We choose his way without constraint
Of threat, coercion's theft will rob
Our souls of will that's truly own.
And then his nascent spark of love
Would fade away and leave us cold
To feeling, deaf to needs apart
From selfish drives alone. As beasts
Without the grant of grace we'd sink
Below the human Plimsoll Line
And end our days as soulless junk
Beneath the ocean's heartless swell.
Our lives are only means to end.
I've had my say". The preacher's stunned.
Before riposte he hears his wife
Respond "Amen. I hear the Word at last!"

To me there are three great 19th Century scientific insights that clear away
much past misconceptions in both science and theology. The Darwin/Wallace
theory of evolution by natural selection (more than vindicated in the 20th
Century by advances in molecular biology); the Pasteur, Koch/Lister microbial
theory of infectious diseases; and the Manson, Theobald Smith/Ross discovery
that many parasites of man and other vertebrates require a developmental stage
in an invertebrate host (such as a mosquito). In the 20th Century we gained the
theory of plate tectonics and an understanding of the antiquity of the earth and
even greater antiquity of the universe. Any theology that rejects these gains is
to be rightly condemned and dismissed as being essentially stupid. One can but
feel sorry for such deluded fundamentalists.

This first-hand experience of a valued colleague turning her back on science in favour of a narrow fundamentalist, judgmental creed contributed to me gaining a sense that my vocation had been genuine but misdirected towards the priesthood. My experiences to date had gifted the ability to communicate the Gospel that was compatible with science and varied human conditions. My increasing use of poetry to articulate my perceptions also bridged the supposed gulf between science and the arts. This sense of a special ministry gradually increased along with my growing standing as a productive scientist. Rather than scholarly works on science and religion my poems explore and reflect upon my varied experiences prior to, and subsequent to, me becoming a scientist and a Christian best characterized as being a 'Lapsed atheist' (see chapter 9 and my third collection of poems published in 1995).

In 1981 close to the end of my second three year term as a Ministerial Appointee on the Yorkshire Dales National Park Committee I received a letter from the Minister for Local Government. I was expecting a routine renewal for my third (and final) term as a member of the Committee. Instead it was thanking for my service but terminating my appointment. Over the next few days I learned that all but one of the eight Ministerial Appointees had been similarly dismissed! Then I was phoned by the National Park Officer to ask if I had seen a particular application due to come before the Committee and if so what did I think of it? I replied that I had read it and I had certain questions that I thought needed addressing before a decision could be made. He then wrote down my questions and thanked me, adding that he would ask the Chairman to put the item on the agenda for the afternoon session so that he (the NP Officer) and I could discuss it further over lunch. Surprised, I replied "you haven't heard then. You have lost seven of your eight Ministerial Appointees". He was astounded when I told him about the letters from the Minister. Nobody had told him. He subsequently learned that the remaining Appointee had been renewed for two years only instead of the normal three years term. It transpired that the Government wanted the seven who lived in the National Park removed before the local council elections but the eighth, who lived outside the National Park, to be removed before the General Election! The Thatcher Government evidently thought we were too independent minded as evidenced by our records for what we had voted for or against. In my case it seemed that an additional black mark was that Audrey had stood as a candidate for the Liberal Party in a District Council election! (Incidentally, when Audrey and another lady, for the local Tory Party, were recording people as they went into the village hall to vote in this District Council election it started to rain. So they agreed there was no point in them both getting soaked and they would take it in turns to remain outside the village hall and share their records. The other lady added "Don't tell my husband, but I never vote Tory anyway!"). Later the result of a questionnaire sent, by a former National Park official then at Sheffield University, to all past and present Ministerial Appointees, revealed that a similar dismissal of Ministerial Appointees had occurred on the Committees of the other National Parks and their replacement with members more in tune with

Thatcherite notions. The Government was incensed when these findings were published in an environmental magazine!

An unexpected result of my own dismissal was when the Yorkshire Dales NP Committee decided to commission a report on the environmental values of the Malham Moor complex because of its national and indeed international importance. The National Park Officer persuaded the Committee to give the commission to me. I put my staff onto it and we produced a set of transparent overlay maps for an overhead projector. Each map represented a different set of values (vegetation, archaeological, geological. etc.) with each OS field coloured black for Grade 1, grey for Grade 2 or left blank for Grade 3. The justification for the grades was then provided in a supporting document for each map. I was told this influenced decisions for several years at least.

My involvement with the Yorkshire Council for the Environment and then the Yorkshire Dales National Park Committee taught me much about politics and what is involved if one is to influence the decision making process. Many well-intentioned representations to the Committee had little chance of influencing a decision by not indicating how a proposal related to alternatives. My 3-point ranking in the above example exemplifies how such a representation is more likely to assist the decision making process than a bald assertion that a site is of importance in terms of its archaeology. One is left wondering – How important? Is a proposed use for the site more or less important? Those are the sorts of question a decision maker needs addressing by someone making a submission. Often the preferred choice was far from clear. I recall the occasion when the Initial Draft National Park Plan was being subjected to public consultations that included a meeting in Skipton. The proposed plan regarding sites for tourist caravans in the National Park was challenged. The Plan proposed a limited number of tightly regulated sensitively chosen sites be allowed. A farmer said that all tourist caravans should be banned from the National Park. A representative of a caravan club objected, and said there should be unrestricted access throughout the Park. Meadows and pastures should be accessible to all. The Chairman smiled and observed that the proposed policy in the draft Plan was about midway between those two views!

1982: my second poetry collection published – QUESTINGS (Chester House Publications, 54 pages).

In 1982 Michael Usher (then at York University) and I ran a ten day course primarily aimed at advisors from the Government's Agricultural Development and Advisory Service on evaluating the conservation value of habitats, especially farmland. From the discussions at the end of this course was born the proposal for what became a landmark book on this topic. It was edited by Michael and I contributed a chapter (Disney, R. H. L., 1986. Assessments using invertebrates: posing the problem. Chapter 12: 271-293. In Usher, M. B.

(Editor). Wildlife Conservation Evaluation. Chapman and Hall, London. 394pp).

In 1982 we had a memorable holiday for the whole family at Aviemore in Scotland. By now the children were starting to depart from home for much of the year. It had started when Audrey had spotted a notice about it and Trudy had won the North Yorkshire scholarship to Atlantic College (the first of the United World Colleges) in South Wales. Adrian was to follow her there, but on a bursary. Little did we expect that after his prolonged stay in hospital in 1997 (see chapter 9) he would return to Atlantic College as a biology teacher.

In 1983 the first four titles of the Naturalists' Handbooks commissioned and co-edited by Sally Corbet and myself were published (see appendix G) and were well received by the reviewers.

Also in 1983 I was asked to contribute to a special volume of the journal Field Studies and decided to respond to requests from teachers to give a simple introduction to taxonomy and the recent developments in taxonomy and the arguments about how to classify species in higher categories (genera, families, etc.) (Disney, R. H. L., 1983. A synopsis of the taxonomist's tasks, with particular attention to phylogenetic cladism. Field Studies 5(5): 841-865). This was also well received.

The year 1983 was to be remembered for a very different reason by not only myself but by Audrey and the children, as it unexpectedly was to prove to be our last year in Yorkshire.

Leaving Yorkshire

In 1983 I was the Unit Manager next in line for a three month sabbatical. I was in fact exploring the possibility of an overseas entomological trip (see chapter 9) when the following unexpected event came out of the blue.

The move from Malham Tarn was precipitated by a misapprehension by the then Chairman of the Field Studies Council Executive Committee. During 1983 he dropped in at the Field Centre and I had briefly chatted with him in the staff dining room during a coffee break. Otherwise we did not encounter each other during his brief visit. I only later learned that he had concluded that I was doing my own thing at home (half a mile from the main centre). He had failed to take in that I was on holiday but we had decided not to go away but to catch up on things and to make local excursions and visits with the children instead. Added to this misapprehension the Chairman was known to have been somewhat annoyed when I had been appointed to the post of Warden of the Field Centre in 1971 instead of his strongly backed candidate for the post. He had been further annoyed when he had sent a memo to all Unit Managers with certain proposals which required a response before the next Senior Staff meeting. My fellow Unit Managers rightly perceived the proposals to be based on false assumptions and unrealistic predictions and so had binned the memo. I, however, had sent a response pointing out why his proposals were unacceptable. At the subsequent Senior Staff Meeting he first reprimanded my colleagues for not responding to his memo. He then thanked me for responding but added that he rejected my response. My colleagues, however, supported my response to his memo!

The shock came at the end of the year when the Unit Managers of the Field Centres and other FSC units assembled at a field centre for a weekend. During this annual event each unit manager was interviewed by a subset of the Executive Committee in order to review the performance of his or her Centre. In my case the EC subset was chaired by the Chairman. He opened the proceedings by saying he was going to read me a statement before handing me a copy. I would not be allowed to ask any questions and the meeting would then be closed. What he read out was a notice of dismissal. No explanations, no reasons, no evidence. I departed in a state of shock. Apart from anything else his action was contrary to the law relating to unfair dismissal and I had been denied a colleague of my choice as a witness to the proceedings.

On return to Yorkshire the FSC Research Director, Jenny Baker, sent me photocopies of the legislation about unfair dismissal. So I then consulted a politically Liberal, woman solicitor. She sent the Chairman (said by some colleagues to be an admirer of the ruthless type of management that became common during Thatcher's time as Prime Minister) a letter telling him that if we went to Tribunal I would win as his act of dismissal had been illegal on several counts. He sought legal advice and was told my legal advice was correct. Meanwhile colleagues at other Centres were urging me to go to Tribunal. Instead I circulated members of the Executive Committee with my perceptions of the situation. Several contacted me expressing their shock. The Chairman, determined to have me removed from Malham Tarn, managed to obtain funding to set me up as a Research Fellow, by preference in the Zoology Department at Oxford University. The Director was sent to Malham Tarn to put this proposal to me. By now we were deep in snow. The Director had to abandon his car about a mile from the Centre, because of the snow, and to walk the rest of the way. He laid the proposal before me and asked what I thought of it. I replied that it was an interesting idea. He then asked was I going to accept. I replied that I would consider no proposal, however attractive, until the notice of my dismissal had been rescinded by the Executive Committee and this had been recorded in the minutes. A disconsolate Director returned to his car to report my response to the Chairman. Incidentally, I had appointed the Director as a tutor at the Field Centre, he then became my Deputy before he went on to become in charge of another FSC Field Centre prior to becoming Director of the FSC. He, therefore, well knew I was an obstinate so-and-so when it came to standing up for what I considered to be a right course of action.

A special meeting of the Executive Committee was convened in London, with the President of the FSC in the Chair. Myself and staff representatives were excluded from the morning session. Audrey had come to London with me and when I was admitted she gate crashed the meeting and gave forth her condemnation of the Chairman's attempt to dismiss me. She then stormed out.

233

A colleague went out and caught up with her and brought her back to wait outside the committee room. The dismissal notice was formally rescinded. Afterwards Audrey wrote to the President apologizing for her intervention at a meeting to which she was not entitled to attend, but not apologizing for what she had said. He replied with a long hand written letter with apologies expressed, on behalf of the FSC, for the stress to which she and I had been subjected for three months. However, he added at the end that the Chairman would still prefer me to leave Malham Tarn. Audrey and I considered this carefully and concluded I would be like a mouse with a cat watching the entrance to its refuge waiting to pounce if I emerged. So I agreed to accept the Research Fellowship.

As instructed I wrote to Professor Sir Richard Southwood, Head of Zoology at Oxford. Professor Bob May (later Lord May) replied that Sir Richard was on sabbatical and he was Acting Head. He had been about to say yes when he found Sir Richard had a file on me (I had identified phorid flies for him. Indeed I had named a South African species after him and was later to name a species he sent me from France after him) and thought he had better consult him when he returned from an overseas trip. When a friend at Cambridge learned what was going on he set in motion discussions leading to the Head of Department of Zoology and Director of its Museum of Zoology agreeing to accept the FSC Research Fellowship, which would be based in the Museum.

The sort of treatment of an employee that precipitated this move had become all too common in the mid-1980s. Indeed we learned afterwards that the Chairman had planned to follow my dismissal with that of two fellow Unit Managers towards whom he felt antipathy. Several colleagues said it was fortunate that he picked on me first as I was the one who had been prepared not only to challenge him but had demonstrated that I had known how to set about doing so.

HOLLOW VICTORY? (CO)

The dawn aflame with every shade
Of red and orange hue had caused
Him pause. He knew his time was short,
And early fires in sky foretell
Of storm ahead. Today he's due
To meet with man who tried to sack
Him twenty years ago, because
He feared his independent mind
And couldn't cope with those who stood
Their ground in real debate; despite
The fact he'd made a token call
For comments on his crazy plan
For change. Our friend had called his bluff.
By taking every clause apart,
His logic won the day. Today
They come in different roles to play
Another game. It seems a rage
Those many years ago remained
Beneath the surface charm that's thin
As varnish film on portrait hung
On panelled wall behind. Revenge
Now seeped from every pore. He saw
A chance to scupper scheme our friend
Proposed for good of all. The tricks
And ploys he now employed were black
Indeed. The playground bully strode
From field of sordid gain with smirk
Of triumph sprawled across his face.
Our friend beheld his years of work
In shards and knew antipathy
To him alone, not reason, won
That day. With sorrow in his heart
He left the room. He pities man
Who treated folk with such contempt,
When loss of face required retreat
From all he wanted in the end.
Our friend, with broken will, now heeds
The call to cross the murky deeps
Of swirling river in a boat,
As western sky with every tint
Of red and gold made welcome blaze
Announcing better life beyond.

FROM NATURE'S BOUNTY (GK)

It may be figments in the mind
When I rejoice in scene of hill
And dale, with lake reflecting sky
And trees, and hear the dancing rill
Beside the grazing sheep whose lambs
Express the joy of spring in games
Of pure delight. And at my feet
The flowers bloom with ancient names
Invoking past when each was thought
To signify a blessing sent
By God, who'd chosen each in turn.
The loss of such beliefs that went
When science told a different tale
I don't lament, for Darwin gave
Us key to understand that death
Is need of nature. When we crave
Forbidden fruits it's not because
A devil tempted Eve, it's part
Of way we stay alive. We're free
To try our luck or heed our hearts,
In which the secret seeds of grace
Await response. We're called
To open doors that lead to births
Of souls, where lasting love's installed.
What they select for praises now,
From nature's bounty on display,
We will embrace, imbue with joy,
Despite the darker side to play.

It was difficult to accept that we were to leave Malham Tarn. Not only would I miss it, but also for Audrey and the children it would be especially hard. For the children it was home and their friends went to school with them. Audrey was much appreciated in the local community and at the Field Centre. Indeed she was the best Field Centre Secretary not only as far as I was concerned but also according to our visitors, who greatly appreciated her cheerfulness and helpfulness.

REGRETS (TL)

'I've no regrets' declared a man
Whose wife had left him long ago.
If only I, with hand on heart,
Could say the same as he. But no.
There's much that I reproach myself
For saying out of turn. I'm like
A clumsy kid, retrieving ball,
Who treads on precious plants I've raised
With endless care. He's unaware
Of grief I feel as hulking feet
Now crush my pride and joy. It seems
It's only as I learn to curb
My thoughtless tongue I earn the right
To stay with she I love beyond
All else I've known, or ever wished.

CHAPTER 9

CAMBRIDGE ONE

1984-1998: Field Studies Council Research Fellowship, Department of Zoology, University of Cambridge (until 1991 funded by the Mary Snow Trust: from 1991 to 1993 funded by the Isaac Newton Trust of Trinity College and the Wingate Foundation: from 1994 to 1996 funded by the Leverhulme Trust and the Isaac Newton Trust: from 1997-1998 mainly funded by the Isaac Newton Trust with some funding from the FSC).

The cost of housing in Cambridge was at least twice what it was in Yorkshire and with the FSC being a charity, the salaries were adequate but not sufficient for a straight forward mortgage. The option was to live in Ely or a village away from Cambridge or dispense with our car and live in Cambridge. We went for the latter option. It proved to be the right decision. In Yorkshire we were dependent on our car as we had lived beyond public transport. In Cambridge if we needed to get to a remote village for a wedding or whatever we hired a car for the day. With the rising costs of running a car we reckoned we ended up saving several thousand pounds per year. While I made a little extra money doing occasional editorial jobs it was money earned by Audrey that enabled us to survive financially, allowing us to just keep up the regular payments on the house. Initially she did a number of cleaning jobs, etc., until more interesting employment (office assistant, secretarial, etc.) came along. By this means we just managed on a very tight budget for the twenty years of our mortgage, with typically the last week of each month our bank account dipping a little into the red. Fortunately it wasn't long before Audrey progressed from the boring chores of office cleaning to jobs utilizing her secretarial and other skills. Initially she moved to a job at Tyndale House (in Selwyn Gardens west of the Cam). While this involved cleaning and additional chores she met the residents and others and organized coffee breaks, etc. It was an odd experience. There were one or two genuine Biblical scholars and a very down-to-earth cheerful gardener. Most were over earnest American PhD students working on highly obscure bits of the Old Testament. They seemed almost idolatrous of Scripture with a capital S and deficient in humour. When one day Audrey put out no biscuits for the morning coffee break, but instead displayed a book from the library entitled A CELEBRATION OF DISCIPLINE it took them a while to realize it was a joke! Later she moved to more agreeable work; as an

239

Assistant Librarian in the Haddon Library of the Faculty of Archaeology and Anthropology, and then in the Office of the Scott Polar Research Institute until retirement from University employment. She was in fact somewhat past retirement age when the SPRI received a memo from the Old Schools (the central administration of the University) demanding to know why Mrs Disney was still being employed well past the obligatory retiring age. The SPRI had not realized how old she was as Audrey was always so cheerful, friendly to all and frequently singing away to herself as she went about some task!

After 'retirement' Audrey was then the first Secretary for the Milton Children's Hospice at the stage when they were raising money in order to get the project off the ground. Later she became secretary to the Link House Trust, which provides a residential community for overseas research students who lack a college placement. She continued doing voluntary work for the Trust after her retirement as well as being a volunteer in the Amnesty second-hand bookshop, giving extra tuition to a girl in a local secondary school (the girl being quite bright, but her single mum had gone off with another woman's husband before leaving her daughter in the care of his wife and another man she had then teamed up with); and at the University's Botanic Gardens, where she helped in the shop and with the collection of seeds.

The move from the Pennines to the flat lands of East Anglia was quite a contrast. Indeed one fine Saturday I suggested to Audrey that we cycle to the Gog Magog Hills south of Cambridge, as I recalled that as a student I had found it was a good place to walk and see some unusual wild flowers. After cycling some time I paused and said I was sure it wasn't this far. The 'minor' hill we had passed had not registered after living above 300 metres altitude! The Pennine landscape had become a part of my mental landscape:

FOUNTAINS FELL, YORKSHIRE (GK)

You thought this windswept fell was bleak
When walking on a summer's day
In gentle breeze when skies were blue
And sheep were grazing by a stream,
Which drains the peat that blankets cap
Of millstone grit. I relish slope
Of varied hues reflecting bands
Of different rocks that underlie
The patchwork quilt of diverse plants.
Its many moods, from gentle sun
To driving rain, to drifting snow.
To thunder storm with bouncing hail
In fearsome rage, before a calm
In which the larks proclaim that spring
Is here and grouse demand that we
Retreat – 'Go back! Go back! Go back!'
They cry. As I recline beside
A wall of drystone blocks, all laid
With skill and care, the view of dale
Below becomes a living map
That's shaped by years of patient toil.
It seems to be I'm lifted up
Above the petty squabbles, loves
Awry and gossip marring peace
That should prevail in such a scene.
I've learned romantic view of life
Requires a distant view or else
The truth is likely to intrude
And topple lofty thoughts. Despite
This constant risk, I still insist
To walk this fell revives my soul.
I don't know why, but in my dreams
I often wander here alone.

CONTINGENCY AND DESIGN (MC)
(First published in 1997 in FSC Magazine 13: 5.)

A Pennine wall of limestone blocks
Is symbol deep within my mind.
It feeds my wish to comprehend.
The way old Joe contrived to build
This work of art, from trailer load
Of random rocks, recalls the means
That God employs to utilize
Ourselves. Each piece a hopeless choice
For those who claim that only bricks,
Or stones all sawn and shaped to rule,
Are good for building walls to last.
But Joe prefers his jumbled heap.
With practiced eye, and sometimes curse
At accidental forms, he knows
That once the first is put in place
Adventure lies ahead. The space
Defined at every stage directs
The choice to come. An awkward slab,
Of stubborn weight, becomes a beam
That tames discordant tearaways,
Until the capstones bind as one
The two opposing teams of stones;
For each of which more ruly minds
Might just discard as worthless trash.
Likewise the rubble that remains
Now fills the potholes in the track,
Which runs beside the splendid wall,
And thus performs a humbler role.
Our Joe does not believe in waste.

Gradually, with time the grounds of the college gardens and the flat fenland landscape became a part of my mental landscape:

A CAMBRIDGE COLLEGE GARDEN (RE)

No need to roam in wind beside
A lake to find a joyful dance
Of glory daffodils. In spring,
In Peterhouse's garden, squills
And awesome spread of yellows, white
With orange trumpets, take one's breath
Away. It seems that nature tamed
Creates a feeling only dreams
Convey. One's child again in tale
Of secret garden. Time has ceased.
We half expect an elf to dance
With joy beyond a tree bedecked
In blossom sprinkled from the wand
Of fairy queen. We pass a seat
With don who's laid a heavy tome
Aside to drink the scene in calm
Repose. He's found a gentle peace
With wisdom reaching back to past
Before the days of learning stored
In books. He watches thrush with snail
It strikes against a stone. He sees
A squirrel's agile run deflect
A bough all hung with catkin tails.
A ladybird enjoys the sun
On gravel path. He feels his mind
Relax as warring thoughts subside.
This garden's greater work of art
Than much that's hung on walls within
The museum backing eastern edge
Beyond this gently healing spread.

EXPLICIT RECOGNITION (CW)

I'd walked this way a thousand times,
But not until a painter froze
The scene did I perceive how well
It is composed, how apt the blend
Of trees and buildings well designed,
How right that moody river flows
Below to mirror sky and all
Beneath. Since artist's eye discerned
Its worth, so now I slow my pace
To relish daily walk. I sense
That I, at last, am now a part
Of piece of paradise on earth,
In which I've long so felt at ease.

Coming after working in Cameroon, the move from rural Yorkshire to the city also required a change of habits and expectations. In Yorkshire everyone knew everyone else who lived nearby and one always greeted people walking the Pennine Way along the Estate Road. If approached by a stranger one assumed they had some legitimate enquiry. In Cambridge one knew only a few who lived in the same road, passing strangers looked surprised if one greeted them and one was sometimes embarrassed when one was approached by strangers:

ACCOSTED (CW)

Her face was overdone.
Her dress was quite reverse,
As bosom half exposed
Invited lustful glance.
She plucked my sleeve and smiled
A pleading look and asked
If I desired a fling.
It's only then I grasped
Her lowly trade. I made
Excuse and fled in haste.
But now I wonder how
She'd come to sink so low.
What failures, sorrows, pained
Her so? Has man, whose child
She bore, deserted just
As soon as need was most
Acute? Should I have stayed

And tried to help her find
Support to free her from
Her present plight and fate?
Or would she laugh at my
Concern and quickly leave
Me feeling meddling fool?
Perhaps she chose her life.
Perhaps the risks involved
Provide a fleeting thrill
That tempts her empty heart.

NEEDY? (TL)

A man in evident distress
Approaches me and pleads for help.
He's just been mugged and needs the fare
To get the train to where he lives.
He writes his name and home address
On scrap of paper in exchange
For cash. It's only when my card
Returns, 'address unknown' is scrawled
Across its face, I learn that guy
Could earn an Oscar for his skills
As actor born and bred. I shrug
The rat aside. But now I know
Not how to tell apart a man
In want and con. To former I'm
A mean and hardened bloke who thinks
Of self alone. To latter I'm
A target for his oaths and spleen.
It's thus the Government betrays
Its values posed in Conference speech.
As they kill hopes of those who seek
Asylum here, they're baiting hooks
With fascist views to catch the votes
Of mindless yobs. They fail to sort
The wheat from chaff, ejecting men
Of youth with skills our nation needs,
While squeezing pensions aimed at us
Who swell the ranks of growing load
Of aging folk. Their promised new,
And joined-up, rules across the board
They've shelved. For those in need now feel
They're being branded scrounging frauds.

It seems that Blair and gang have lost
The plot as focus groups concoct
Their latest gruesome, ugly spins.

It took us time to readjust to the constant of risk of theft that characterizes urban living. Audrey was always helping charities raise funds by making cakes and helping out in serving them with drinks at some venue in town. Indeed on one occasion a couple came in and the woman chatted while the man passed the kitchen to visit the toilet. On his return the couple hastily left. We then found Audrey's small shoulder bag with her purse had gone from the hook just inside the kitchen door. The empty bag and empty purse were later found abandoned in a shop nearby.

OFFENCE (CO)

When wife and I were selling cakes,
With cups of coffee, tea or squash,
To raise some funds to aid the poor,
A steady stream of people came.
But then a woman stalled the queue
To play her tape of fancied ills.
At last she leaves, with scruffy bloke
Not far behind. It's then we find
The bag my love had hung on peg
Has gone. It seems that bitch's tale
Of woes was all a con to screen
Her shifty partner's theft. It makes
Us wonder how that pair can sleep
At night. Do they not feel a sense
Of guilt? Or do they cackle long
Beyond our ken, until the law
At last delivers just deserts?
Will then remorse dissolve their crust
Of hard contempt for other's needs?
Or will regret at being caught
Be sole concern? And how did they
Become the way they are today?
We know there is no gene for crime,
That fates are not controlled by stars,
Despite the bilge from those who claim
It's so, and jargon labels by
Some shrink do not explain. Perhaps
Their homes were fraught with fear, so growth
In self-esteem was crushed from birth.

Perhaps decay lay further back
In time when parents suffered from
Neglect as kids, because of drink.
And so we shift the blame, instead
Of calling 'crooks' without excuse.
Our soggy liberal views may seem
Benign, but thieves all know they're crap.
To them offence is getting caught;
As when a soldier I was taught
By sergeant, who was artful rogue
Who milked the system not his men.

I still found it strange ignoring those I passed on the pavement without a greeting. But on our own road I continued to greet some:

STRANGERS (TL)

I pass a lady with her dog
Each day when walking to my work.
We greet each other like lost friends
And yet we know not who we are.
I'm just the man who lives along
The road on other side: and she's
The cheerful lass with friendly pug.
If we one day put on the news
And saw the other found to be
A wanted swindler caught at last,
We'd both be shocked beyond belief.
Yet that's how small is what we know,
Beyond their names, of most of folk
Encountered in the course of day.
We're like autistic kids alone
In crowded playschool's noisy din.
Perhaps our secret lives are just
A ruse to hide our empty hearts
When childhood's dreams have left no mark.
But I for one rejoice I'm known,
In part, by wife I love and kids
We've raised and launched on life. And so,
With thanks for them and friends, I'll still
Extend my daily greetings to
The stranger lady with her dog:
Despite the fact we're only each
A fleeting part of other's scene.

In parts of world our daily nod
Would cause dissent or even spark
An angry row as rumours grew
And ran amok. On England's streets
We're just a sentimental pair
Without a whiff of scandal's shame.
And still I do not know her name!

By complete contrast were the encounters experienced when dining at
Sidney Sussex College, which granted me generous dining rights on my return
to Cambridge.

INDULGENCE (CO)

Today I dine at college, where
I meet with those who study stars,
Or history's muddles, genes, or trends
In shares, or cancer drugs, or role
Of symbols in the Cantos Pound
Inflicted on the world. Our talk
Embraces anecdotes, the crap
Our politicians serve, a new
Device for finding faults in plane's
Electric systems, gossip laced
With rumour going rounds, and jokes
From lawyer fresh from Brussels trip
Advising Euro bureaucrats.
We come from many lands, but all
Are geared to searching out the truth
Or solving problems in their field.
For each has reached esteem by climb
Of ladder's academic rungs
With ease or patient slog. But some,
It seems, have never paused to ask
Themselves about the aim of life
And whether chosen niche in sphere
Of learning really serves a want
In wider world or if it's flight
For lonely child behind the mask
That's now displayed. For all the words,
As claret's passed around, I note
That few reveal their inner hopes
And fears. Unwritten code forbids
Embarrassments unlocking tears

Or calls to heed the needs of those
Whose lot reveals us as remote
As Pound's allusions in a tongue
We do not know. Our comfort seems
Almost obscene as news of AIDS
In Africa or else a threat
Of yet another Balkans war
Is headline news. Perhaps as youth
My brush with death in Cyprus mess
Has left me scarred, and shaped me so
I feel too much for those whose lives
Are upside down, because of those
Employing bomb and bullet's threat
To get their way; despite the cost
To all who wish to live in peace,
Despite their legacies of hate.
Perhaps we need escapes to keep
Us sane. A scholar's lonesome role
Requires respite from focussed mind,
A freewheel ride to help unwind.
I'll play my part in pampered rite.
I'll pass the port with conscience clear.

We gradually came to appreciate living in suburbia and going everywhere on our bikes.

SUBURBAN COMPANY (TL)

Rejoice, I say, rejoice again
I plead. The springtime sun today
Is rousing joy from winter's gloom.
The daffodils, despite the praise
Of Wordsworth's words, survive his song
That's now a cliché killing hope
Of modern poet's fresh attempt.
Our garden is no northern vale,
But, gazing down its length, the dance
Of yellow heads is pure delight:
And what is more, despite the threat
Of April shower, I'm relaxed
In calm of comfy chair behind
The glass of sliding door in warmth
And dry; and she I love beside
Me sits and shares this tranquil scene,

As glossy starlings scour our lawn
All unaware of us or kiss
Of light upon their restless backs.
We gladly leave our Lakeland bard
To haunt his windswept fells alone.

SUBURBAN LIFE (RE)

By early May our garden glows
With many rainbow blooms to bring
A sense that life is good. Too soon,
As courting birds now nest and sing,
The weeds begin their march, intent
On waging ceaseless strife. We start
Relentless counter strike with hoe
And other means. But weeds are smart.
They're skilled in bandit tricks. Some creep
Along the ground or climb aloft
By twining round our favoured plants.
But sometimes when I'm feeling soft,
I think a garden full of weeds
Becomes a mini nature park
With bindweed trumpets, yellow spread
Of dandelions, or dance to mark
The edge of lawn a lacy dance
Of umbels named for Queen we've long
Forgot. While nettles may be dull,
And threat to child, they still belong
As food for infant butterflies.
But hoverflies and bumble bees
Enjoy exotic blooms as well
As us we who cherish all of these
We've nurtured right from seed with care
And patient hope. Perhaps the best
Is compromise as shown by lawn
That's far from grass alone. It's blest
With many daisies, yellow dance
Of composites and bugle clumps.
And in the spring the violets give
Us joy along with little humps
Of moss the birds employ to pad
Their nests. Today I drew a line
When rat appeared. I set a trap.
For some of nature's not benign!

Indeed, at scale of ants, the world's
A constant fight to stay alive.
From dawn till dusk, throughout the night,
To eat and not be prey, survive
Is only task of real concern.
It's from a jungle we emerged,
With beastly instincts still intact.
But God desires that we be purged.
By grace the weeds of self-regard
Are slain as Holy Spirit's gift
Ensures that love is freed from drives
And life's no longer aimless drift.
Emergent souls are what survives,
As that's the goal of human lives.

SUBURBIA (CW)

A know-all lass of twenty three
Proclaims 'suburbia is hell
On earth. It gobbles land,
Destroys community and kills
Desire for radical reform.
A muzzling mortgage stretched across
A span of twenty years has quenched
All fires of youthful zeal. To them
Our views are antigens of wild
Excess. Instead they're more concerned
With weeding beds of chosen blooms
Than curing world of blatant ills.
Our road's become a clone of drones.'

Her scorn has skated past the facts
That contradict her cartoon sketch.
Her mum has toiled for years to raise
A mound of funds for Christian Aid.
Her dad has tithed each month to give
Support to work that strives to find
A cure for cancer's scourge and care
For kids without a home. She's blind
To beauty on display in street
Without a plan imposed by those
Who rule. While each is free to be
An island on their own, they each
Belong to intersecting rings

Of friendship groups. There's mums whose kids
Attend their local school, there's those
Whose mates are found at work, at church,
At club or evening class. There's some
Who play at politics or toil
For cause. A web of gossip means
That those in need are not alone.
It's only parasites, who win
Their own estates, and those whose wage
Condemns them to a tiny flat,
In ugly concrete block, who may
Resent the ordered life our lass
Derides – until she bears a child
Of own and starts to build a home.
She's now a thankful member at
The church's group for mums and kids.
She now delights, through eyes of child,
At daily wonders they perceive
On every trip along their road –
That once she viewed with rich contempt!

When my GP tested my hearing I explained that it had been damaged by a couple of terrorist bombs in Cyprus in 1958 (see chapter 2). He said that as it was on active service then the Ministry of Defence should pay me compensation. So he sent me to Addenbrooke's Hospital where a battery of tests were carried out. The senior consultant reported that the top third of my hearing range had been damaged and that the bombs were undoubtedly the cause. My GP got the forms from the MOD and these were duly completed and dispatched along with a copy of the consultant's report. In due course I received a letter from the MOD instructing me to go to March where a technician in a caravan by the railway station would carry out a test. With one out-of-date piece of equipment he did a single test. I then received a letter from the MOD stating that as I had lost less than 10% of my hearing range I did not qualify for compensation! Furthermore on the back in small print it stated there was no appeal against this adjudication! If I had had the funds I would have taken the MOD to the European Court. In all my dealings with the MOD I have been led to regard them as the 'Ministry of Deceit', as evidenced, for example, with other exchanges with the MOD relating to the Dervish (see below) and the reporting of low flying jets (in chapter 8).

The publication of the first of the Naturalists' Handbooks in 1983 (see chapter 8 and appendix G) was to result in another piece of nonsense from the Inland Revenue (for the first see chapter 8). They sent me a letter demanding details of my co-editor's royalties. I replied with copy of my letter instructing the publisher to pay these direct to a charity. The IR replied that my letter had not employed the correct wording for such an instruction. I responded by asking the IR as to what was the correct form of words. They replied that they were not competent to specify the correct form of words! So I then asked how was it that they were evidently competent to say my form of words was incorrect when it was perfectly clear to the publisher as to the meaning of my instruction. Having got a stupid reply I copied the correspondence to the then Chancellor of the Exchequer, who once again told the Inland Revenue to stop being stupid!

In 1984 Zakaria (Zak) Erzinclioglu embarked on a six year postdoc with me before becoming the UK's leading forensic entomologist until his untimely death in 2002. I first met Zak when he came up to me after I had given a lecture at the Natural History Museum in London. It was clear that he had a real commitment to studying flies, especially blowflies (Calliphoridae), in his spare time. I suggested he join my annual week's course on Flies, Midges and Gnats at Malham Tarn (see chapter 8). He became one of my regulars. He then decided to return to academia to undertake a PhD on blowflies at Durham University. It was through his work on blowflies, especially his detailed studies on their eggs and larvae, that he had become involved with forensic work. It was when he encountered larvae of scuttle flies (Phoridae) that I was subcontracted to deal with them.

At Durham Zak met his wife to be, Sharon Davies, who was doing a PhD on mink. They married soon after the move to Cambridge. At Durham he got on well with his fellow research students, but a few failed to appreciate his sense of humour:

A CULTURAL DIVIDE IS NO JOKE (RE)

When Jock pronounced a haggis king
Of meals his Arab friend declared
He'd never heard of same. So Joe
Replied "It's best when freshly snared
At night when moon is full". "But what's
It like?" Hussein demands again.
"It's size of rabbit, golden brown
Its fur. It lives within domain
Of Scotland's fiercest clan, who guard
It close from risk of English men intent
On shooting grouse. The male has limbs
On left of greater length's extent
Than those on right and clockwise runs
Around the hills; but female's legs
Are quite reverse. She races round
The other way. When chased by clegs
They dash to edge of burn and take
A swim. They feed on bracken fronds

At dawn. By day they play and make
A moaning sound to strengthen bonds."
By now Hussein has look of child when told
That Santa comes with gifts on eve
Of Christmas – IF she's good. When week
Had passed he learned to not believe
A word of tale he'd swallowed whole.
Instead of laughing at the joke
He loses rag with Joe, who fears
Hussein's at risk of having stroke.
But saying sorry can't appease.
The loss of face has built a wall,
Has lit desire for dire revenge
That brings about a friendship's fall.

While it was only a minority of cases where the scuttle fly specimens
proved to be significant, they sometimes provided key evidence helping to
secure the conviction of a murderer:

FORENSIC CASE (CW)

As I contrive to weigh the facts,
Infer from slender clues I can
Deduce from maggots taken from
The corpse at morgue, my thoughts are tuned
To tiny details only mind
Prepared discerns. I find I need
To stay detached, or else recall
That insects came from body dumped
In shallow grave, by man who killed
His partner's child, inflames my heart
With rage until I start to twist
The facts to nail his sordid lies.
To scuttle flies her corpse is gift;
To him it's problem out of way;
To me it's not just challenge posed
By those who wish to solve this crime;
For me she's daughter's child defiled.

'LIES EXPOSED BY MAGGOTS' (CO)

A hardened, selfish, bitter face
Beheld me in the witness box
With cold contempt at first. She thought
Her fibs remained intact until
My answers slowly chipped away
Her crass defence. She'd not conceived
That tiny maggots told a tale
At odds with hers. Her features now
Revealed despair. Indeed her life
Has been a chain of woes and now
This man, who studies flies, was there
In court to say she lies. My heart
Begins to feel a slow concern
For her as she perceives she's lost
Her case. Beneath her shell it seems
A frightened girl had learned as child
The world is not a place to give
A care for kid abused behind
A door that shuts her out of joy.
And I, who move in spheres beyond
Her ken, are just another man
Who's come to put her down again.
While justice takes its course the role
Of warm compassion stands aside.
I can but feel it's father, who
Abused her years ago, who should
Be in the dock instead of her.

1985: Project Wallace expedition to Sulawesi (Royal Entomological Society of London).

A trust had provided a fund to allow long serving employees of the Field Studies Council to take a three-month sabbatical with funds for an approved project. I was due my sabbatical in 1984 before I left Malham Tarn Field Centre. I had recently been approached by Brian Stuckenberg, the Director of the Natal Museum (later to be called the KwaZulu Natal Museum) in Piertermaritzburg, wanting me to become Head of Arthropods. I had thanked him for the offer but said I would not consider it as long as Apartheid remained South Africa's government policy. He replied that I had been misled by the BBC's exaggerations! I responded that my sister and brother-in-law (Diana and John) had visited South Africa under the auspices of the Quakers and reported that the BBC, if anything, underplayed the effects of Apartheid. When the then

Head of Arthropods came to visit the Natural History Museum in London he phoned me to ask if he could come to talk to me about the situation at the Natal Museum. I said he would be welcome and booked him in for a night's stay at the Field Centre. For the evening meal I reserved a place for him beside my Warden's chair at the end of the centre table. It was only as I led him into the dining room that I realized that he was undergoing some sort of culture shock as I showed him to his seat beside a Malaysian and opposite a Nigerian. It happened to be the week of the London School of Hygiene and Tropical Medicine's annual field course (see chapter 8) and we had more than twenty nationalities in the Centre! I learned later that on his return to South Africa he had reported to the Director of the Natal Museum that my objections to Apartheid were not theoretical and that the Centre had been crawling with Africans! The Director then wrote to ask me to visit South Africa at their expense so that I could see the situation for myself and undertake some entomological fieldwork. I replied I was agreeable as long he fully understood that I would not consider a move to South Africa as long as Apartheid was still in force and that where I went on a visit would be decided on scientific not political grounds. After some delay he agreed. I then put the proposed visit to the FSC Committee for approving proposed sabbatical projects. They decided that because the FSC's Oil Pollution Research Unit had contracts with Nigeria and the Gulf States that a visit by me to South Africa might jeopardize future, if not then existing projects (despite Nigeria was known to be covertly flouting the embargo on selling oil to South Africa). I was told to propose another project and my sabbatical was postponed a year, by which time I had moved to Cambridge. My participation in Project Wallace was then approved for my overdue sabbatical.

A later postscript to this episode was when I was asked to contribute to a Gedenkschrift special volume of the journal in honour of the Director (Brian Stuckenberg) who had died in 2009 (Disney, R. H. L., 2012. Five new species of scuttle fly (Diptera: Phoridae) from southern Africa. African Invertebrates 53: 113-124). In this paper I named two of the species after Brian.

The 1985 Project Wallace expedition to Sulawesi in Indonesia was a major, yearlong expedition with scientists coming and going for limited terms. It had an enormous attraction over many other expeditions in that survival (physical and political) would be looked after by an army, navy, air force and Gurkha support team, so that the scientists could concentrate on their science. I signed up for the first three months. It proved to be a welcome therapy after all the stress of the events leading up to the move from Yorkshire. It also became a wonderful stimulus to my growing interest in the astonishing diversity of the natural histories of scuttle flies. My programme aimed to concentrate on acquiring novel natural history data, especially on species parasitizing other invertebrates. In the event the sophisticated habits of scuttle flies parasitizing or invading the colonies of ants and termites became a major focus of my research and thereafter on my return to Cambridge.

A dozen papers were spawned by this adventure. These covered new genera and species; with the descriptions of some of these requiring new keys for the Oriental species of half a dozen genera. I also obtained many new natural history data. Of especial note were two new species that parasitized termites. They got given the name of 'con flies' by some of the soldiers to whom I was able to show a female in action. The latter prods a termite exposed on a tree trunk and then leads it down to the ground where it renders its victim comatose. She then inserts an egg, covers the termite with soil and guards it for a week. A new adult fly then emerges from the remains of the termite. I named one of these flies after the Royal Marines padre who took a photo of a fly leading a termite down a tree trunk. This gave rise to a piece in the Royal Marines newsletter – 'con artist named after padre'! This in turn caused the RM director of Music to compose a Con-fly March!

Many of my Sulawesi publications are cited in the subsequent symposium volume (Disney, R. H. L., 1990. Phylogenetic implications of some features of Sulawesi scuttle flies (Diptera: Phoridae). Chapter 12: 103-105 and Scuttle flies (Diptera: Phoridae) associated with ants and termites in Toraut Forest, Sulawesi. Chapter 26: 301-304. In Knight, W. J. & Holloway, J. D. (Editors). Insects of the Rain Forests of South East Asia (Wallacea). Royal Entomological Society of London. IV + 343 pp).

After my departure from Sulawesi David Kistner from California took part in the project. He was a renowned specialist on the small beetles that inhabit ant and termite nests. He also collected any other insects, including scuttle flies. These duly arrived on my lab bench and resulted in a joint publication (Disney, R. H. L. & Kistner, D. H., 1988. Phoridae collected from termite and ant colonies in Sulawesi (Diptera; Isoptera, Termitidae; Hymenoptera, Formicidae). Sociobiology 14: 361-369). From then on a steady stream of phorids arrived from California (e.g. Disney, R. H. L. & Kistner, D. H., 1989. Neotropical Phoridae from army ant colonies, including two new species (Diptera; Hymenoptera, Formicidae). Sociobiology 16: 149-174) and a long collaboration continued. Indeed we published a dozen papers together before we ever met! Among the papers resulting from the trip to Sulawesi was one on the tiny flies of the genus Chonocephalus, in which the flightless females are about 1 mm long and the winged males about 1.5 mm long. I had first become intrigued by this tropical genus when in Yorkshire and I had been asked to identify some specimens from Panama and shortly afterwards a species from a hothouse in Middlesex (Disney, R. H. L., 1981. An exotic scuttle fly, Chonocephalus heymonsi Stobbe (Dipt., Phoridae) from Middlesex. Entomologist's Monthly Magazine 116: 207-212 (1980)). In Sulawesi the species collected (Disney, R. H. L., 1986. Morphological and other observations on Chonocephalus (Phoridae) and phylogenetic implications for the Cyclorrhapha (Diptera). Journal of Zoology, London (A) 210: 77-87) made me realize not only were the male genitalia (hypopygia) very complex but the taxonomy of the genus was in chaos because males and females had often been treated separately. Furthermore the morphology of both sexes retained ancestral features not reported for other Phoridae. Accordingly, when I had completed my 1994 book (see below), in which I had commented on the confused state of the taxonomy, I decided that I must try to tackle these confusions in due course. This became a major project in my 'retirement' (see chapter 10).

1985-1990: I served as a member of the Wicken Fen National Nature Reserve Management Committee (National Trust).

The Chairman of this committee was Sir Norman Moore, with an international reputation with regard to conservation management and pollutants affecting wildlife. As a result of the record of my relevant appointments in Yorkshire and my publications on the environment and conservation (see chapter 8) I was appointed to this committee. Because of these credentials the Bishop of Ely decided that for his last Diocesan Synod before his retirement it was time to put concern for the environment and wildlife conservation onto the Diocesan agenda. After taking advice as to who in the Diocese would be suitable persons to address the Synod on this topic, he invited Norman and myself to undertake this task. Under the next Bishop the Diocesan Synod established its committee to advise on the environment and wildlife conservation. It was gratifying to see the Church of England taking these concerns seriously at last. After all I had been roped into editing a chapter on this topic for a report commissioned by the Methodist Conference and published in 1981, apart from having been signed up previously to give the First of the annual Charles Coulson Lectures at the Methodist's Luton Industrial College in 1975 (see chapter 8). When I had been asked to undertake these assignments I had responded by pointing out that I was not a member of the Methodist Church. The reply had been that that was an irrelevant observation!

Shortly after the move to Cambridge I acquired my first desktop, very basic, computer. This was progressively replaced, with each new model getting ever more sophisticated. Word processing became one of the great advances that did away with typing and retyping draft papers and doing carbon copies with final versions. Later on there came the Internet and the use of e-mailing. Again this was a huge advance, but something of a mixed blessing due to the growing amount of junk mail. It became routine that I would spend about two hours each week dumping spam, despite the University's computing centre screening out hundreds of dubious e-mails before they ever reached my mailbox. Gradually it became easier to block further e-mails from each new unwanted spam and scam.

REASSURED (CW)

As I attempt to clear my desk
It seems a ballcock operates
And papers deluge once again
In filling tank at rate at which
I open tap to drain it dry.
It's same with e-mails on the screen.
As soon as daily flood is scanned,
And junk is binned, another spate
Appears and most are scams or filth,
Or both. It's like the news that gives
Us no respite from crimes and deaths
By accidents or wars, with few
Reports of good or fun events,
Or both. And yet in daily round
The balance tips the other way.
The people I engage are worth
The time of day, except for few
On rare occasions once a month
Or two. The daily drip of gloom
Corrodes belief we'll ever make
The world a better place. But when
I read of former times when men
Were building mansions on a scale
They could afford because of slaves
Who toiled abroad and out of sight,
Of children wheezing down our mines,
Of pittance wages women won
By minding noisy looms for all
The daylight hours and more, it's then
I'm reassured that things improve,
As long as some are heeding call
To serve the cause to make it so.

REACTIONS (RE)

I published a paper on flies
That helped the police expose lies
So now I'm e-mailed
By cranks who have failed
With pleas that their logic defies.

By some I am asked to be source
Of thought for a student whose course
Is learning the facts
Without the impacts
Of reason as synthesis force.

What's more there are fools who believe
They're sure I can help them retrieve
The purse they mislaid
Their cat that has strayed
The future that man can't perceive!

SPAM (GK)

When e-mail box is gorged with spam,
I bin the bulk without a need
To scan. Their titles tend to let
One screen the junk without delay.
Today a label read 'reply
To yours of yesterday' but when
Exposed it proved the usual scam
For fleecing me of all my funds.
It seems sufficient fools abound
To swallow blatant cons as these.
Or else one wonders why they try
Their luck each day for months on end.
It's like the spread of silly fads
For crystals meant to cure all ills
Or loony rites designed to wipe
Away one's angsts. The sermon's flow
Employed to sell these wares purports
To be rebirth of ancient ways
Imbued with mystic wisdom lost
When science reared its head. When asked
If double blinded tests had proved
Their claims they lose their cool;

Without the wit of sharp riposte
To heckler halting stream of speech
Designed to hook your votes. I doubt
Their faith is based on fact, for some
I doubt their words are more than sham.
Apart from those whom Mammon rules,
It's relished power they exercise
That underpins their sordid games.

As the computers got more sophisticated, with many additional options, I was able to move from photographing my figures labelled with Lettraset, to scanning them and labelling them on screen. One could then e-mail text files and the figures to journals instead of posting photos and typescripts. With the increasing options (many of which I did not require!) they also got temperamental and would suddenly seize up for no apparent reason. I would then crash out and restart the computer:

P.C. (RE)

(In fact I have always used Apple Mac computers except for the advance imaging system for my microscope acquired when I went three quarters blind – see chapter 10)

The menu bar has choice called Help,
But it's a farce.
Whenever aid is needed fast
She fails the test,
For when a fault occurs she states
It's error 'X',
Without a clue to indicate
What 'X' might be!
Another time the screen will freeze,
And cursor too,
And so I pull the plug and start
Again. She tells
Me then to follow proper form
When closing down!
Indeed machine is most perverse.
She's like a kid
I knew whose know-all head was crammed
With random facts,
Without attempts to synthesise
The piles of junk.
And yet I cannot live today
Without the beast.

She's got me hooked for rest of life
For good or ill.
She saves me hours of time and sweat,
Besides she's fun!
And so I'll love and hate her guts
With equal whim.
She's just a lass one loves despite
Her fickle moods.

The other big change was when our children started to leave home for university and beyond.

RELEASE (TL)

The feeder hung for birds is filled
With nuts and seeds conveying joy
To tits and we ourselves. Today
We found a lively mouse who's coy
And scared by turns within the cage
Embracing feast beyond its dreams.
Its race for cover when released
Is like a toy on wheels that seems
Alive when aimed by child across
The floor towards his mum. But now
He's gone we feel deprived; recall
Our children leaving home, so now
We feel we never knew their selves
Beyond endearing ways; their hearts
Concealed from prying world. It's strange,
It's only when each one departs
We gain a gaping hole, and yet
The bonds remain despite their slow
Maturing selves that travel way
Beyond the routine ways we know.
Through them we share a glimpse of minds
Of lively youth to whom this life
Is still a feeder filled with good
And wholesome fare and free of strife.

With the passing of the years this dispersion of our family increased our ambiguity of feelings at our loss but also of our sense of pride in them making their own ways in life.

Trudy started out her medical studies at Southampton University, but in 1986 she transferred to Sydney University in Australia in order to marry

Andrew F. The date for the wedding was set when our commitments meant we had not been able to attend. We had our doubts about the suitability of the marriage but did not feel it wise to say so. In fact the marriage did not last long. After qualifying as a doctor, in 1992 she married Andrew Climie, who worked in Accident and Emergency in the central hospital in Hobart (Tasmania). We flew out to New Zealand to meet Trudy's future parents-in-law before proceeding to Australia. Trudy and Andrew took us on a grand trip in mainland Australia before we proceeded to the wedding in Tasmania.

The highlights of this tour was experiencing a diversity of birds and mammals while staying in a farmhouse in the Outback, in a lodge in high forest in south Queensland and a visit to Heron Island. The boat to the island had intended to be longer, but the cost had proved insufficient so when three quarters complete during its construction it had been shortened to save money. The result was it had a curious motion that brought on my old seasickness sensation (see chapters 2 and 5). After enjoying the island's wildlife, especially the turtles coming ashore to lay their eggs, Andrew managed to secure a place for myself on a helicopter for my return to the mainland. From this vantage I had spectacular views of huge rays swimming along the edge of the coral reef. We then visited the Parliament buildings in Canberra before proceeding to Sydney, where we visited the Botanic Gardens, before flying on to Hobart.

'SHRUNKEN' WORLD? (TL)

Today I saw a pair of swans
When walking towpath by that flow
Of friendly river that's become
A daily joy for me. Of course
A swan is part of scene that brings
Delight. But those I met today
Were black. Their proper home is far
Away Antipodes, where two
Who bring us joy at slightest hint
(The children born to daughter long
Removed from frequent sight, except
In mind) now dwell. The world is said
To be a shrunken, closer, place
Than in the past, but now our kin
Are scattered far and wide. To us
Our own are now as rare a sight
As these exotic birds, while those
We meet at work each day are known
As normal as a swan that's white.
Our world remains too large for smiles
To reach across intruding miles.

SCATTERED (CW)

Attention's held by photos ranged
Along the bookcase top, for there
Our children, also theirs, are on
Display. Oh how we wish them near,
Instead of being far away.
Our brief encounters in a year
Can only serve to make us wish
That daily sight, and also ear,
Could share their steady growing up.
We'd slowly learned our very own
Are each unique and still surprise.
It's plain to all they're not a clone
Of either mum or dad or both combined.
The fact they came from single nest
Could not be guessed by those who meet
Them now. We feel we're more than blest
In them and in their bonus kids.
But in our frantic modern times

We scatter far and wide, with some
Across the globe in foreign climes.
In past one's children, cousins, aunts
And uncles, parents, theirs as well
Were all within a mile or two
Of where we lived. But truth to tell
The choice of jobs was poor indeed
And gossip often opened rifts.
Perhaps the present state ensures
Infrequent meetings come as gifts.
But still we're left with sense of loss.
From babes to adults twenty years
Accomplished all the many joys
As well as sometimes darker fears.
But that was best of times, when home
Was where we lived to full and more.
But since, our routine ways, devoid
Of sudden squalls, now seem a bore.
And yet with creeping age we need,
Perhaps, a time to pause before
Embarking soon for glory's shore.

Following our move to Cambridge I had written to the then Bishop of
Bradford to let him know that, as one of his selectors of ordinands (see chapter
8), I had moved to Cambridge. He asked me to complete my five-year
appointment on behalf of his diocese. In 1989 the then Bishop of Huntingdon
(on behalf of the Bishop of Ely) came to see me at my lab. The then Advisory
Board for Ministry had pointed out that the Diocese had a vacancy for a pastoral
selector of ordinands and had recommended me. After a wide ranging
conversation the Bishop of Huntingdon supported this recommendation to the
Bishop of Ely. Several colleagues in the Department of Zoology were surprised
to find a bishop loose in the Department asking the way to my lab. They were
even more surprised to learn of the reason for his visit!

As a medical entomologist in the 1960s I had quickly learned that unless I
mastered the taxonomy of the flies I was studying I would be wasting my time
(see chapters 5 and 7). My editorial commitments (see Appendix A) reflected
my growing concern at the lack of realization among many ecologists and
naturalists as to how little we know about the species on planet earth. Even with
the well documented fauna of the British Isles we are constantly adding species,
describing hitherto unknown larvae, etc. When I started contributing to our
knowledge of the natural history of scuttle flies I, of necessity, got deeply
involved in the taxonomy of these challenging flies. I was constantly adding
species to the British List, including species new to science. Indeed, in order to
progress in my study of the species of the British Isles I ended up producing a
two volume provisional handbook on these flies (Disney, R. H. L., 1983.

Scuttle Flies – Diptera, Phoridae (except Megaselia). Handbooks for the Identification of British Insects 10(6): 1-81, executed and published while I was still in Yorkshire. However, it quickly became out of date by other species turning up that had not been previously been recorded from the British Isles, including a remarkable genus new to science (Disney, R. H. L., 1986. A new genus of scuttle-fly (Diptera: Phoridae) from England. Zoological Journal of the Linnean Society 87: 85-89). This species later proved to be common in the canopies of oak trees near Oxford (Table 7.4 in my 1994 book cited below). I completed volume two on the giant genus Megaselia after moving to Cambridge (Disney, R. H. L., 1989. Scuttle Flies – Diptera Phoridae Genus Megaselia. Handbooks for the Identification of British Insects 10(8): 1-155). Following my review of 1994 (see below) and subsequent publications this genus has been described as being 'one of the largest, most biologically diverse and taxonomically difficult genera in the entire animal kingdom' (Marshall, S. A., 2012. Flies: the natural history and diversity of Diptera. New York, Firefly Books. 615 pp).

Both my Handbooks increasingly became out of date due to subsequent additions to the British List (including further new species) and revisions. These volumes were followed by many papers on non-British species and by my most cited publication (Disney, R. H. L., 1994. Scuttle Flies: The Phoridae. London, Chapman & Hall. xii + 467 pp). In 2013, despite being twenty years out of date (much due to my own subsequent papers) this was archived on the Internet in perpetuity by Springer Book Archives (https://www.springer.com). The prime motive for the book had been to rectify many misleading statements in textbooks and other reference works. These seemed unaware of the well documented astonishing diversity of the larval habits in this family. For example compare the sole statement on these habits "'larvae live in decaying or putrefying material' (Allaby, M. (Editor), 1985. The Oxford Dictionary of Natural History. Oxford: Oxford University Press) with the fact that more than 150 years before this the parasitizing of the pupae of ladybird beetles (Coccinellidae) by scuttle fly larvae had been reported (Curtis, J., 1833. British Entomology, Volume 10. London). A truer statement of the larval habits was 'it is doubtful whether the life histories of most ...conspicuous Diptera can compare in interest with those of the tiny, dull-colored Phoridae' (Wheeler, W. M., 1901. An extraordinary ant-guest. American Naturalist 35: 1007-1016). Indeed it was my putting the case for the need for a review of our actual knowledge of the diversity of these habits, along with a new key to the genera of the world and guide to the identification literature for the species of each genus, that persuaded the Wingate Foundation to part fund me for two years in order to allow me to write the book published in 1994.

As I increasingly identified specimens from around the world a major challenge was the African species of the huge genus Megaselia. The problem was a monograph published in 1965 by Beyer. The descriptions were poor, the figures even worse and the identification keys to species were riddled with errors, omissions and runs of couplets based on males then a switch to those on females and then back to males again. So one had to keep skipping couplets not based on the same sex as the specimen one was trying to identify. Apart from my first paper on an African species, which I named after Audrey (see chapter 8) I published on only a few African species and one more substantial paper (Disney, R. H. L., 1991. Scuttle flies from Zimbabwe (Diptera, Phoridae) with the description of five new species. Journal of African Zoology 105: 27-48). By now my annotations of Beyer's identification keys were almost extensive as the original text. So I decided to gradually deal with the non-mainland species of the Afrotropical Region as a priority with regard to the Afrotropical Megaselia. Apart from papers on the smaller warm climate Atlantic islands, a more substantial contribution was the following: – Disney, R. H. L., 1991. Scuttle flies of the Cape Verde Islands (Diptera, Phoridae). Journal of African Zoology 105: 205-241.

The species of Arabia and Islands to the east of mainland Africa were to follow later (see chapter 10). Some unusual new species sent by Steve Compton from South Africa had been reared from figs and the adults then preyed on fig wasps emerging from other nearby figs (Compton, S. G. & Disney, R. H. L., 1991. New species of Megaselia (Diptera: Phoridae) whose larvae live in fig syconia (Urticales: Moraceae), and adults prey on fig wasps (Hymenoptera: Agaonidae). Journal of Natural History 25: 203-219).

As I tackled species from across the world, the family had continually sprung surprises. For example, I had been sent specimens of scuttle flies from India that I had been asked to identify. They had been reared from larvae infesting the nitrogen-fixing root nodules of chickpeas (Cicer arietinum), an important crop of semi-arid regions in India and elsewhere. The reared flies raised serious questions about the recognition of genera. The females existed in two forms. One was a typical member of the genus Metopina. The other females were blind and had reduced wings, and were referable to a 'genus' only known from females collected in South America. The males from India, according to the then current concepts, if procured in isolation would have been assigned to a new genus. However, these three entities had been repeatedly obtained in reared series. It seemed that larvae initially invaded the larger root nodules nearer the main stem and gave rise to flightless females that then crawled to the next lot of nodules to lay their eggs. As the nodules exploited became smaller this seemed to trigger the production of winged females that presumably emerged from the soil to seek a fresh chickpea plant. Anyway I assigned the two sorts of female and the males to a single new species (Metopina ciceri) and abolished the South American genus (Disney, R. H. L., 1988. A remarkable new species of scuttle fly (Diptera: Phoridae) whose larvae infest chickpea root nodules in India. Journal of Natural History 22: 611-616). On another occasion I almost made the mistake of assigning two similar forms of a flightless species into separate species until I came across intermediates that indicated that the species was more variable than had been supposed:

CLEARING GROUND (GK)

Today I sorted tiny flies
Dividing 'species' into three
Depending on the size of stumps
Of wings ancestors used for flight.
There's 'shorts' and 'longs' and those between,
With gaps as clear as day. But when
I mounted next on slide surprise
Had left me reeling wild. On left
Its stump was long, but short adorned
Its right! It seemed a simple switch
Of gene was key to what I had
Inferred were sibling species when,
In truth, it's one that varies more
Than most within these flightless forms,
Evolved by losing parts or else
Reducing bits by slow degrees.
Conclusions reached are never firm.
They're just the best explaining facts
At time, before some novel finds
Demolish edifice we've built
With care and silent pride. Perhaps
We need these constant shocks to keep
Us seeking more of light within
The ocean ignorance that meets
Us daily in our ceaseless work,
That clears the ground for those to come.
They'll build the edifice we dream.
They'll win applause that we're denied.
But no regrets embitter souls
That know they've helped advance the plot.

Jenny Baker, FSC Research Director, was very supportive of my Research Unit at Cambridge and its growing international reputation. By contrast the FSC Director was not so appreciative as his legitimate concern was maximizing income for the FSC. He was somewhat perplexed when, at a Senior Staff meeting, we were handed a blank matrix to complete that plotted customers against services. I handed it back commenting that I did not have customers. The return on my output was measured in publications not income. The only way I could improve my financial performance was by doing nothing, because as soon as I did anything I incurred costs!

In 1989 I spent several weeks trying to raise funds for my research. The lack of support for fundamental taxonomy was growing worse. It was apparent that without ring fenced funding other priorities for university biology curricula (the exciting new developments in molecular studies and advanced computer modelling of populations, etc.) would lead to an accelerating decline in taxonomy in universities. Indeed my colleagues and I highlighted this perception in the following: Joysey, K. A., Clack, J. A., Coates, M. I., Disney, R. H. L., Foster, W. A., Friday, A. E., Lister, A. M. & Preece, R. C., 1990. Correspondence (on the inadequate support for taxonomy). Nature, London 345 (6276): 568. I continued campaigning in letters to journals and submissions to the House of Lords Select Committee (e.g. Disney, R. H. L., 2008. Memorandum submitted 20 December 2007. Pages 232-233 in: Systematics and Taxonomy: Follow-up. House of Lords Science and Technology Committee 5th Report of Session 2007-08. HL Paper 162: 1-330). The response to the House of Lords report by the Natural Environment Research Council was evasive, as highlighted in the subsequent debate in the House of Lords that included excerpts from comments I had sent to the secretariat (Disney, R. H. L., 2009. [Quotation from e-mail on NERC's criteria for funding – from speech by Baroness Walmsley]. Lords Hansard 25 March 2009: GC228).

I was getting used to the Establishment being deaf to reasoned arguments indicating a lack of their perception of a situation! A further example is noted below this far happier event.

29th May 1993: Rachel married Alex Holland, a dairy farmer in Pendine, South Wales – Thankfully not as remote as Tasmania!

Following an article in the March issue of Yes (the magazine of the Church Mission Society) on the numerous injuries and deaths inflicted by landmines on non-combatants (many of them children), in the issue of the New Scientist for 9th March 1996 I read a report of a suggestion for a low cost device for the detection and destruction of landmines that, by being operated remotely, did not put the operator at risk. The risk with mine detection by prodding is great (for example more than 80 prodders were killed in Kuwait after the Gulf War). What really caught my eye was that the inventor was Stephen Salter, with whom I had shared rooms as a first year undergraduate (see chapter 3). So I contacted him to ask who was putting up the funds to get his invention off the drawing board. It seemed that was the problem. Accordingly, being a member of the Parochial Church Council of the Church of the Good Shepherd, my suggestion that an appeal be launched in the name of the church (already a charity in law) was accepted and was formally in operation on 25th March. On 20th April, which was NATIONAL LANDMINE DAY, Audrey and I joined a delegation to our local MP for his support of the campaign. On 4th May the New Scientist had an article on landmines and the problems of how to deal with them. In the same issue was a letter by myself announcing the launch of the appeal to get the Dervish off the drawing board.

Following the appeal for funds for the Dervish Project sufficient money was raised, along with a larger amount Stephen had procured, so that there was enough for a prototype to be constructed and put through its paces on a Scottish Hill Farm. It became evident that the next stage would be to try it out in a real minefield to test it and modify it as necessary. My initial approach to the Ministry of Defence was a terse response to say that they had been advised (by, we later learned, the Mines Advisory Group, who supported us in correspondence but opposed us behind our backs) it would never get off the drawing board! When I responded by sending them a video of it in action on the Scottish Hill Farm there was a strange lack of response! The opposition by MAG, along with a lack of enthusiasm by the Halo Trust (following comments by MAG it seems), appeared to be partly a fear that their teams would be put out of business by the advent of the Dervish. This was essentially stupid; as their teams could be readily trained to use the Dervish and their operations would thereby be greatly speeded up and their operators would be at a greatly reduced risk to themselves. The MOD failed to challenge the spurious advice by MAG.

When in March 1998 Stephen exhibited the prototype at the DERA arms fair in England the representatives of arms industries kept guiding the admitted journalists to their own stands. However, the senior military officer present, who had supervised mine clearance after the Falklands war, kept returning to the Dervish stand declaring it was the only truly original device in the exhibition. Indeed this opinion was confirmed on 19th October 1998 when the Royal Scottish Society of Arts awarded its prestigious Keith Medal for Innovation to Stephen for this "exceptional project". When we subsequently applied to the Ministry of Defence for £500, 000 to put the Dervish through its paces in real minefields two referees were strongly, indeed enthusiastically, in support. However, the third referee (we were later to learn represented a group developing a more expensive and more risky device supported by the arms industry) was opposed. The MOD response was to assign our submission to the second priority list, as to be in the first priority list one needed all three referees to support one's proposal. Once again the MOD was too close to the arms industry when it came to critical evaluations of proposed projects and took too much notice of the spurious advice by MAG. It was estimated at the time that the cost of clearing landmines by the then current means being employed was three to four times the cost of that it would involve using the Dervish instead. The MOD, however, has a poor record for getting value for taxpayer's money when vested interests are involved. Stephen has published the design and full details of the Dervish on the Internet. Hopefully it will be taken up in the future or a modified version (such as in conjunction with a subsequently available miniature bulldozer that could attach a Dervish in front and sweep it from side to side as it moved slowly forwards) all operated remotely. A far more expensive Japanese device adopted the remote control element of the Dervish, thus greatly reducing the risk to the operators. An interesting development in the 21st Century has been the Belgian NGO Apopo that has employed an African giant pouched rat with a highly developed sense of smell to locate the mines. They are not heavy enough to explode the mines and are rewarded with fruit each time they locate a mine. They have been employed to successfully clear parts of Angola and Mozambique of land mines.

As the time approached when Zak would cease to be my postdoc I was desperately trying to find new sources of funding. Indeed in 1989 I had written more than 1000 letters before I obtained support (see above). When funding, or part funding, was obtained it was usually for only a few years. A consequence was that requests from potential PhD students had to be declined as I was not in a position to guarantee I would be able to supervise them for three years. I had not been a PhD student myself, having obtained my PhD, in 1971, for my 1960s publications (see chapter 8). While some applicants were clearly good candidates, others struck me as unlikely to show originality but would want to play it safe in order to obtain the qualification. I had come across a few people with PhDs who seemed to be clones of their supervisors but without the latter's flair for originality. Indeed one such, but better than most, provoked the following poem:

BREAKING IN? (CW)

To tell the truth she's getting bored
With tiny topic spread across
Allotted stretch of thirty six
Of youthful months. So much is dross,
She now perceives. As thesis starts
To take its shape at sluggish pace,
A nagging worry sprouts and grows.
Perhaps she'll end in blank disgrace
Of insufficient data points
To make her case. Besides there's what
Will happen next? A postdoc post
With luck or just a job that's not
A challenge, merely means to earn
The cash required to stay afloat?
But now, with thesis bound and prize
Is won, she's proud of what she wrote.
She's offered post exceeding dreams.
Perhaps surviving times of drought
Was what it really was about,
As few will read her tome it seems.
It's just her ticket winning place
In team engaged in work that shares
In search for cure of dread disease.
The pain was gain, she now declares.
But still she wonders whether yield
Was at expense of moulding mind,

To make her clone of rest of team;
Apart from Tom who's different kind.
He'd switched from being software freak
To being one with novel line,
Their ideas man. Compared to rest
He's like a glass of vintage wine.

Sometimes the research student has a more original mind than the supervisor. The good supervisor then has the sense to give him or her a pretty free rein as long as the student doesn't try to spread their efforts across too wide a range. Very rarely a supervisor in this position becomes obstructive:

HIDDEN TALENT (GK)

Her problems spring from simple fact
That he, who's meant to supervise
Her work for thesis, can't admit
She's swimming way beyond his depth.
It's thus he's led to scorn her work,
Demanding cuts and glossary
Of words that any dictionary
Defines. It's simple case that he,
Not student, fails to stay the course.
But on appeal the powers that be
Align themselves behind the fool,
To save their system losing face.
But when her papers make their mark
They're keen to claim they played their part
In spotting talent now acclaimed.
The truth is rarely what it seems
When self-important clowns are those
Who run affairs, or so they claim.
In fact the bulk of work is done
Behind the scenes by nameless folk,
Who flatter those in charge but do
The job with skill, without a fuss.
Perhaps it's always been this way.

Over the years I have refereed many papers. I always try to make constructive comments. Very rarely I have received an intemperate response, when I have commented that an interpretation was a tentative hypothesis and not a conclusion and the author(s) should perhaps reconsider it in the light of published evidence that would seem to contradict it.

AWRY (GK)

I'm at a loss with how to deal
With comments on a paper sent
To referee who seems to think,
Because I disagree with some
Suggestions published by himself,
I'm waging war against his work
And person in attempt to boost
Myself at his expense. Debate
About the facts and what they mean
Is very soul of science at
Its best, as long as we observe
The rule to keep exchange ad rem.
It's he by reading my dissent,
From work he dreamed was way ahead
Of field, as just malign attack
On all he's tried to do, who sinks
To childish tantrum; leaving me
With need to write riposte as best
I may without descent to swamp
Of his subjective damaged pride.
I've learned to heed the rival views
And novel facts that may require
I ditch my own or else I risk
Becoming dinosaur whose fate
Is sealed when youthful ways are claimed
To be the only ones to reign,
To be upheld till end of days.
Indeed I've greater credit gained
When I have changed my mind about
A view I published years ago.
And what is more a guess that proved
To be awry has sparked research
That led to others finding truth.

PEER REVIEW (GK)

Today I got report from guy
Without a name.
He's meant to judge my paper's weight
And point the ways
To help the reader understand.
Instead he carps.
He wants to jargonise my text.
He rules I ought
To add another theme in which
I'll cite his work;
Despite the fact he hides behind
Pretence I won't
Infer it's him I'm asked to name.
Besides, to add
Suggested piece diverts from aim
Of paper's thrust.
So now you know why I insist
On signing when
The boot is on the other foot
And I am judge.
Unless Anon acts gentleman
The game is farce.

EXAM PAPER (GK)

I scrawl these words on sheet from pile
Intended for exam. In place
Of Question one I seize my thoughts
And feelings as they come like birds
To scraps of food from children's plates.
It's forty years since last I sat
To be assessed on knowledge long
Forgot. But first degree procured
A job. On winding road that since
I've walked, I've taught myself the facts
And skills required to serve my needs.
So now it's only I who knows
Enough to mark my latest scripts:
And yet the rules require they're scanned
And criticised by those whose own
Achievements thrive in fields beyond
Horizons bounding mine. I pounce

On helpful ways of smoothing flow,
But pompous challenge to my views
Derived by logic's rules from facts,
Of which reviewer's unaware,
Are plain inane. Despite ripostes,
I've had rejection notes on grounds
"I needs must heed advice from those
I've asked to act as referees"!
Indeed amongst most cited works
Are some that found themselves in print
At third attempts. It's all a game;
As life, it seems, amounts to throws
Of dice from birth until our ends:
And yet we daily make our choice
Between competing calls on time:
But random acts will intervene.
Besides, no comments give us break
To change our minds, no proofs provide
A final chance to make amends.
It's thus we blunder on in faith
With good intents and fragile hopes
Of gains in love and greater light.

I have also come across papers that have not been adequately refereed and thus clog up the literature with nonsense that is then uncritically cited by the unwary.

A LITTLE LEARNING LEADS ASTRAY (CW)

A recent paper came attached
To e-mail. Title caught my eye
As being right within my field.
But when I viewed the figured fly
I promptly saw it wasn't what
The caption said. It's larger far
Beyond the largest kin of fly
They've named. It's though a car
And juggernaut had been confused.
One wonders who reviewed this hash.
I've come across this sort of thing
Before. They're filed as worthless trash.
They're mainly wordy papers where
The species names were fast assigned
By using picture books or keys
Beyond their sell by dates. Resigned
To need to check all papers, texts
And recent works they cite, I've found
There's always one or two are flawed,
Because the names employed aren't sound.
As knowledge grows it often proves
To be the case that 'widespread' kinds
Are really clans of species each
Of which in part of range one finds
Alone. They now no longer teach
Our students how to deal with large
And tricky groups of beasts. The books
They use are only meant to show
Selected few whose diverse looks
Display the range of forms alone.
For each there's dozen more that look
Alike. Providing name's a skill
That's more than telling crow from rook.
To add to challenge man, in planes
And ships, is introducing bugs
From foreign lands, despite the checks.
They enter like illicit drugs.
One's guide is constant doubt until
One's sure the name one's reached is right.
At times an error causes harm,
As when a name was just a flight
Of fancy by defence that gave

276

A guilty man an alibi
Until the error was exposed;
As bogus expert's shown to lie.
I came across another work
Designed to test a notion as
Excuse for trip abroad, despite
An English garden's fauna has
A better known, already named,
Display of beasts. He sampled range
Of fallen forest fruits to count
A chosen insect very strange.
Applying clever maths to scores
He thought he'd proved his point. But when
He asked an expert for a name
He's shocked to learn there's more than ten,
With two or three in every fruit. He'd just
Assumed a single striking beast
Would meet his needs. His counts were waste
Of effort, time and funds at least!

While the majority of species remain unknown to science, ecologists must expect undescribed species to occur in their samples. While I acquired a reputation as a taxonomist, my taxonomic work was primarily a means to the end of advancing knowledge of the diversity of the natural histories of scuttle flies and their role in ecosystems. Inevitably I have described and named several hundred new species. Occasionally the press has decided to report a routine description of a new species without any apparent reason for selecting it as opposed to a new species associated with highly novel habits. Indeed the prevalence of ignorance among journalists as to the astonishing richness of invertebrate species found, for example, in urban habitats (e.g. Disney, R. H. L., 2001. The scuttle flies (Diptera: Phoridae) of Buckingham Palace Garden. Supplement to the London Naturalist 80: 245-258. – with 75 species listed, 53 being in the giant genus Megaselia and with one being new to science). With more extensive collecting I have recorded 87 species of Phoridae, 58 being Megaselia (with several new to science), in gardens (mainly my own suburban garden) in Cambridge.

DO THE MEEK INHERIT THE EARTH? (RE)

The papers make a song and dance
When Oxford don reports a slug
That's new to science, hence to list
For England too. But why the plug
For fellow's routine work, when most
Of smaller beasts on planet Earth
Have yet to be described and named?
Perhaps frenetic press has dearth
Of stories needed fast to fill
A space between the adverts few,
If any, readers scan. Perhaps
The tiny flies I name as new,
On monthly basis, lack allure
Of mollusc munching favoured blooms.
Or else a canny scientist
When needing funds renewed he grooms
His in-house media contact man,
Inflating why his find is news.
Too soon it's wrapping chips, too soon
Forgot. The tales our papers choose
Too often seem a random pick
Of mostly bleak, depressing lists
Of violent deaths or evil deeds.
At least report of slug insists
We need to care for precious earth
Or else we'll lose its rich display
Of varied forms of life. At least
Our mollusc friend is neither gay
Nor straight*. It can't provoke the fools   *Slugs are hermaphrodite!
Who choose to take offence if male
Or female takes the stage and leaves
Excluded sex to rant and rail!
It's not the ant as paradigm
We need to seek, but slug sublime!
It calmly, slowly lives its life
Avoiding any form of strife.

The number of species of invertebrate in the average suburban garden is surprising, as noted above for the scuttle flies alone in my suburban Cambridge garden.

GRAND DISPLAY (GK)

The honeysuckle's in full bloom
On side of garden shed. It lures
A hundred flies and bees in hum
Of sweet content. For me this crowns
The joys of summer days when life
Is feeling good. I've met a range
Of flowering trees and sprawling vines
In humid forests rising high
Towards relentless tropic sun,
And while their blooms were twice as large,
Or more, and often seemed of wild
Design, there's none whose scent and throng
Of dual coloured lyric forms
Have brought me more delight than these
That now adorn suburban view
In English town. But better still
Is when I come across it sprawled
Along a country hedge, beside
A herd of cattle chewing cud
In slow and peaceful scene that seems
Was made for artist's eye and brush.
In winter when I've wandered woods,
Beneath a gloom when skies were grey,
I've found a sapling tree whose trunk
In sculpted corkscrew stands forlorn,
Embraced by honeysuckle stem,
Whose grasping grip induced this art
That brings to mind more languid days;
But also strangler figs I've seen
In forests set in warmer climes,
Where nature's constant wars prevent
Romantic views from taming truths.
These scrabbling shows are deadly race
To claim the light before the rest.

A far more significant advance than recognizing new species is achieving a new insight. However, there may be few, let alone journalists, who are in a position to appreciate it. For example the scuttle flies belong to a group of flies, the Achiza, that lack a feature on the head associated with a balloon like structure (the ptilinum) that helps the adult fly (of families in the Schizophora – such as house flies) escape from its pupal stage. I realized that an African genus of Phoridae in fact has this structure and probably represents an example of independent (convergent) evolution (Disney, R. H. L., 1991. Aenigmatistes (Diptera: Phoridae), Aschiza with a ptilinum! Bonner zoologisches Beiträge 42: 353-368).

ONE CULTURE? (CO)

I've spent some weeks in mental toil
Extracting signal from an ore
Of data that conceals the thread
Revealing evolution's path.
With logic's thorough sieves, and bins
That overflow with crumpled thoughts
I'd seized at first but found were flawed,
At last I serve the finished dish
In polished prose. It's end of long
And tricky road to reach a goal
For long I'd sought. But now I know
There's less than dozen round the world
Who'll understand achievement gained
Is crown of years of slog. For most
Will take conclusions as they stand,
Without concern for how they came
From hours of sweat and constant turns
That proved to be all cul-de-sacs.
It ranks along with art we take
For granted at a glance without
Regard for skill and flair beyond
The normal run for mortal man.
It's only those who've had a go
Themselves can truly judge such works.
Some science ranks with greatest verse
That only other poets know
How deep the dive to fetch such pearls.

With the completion of my 1994 book (see above) I was becoming increasingly intrigued by the extremely peculiar flightless females of the scuttle flies (assigned to the subfamily Termitoxeniinae) found in the fungus gardens of termites. With funding from the Leverhulme Trust and Isaac Newton Trust, and with many new specimens collected by David Kistner (based in California but constantly traveling abroad to collect his favoured beetles and other creatures from the colonies of ants and termites), I set about a revision of the species of the Afrotropical Region culminating in the following monograph: – Disney, R. H. L. & Kistner, D. H., 1995. Revision of the Afrotropical Termitoxeniinae (Diptera: Phoridae). Sociobiology 26: 115-225.

I then turned my attention to the species of the Oriental Region. However there was a problem. In 1925 Shiraki had briefly described some of these aberrant flightless female scuttle flies from the fungus gardens of termites in Formosa (today's Taiwan). He said he would provide fuller descriptions in another paper, but never did. The problem was that all but one of the species he had assigned to a genus we now know is restricted to Africa. I had tried to borrow his specimens from the museum in Taiwan, but after a lengthy correspondence it transpired that they had been destroyed in the Second World War when the Japanese had bombed the museum. So in 1995, with the Leverhulme and Isaac Newton Trust funding, Audrey and I based ourselves in the Chinese University in the New Territories of Hong Kong. We then travelled by train to Ghangzhou, in the Ghangdong Province of Mainland China, where we were guests of the Entomological Institute adjacent to the University. Dr Gui-Xiang Li at the Institute was the leading specialist on termites in China and I greatly benefitted from his expertise with regard to their taxonomy and the recognition of their nests in the field. Unlike many relatives elsewhere that construct conspicuous above ground mounds (some taller than a person) the nests of the Chinese species I was interested in are entirely underground. Dr Li showed me how to recognize the sealed entrances that are only opened for the nuptial flights of the brief emergence of the flying stages of the adult termites. We excavated termite nests in the upper reaches of the Pearl River. We found the first specimens of one of Shraki's species, after digging down a little more than a metre to reach the fungus gardens of the termites. Audrey reacted by expressing great surprise that we had come all the way to China to collect such tiny flies! After returning to Hong Kong, we proceeded to Taiwan. There we not only procured further specimens of Shiraki's problem species but also in addition related new species and new genera. One of the new species became the third species of fly that I named after Audrey (in the 1997 monograph cited below)! In Taiwan we were guests of the Forestry Research Institute in Taipei. The whole trip was extremely productive and not only culminated in a monographic revision of the Oriental species of Termitoxeniinae (Disney, R. H. L. & Kistner, D. H., 1997. Revision of the Oriental Termitoxeniinae (Diptera: Phoridae). Sociobiology 29: 3-118), but this in turn gave rise to a paper on Japanese species that went on to win an award in 2012 (see chapter 10).

Apart from the scientific gains of this trip the whole adventure was an unforgettable experience. In mainland China we had been asked where we wanted to stay and to eat and we had replied that we would be pleased to join with them. When we went to the upper reaches of the Pearl River we stayed in the hostel for the engineers responsible for overseeing the flood control. When we went upstream to excavate termite nests in the flood control banks the residents of the last village we passed through all ran away, apart from one old woman. They had evidently not encountered Europeans before. Audrey, using sign language, managed to engage in conversation with the old woman. Another interesting experience was with regard to the driver. He was a somewhat bumptious young man. At one stage we got a puncture. The driver removed the wheel and took into a nearby dwelling to fix it. In his absence a professor from the university started talking politics, but as soon as the driver reappeared the professor loudly drew my attention to some butterflies. It seemed the driver was a plant by the Party to keep an eye on these independent minded academics! Such a perception was reinforced by the fact that we were tailed by an official looking van with uniformed occupants. When asked who they were I was told, somewhat unconvincingly, that they were 'friendly' policemen curious as to what we were up to. When we had dug down to the fungus gardens of the termites and I produced the flies I had come to China to collect, the excitement of the professor and members of the Institute was obvious. Up to that point they had only known these strange scuttle flies as illustrations in textbooks. We eagerly collected samples of the flies. When we paused, we noticed the 'friendly' policemen were no longer with us! Back at the hostel the professor announced at the meal that after a brief meeting with his colleagues I was going to give a seminar on the peculiar flies! When I was about to start the professor turned to the young rodent control officer who had been assigned to us as interpreter and told him and myself that he, the professor, would undertake the translation as the technical entomology needed an academic to get it right!

When back in Hong Kong the young English lecturer, our host, asked me to give a seminar on the scuttle flies from the termite nests for his postgraduates. I started off by saying that as postgraduates I presumed they realized that much in textbooks was out of date or actually wrong. I then reviewed a series of hypotheses about these strange scuttle flies that had been put forward by Wasmann early in the 20th Century, some of which were in the textbooks. One by one I explained why all but one I had been shown to be incorrect. However, I pointed out that the erroneous hypotheses had nevertheless generated much detailed knowledge of the anatomy of these flies, albeit with misinterpretations of some structures. When the students left the lecturer could contain his mirth no longer and declared his students had never had a seminar like that before. When I asked what was amiss with my exposition he replied that nothing at all was amiss, but his students tended to regard the textbook as sacrosanct and I had challenged that assumption in a way they had not experienced before!

In Taiwan I had made all the arrangements with the entomologist, Dr Jung-Tai Chao, at the Forestry Research Institute. On arrival he welcomed us but said the Director was very busy and would be unlikely to be free to greet us himself. So I presented Dr Chao with a copy of my 1994 book and copies of papers on scuttle flies relevant to China with a request that he give them to the Director with my compliments. The next day Audrey and I were summoned to the Director's office and he presented Audrey and myself with gifts. I was then required to sign the next blank page in the VIP's visitor's book. The previous page had been signed by Professor Sir Richard Southwood. It seems that the Director had looked at my 1994 book and spotted that Sir Richard was the author of the Foreword to the book! It was during his sabbatical that Sir Richard had visited the Institute, and it was this absence from Oxford that had resulted in the FSC Research Fellowship ending up in Cambridge instead of Oxford (see chapter 8)!

After China we flew to Australia to stay with Trudy and her family. At the customs clearance in Australia a lady in front of us had made a scrapbook of post cards, pressed flowers (sealed under transparent plastic) and other mementos of her holiday in China. The official just ripped out the pages of pressed flowers and consigned them to an incinerator. When I declared my tubes of scuttle flies and termites preserved in ethanol and explained that we had been excavating termite nests in China he insisted on inspecting my shoes for evidence of Chinese soil! I didn't like to tell him the shoes I had worn for fieldwork, after being cleaned before packing, were in my suitcase! The Australian authorities are rightly concerned about accidental introductions of alien species and are critical of other countries not so concerned. However, they themselves are not without blame in transporting species. Thus I subsequently reported examples of a species of scuttle fly transported in Australian ships from Queensland to New Zealand (Disney, R. H. L., 2008. Natural history of the scuttle fly, Megaselia scalaris. Annual Review of Entomology 53: 39-60) in a cargo of melons; and from South Africa to the Antarctic (Nickolls, P. & Disney, R. H. L., 2001. Flies discovered at Casey station. Australian Antarctic Magazine 1: 54) in trays of eggs (some of which had gone bad) in a container that had been loaded in Perth but invaded by the scuttle fly in Cape Town; and in a consignment of wheat meal animal feed from Australia to New Zealand! Small insects whose larvae develop in decaying organic materials or fruit, or are pests of crop species, are most at risk of being unwittingly transported around the world by man. If a species whose larvae are parasitic on a particular species of ant is accidentally introduced it will only get established if its host is already there. For an example of species most prone to being transported around the world by man see the report of the scuttle flies of the Galápagos Islands in chapter 10.

Pest species are especially prone to being accidentally transported across the world by man. Thus the pests of our white cultivated mushrooms (Agaricus species) in Europe have been transported to Australia and New Zealand; while their American pest species have been transported to India as these mushrooms became popular amongst the rising affluent classes in India. Likewise oyster mushrooms (Pleurotus species) have long been a cottage industry in India, but during the last few decades of the 20th Century became popular in Europe. It was not surprising, therefore, that a pest of oyster mushrooms in India, that I had named Megaselia tamilnaduensis in 1996, in a note of 1999 I reported it to have turned up on two oyster mushroom farms in Poland.

1995: my third poetry collection published (LAPSED ATHEIST and other poems Rockingham Press, 40 pages).

The blurb on the back cover said of me 'He regards the Darwinian revolution as a gift to theology and considers doubt to be essential for discoveries in both science and theology. He regards observable facts and authenticated experiences as sacred, and all interpretation as provisional.' This was a quotation taken from my contribution to correspondence under the heading 'God's razor' published in the New Scientist (15 May 1993, volume 138 No.1873: 52). The title poem of this collection is reproduced in chapter 3, where it and a number of other poems demonstrate that a period of atheism was beneficial in allowing me to reject atavistic dogmas and practices that tend to obscure the Gospel call to embrace a life of compassionate service and just dealing in place of self-centred living.

31st May 1996: our grandson Alistair born.

I became involved with leading the children's groups at the Church of the Good Shepherd. This was challenging but rewarding. The materials supplied to us leaders gave us a topic, a Bible reading, commentary upon it and suggested questions for each week. However, there was a tendency to be simplistic and verging on an over literalistic interpretation of Old Testament Scripture. Having experienced Sixth Form students of biology realizing that Sunday school teaching they had received when younger was at odds with modern science, and thereby their faith diminishing, I was determined to avoid this. I therefore edited the prescribed commentary and answered the children's questions as honestly as I could. At the same time I had to avoid being too technical and comprehensive in relation to their level of knowledge and understanding. The vital task was to share what being a Christian involved and not confuse them with theological abstractions. Thus I wrote this prayer for them:

A CHILDREN'S PRAYER (RE)

Let's thank our loving Father God
For food and homes, for caring mums
And dads, and grown-ups everywhere,
For teachers too, and special chums.

Let's thank our loving Father God
Who helps us learn to love and care,
To tell the truth and do what's right,
To not be greedy but to share.

Let's ask our loving Father God
To help us welcome stranger boys
And girls from other lands and ways.
For they, like us, have hopes and joys.

Let's ask our loving Father God
To help us when the going's bad,
To ease our pains, and when at times
We're just upset or feeling sad.

And so, oh loving Father God,
We give you thanks that Jesus came
And showed your love throughout his days.
We ask your help to do the same.
Amen.

I also rewrote the hymn 'All things bright and beautiful' (see chapter 10). With the younger children, of course, one needed to meet them at the level they were at in understanding. Abstractions were virtually taboo and distractions all part of the fun:

MATCHING KNICKERS (MC)

I'm telling kids about the love
Of God and how He spurns the sin
But not the sinner, when a girl
Of four declares her dress is new
And what is more her knickers match -
As she displays! We fail to keep
Our faces straight while we admire
The dress before I gently bring
Them back to thoughts of Christ; who showed

A special love for children when
On earth He strove to sow His view
Of God as loving Father – not
Demanding tyrant as conceived
In minds of those for whom the Law
Concealed the truth of God's desire
That we should tend compassion's seeds
Within our souls. Besides, I sense
That He delights in joy of she
Who wants to speak her praise of dress
He mum acquired for her last week!
I'm sure He smiles with us at show
Of matching knickers too! Indeed,
As we rejoice with her, we share
Her bashless bliss infecting all:
We catch a glimpse of grace behind
Distorting masks we all parade;
But now resolve our outer garb
Will be at one with hidden selves.

I and my fellow leaders seldom knew what we were achieving.
Occasionally one was surprised:

SOWINGS (RE)

The precious seeds she scatters blind
When taking kids in Sunday school,
Enshrining truths of Gospel's gold
In simplest words; but all a child
Of six responds – 'my frock is new'!
She talks of being kind to all, when boy
Of eight delivers punch to one
He thinks is in his way. But then
When final hymn is sung and hall
Becomes awash with drinks and hum
Of voices sharing news, a lad
Who years ago was just as wild
Informs her now he wants to teach,
And R.E. is his chosen field.
Another child, who always seemed
To pay attention all the time,
Is now a dropout from the church
And only lives for kicks. It seems
Her earth was stony ground or else

She needs to freely find herself
For while. Perhaps we're each on search
For path that only we discern
Amid the jumbled scene ahead.
We're each a bloodhound running free
In restless hunt for trail that leads
To prize we half believe since Christ
Proclaimed at Eastertide it's not
A joke, or fairy tale, but real.

Apart from leading the children's group at church I was also involved with undergraduates. Those in their final year undertook research projects. If they chose one set by me I would make them carry out a small taxonomic investigation involving description of at least one new species, but involving some extra element such as an example of convergent resemblance to a genus in a different subfamily or with some applied aspect. I required them to employ more than one method of illustration apart from drawing (black and white photography and/or scanning electron micrographs). They were required to format the main part of their report for a named journal, and when approved by me it was submitted for publication. They thus had a paper in press when applying for a postgraduate position (e.g. Coomer, R. P. C., 1999. A new species of Tubicera Schmitz, 1920 (Diptera: Phoridae) from Algeria. Entomologist's Gazette 50, 109-114. Woolf, G. E., 1998. A new species of Phoridae (Diptera) from Brazil. Giornale Italiano di Entomologia 8, 207-211 (1996)). In addition I felt that a part of their training should be learning how to deal with the comments of an editor and referees.

I also gave four lectures on flies (Diptera) to the final year undergraduates until austerity required the Department to cut back on lectures by non-University employees, as they had to pay a fee to people like myself who were based in the University but not employed by them. However, undergraduates and research students often came, or were sent by their supervisors, to consult me about flies and other matters.

Research assessment exercises, etc.

During the 1990s academia was afflicted with attempts to assess the contributions to knowledge made by those engaged in research at universities. The problem was that the assessments made by the initial Research Assessment Exercises were perceived to be too subjective. The result in the 21st Century was a preference for a more 'objective' set of measures – 'citation indexes', 'impact factors', etc. But these have proved even more misleading.

Under the RAE system one was required to submit a list of the six publications that best represented your contribution for the period in question. I included the following paper – Disney, R. H. L. & Cumming, M. S., 1992.

Abolition of the Alamirinae and ultimate rejection of Wasmann's theory of hermaphroditism in Termitoxeniinae (Diptera, Phoridae). Bonner zoologische Beiträge 43: 145-154. Among the reasons I included this paper was the fact that Paul Dessart in Belgium, who edited a quality magazine on natural history, was so intrigued by our paper that he wrote an article about it (Dessart, P., 1993. Histoire des Termitoxéniides ou les errements de la science. Les Naturalistes Belges 74: 61-75). However, I was instructed to remove this paper in an 'obscure' German journal and to replace it with a note in Nature (Weissflog, A., Maschwitz, U., Disney, R. H. L. & Rosciszewski, K., 1995. A fly's ultimate con. Nature, London 378 (6553): 137). However, as Nature has a severe limit on the number of pages for a paper, the prime purpose of this note was to direct readers to the detailed treatment of these extraordinary flies that was being published in California (Disney, R. H. L., 1996. A new genus of scuttle fly (Diptera; Phoridae) whose legless, wingless, females mimic ant larvae (Hymenoptera; Formicidae). Sociobiology 27: 95-118). It is worth noting that the note in Nature gave rise to articles across the world, me being interviewed on a BBC Radio 4 science programme and the fly ending up in the Guinness Book of Records! Furthermore I was invited to write an article to illustrate why taxonomy was a challenging science and not 'merely descriptive' (Disney, R. H. L., 1997. Fantastic flies and flights of fancy. Journal of Biological Education 31: 39-48). The paper in Sociobiology scored two orders of magnitude less than the note in Nature!

Many have criticized the fashion for the simplistic ranking of journals and scientific papers by measures such as impact factors and citation indexes (e.g. Sparagano, O. A. E. 1998. Publication records. Biologist 45: 55). I have joined in this criticism. The impact factor of a journal is particularly silly as it ignores the restriction on the number of pages allowed by many journals. For example, the single page note in Nature referred to above scored orders of magnitude more than a monograph of more than 100 pages that took up the entire issue of a journal. This I subsequently likened to assessing the pictures in the National Gallery by ranking the quality of their frames only (Disney, R. H. L. 2000. The relentless decline of taxonomy. Science & Public Affairs October 2000: 6. Disney, R. H. L. 2001. Evaluating scientific papers and research proposals. Cortex 37: 583-584).

RATINGS (GK)

The chatter never stops its flow
As we partake at coffee beak.
It's mostly little things we're on
About. There's skirt that's new, a guy
Who's feeling blue, a cake that's made
To celebrate a birthday, price
Of food, a child who's hurt her knee,
The latest film at cinema,
The traffic jam on way to work.
You'd never guess Department's head
Of list in latest round to rate
The 'best' of science of our kind
In 'leading' journals in a year.
Perhaps because our work is not
A drug we take each day, but cause
Consuming like a fire, we need
To turn our minds to lesser things
To keep us sane. Besides, we know
Assessments made of papers, judged
By silly rules and those without
The special knowledge gained
By those in field, are little worth.
My longest papers far exceed
The bulk and length accepted by
The 'top of range' of journals held
In high esteem. Indeed they score
Away below my minor note
In Nature's fashion-conscious game.
It's all a con. They scrutinize
The frame but not the painted scene.

With regard to citation indexes these are frequently misleading with regard to the change of direction in a field of science. The highest scores are frequently allocated to subsequent review papers rather than the papers responsible for initiating the changes of direction.

CITATION'S GAME (GK)

As rival aims to raise his name
At her expense, in growing rage
She quietly grinds away to cull
Her data till she knows her case
Is sound beyond dispute. For him
The search for truth is just a game,
A war to win in hunt for grants
And accolades. But soon he starts
To just ignore some awkward facts
That fail to fit his favoured scheme.
She fears his skill with words will win
Debate unless she overwhelms
Tirade with novel truths. She bides
Her time as notebooks fill and one
By one her numbers march across
Computer's screen to be assessed
By careful tests. At last she drafts
Her paper, line by polished line,
Until content. She e-mails all
Her hopes to chosen journal's box
Across the world. Her rival's asked
To referee her script. There's clash
With other given task as well.
At length this other's view prevails.
At last her efforts see the light
Of print. But he inters, conceals
His former work, in which he erred,
In long review of field. It's this,
Which crosses every 't' and dots
Each 'i', that those who follow cite.

Furthermore, the end point of a change of direction in a field of research may be a change in policy, or even a change in the law, rather than a review paper that cites the initial change of direction of research that was the catalyst for the subsequent outcomes. Such an undoubted 'impact' is seldom registered by our current impact factors. For example, when l was a medical entomologist in the forest zone of West Cameroon, but was on leave in 1969 in the City of Bath (Audrey's home city), I was struck by one respect in which Bath was less hygienic than the large market town of Kumba. In the latter, people openly urinated against the boundary wall of the market and deposited faeces in the drainage channels. Likewise, dogs deposited excrement everywhere. However, within a matter of a few hours at most the dung beetles rolled up the dung into balls and buried them along with their eggs. By contrast one could not walk ten metres along the streets of the salubrious City of Bath without passing a deposit of dog faeces. I therefore recorded which flies were visiting these deposits, which fly larvae were developing in them and which of these (such as the lesser housefly Fannia canicularis) were also commonly found in the kitchens of our houses. I suggested that the prevalence of dog dung in English cities was directly related to the then frequency of human enteric infections in England (Disney, R. H. L. 1973. Some flies associated with dog dung in an English city. Entomologist's Monthly Magazine 108: 93-94 (1972)). I published a further paper to show that the insects associated with dog turds varied with the habitat context (Disney, R. H. L., 1976. Some Diptera and Tineidae (Lepidoptera) associated with dog dung on the Yorkshire Pennines, with some comments on animal habitat classification. Entomologist's Monthly Magazine 111: 41-45 (1975)). Zakaria Erzinclioglu read my notes and carried out a more extensive study in a north London suburb, confirming and extending my findings (Erzinclioglu, Y. Z., 1981. On the Diptera associated with dog dung in London. London Naturalist 60: 45-46). The curiosity of neighbours observing him collecting samples gave rise to his work coming to the attention of one of the London evening papers. In the subsequent correspondence it was pointed out that a parasitic infection of the eye (Toxocariasis), then more frequent among children, was also commonly derived from dog dung. The result was the introduction of the requirement of dog owners to collect up their dog's excrement and for local councils to provide bins for its deposition. The end result has been a reduction in the infections derived from dog dung. This undoubted impact of my initial note is not reflected in the scores used to measure the value of a scientific publication. Indeed, according to these measures my note was of no significance whatsoever!

Increasingly my research was driven by requests to identify specimens with novel biological data (reared from a named fungus or invertebrate host, visiting a named flower, preying on a named insect, etc.) from around the world. The species frequently proved to be new to science and when a known species the biological data were new. The resulting papers typically included the correspondents as co-authors. The new data were frequently surprising.

'HISTORY IS JUST ONE DAMN THING AFTER ANOTHER' (GK)

In jungle's gloomy scrum of plants
That strive to reach the light he finds
A vine with several swollen twigs.

A closer look reveals each bulge
Is hollow tipped with tiny hole
From which a stream of ants emerge.

They lick the gifts of nectar placed
At base of leaves and in return
Patrol each branch removing pests.

But tiny flies observe the scene
Awaiting time the flying ants
Emerge to light for nuptial flight.

It's then they strike and lay an egg
In victim's rear, and when it's shed
Its wings the larvae hatch and feed.

By eating non-essential parts,
Before they reach the vital brain,
Its death's postponed, the meat stays fresh.

When fully grown they finish task
And use the emptied head as shield
In which the pupa bides its time.

Today the daughter flies emerge
To find a mate, and then a vine,
And so the cycle starts again.

There's something neat and clean about
This dreadful tale of vine and ants
And cunning fly that links the three.

With men, for everyone that's kind
There's yob impelled by ill intent,
Exploiting every chance for con.

'NERDY BORE'? (GK)

Today at microscope I saw
A marvel never seen before,
A wondrous insect on a slide
Of genus new to science. What
Is more it fills a gap in scheme
Of evolution's tale. Besides
Its elegance conveys delight
And sense of awe. The many hours
Of patient toil received reward.
The snobs, who think a scientist
A threat to way of life we share
Or nerdy bore devoid of heart,
Have never heard the secret praise
I sing when novel truths emerge
From days of work for small returns.
Perhaps they fail to grasp that dry,
Concise account on journal's page
Conceals the sweat, the fun, the long
Sustained enthusiastic quest
For clues, despite the odds and blocked
Off ends to tracks that seemed to lead
To heights ahead. The hunt is half
The gain, along with beauty's crown,
The glow of thanks for knowledge won,
And pleasure shared with fellow 'nerds'
Who know their science feeds the soul -
That hidden child who dwells behind
The 'boring' mask the world perceives.

In 1996 I was pleased that a book Zak had started when he was doing his postdoc with me was at last published: – 23. Blowflies. Naturalists' Handbooks by Zakaria Erzinclioglu. 1996.

Requests to identify scuttle flies caught in flight interception traps, etc., without biological or quantitative ecological data I had, regrettably to now decline. The time required to process my backlog of such material (which evidently includes many species new to science) had by now exceeded my life expectancy:

SUCH REGRETS (TL)

It's with regret I must refuse
A Turkish man requesting days
Be spent on naming flies he'd caught
In olive grove. Despite he says
The list of scuttle flies for where
He lives is short, and claim his catch
Includes a range of forms, the queue
Extends beyond my death's dispatch.
The things I've left undone are now
A load I have to bear. The worst
Are times I should have spent with those
I love – instead of work. I'm cursed
With thoughts of 'urgent' tasks I now
Perceive as mostly wasted hours.
But such regrets have come too late.
Today there's risk the past devours
My present joys and future hopes.
Perhaps that's why I fritter time
Away instead, perfecting tropes,
Or otherwise, and search for rhyme,
Attempting grasp of things sublime
Before my final knell's lone chime.

SERVICE (GK)

I burden self with mounds of work
Because I'm now too soft to say
To each request for help a "no.
I'm sorry, time does not allow.
My backlog now exceeds the span
Of life I can expect before
I die". And so what once was fun
Becomes at risk of being grind.
And yet in every sample sent
I find a new delight or else
The facts that sender writes are new
And need a name attached to see
The light of print. It's thus I find
I'm working faster than before.
I'm like machine providing aid
To those who set agenda, stoke
My fire, to serve their ends not mine.

And yet the gains from service, not
Pursuit of narrow road to fame,
Fulfil a deeper need. So why
Complain? It's idle folk who pine.
Besides the warmth of peers' respect
Is worth far more than fashion's prize.

1997: Sc.D. (Cambridge University)

As with my PhD, this award was for published work. It was given for publications (on scuttle flies) published since my 1960s publications that were assessed for my PhD. What was most unusual was that, for the research involved, not one of these publications had received a penny from a Research Council. All the work had been funded by private trusts. After being awarded this higher doctorate (the highest examined award a scientist can attain) colleagues suggested I inform NERC (the Natural Environment Research Council) that the University had rated me worthy of this award but NERC had repeatedly turned down my applications over a quarter of a century. Each rejection had informed me that my application had been 'highly regarded' by the Review Panel but – waffle to the effect that my field of research was not fashionable. So I contacted NERC and told them I had been awarded a Doctorate of Science and colleagues had suggested I apply for funding support. I asked whether it would be worth the effort involved in view of the past record of fruitless applications. They replied that they would get back to me with a response to my question. When they did so they encouraged me to apply. In due course I received similar letter of rejection to those as before plus the addition 'We wish you well in your chosen career'! This was a crass addition in view of the fact that I had just turned sixty and was being forced into early retirement due to a failure to obtain research funding that included a component for a salary. Thus the principal effect of the award of the Doctor of Science degree was that I was now required to wear a red gown when attending formal occasions at the Senate House!:

INTO LINE (TL)

Today I queued at Senate House
To hear a lecture given by
A colleague for the Prince who's named
As Head of Alma Mater. High
Above the Royal Standard flew,
While I below was clad in gown
Of scarlet like a Santa Claus,
But feeling like an awkward clown.
I ponder why we had to dress
For pantomime to hear a talk
On watching deer on Scottish Isle.
I don't suppose the Duke would balk
Event if all had dressed in garb
Of daily choice. 'Tradition' came
Reply when asking reason why;
Since colleague's words would be the same
Whatever clothes we'd worn! He winced
And added more 'we dress for wake
Or wedding, so it's right to do
The same today – for old time's sake.
A solemn tone is what sustains
And links the past to future gains.
Besides it's what the rule ordains'.
My feeling not myself remains!

CONTRIBUTION (CW)

When first I'd tried to name a fly
I'd reared I'd been in awe of tomes
I'd used. But as I came to see
The need for handbook up to date,
With novel key to scuttle flies,
I'd learned of flaws in former works
That I'd employed. My awe remains
At how those early workers had
Progressed, despite the fact they'd pinned
These tiny beasts. It's only when
I mounted them on slides, and moved
To compound microscope, that sense
Began to dawn at last. Despite
The strides I've made, and steady shift
From those I caught on local patch

To many sent from distant lands
Across the seas, it seems I'm just
Consuming crumbs of tiny slice
From cake we've only just begun.
Today I'm king of scuttle flies,
But when I'm gone my name will fade
Until I'm just a passing note
Or two in monograph at which
I'd aimed as mirage dream I'd known
I'd not attain in several lives.
We strive and goad ourselves without
The gains we'd glimpsed as youths and now
Accept as out of reach. Enough
To set our hands to plough so time
May yield a harvest for our heirs.

AT RIVER'S EDGE (CW)

I sometimes ponder how it's come
To be I've published more than all
The fellow workers in my field.
On looking back I can recall
An early wonder as a child,
As I observed the creatures in
A magic garden's other world.
I quickly learned I'd never win
The prize for being top of class,
As I was not above the norm
In terms of high I. Q. As boy
I'd no desire to just conform
To bragging, shallow views of rest
Of herd. They thought me cat that stalked
Alone, they deemed aloof. In truth
A curbing shyness meant I baulked
At joining in. Instead I found
Delight in nature's rich display
Of varied forms of life. The world
Of pop and football stars, the way
Of jeering scorn of those who lacked
The perks we took on trust, were not
For me. Instead I wandered hills
And lanes, or else my favoured spot
At river's edge is where I sat
To watch the dragonflies, the fish,

The water voles and birds. It's thus
There slowly grew the stubborn wish
To spend my days researching lives
Of lowly beasts whose beauty brought
Me such delight. Despite a lack
Of grades it's still believed I ought
To need, I muddled through exams
And carried on recording ways
Of lowly insects on my own.
And so I've spent my rest of days.
In retrospect it seems so strange
I'm now a doctor twice, despite
I've never written thesis, gained
A grant from NERC, or chosen right
Amongst the shiny topics judged
To be within the current flow
Of fashion's stream. Instead I've worked
At water's edge and there by slow
Degrees and dogged will have made
My mark, attaining highest grade.

Some of the novel habits reported by my co-authors of papers where I have described the previously unknown species involved have continued to surprise. For example three species associated with the huge tarantula type spiders of South America that feed on birds, frogs, etc. The larvae of the associated flies go down the jaws of the spider to share its meal when it has caught its prey, and then return to pupate on the sides of the spider (Weinmann, D. & Disney, R. H. L., 1997. Two new species of Phoridae (Diptera) whose larvae associate with large spiders (Araneae: Theraphosidae). Journal of Zoology, London 243: 319-328. Disney, R. H. L. & Weinmann, D., 1998. A further new species of Phoridae (Diptera) whose larvae associate with large spiders (Araneae: Theraphosidae). Entomologica scandinavica 29: 19-23). These observations made me wonder whether I would have found such larvae if I had examined the spiders that used to observe Audrey as she nervously hung the washing on the line by our house in Belize (chapter 5). But those were the days before I had ever tried to identify a scuttle fly!

1997: Adrian falls about thirty feet in Glen Nevis and spends six months in hospital in Glasgow before facing life in a wheelchair.

LIFE SENTENCE (TL)

As gale subsides and trees have ceased
To toss and sway
I once again can lay to rest
My anxious fears;
As when my son's intensive care
Had ceased at last
And slowly nature healed his wounds;
But left him tied
To irksome life in wheelchair's thrall,
And dream's demise.
A moment's fall had changed his hopes
For once for all.
It's heavy price to pay for rest
Of days; despite
His will to carry on with guts
And anger reined
Beneath his witty dry asides,
Concealing voids.
His zest for life once overflowed
Amongst the hills
He loved to roam or climb with friends
Who shared the thrills.
He's now a tethered hound who hears
The pack give tongue
As scent of fox now lures them on
Across the fell.
I pray he'll find a friend to feed
His need to love.
I pray research will find a way
To mend such states.

Audrey and I never understood Adrian's passion for rock climbing. It was the one unfortunate legacy of living on the Pennines as rock climbing was a popular pastime at Malham Cove and other limestone scars in the district. Apart from urging him to be careful, it was not our way to object. When he was a student at Bangor University he had a nasty fall that landed him in hospital. We were so relieved when he appeared to have recovered completely. What we did not know, nor Outward Bound (his employer in 1997), was that it had left a legacy of occasional momentary blackouts. In Glen Nevis he had set up a relatively easy abseil for his party of young people and leaving them under the supervision of his assistant he went round a bend to set up a harder one. He was stood on a relatively wide, safe, shelf of rock. It seems that having completed

299

his task he stood up too quickly and triggered a momentary blackout. The result was a thirty-foot fall and, following six months in hospital in Glasgow, life confined to a wheelchair thereafter.

ENDURING ACHE (TL)

It's hard to come to terms with fact
Of son confined to wheelchair all
His days. Before that numbing blow,
Before that life reducing fall,
He'd seek the mountains. There he felt
As free as bird who soars above
Frenetic ways of man below.
It seems that no amount of love,
Expressed in pleas to distant God,
Avails. And yet we harbour pride
In way he copes. And while our hopes
For cure begin a steady slide
To dull despair, we pray that new
Research will culminate in cure
For other victims so impaired.
But still we daily must endure
The shackled life of son for whom
The hills, the wildest foaming streams
And walls of rock were calls to test
His skills and feed his favoured dreams.
I sometimes wish it could have been
Myself confined to chair on wheels,
In place of son. For me research
Provides the challenge that appeals,
Without the need to be as fit
As son before horrific fall.
Instead we can't escape the fact
He's chained to chair for rest of all
His days. But still I cling to hope
In afterlife, when all are healed,
All fractured lives are made as new,
And all unknowns will be revealed.

DEAR STRANGER (CW)

When son's return has been delayed
And not a word of why, or when
He will arrive, it's then in mind
We pace the cage of fear. It's then
I start to see myself as dad
Who failed to pass the test a boy
Expects a father should attain.
As we recall the priceless joy
His birth bestowed it seems bizarre
We slowly found we never felt
We understood his different ways
Of seeing world. It's though he dwelt
On other side of ocean's vast
Expanse. Despite this seeming rift,
We ache with hope he'll live his life
To full. To us he's still a gift.

PIANO'S BALM (TL)

She plays her favoured hymns with verve
And tackles classic works with skill
And quiet delight that soothes her soul
And swamps her throbbing thoughts of son,
Confined to wheelchair since he fell
That fateful day. By losing self
In such employ her pain is eased.
For me the realm of music's strange
And foreign land: perhaps because
Of faulty hearing since my youth.
For me the microscope has been
Escape from woeful thoughts. It takes
Me into worlds no artist dreamed.
A tiny fly emerged from corpse
Becomes a gem without compare.
Its compound eyes and golden hairs,
The intricate device to clasp
Its mate in nuptial flight, its palps
And probing snout proclaim its way
Of life. Its span is short but filled
With purpose lacking doubt. But we
Cannot avoid the nagging wish
To know the point of all when robbed

301

Of youthful dreams by sudden blow
Condemning rest of days to trap
Of constant paraplegic thrall.
We know he could be cured if cash
Consumed by crazy wars were used
Researching ways to make as new
Such shattered lives that crush our hearts.

Audrey sought solace in her piano playing, in avidly reading novels from the public library and helping with fund raising for charities, especially the Link House Trust (which provides a residential community for overseas postgraduate students without a college attachment). I endeavoured to bury myself in my research in order to take my mind off this tragedy. The result was an increase in my rate of publication of papers on scuttle flies as I dealt with a backlog of specimens sent by others. We both tried to keep on top of the garden and to add to it bit by bit. Audrey had a deep love of flowers, especially the smaller, less showy ones. Together we watched dramas and documentaries on the television. Once a year in the summer Audrey was glued to the television for the annual tennis championships at Wimbledon. Otherwise we did not follow sport in the media. We both became ever more proficient at the computer, but mainly by a process of muddled trial and error. By contrast, some years on our grandchildren seemed to take to computing like ducks to water!

SETBACK (CO)

Today, when my computer crashed,
I felt deprived. It seems I've been
Entrapped, I'm tied to cursed machine.
It's worse than being child who screams
When mother's out of sight. It's total loss.
I've many chores in queue but still
I don't embark on single one.
I pace the room. I pause to stare
At empty screen. My mind amok,
I wonder what important files
Are lost. I'm sure I copied lot
To disks in box, or did a lapse
Ensure the vital one's forgot?
I cannot check as long as beast
Will not perform. It's like the time
My train was late when on my way
To interview. Although in sweat,
Despite I'd just arrived a tad
Before they called my name, my brain

Remained in panic mode. I'm not
My best when angst prevails, or so
I feared. But I recall when fear
Was norm in days as youth I served
As soldier on patrol, in distant land,
Against a ruthless foe. For then
The constant need to watch my step
Ensured I was at concert pitch
By day and night. But as my rage
Began to cool at last, I turned
To long neglected task instead.
To my surprise a stubborn block
Began to shift and sudden dawn
Then shed its light on problem left
As fallow for a time. Perhaps
A setback has its own reward:
As when neglectful son had fall,
And learned of love concealed beneath
His caring father's dumb reserve.

2nd January 1998: our granddaughter Samantha born.

When our son-in-law Andrew phoned to give us the news that we had a new granddaughter, he concluded by saying she had been "born yesterday, today" because of the time difference between Tasmania and England!

In the autumn we flew to Hobart, via Sydney, to visit Trudy and her now complete family. On the way, as usual, we visited my cousin John at Berowra (north of Sydney) before proceeding to Hobart. I have collected a number of new species from John's garden over the years as well as from the nearby National Park (e.g. Disney, R. H. L., 1999. Two new termitophilous Phoridae (Diptera) from Australia. Sociobiology 34: 87-97).

We returned to the last few weeks of the FSC Research Fellowship before my 'Retirement'. Audrey doubted I knew the meaning of the word as we faced the future together on our modest pensions (modest because the FSC is an educational charity and I was retiring prematurely at sixty); and we still had half a dozen years to go before we paid off our mortgage!

CHAPTER 10

CAMBRIDGE 2

RETIREMENT AT CAMBRIDGE UNIVERSITY

From 1999: Senior Research Associate, University Department of Zoology, Cambridge (funded by the Isaac Newton Trust of Trinity College until 2003. The INT required matching funding and a new precedent was established when they treated my pension as matching funding).

To mark my enforced retirement at sixty, the FSC Executive Committee made me the FSC Honorary Research Fellow. It is perhaps worth asking the question – had the trauma of the enforced move from Yorkshire to become the FSC Research Fellow given rise to scientific and other benefits?

RESTORATION (TL)

When post-traumatic stress had clamped
The lid on inward screams it took
A while to ease the pressure thus
Contained. A lack of valve, or book
To guide me back to normal ways
Of seeing world, delayed return.
My mind would fail to concentrate,
Became a cage of hounds I'd turn
Adrift to roam at large in search
Of gain. Exams ahead became
Another threat to sense of worth.
Regained composure only came
Too late. My marks did not attain
The level rules required to win
A grant to fund desired research.
In other work I then begin
To climb the walls of pit in which
I'd dwelt too long. On finding girl
I've loved, I've wed, who's shared both joys

And sorrows, learned both plain and purl,
The cure became complete. We went
Abroad. We raised our children, while
I quickly learned research away
From academe, acquired a style
That's proved productive down the years
As papers flowed from pen and time
Has quite restored my self-esteem.
So now I feel I'm in my prime,
Despite my greying hairs and slow
Decline towards horizon's glow.

I have been first and foremost a naturalist. As people had learned I was
working on scuttle flies (Phoridae) I had increasingly received requests from
around the world to identify specimens of applied importance (pests, from
forensic cases, potential biological control agents, etc.) or with novel data on
the larval habits or whatever. As new (hitherto undescribed) species were
frequently encountered I often had to revise the members of an African genus
or an Oriental tribe. Furthermore standard works of reference ignored most of
the literature on the larval habits of the scuttle flies (see chapters 8 and 9 and
the motive for writing my 1994 book).

I WONDER (CW)

In youth I travelled world
To work abroad. I learned
How others lived their lives.
Today our home is where
I want to be for most
Of time. But samples come
In post from many lands,
And so in mind I range
Across the globe. Beneath
The microscope I view
Some strange and wondrous flies
Of diverse habits way
Beyond the reach of what
Imagination dreamed.
There's those whose larvae dwell
On sides of largest, dread,
Grotesquest spiders known.
There's others feed on eggs
Of frogs, and some on stores
Of bees, and few who take

The easy way of taste
For rotting flesh. There's more
Are parasites, of ants,
Of worms, of snails or men.
There's even some in mud
Below the sea. As I
Delight in sorting these,
I wonder if my life
Has drained away in play
While much of world's in pain.

In Belize I had become intrigued by the leaf-cutter ants (see chapter 5) and had published a few papers on specimens I had been sent for identification (e.g. Disney, R. H. L. & Bragança, A. L., 2000. Two new species of Phoridae (Diptera) associated with leaf-cutter ants (Hymenoptera: Formicidae). Sociobiology 36: 33-39). I was therefore pleased to oblige when Professor Patricia Folgarait in Argentina asked if her bright research student, Luciana Elizalde, might come to spend part of a summer vocation learning how to identify Phoridae parasitizing leaf-cutter ants. It was decided that we would start by revising the genus Myrmosicarius whose species parasitize these ants, as Luciana had many new field observations and needed to name the species observed, which she brought with her preserved in ethanol with their code numbers that related to her field notes and the species of ant involved. The name Myrmosicarius literally means ant assassin! We duly accomplished this revision (Disney, R. H. L., Elizalde, L. & Folgarait, P. J., 2006. New species and revision of Myrmosicarius (Diptera: Phoridae) that parasitize leaf-cutter ants (Hymenoptera: Formicidae). Sociobiology 47: 771-809). This was only the start of a continuing collaboration. When Luciana found members of the parasitic genus Apocephalus (the name referring to the fly larva decapitating its ant host when it enters its host's head) were attacking the ants she had been observing in the field, we got Brian Brown (from the Natural History Museum in Los Angeles) to join us in writing the paper, as he had published much on the South American species of this genus (Brown, B.V., Disney, R. H. L., L. Elizalde, L. & Folgarait, P. J., 2010. New species and new records of Apocephalus Coquillett (Diptera: Phoridae) that parasitize ants (Hymenoptera: Formicidae) in America. Sociobiology 55: 165-190).

Ever since the extraordinary legless and flightless female scuttle flies associated with Old World army ants had landed on my lab bench (see chapter 9) the Phoridae associated with the formidable South American predatory army ants became equally intriguing (e.g. Disney, R. H. L. & Berghoff, S. M., 2005. New species and new records of scuttle flies (Diptera: Phoridae) associated with army ants (Hymenoptera: Formicidae) in Trinidad and Venezuela. Sociobiology 45: 887-898. Disney, R. H. L. & Berghoff, S. M., 2007. New species and new records of scuttle flies (Diptera: Phoridae) associated with army ants (Hymenoptera: Formicidae) in Panama. Sociobiology 49: 59-92).

The studies of the associates of these army ants progressed with two large papers with Carl Rettenmeyer, the acknowledged expert on South American army ants. Sadly he died as we were finalizing the second paper (Disney, R. H. L. & Rettenmeyer, C. W., 2007. New species and revisionary notes on scuttle flies (Diptera: Phoridae) associated with Neotropical army ants (Hymenoptera: Formicidae). Sociobiology 49: 1-58. Disney, R. H. L. & Rettenmeyer, C. W., 2010. New species and new records of scuttle flies (Diptera: Phoridae) associated with Neotropical army ants (Hymenoptera: Formicidae). Sociobiology 55(1A): 7-88) and continued with my Argentinian co-authors (Disney, R. H. L., Elizalde, L. & Folgarait, P. J., 2008. New species and records of scuttle flies (Diptera: Phoridae) associated with leaf-cutter ants and army ants (Hymenoptera: Formicidae) in Argentina. Sociobiology 51: 95-117). These studies exemplified the continuing, indeed increasing, requests to identify specimens from around the world. They resulted in numerous unforeseen publications and a growing list of co-authors. This meant my own plans for a major monograph were constantly being delayed. On the other hand, if eventually accomplished it would be far more comprehensive! Besides I was continuing to add species to the British List, including species new to science. Some of these additions included novel natural history data. For example a species whose larvae are subjected to inundation by seawater at high tides but with freshwater by rain at low tide (Disney, R. H. L., 2002. A new species of maritime scuttle fly (Dipt., Phoridae) from East Sussex. Entomologist's Monthly Magazine 138: 19-22).

Arabia was a region whose scuttle fly fauna was virtually unknown, with only four species recorded in the literature, so when Dr Tony van Harten who previously had sent me collections from the Cape Verde Islands – see chapter 9) asked me to examine collections from Yemen I was pleased to do so. Along with smaller collections borrowed from museums this work was progressing well when on the 11th of September 2001 the suicidal attack on the World Trade Center in New York set in train the madness of the West invading Iraq and subsequent interferences in the Muslim world (see poem WORLD TRADE CENTER below). It was too dangerous for Tony to stay in Yemen so he fled to the Cape Verde Islands until things had calmed down. However, when he returned he was told it was still too dangerous for him to engage in further fieldwork and he must only undertake office work. So he resigned and signed up to edit a proposed set of volumes on the Arthropod Fauna of the United Arab Emirates. So I was soon receiving many specimens from the UAE. The consequence was that my coverage of Arabia extended from the West coast to that of the East. This resulted in a two volume monograph on the Arabian scuttle flies with the unexpected bonus of a chapter in the second volume of UAE series (Disney, R. H. L., 2006. Insects of Arabia scuttle flies (Diptera: Phoridae) Part I: all genera except Megaselia. Pp 473-521 in Krupp, F. (Editor-in-Chief) Fauna of Arabia 22: pp 530. Senckenbergische Naturforschende Gesellschaft, Frankfurt a.M, Germany and King Abdulaziz City for Science and Technology, Ryadah, Kingdom of

Saudi Arabia. Disney, R. H. L., 2008. Order Diptera, Family Phoridae. In Arthropod Fauna of the United Arab Emirates, Volume 1. Pp 604-635 in A. van Harten (editor), Dar al Ummah, Abu Dhabi. (2007). Disney, R. H. L., 2009. Insects of Arabia scuttle flies (Diptera: Phoridae) Part II: the genus Megaselia. Pp 249-357 in Krupp, F. (Editor-in-Chief) Fauna of Arabia 24. 405 pp. Senckenbergische Naturforschende Gesellschaft, Frankfurt a.M, Germany and King Abdulaziz City for Science and Technology, Ryadah, Kingdom of Saudi Arabia). This work is not definitive. In particular a major gap in sampling remains Iraq. Until political mayhem ceases in the Arab world our knowledge of its scuttle fly fauna will remain incomplete. However, Parte II added greatly to our knowledge of Afrotropical Megaselia along with the following publications: – Disney, R. H. L. 2005. Phoridae (Diptera) of Madagascar and nearby islands. Studia dipterologica 12: 139-177 and Disney, R. H. L., 2009. Superfamily Platypezoidea Family Phoridae. In Gerlach, J. (editor) Seychelles Fauna Monographs. The Diptera of the Seychelles islands. Chapter 11: 167-236. Pensoft Series Faunistica 85. Sofia-Moscow, 431 pp. These together with papers on some smaller islands increasingly rendered obsolete parts of Beyer's poorly constructed keys (see chapter 9). Only when we can replace his keys entirely will our knowledge of the Afrotropical species advance more rapidly.

Ever since I had realized that the role of Phoridae as flower visitors had been under appreciated (see chapter 8) I routinely recorded the species observed visiting species of flowers and summarized the then knowledge of this habit in my book of 1994 (see chapter 9). So when I was asked to examine a collection reared from larvae from the extraordinary flowers of Aristolochia I readily agreed (Disney, R. H. L. & Sakai, S. 2001. Scuttle flies (Diptera: Phoridae) whose larvae develop in flowers of Aristolochia (Aristolochiaceae) in Panama. European Journal of Entomology 98: 367-373). This was followed by further requests that resulted in the perception that scuttle flies were the major group of insects involved in the pollination of these flowers across the world. (Bänziger, H. & Disney, R. H. L.. 2006. Scuttle flies (Diptera: Phoridae) imprisoned by Aristolochia baenzigeri (Aristolochiaceae) in Thailand. Mitteilungen der Schweizerischen Entomologischen Gesellschaft 79: 29-61. Disney, R. H. L. & Bänziger, H. 2009. Further records of scuttle flies (Diptera: Phoridae) imprisoned by Aristolochia baenzigeri (Aristolochiaceae) in Thailand. Mitteilungen der Schweizerischen Entomologischen Gesellschaft 82: 233-251. Disney, R. H. L. & Rulik, B., 2012. Scuttle flies (Diptera, Phoridae) trapped by flowers of Aristolochia L. in Italy. Entomologist's Monthly Magazine 148: 234-236).

In addition I have records of Phoridae from Arsistolochia flowers in Burma (but the taxonomy of the species has yet to be resolved). All this showed that a paper I had cited in my 1994 book (Hall, D.W. & Brown, B.V., 1993, Pollination of Aristolochia littoralis (Aristolochiales: Aristolochiaceae) by males of Megaselia spp. (Diptera: Phoridae), Annals of the Entomological Society of America, 86: 609–13) had been the start of this subsequent demonstration of a worldwide importance of scuttle flies in the pollination of these extraordinary flowers.

A continuing concern was the affinities of the genera. I was often encountering evidence that a genus was misplaced in its assignment to a tribe or subfamily. In the case of the 'family' Sciadoceridae, represented today by one species from southern Australia and New Zealand and one South American species, but otherwise showing affinity with fossils dating back to Cretaceous, aroused my interest when I received specimens from New Zealand. They clearly retained features possessed by the ancestors of scuttle flies along with more advanced character states. The two living species had been assigned to a separate subfamily (Sciadocerinae) of the Phoridae by Tonnoir in 1926. However, Schmitz in 1929 had strongly argued that they should be assigned to a separate family, and his view tended to be adopted by textbook writers. When I reviewed the specimens from New Zealand I concluded that the character states selected by Schmitz in support of his view were all ancestral states. By contrast the derived states strongly indicated affinity with the Phoridae and thus supported Tonnoir's position (Disney, R. H. L., 2001. Sciadoceridae (Diptera) reconsidered. Fragmenta faunistica 44: 309-317). This revised view was an example of the application of the principles promulgated by Henniig that had so excited me when I had first read his classic text (see chapter 8). A paradigm shift had rendered Schmitz's case untenable! Likewise the consideration of morphological features not considered before was sometimes revealing (e.g. Disney, R. H. L., 2003. The dorsal abdominal glands and the higher classification of the Phoridae (Diptera). Zootaxa 293: 1-16). Furthermore molecular data were increasingly indicating the true affinities of problem groups. For example the affinities of the highly peculiar Termitoxeniinae (see chapter 9) were resolved by this means (Cook, C. E., Austin, J. J. & Disney, R. H. L., 2004. A mitochondrial 12S and 16s rRNA phylogeny of critical genera of Phoridae (Diptera) and related families of Aschiza. Zootaxa 593: 1-11).

I was asked to identify a collection from north of the Arctic Circle in the Kola Peninsular, as part of a Finnish project monitoring the impact of the smelting of copper and zinc in this most polluted region of the Russian Federation. I was expecting only a few species as in Greenland there were only three species of scuttle fly known from north of the Arctic Circle (as reported in the publication delayed by ten years by authors of other chapters who failed to meet deadlines! – Disney, R. H. L., 2015. Diptera Phoridae (Scuttle Flies). In Böcher, J., Kristensen, N. P., Lyneborg, L., Michelsen, V., Pape, T. & Vilhelmsen, L. Editors) Identification handbook of the Greenland entomofauna. Copenhagen. Chapter 17-15: 582-588.

However there were more than sixty species (Disney, R. H. L., 2013. An unusually rich scuttle fly fauna (Diptera, Phoridae) from north of the Arctic Circle in the Kola Peninsula, N. W. Russia. ZooKeys 342: 45-74). The adult emergence is brief in late July and August with the rest of the year being spent as larvae and resting pupae below the snow and permafrost despite temperatures of -30°C or lower above the snow.

When helping to run a course on insects we obtained a new species when fogging the canopy of an oak tree with insecticide (Disney, R. H. L., 2002. A new species of Megaselia (Rondani) from Hayley Wood, Cambridgeshire (Diptera: Phoridae). Entomologist's Record 114: 189-191). I named the species after my colleague Ray Symonds who in his spare time was a volunteer for the nature reserve. It added to the perception that collecting at ground level in woodlands only obtained a subset of the fauna (see chapter 9). This was subsequently confirmed when collections from the crowns of ancient pollarded trees turned up additions to the British List, including four new species (Disney, R. H. L. & Russell-Smith, A., 2015a. Additions to the British list of Megaselia Rondani (Diptera: Phoridae), including two new species, from the crowns of ancient pollarded trees, Journal of Natural History 45(25-26): 1599-1626. Disney, R. H. L. & Russell-Smith, A., 2015b. Further records of Megaselia Rondani (Diptera: Phoridae) including two new species, from the crowns of ancient pollarded trees in England. Entomologist's Monthly Magazine 151: 169-175).

A collection from Norway added to evidence that sampling the crowns of trees produced species not, or only rarely, encountered at or near ground level (Disney, R. H. L., 2015. Scuttle flies (Diptera: Phoridae) from the canopies of oak trees (Fagaceae) in Norway, including 13 new species. Norwegian Journal of Entomology 62: 20-52).

Since my work in Belize (chapter 5) I had been familiar with the phenomenon of a different set of species occurring at ground level compared with those found up above, with some being confined to the tree canopy. However, invertebrate fauna lists for most nature reserves in Britain, and elsewhere, are dominantly based on collecting at ground level only. The result is that some species considered to be 'rare' are really canopy species only rarely caught lower down. Likewise species reared from rotholes in trees produced novel species (e.g. Disney, R. H. L. & Withers, P., 2011. Scuttle flies (Diptera, Phoridae) reared from tree rotholes in France, including three new species of Megaselia Rondani. Fragmenta faunistica 54: 29-41).

Another project on the backburner was the genus Chonocephalus whose confused taxonomy had caused me to publish a baseline paper as a basis for moving forward (see chapter 9). I then undertook a paper on the Afrotropical species (Disney, R. H. L., 2005. Revision of Afrotropical Chonocephalus Wandolleck (Diptera: Phoridae). Journal of Natural History 39: 393-430). This was followed by a treatment of the more species rich South American species (Disney, R. H. L., 2008. Review of Neotropical Chonocephalus Wandolleck (Diptera: Phoridae). Zootaxa 1772: 1-54). I then embarked on the even more species rich Oriental and Australasian species. However, this ground to a halt when I went three quarters blind in 2012 and was only resumed when I acquired the digital imaging system for my microscope (see below).

PROLONGED GESTATION (GK)

I dream of monograph, that's half
Complete, at last is done. But when
The work resumes again I find
Another letter, making ten
This year, requesting once again
I process batch of flies for which
Are needed names before results
Are fit to print. I'd sure be rich
If all requests had claimed a fee,
But only when police or large
Commercial firms require my skills
Is invoice sent. I never charge
My fellow scientists. Attempts
To raise a grant for major work
I've planned have always failed. But still
My expertise is seen as perk
That's always free to academe.
The tome I have in mind would let
A novice name the bulk now passed
To me instead. I don't regret
The time I've spent on other's flies
When data linked to each advanced
Our knowledge, filling gaps about
Their lives, and gifting awe enhanced.
Besides, the final weighty book
Will be as river formed by each
Of many a small and dancing brook,
As many words compose a speech.

IN HOPE (CW)

I find it hard to give a 'no'
To those who ask me will you please
Identify intriguing flies
They've reared from novel source. I squeeze
The sample into scheduled queue,
And let my favoured project fall
Behind again! And yet the new
Is adding bricks to growing wall
That's rising slowly, week by week,
To build the house of knowledge gained
To date. But still we only see
The ground floor plan. But I'm sustained
By hope of what's to come. Perhaps
A future team will add its roof
And then proceed to build afresh.
But on this earth the warp and woof
Of aim and chance remain a game
We can't predict. We build with good
Intent and move aside for those
To come. They'll start from where we stood
To view our handiwork before
We died. And if a storm destroys
My wall at least foundation laid
Provides the base for future joys.

SLOWING DOWN (CW)

I wonder why he can't accept
I'm getting old and slowing down.
He knows my record shows I've won
Acclaim, and even some renown
Beyond the special field in which
We toil. As old ambitions wane
I'm now content to tidy ends
Remaining loose. I don't complain
As others seize the reins and drive
Along enticing paths I'd put
On map but not explored for lack
Of time. But now my end's afoot
I most regret the paltry care
I've shown for those I love. At time
I'd thought the hours must be employed
On other things. Insistent chime
Of duty's sacred calls had caused
Me being deaf to lack of need
To let the minor tasks await
Their turn in queue. I failed to heed
The speed with which my children grew
Until, in blink of eye, they'd left
Our home to spread their wings beyond
Our care, and left me quite bereft.
It seems we take a life to learn
To be a human fully fledged, with mind
And body, will and heart all fused
As one, with constant love aligned.

STAID! (CW)

I've had unusual life, but now,
Perhaps, I'm just an ageing bore
Content with being chained to wheel
Of routine rites from day to day.
But then I must admit if life
Were otherwise I'd be in state
Of ever frequent fret. Besides
I use my time to good effect,
Inflicting world with stream of verse
And scientific works that build
The solid walls of facts on which
Advancing knowledge feeds. I'm not
A name of poet known to those
Who pride themselves on being up
To date regarding avant-garde.
But those who read my published works
Profess they like my style, its lack
Of sloppy sentiment, its want
Of dark allusions, purple bits
Of wild flamboyant tricks. At times
I feel a need to scream 'Oh let
Me quit this dreary rut', but then
Return with sigh of deep relief
To daily pulse of ordered ways.
To be a household name, or rich
Beyond one's dreams, would not have brought
The inner peace I now enjoy;
And so I offer up my praise
Of thanks for steadfast wife I love,
Our children and their lovely kids.

Despite the dire predictions in the media that the advent of the New Millennium would cause the Internet to fail and that planes would be unable to navigate, the event that really heralded a new era was the news reports of the attack on the World Trade Center in New York. It shocked us all and revealed some unexpected reactions among some colleagues. My own response was as follows:

WORLD TRADE CENTER (CO)
11th September 2001

When chilled fanatics flew those planes
To sudden death for them, for those
On board and thousands unaware
Their days on earth were done, the world
Was stunned. Heroic rescue work
Redeemed a gleam of hope. But soon
The media swamped us all in flood
Of relished scenes and pundits, whose
Recycled, cliché ridden, views
Became a steady chant for crude
Revenge by means of war. The rage
Aroused soon stifles wiser words
From being heard. Unless the cause
That drove those men to kill themselves,
In balls of screaming fire, is seen
As howl of anguish wrung from pit
Of bleak despair, we'll merely reap
A steady harvest of the dead.

But who am I detached from scene?
Across the seas, in comfort, I'm
Remote from flames; despite the fact
That in my youth a pair of bombs,
A terror gang had placed in tent
Across the way from me and mates,
Impaired my hearing to this day;
Despite the fact my wife was dug
From choking dust and dark remains
Of home destroyed by Nazi bomb;
We're merely distant ghouls at rim
Of hell. It's hard to comprehend.
My daily routine hasn't changed.
I wrestle problems as before,
Researching flies, in work that seems
To most divorced from daily life.
It makes one wonder if one's sane.
And yet it's clear I have a flair
For culling yields from tiny field
Of scholarship. Besides, most tasks
Are done to aid a colleague clinch
A puzzle, advise about a pest

Abroad, or help police to solve
A crime. At times I seem denied
The hours to work on projects I
Desire to do before I die.

When I review the varied lives
Of scuttle flies I'm filled with awe,
In sense of wonder and of fear.
I'm glad I'm not an ant who's slow
Consumed by maggot feeding on
My non-essential organs first,
Before it eats my brain, and then
Employs my empty shell of head
As shelter for its pupal pause
Before the fly is born to hunt
Another ant in turn. The pain
And death these tiny flies dispense,
In human terms, reflects the vile
Effects of those consumed by hate.

They flew those planes with grim intent
To further cause, to kill and wound
Whose names and loves and lives remained
Of no concern. Their mates rejoice
As outraged headlines scream revenge.
Their cold indifference, to death
Of infants, husbands, wives and those
Whose duty is to help the maimed,
Erodes the urge to heed the hurts
And ills that they perceived as spur
To act with such disdain against
Those helpless folk whose daily wish
Was peace. As long as violent means
Are used by those in power, blood
Is spilled by those denied all hope
Of better lives. No interchange
Of views prevails in search for rights
And justice in our time. For hate
Is like a maggot eating first
The feeling heart, until the head
Is deaf to reason's cries for calm
Reflection on the way to reach
The promised land of common good.
Instead revenge prevails and death
Is laughing at its cheap success

In ceaseless cycle of despair.

When Bush, supported by Blair, decided to invade Iraq the country was instantly divided. I, along with many of my colleagues and friends were strongly opposed; while others relished this madness.

IN PERSPECTIVE? (TL)

As boy I once was asked to ride
To hounds on borrowed horse.
I only just completed course
As steed was frisky, ditch
And hedges nearly caused a fall.
By time I'd reached the copse
At end of chase the wily fox
Was torn apart by hounds
In ecstasy at last. I'm pleased
I'd missed the kill itself,
But glad I'd tasted thrill. I've no
Desire to go again.
Besides it's silly way to deal
With pest, or else for why
The gun is used when cunning rogue
Is raiding chicken pen.
The hunt is merely sport that's choice
Of some, but causes angst
To others pained by thought of fox
On run in frantic fear.
What really gets my goat is hours
Of stale debate before
The vote to ban the gruesome game,
While children die from rain
Of bombs and shells our troops employ
Against Iraqi towns.

MATCH OF THE DAY (CW)

The news reports of war against
Saddam are relished as a sport
To entertain, designed to keep
The ratings high. They bring to mind
The time, some forty years ago,
When I was called to fight against
The terror gangs that Grivas led
In Cyprus, fired by foolish cause
Conveying fear to those who wished
To tend their vines and goats in peace.
We lacked the high-tech means that now
Have turned our TV screens to scenes
Of Sci-Fi nightmare games.
Indeed, we left our heavy guns
Behind on Salisbury Plain, for then
We wouldn't hazard death of child
From faulty aim. Instead we put
Ourselves at risk in constant hunt
On mountain tracks, in narrow streets,
Dispersing seething mobs, in stop
And search of dodgy trucks and cars.
At times our lives were put on line
By planted bombs or ambush tricks.
We could be rough when searching homes
At dawn, but sat the kids upon
A wall and gave them sweets. Our means
Denied the need to shed a tear
For people felled by random shells
That went astray. Today, it seems,
It's common folk must pay the price.
But I, for one, will have my say -
It's time that Bush and Blair were shipped
Away to distant isle to spend their days
Compiling memoirs full of self
Deceit, for readers just as blind.
March 2003

I am sent small packets of scuttle fly specimens, preserved in tubes of ethanol, from around the world. Following these events a number of these packets were being opened by the authorities on arrival in England.

OUTSMARTING RISKS? (GK)

It's since that 9/11 crime
That Bush and gang have been hell bent
On showing world its bloodied claws
With constant warning of intent
To crush those nations viewed as threat;
At least those small enough to be
An easy target, so they think.
But since inept attempt to free
Iraq, our lives are now at more
Of risk. And stoking fires of fear
Allows our Tony Blair to shave
Away our freedoms, won so dear.
So simple package from Iran
Is seized as suspect, held despite
The contents clearly labelled 'Tubes
Of insects' and below, and quite
As clear, 'For science only. Treat
With care.' The packet's torn apart,
And contents mixed, before resealed
And sent on way. But sender's smart.
His further samples go to friend
In Turkey. Wrapped anew it clears
The Customs, freed from hijack risk
By those consumed by ersatz fears.

AFTER THE STORM (RE)

Yesterday the garden sang
With poppies flaming forth.
Many smaller gems in dance
Of sun and dappled shade
Added sense of ease and praise.
Today a gale arrived.
Havoc rules as lightning, hail
And heavy rain destroy
Much that hours of work contrived.
It makes me want to weep.
Dredged from past, from time a brute
Decides to give me push,
Garden scene now seems is like
That day my chosen world
Fell apart, because that yob

319

Of pompous, narrow views,
Whims, antipathies, proceeds
To weed his small domain.
Awkward guys, who challenge plans
He builds on sand, must go.
Since, I've planted other blooms,
But miss the former scene.
Space allowed a richer spread
Than exile in the town.
Still, from smaller plot I've culled
A harvest never dreamed.

SUSTAINED ENTHUSIASM (TL)

Today my work is on a high,
I feel my hours are being spent
In fruitful way. A week or two
Ago it wasn't so. A blank
Was all I had to show for days
Of tiresome slog. It's then I saw
That all my gains could just as well
Be won by others with less pain,
As I am not the brightest lad
Around. I'm merely focussed like
A hound upon the scent. I'm just
An obstinate old fool who, when
At school, did not perform above
The norm. I've reached the top at end
Of steady dogged climb. Today
I'd not be given chance to try.
The standards set allowing foot
On lowest rung are now too high.
And yet I see that many armed
With shiny first and PhD
Proceed to settle down, beyond
Their postdoc stint, to gentle ease.
It seems they lack my drive and thirst
For novel knowledge wrenched from depths
Of ignorance in chosen field.
Or else they go for fashion's lure
Of fancy methods misapplied
To minor themes, or complex maths
That's utilised to raise a dome
Of theory built on sands of frail

320

Assumptions buried deep within
Computer's programmed rites and rules.
For cleverness displayed's preferred
To patient toil of laying bricks
Upon the walls of solid yields.
Because I've taken risks to fill
The gaps, and sometimes failed, the house
I've helped to build will stand and live
As monument to wonders shared.

However, being a naturalist and lover of countryside and wilderness at heart, there remained a part of me that regretted the move from Yorkshire.

CRAVEN UPLANDS (CW)

It's many years we left our home
On hills astride the Yorkshire Dales.
We now abide beside the Cam,
Which slowly crawls across a land
As flat as any England claims.
In dreams I roam those Pennine fells.

It's many years we left those lands
Of jungle forests rich in beasts
And birds, and stealthy snakes, and flies
That sought our blood by day and night.
As naturalist I relished feast.
In dreams I roam the Pennine fells.

It's many years I left the downs
Of boyhood's days. The rolling chalk
Beneath a springy turf, the streams
With flinty beds, the lazing fish,
The darting dragonflies in sun.
In dreams I roam the Pennine fells.

It's many years I've lived on earth
Designed, it seems, for those like me
Who banquet daily at the spread
Of nature's rich display. But when
My spirit passes out beyond,
In dreams I'll roam those Pennine fells.

FUTURE PERFECT

*(First published in Good Shepherd News, Church of Good Shepherd,
Cambridge, November 2014)*

At start of life I'm chip of stone
Without a heart, with edges sharp
As knife. Erosion soon began
Its work before, dislodged from scarp,
A winter storm conveyed me down
The slope to enter torrent stream's
Relentless onward flow to death,
Which then I feared in nightmare dreams.
But now I know is not the end.
And yet there's much I wish to do
Before I go. On looking back
I now regret I never knew
The simple truths I now embrace.
But then, perhaps, I've only grasped
Them just because of lapses made
That slowly battered, shaped and rasped
Those awkward edges. Pebble smooth
I may appear today at last.
But don't be fooled. It wasn't so
Throughout my awkward, youthful past.
Recalling then I now perceive
My childhood's joy in world and life
Had slowly withered bit by bit
As living seemed an endless strife.
But now delight is creeping back,
As restless time is running out,
Despite there's still so much undone.
And furthermore I'm less devout
In reading Bible, much of which
Is past its sell by date. But sense
Of God's abiding love has since
Been growing ever more intense.
What's more a wonder cause for thanks
Derives from time my lovely wife
Agreed to marry, even though
I'd yet to make my way in life
And hardly understood the ups
And downs apprentice love entailed.
As childhood brought me stress and joys,
At times I felt as though I'd failed.

But looking back I now can laugh
As cheap success was foolish aim
Beside the gain of gifts of grace
That's rendered much a pointless game.
Embrace of ocean death ahead
Is nothing now to fill with dread,
Released at last emergent soul
Will find its way to heaven's goal.

HOMELY (TL)

Astride the garden's grand display
A line of washing screens the scene.
And yet the items summarise
The basic drives that keep alive.
The cloth I used to dry the knives
And forks when meal was done, the socks
Refreshed again, the pants, the bras
And stockings frisky in the breeze,
The shirts and blouse recalling sweat
Of daily wear and tear. The sheet
That flutters like a flag reminds
Of bed in which our love expressed
Itself in long embrace. Our joys
And rows of choicest blooms depend
On ceaseless toil performed without
A fuss. For those divorced from such
By wealth the world's a brittle place
In which the swarms of parasites
Prevent the cosy trust that builds
When daily chores are shared with those
We daily greet with kiss, caress
And gentle words. The 'ideal' home
In magazine is sterile spread
Devoid of daily mess, give
And take, forgiving sweet neglect
Of fallen petals, lonely bowl,
Forgotten mug beside the book
She reads instead of dusting shelf,
As tale allows her fancy flight.
Her echo sings from every clue.

While in full time employment I had resisted the pressure to become a churchwarden at the Church of the Good Shepherd in Arbury (north Cambridge). I no longer had that excuse.

A consequence was that I ceased to be a leader of the church's children's groups. For them I had rewritten Mrs Alexander's Paleyite (Creationist) hymn 'All things bright and beautiful':

ALL THINGS BRIGHT (MC)

All things bright and beautiful,
All acts for good of all,
All things wise and wonderful,
They help us heed God's call.

In past delights of nature
Enchanted eye and ear,
So some believed each creature
Designed by God to cheer.

But nature's not all roses
When microbes lie in wait,
Or cancer fast disposes
Of dearly cherished mate.

But still it's mighty wonder
That God's concerned at all
With peoples prone to blunder
And still defy his call.

He showed His love in Jesus,
Whom Mary nursed as child,
Who grew to be colossus
Before by cross defiled.

But Easter's joy astounded,
Restored the light again,
So now our faith is founded
On hope that's not in vain.

His Holy Spirit giving
To each His caring grace,
Now feeds our souls while living,
And frees from death's embrace.

As indicated above (chapter 9) a major concern I had as a leader of children's groups was derived from having taught numerous Sixth Form students at the Field Centre in Yorkshire. Many who had attended junior church groups when they progressed to secondary school and started to learn about evolution, the antiquity of the earth and universe, and parasitic infections such as malaria, they realized that they needed to unlearn much of what they had been taught. Likewise at Cambridge many undergraduates and research students had reached the conclusion that religion was adherence to myths and legends that science had disposed of long ago. A few who progressed to becoming scientists of note seemed to be consumed by a stultifying ambition and corroding scepticism.

FELL WALKS (LA)

The hills had fired his youthful dreams,
As when by unpolluted streams
He wondered at a wary trout,
Rejoiced at brood of ducklings still
Astonished by a world so filled
With timeless dance of fresh delights.

His childhood's song sustained by God,
In tune with nature's rich display,
No shadows stayed his roving eye.
The reddened fang, the deadly germ,
The creeping maggot's silent psalm,
Had failed to lodge in carefree mind.

Relentless race to make his mark,
In jungle world of peers' esteem,
Corrodes his awe, erodes his dreams.
The distant line, where sky and plain
Embrace, became obscured by mist.
His joy in wilderness had dimmed.

His fells became another goal
To gain. The climb was all. The views
From top now caused him little pause.
He seldom stopped to relish bird,
Or bumblebee who worked a choir
Of blooms on sultry summer's day.

But still the lure of nature held,
And still he yearned to share her truths,
Until his ruthless mind was tuned
To facts to pluck from secret ways
Of bug and butterfly. He logged
Them coldly onto disk. Then graphs,

Derived from cunning tests for each
And every hunch, adorned his piles
Of publications – solid gains,
Which served to raise him high above
The ruck; until he found respect
Was wrapped in lonesome foil.

The honours came, but little joy
Or solace brought. His hollow heart
A cup of self-disdain became.
But then his long-neglected God,
By joyful wonder in the face
Of daughter's child, revived his fire.

And slowly grace restored his soul,
And quietly love embraced his goal,
Until a peace derailed his drive.
Returning vision lights his eye.
He finds a joy in sharing skills,
And learns that God still walks his hills.

But now he knows it wasn't God
Who made all creatures great and small.
Since Darwin's day a grander view
Has shown us why the call of Christ
Transcends our fumbling thoughts and words,
Eluding hope of holding Him

Within our hungry minds. For now
We know the feckless search for light
Is vain, unless the soul first quits
The hidden throne of self – to let
Incarnate love redeem the will;
Let Spirit's flame direct our gaze.

However, despite a loss of childhood's simplistic belief in God, many teenagers increasingly exhibited a commitment to environmental conservation and reducing human impacts on ecosystems. This was encouraging but there was a tendency to a certain degree of romanticism.

HUMAN DELUGE (TL)

A handsome beetle, red and black,
Is crawling on our lily's leaf.
So with regret I seize it fast
And crush it flat. Its life was brief
Because it's known as irksome curse
Whose larvae damage lily leaves.
I must not feel regret at need
To cause its death, for no reprieves
Are handed out to those intent
On harming favoured plants. But still
I wish it weren't so well attired,
I wish I didn't need to kill
Exquisite beast. And yet the food
I eat requires demise of pests
Galore, from aphids, wireworms, gangs
Of caterpillars, other guests
Refused a place at table's spread.
The vegans can't escape the fact
Their meals demand the deaths of hordes.
Organic farmer's every act,
From ploughing fields to hoeing weeds,
Destroys a range of varied lives
Displacing countless beasts with crops
So each of them and us survives.
The greatest threat to nature's rich,
Diverse display of other forms
Of life is us. Our numbers long
Ago exceeded proper norms.
So now it's people spoiling song.

HUNGERS (TL)

She purchased costly skirt that came
From distant Asian land where laws
To curb the curs exploiting poor
Are just ignored when boss conveys
A wad of notes to prying man
Required to check the rules are kept.
But child who stitched her party piece
Is underfed and always tired:
And she is garbed in tattered rags.
Her feet have never felt a shoe.
A little rice and sometimes beans
Is all she ever gets apart
From scraps she gleans from bins on route
To work. On lucky day she'll find
A fallen fruit. The way of life
Of she who's bought attire she sewed
Is out of reach of mind that's starved
Of schooling other than the fight
To stay alive, along with those
Who share her flimsy home of card
And plastic sheeting gleaned from dump.
Her parents dead, she lives with old
And fever-ridden aunt and boy
They found as gift of flood. Deprived,
They're rich in caring love that she
Who wears her tailored cloth can not
Conceive, as all alone she paints
Her face in hope of catching eye
Of man who hungers for a wife.

HUNTING (GK)

A piercing running scream aroused
Me from my sleep as hint of dawn
Was tinting sky. On peering out
I see a fox is chasing cat
Around a yucca plant and bed
Of roses past their prime. As prey
Endeavours to escape its fate
Its foe is on its tail as now
The hunt is moved next door and then
Beyond my sight, but not that sound
Of purest fear that chills one's spine.
At last it ends as out of sight
The fox procures his tasty meal
To end frustrating night. By day
Suburban calm's restored, apart
From yet another card on post
Along the road announcing loss
Of favoured puss and promised sum
To finder for return, which now
I know will never be. But should
I ring the bell to tell my tale?
I know they fed their cat on meat.
I know they march with those who wish
To stop the dreadful death of fox
At end of fearful hunt with hounds.
Our local fox is safe from that
At least, and now their cat's at peace.

In the light of these perceptions I tried to avoid teaching the children
nonsense, such as taking some Old Testament tales as though they were
historical events, while not confusing them with insights from science before
they were in a position to comprehend more abstract notions (see chapter 9).

329

DODO TEXTS ARE OUT OF TUNE (RE)

Selections culled from Pentateuch
For children under ten is all
We need to know of myths and spin,
The pointless laws and treating fall
As real event. The Gospel's light
Is what we need to walk the way
Of Christ, who taught that God is love
That's unconstrained. I cannot say
I see the point of spending time
In sifting through accounts of wars
And nasty crimes to glean a grain
Of true insight. If one ignores
These ancient texts it frees the time
To relish books that speak to place
And times we now endure. Our call's
To live our lives by letting grace
Of Holy Spirit's fire provide
The means to live as part of team
That seeks to build the Kingdom Christ
Desires today. Embrace the dream
Of peace, of justice, true respect
For all, whatever colour, creed
Or race, or straight or gay, they be.
Dissecting ancient texts, that need
A scholar's years of toil to grasp
Their sense, is mere escape from call
To walk the way of Christ today
And cope with ills that will befall.
The Holy Spirit can't be chained,
But ranges where it will. Our rites
And creeds cannot restrain its fire
That daily diverse souls ignites.

IT'S TIME TO PRUNE (GK)

Do we espouse her latest cause?
Or do we go to meeting called
By Ann because we would offend
If we declined? Perhaps it's just
The same when we recite the creed
In church. Its rolling rhythms hide
The long discarded paradigms
That underlie its crafted words.
I much prefer the mini text
We use at children's service, when
We just affirm the love of God
The Father, the hope and truth
That Christ revealed and grace that's gift
Of Holy Spirit's silent voice
Within our hearts. It's same with psalms
Invoking aid in zapping foes,
Or hymns that praise the rich display
Of nature's ways but skip the facts
Of being red in tooth and claw.
I'd like to prune a high percent,
Along with chunks of text from books
Of Bible long before the light
Of Jesus seized the golden thread
Of past and turned our pilgrim feet
Towards eternal light ahead,
Beyond horizon where we'll meet.

Anyway, my fumbling ministry to the children ceased when I became a churchwarden.

Having been a churchwarden in Yorkshire I had a fair idea what I was letting myself in for (see chapter 8). However, unexpectedly our vicar left and my fellow churchwarden and I found we were more heavily committed during the interregnum.

As a churchwarden I was surprised by the number of relatives who chose the original sentimental and atavistic version for one of the hymns at a loved one's funeral. It has to be said that a surprising number of hymns still seem to be at odds with the Gospel:

DIVERTING THOUGHTS (GK)

I sometimes wonder why the hymns
We sing in church are mostly full
Of windy words, recycled thoughts,
And hackneyed platitudes, or else
Are merely padding while we reach
For rhyme. Perhaps there's nothing more
To add to Easter's song of hope or thanks
For mercy, love and grace that God
So freely gives. Before the rout
Of ancient rites designed to earn
The prize of place in sun, or just
Placate capricious god whose wrath
Was feared before all else, our chants
At least were often poems worth
The name; despite their misplaced view
Of despot god. Or else there's those
Who tired of praising God and sing
Instead in psalms applauding bits
Of rich display of nature's works,
Ignoring shadow blood and pain.
Perhaps a Quaker time of quiet
Would better serve the need we feel
To worship God with thanks and praise.
Or is our deeper want to sense
The will of Christ as light to guide
Our shuffling steps beyond the night?
If so then singing facile phrase
To feeble tune will not suffice:
Unless our straying minds entice
Our fickle thoughts to roam adrift.

Some Harvest hymns are especially in need of revision.

HARVEST HYMNS (MC)

When thanking God for food we eat
Remember those for whom a meal
Is only dream, as they subsist
On surplus crumbs we'd throw away.

In past we sang of God we thought
Sustained each plant and gave it life.
But since, we've learned it's been a tale
Of struggle, pointless death and chance.

It's only when we'd wondered why
We're here at all, we sought for cause
And aim of all this awesome world
And what our lives here signify.

At first we guessed designer Lord
Was architect supreme, and when
Disasters struck we tried excuse
Of giving mythic Satan blame.

Today we know we're lowly beasts
Whom Christ invites to sacred feast
If we allow the seed of love
To be transformed to angel's soul.

As the parish church we were asked to conduct baptisms of children of parents who were not regular churchgoers. We maintained a policy of welcome to all subject to the parents attending a session or two of explanation and instruction. One did sometimes wonder how much of the latter had been taken in!

AMEN (TL)

A nervous crowd is milling round
The church's door, with some engaged
In final smoke before they brave
An entrance where the scene is strange
To most, where candles shine their points
Of light on altar's spread and by
The font at other end. They've come
To witness child of friend to be
Baptised to please her gran. The words
The curate reads and then explains
Belong to fiction's page. The sign
Of cross on baby's head awakes
A sudden cry of loud protest
From she at centre stage. But now
The rite's complete they gather round
The font relaxed, arranging groups
For photo album's sacred realm.
They think their pictures never lie,
But theirs conceal the ill-at ease
Performance just survived, as smiles
Display relief the thing is done.
The priest and they inhabit worlds
As wide apart as here and far
Antipodes. And yet if two
Or three alone began to glimpse
The Gospel's golden light, perhaps
A loud 'amen' should be response,
And hope that seeds of faith may sprout
Where roots can reach the unseen depths,
Where patient God embraces all.

Reflecting on the experiences of myself and my fellow churchwardens in Yorkshire and Cambridge spawned the following:

CHURCHWARDEN (TL)

The pressure came from friends and those
She scarcely knew, except by name,
To serve her turn as warden if
The vote allowed at A.G.M.
But on the day she's unopposed;
And so her sentence was decreed.
At first it seemed the job was chain
Of petty chores that any fool
Could undertake as long as all
Was done in line with detail set
In black and white like army's rules.
But soon she finds there's secret wars
Beneath the surface smiles and charm.
There's silent tugs of war for gain
Of Brownie points in eyes of Lord
Of all, at least in vicar's mind.
She finds she's learning fast to read
Between the lines. They're just a bunch
Of sheep who've glimpsed the light but find
It hard to shed their infant selves
Who think the world exists for them
Alone. They're each a pilgrim filled
With good intent, but slow to move
Ahead until their sense of worth
Has been affirmed. They know they need
To leave themselves to care of grace,
But dare not trust to such alone.
The warden slowly learns to love,
Instead of losing patience, as
She sees herself as one with them.

RICH SURPRISE (MC)

As bulbs announce that spring is nigh
We start to plan the garden's year
Ahead. In ordered sequence whites
And yellows, blues and reds, orange
And purples too, against a screen
Of many shades of green, will bring
Us joy. But strange to say there's much
We never planted there and much
We did that's failed; and what is more
The weeds are waging constant war.
In truth display of dandelions,
And spread of daisies on the lawn,
Are pure delight. The bindweed blooms
Are festive trumpets decking hedge
As novel garlands at a fete.
The bumble bees can find no fault
With compromise that we bemoan.
Our garden's like the wider world
Beyond, in which ambitious men
Aspire to order all our lives
To fit their ideal schemes. They rant,
And seek to pin the blame, when ends
Are not achieved. It seems they're blind
To fact that native woods appeal
But blocks of spruce in ranks appal.
Our garden's like my local church.
The actual play departs from script
To improvise a rich surprise.

An important part of being a member of a church is that one mixes with people from every sort of background and of all ages. It is as one joins together in a fund raising or outreach event that one discovers unexpected talents in others and the way these complement each other in achieving the desired outcome:

TRIVIAL PURSUIT? (CW)

The heavy mob is lugging chairs
And tables for the coming fray,
While other folk unpack their bags
Displaying cakes, old books, a range
Of varied bric-a-brac we've seen
Before, along with needlework
And cuddly toys from hours of toil,
With cups of tea and gossip's oil.
The scene is set, the bolts are drawn.
A frantic scrum engulfs each stall.
And soon the dregs alone remain –
A ghastly china dog, a guide
To eating out in France before
The War, a gadget for a task
Unknown, a jar of pickled fruits
And half a children's game for four.
As floors are swept and plates are wiped,
The money's bagged with quiet content.
The church is solvent once again.
But more to point our plans have worked,
And people worked with will as team,
And even raised a sum for poor
For whom our way of life's beyond
Their wildest dream. Too soon we'll start
To work afresh for next year's bash
At raising record piles of cash.
But now we pour a cup of tea
And watch the box before we see
To chores neglected while our Fair
Consumed our energies and hours.
I'm glad this annual jamboree
Is only once a year for me!

My fellow members of the Church of the Good Shepherd were essentially caring, kind people. However, there were some who tended to automatically oppose change. I encountered this personally when the Diocese decided to urge the churches to consider how their policies affected the environment and how the way they managed their church grounds benefitted the conservation of wildlife. In view of my record (see chapter 8) the Parochial Church Council asked me to draw up a policy with regard to the latter. Others put forward proposals for solar panels on the church roof. The PCC twice turned down the solar panel proposal on the grounds that other calls on their finances must take priority for the time being. My proposals for the church grounds included setting aside one area to remain unmown in order to develop a different flora and a tussock structure. The latter encourages a soil surface community of invertebrates requiring a more humid situation than the large areas of mown lawn. I also proposed that one corner be used to accumulate fallen branches as dead wood is a major resource for some fungi and a rich assemblage of invertebrates. When it was suggested that the Chairman of the Diocesan environment committee should be asked to approve my proposal it turned out he had first become enthusiastic about wildlife conservation when I had taught him when he had attended a field course at Malham Tarn! The PCC adopted the proposed policy. However, in 2014 a small group were determined to overturn this in the interests of tidiness. At their first attempt they put forward a spurious argument that the unmown area encouraged an increase in the frequency of uncollected deposits of dog dung. They were unaware of my record with respect to the problem of dog dung (see chapter 9) and my survey of the grounds did not support their claim. At their second attempt the PCC rejected their former endorsement of my proposals in defiance of Diocesan policy. At the following AGM I invited the PCC to think again as they had seemed unaware of the context of the Diocesan policy. I was pleased that the PCC restored the unmown area.

In July 2000 we flew to Bangalore in India.
I gave a lecture at the Institute of Science and at an agricultural university on the edge of the city, before we boarded a train to the extreme south of India. We passed through Kerala, where Audrey had spent two years as a governess to a young boy (see chapter 4). Our prime aim was to visit the Rural Development Movement at Prakkanvilai. We initially stayed at the Church of South India hostel at the extreme southern tip of India. On attending church on the Sunday we were warmly greeted and I was unexpectedly informed that I was giving the sermon! We then went on to the RDM base itself. This charity was conceived and founded by Revd Dr Israel Selvanayagam, of the Church of South India, when he was attending the Church of the Good Shepherd when in Cambridge while on a visit to use the University's rich library resources to complete the research for his PhD. Our church has supported the project from the beginning. Audrey and I were impressed by the fact that the committee comprised not only CSI members but also moderate Hindu and Muslim members. Furthermore, the agenda of projects was set by the local committee and not imposed by some well-meaning external NGO. The royalties from my first seven collections of poems have gone to the RDM ever since.

Following our visit we proceeded to Western Australia to visit a friend from my student days at Cambridge and his wife, who had been my Aunt Sheila's deputy before her marriage. Audrey mainly remembered the visit because of the red-back poisonous spiders everywhere. Fortunately they were not aggressive. We then proceeded to Tasmania to visit Trudy, Andrew, Alistair and Samantha. It was great to get to know our lively grandchildren.

It was my habit when visiting Tasmania to set traps for scuttle flies in the garden, which I visited before breakfast while the children were not yet active. The specimens were preserved in ethanol for processing back in Cambridge. I also collected specimens at windows, etc. After this visit I decided it was time to write up the results of these collections. The eventually completed paper (Disney, R. H. L., 2003. Tasmanian Phoridae (Diptera) and some additional Australasian species. Journal of Natural History 37: 505-639) described a new genus and twenty-seven new species, two of which were named after Sam and Ali (see Appendix E).

16th October 2000: our granddaughter Zoe is born in Wales.

Witnessing grandchildren growing up is not only a blessing in itself but it brings to mind incidents in the childhoods of one's own children. These poems tell of incidents in Zoe's childhood.

PART OF PLOT (TL)

With leaf of heliotrope as hat,
And then reversed as parasol,
A child of two creates a realm
Of fantasy. She shares delight
With us for whom this world's become
A place of threats, of rampant greed,
Of cynics knocking all that's good.
It's through her eyes we come to see
That joy's alive, the future's bright.
Despite we know there'll still be tears,
Each night is only pause before
The dawn invites anew desire
To choose to walk within the light,
For sake of she whose smiles are real.
We dare not steal her right to see
The road ahead as way to land
Of future plans that will be more
Than paper dreams. For her it's still
A time to relish blessings now.
With her as guide the clouds disperse.
Desire to hear the wheels of hearse
Declines as we become a part
Of plot to scatter seeds of hope.

PERSPECTIVES (GK)

Today the sky is overcast
With pall of grey, which suits my mood.
My wife's in pain, research is stalled
By knotty problem unresolved,
Our son-in-law has herd of cows
In path of foot-and-mouth's advance
Across the land. But then I play
With daughter's child and soon the sun
Imbibes the clouds. To her the world's
To understand. It's full of fun
And wonder too, enough to fill
Our cups to brim and more. So come,
Forget the gloom and let us praise
The gifts of joy, resolved to drink
Of life, with those we love, to end.

WORLD APART (RE)

The sun is shining through the pane
Of sliding door whose outer side
Was polished bright a week ago,
But now the golden light reveals
The handprints daughter's child had left
On inside face when sticky touch
And lovely smile conveyed her joy
At squirrel eating nuts it clasped
In dexterous hands, while bushy tail
Was flagged aloft. To me the beast
Was pest. To her its presence, just
A pace beyond the glass, was gift
Of magic brought to life. To her
Suburban garden's world apart.
To us, as age begins to slow
Our pace, it's now a growing chore
To cut the grass and keep the weeds
At bay. To her it's realm of birds,
A scene of varied hues, a place
Where making mess is not a crime.
Her pure delight in these has made
Us relish what we took as read.

RESTORED (TL)

When grandchild's taken ill
And lies in bed with drip
Attached to arm and face
Has lost its bloom, it's then
The nightmare fears invade
Our minds. They race around
With taunts that drain away
Our peace and calm until
Our thoughts are numb. But when
Her smiles return and once
Again she's full of fun
And mischief, then we feel
The sun is here again.
But when relapse occurs
It seems the end of world,
And hope's forever dead.
At last she slowly gains
Her strength again. Today
Relief is tide of joy
That drowns the rasping dread.
The light returns once more
To eyes of she we love.
She's cherished more than's good
For child, as though she's born
Afresh, a precious gift.

I have deliberately omitted my overtly political poems from this sketch of my life. However, I decided to include the following as the politician referred to is Cyril Smith, who was to be exposed, after his death, as a sexual pervert. My brief encounter with him convinced me that he was not a man to be trusted, despite my sympathy with much of the politics of his party. I had no idea at the time as to the depths of his depravity.

ELECTION 2001 (CO)

I shook a politician's hand
At time of campaign for our votes.
In line we queued for 'privilege',
But when it came my turn his gaze
Was straying past to pretty girl
Behind. His muttered words were worn
To hollow shell by constant chant.
At question time he ducked and weaved,
Maligning other side when called
Upon to face a tricky ball.
I made a note to put my cross
In other's box. But then I heard
His rival on the radio.
It seems she's clone of first.
They really must incline to view
We're fools, who only wish for less
In tax but more on schools and health.
But wider issues bother me.
I want to know the reason why
The war in Kosovo was not
A crime; and why we bleed
Some poorer lands to fill the gaps
We have for nurses, doctors, skilled
Computer folk and engineers.
Why favour purblind trade with those
Whose human rights are brazen snub
To UN code? And why the play
Of market, unconstrained, is free
To sacrifice our jobs at home;
Because abroad some wages paid
Are lower than a slave who gets
His board and keep? They glibly talk
Of level playing fields, despite
Disparities of tax and wage.
And why are worthy MPs not
Allowed, by whips, to vote in line
With conscience, just because the few
Who form the Government desire
An easy ride? And why, oh why,
The silly spin in place of frank
Discussion free of cant and lies,
Disguised as 'facts', about their foes?

No wonder politicians seem
To most to be a form of life
Akin, or scarcely higher than,
The slime from which we all arose.
Perhaps it's only just deserts
For nation where success means wealth.

2001: A Royal Society/NATO Fellowship awarded to Dr Mikhail ('Mike') Mostovski (Moscow) for him to work with me for a year. These fellowships were to enable postdocs from the former Soviet Union to work with a scientist in the West.

Mike was a hard worker and arrived with some interesting specimens to process from museums in Moscow and 'Leningrad'. We produced a number of papers together. Perhaps the most noteworthy was a species with flightless females collected on snow in winter, along with its males, in Kazakhstan
(Mostovski, M. B. & Disney, R. H. L., 2002. A remarkable new species of Triphleba Rondani (Diptera: Phoridae). Studia dipterologica 8: 557-562 (2001)).

Another interesting species from mountains in Tadjikistan and Uzbekistan seemed to possess a number of features reflecting ancestral states (Mostovski, M. B. & Disney, R. H. L., 2003. On a peculiar new species of Megaselia (Dipt., Phoridae) from Middle Asia. Entomologist's Monthly Magazine 139: 83-86).
While he was with me his boss in Moscow died. When Mike returned to Russia he found himself inundated with administration that would have been done by his boss. He had almost no time to continue his research, so started applying for posts elsewhere. He then landed the job of Head of Arthropods at the Natal Museum in Piertermaritzburg. This was the appointment I had turned down, when I was not prepared to accept it while the Apartheid regime still ruled in South Africa (see chapter 9). Mike settled in well and started to make a significant impact. Ashley Kirk-Spriggs and Mike decided to edit a MANUAL OF AFROTROPICAL DIPTERA and Mike suggested I and himself should undertake the chapter on scuttle flies. However, Mike's position in Piertermaritzburg started to unravel during 2014 following the retirement of the Director of the Museum. His replacement as Director of the Museum (now renamed the Kwa-Zulu Natal Museum) was by an African chosen on political grounds rather than by an African with far better scientific credentials. Mike's reputation as an entomologist, as well as Mike being a Russian Jew, seemed to irk the new Director. This situation coupled with the exceptionally high crime rate, which Mike had experienced first-hand more than once, precipitated Mike's sudden resignation and his move to Israel with his family.

6th August 2002: our grandson Max born.

From an early age Max was intrigued by how things were put together and how they could be taken apart! In time this developed into an interest in how things worked. He developed an extraordinary memory for technical details.

DUXFORD IMPERIAL WAR MUSEUM (CW)

Our trip with lovely daughter's kids
To Duxford's sheds of planes and tanks,
Of guns and other tools of war,
Had subtext urging ceaseless thanks
For peace secured by means of all
This kit. As children learned a lot
From clever, even elegant,
Designs displayed, one soon forgot
Obscene amounts of cash, of work,
Creative skills were just employed
To better zap the other side
Before ourselves could be destroyed.
Resources spent could conquer want
For many still deprived of dream
Of daily bread. The title irks.
Recall of empire, I would deem
As out of place as time when slaves
Provided wealth for lavish homes
The National Trust now owns with pride.
The shop is stocked with many tomes
And tacky toys that take delight,
One feels, in war; as though it's all
A children's game. Resort to force
To foster peace is not a brawl
Between opposing gung-ho knights.
Today it's mothers, children most
At risk from missiles, bombs, the rest
Of ghastly ordnance here they boast
Was fastest or the best for task
Of wreaking havoc on the foe.
Recoil from war is reinforced
By all this slick design on show.
If only all those able minds
Had planted wisdom seeds that grew
To give us lasting peace. Instead
This ugly beauty, old and new,
Confirms our need to heed the voice
Of Christ from long ago to try

To love our foes, placate their fears,
Address complaints. If not we die.
The urge to seek revenge for wrongs
Perceived becomes as drug to drain
Concern, destroying trust, until
Our fears and sense or anger gain
Control and overwhelm desire
For seeking calm and common cause.
It's those who try to mend esteem
Who should deserve the most applause.
And yet to witness pure delight
Of grandson's eager eye for ace
Displays has made our day. We pray
He'll never join the fighting race.
My lasting hate of war derives
From time in youth, as soldier sent
To play a minor part in fight
Against the vicious gang who rent
Apart idyllic Cyprus all
For nowt. I honour those who served
In thankless game restoring peace,
With hope it might be long preserved.

GENERATIONS (RE)

The joys, the worries, pains and hopes
Were intertwined as we beheld
Our children growing up, and now
They find their ways in work and play.
And even if we'd had our time
Again, we cannot tell we'd not
Have blundered, stumbled just the same.
The single thread that links it all
Is love sustained through times of cold
Despair and fear. But now we know
It's they who've made us what we are.
It's being parents makes us learn
That school is part a farce designed
To give all mums and dads a break,
Before return to daily game
That renders sport a childish prank
And novels empty skeins of words.
The rich returns we gain are not
Conveyed by clever phrase or tropes.
The smiles of grandchild say it best.
In them we know we're truly blessed.

26th September 2002: Zak died.

Some days before he died Zak phoned to say he was unwell in bed and that he did not think he would be fit enough to give a lecture at the Law Faculty as part of the Alumni Weekend that takes place just before the start of the new academic year. He asked me to agree to him suggesting that I take his place and that I talk about the work I did in Belize (British Honduras). He was to have talked on the consequences of the Home Office Forensic Science service being given agency status and opened up to competition from private companies. He had warned that subjecting forensic science to market forces would create a charter for sharks. Indeed he had published the following: – Erzinclioglu, Z., 1998, British forensic science in the dock. Nature 392: 859-860. The response of the Establishment was to grudgingly agree but said unless such charlatans were named and evidence given they could not act. Zak expanded on his concern, and the basis for it, in the last chapter of his best-selling book (Erzinclioglu, Y. Z., 2000. Maggots, Murder and Men. Harley Books, Colchester, 256 pp). However, when I, as an expert witness for the prosecution, was challenged by such a charlatan the Establishment failed to act (see below).

Zak died a few days before I gave my talk at the Law Faculty. I preceded my talk by showing a slide of the cover of the above book and paid tribute to him. I concluded with reference to the last chapter of the book in which he presented his criticism of the Tories subjecting forensic science to market forces. Four soberly dressed, middle aged, men got up and walked out! A distinguished colleague remarked "Splendid! Zak is still ruffling the feathers of the Establishment from beyond the grave!"

DOUBTLESS (RE)

In lecture I referred to piece
In which my colleague stated how
The Tory Government's reform,
By which Forensic Science had
To move to market place, had been
A charter sharks embraced. At once
A group of four, with scowling looks,
Arose and strode from lecture hall.
It seems they disapproved of truth
That punctured myth their party's white
As freshly fallen snow. It's plain
To all impartial minds that bricks
Are dropped by Governments of left,
Of right, and muddling middle way.
I'd merely cited mess that lacks
A mop. By walking out on me
They'd shirked the chance to face the truth
That all are prone to blunder's lure.
I know it's so with me. There's none
So deaf as those who won't confront
The awkward facts revealing need
To think again, despite the pain
This might entail in eating words
They once considered right and sane.
It's only those prepared to doubt
Who'll ever learn from past mistakes.

I was asked to write Zak's obituary for The Times (7 October 2002). The authors of obituaries in this paper are traditionally supposed to remain anonymous for fifty years. However, I received a series of phone calls saying that they had gathered that I had been the author!

I then published the following tribute to Zak in the Royal Entomological Society's journal Antenna (2003, 41: 302-303).

ZAKARIA ERZINCLIOGLU (RE)

To me he was a friend without
Compare and colleague who perceived
Our field of science through the same
Concern for detail slowly won,
Instead of shaky theory's con
Selecting only facts that fit.
To me he was a man as straight
As any man I've known. I'd trust
Him long beyond all doubts about
Myself. His courage fighting lies
In courts of law: his war on those
Who charge police for expertise
They lack, or fabricate for fee,
Was undeterred by those who tried
To black his name behind his back.
His lust for reading way beyond
His chosen sphere was rare indeed.
But I recall his love of wife
And lovely kids, for whom his pride
Was fully justified. Their dad
Was one they'll come to see as giant
Whose heart with pure compassion flowed.

I was asked to write a further four obituaries for Zak, culminating in:

Disney, Henry, 2006. Erzinçlioglu (Yahya) Zakaria (1951-2002), Oxford Dictionary of National Biography Article 77385.

The last case in which Zak was involved with myself was the one referred to above in which I subsequently exposed a charlatan 'expert witness'. It became a high profile case, featuring on the BBC's CRIMEWATCH programme twice and, following the court case, was featured in the Channel 4 series THE REAL CRACKER and the accompanying book (Stephen Cook, 2001, the Real Cracker. Channel 4 Books, 224 pages). The essentials of the case were as follows. A burglar entered the house of an old lady in Sussex and stole some antiques. As there were still plenty left he returned some days later for a second go. However, the lady had changed the locks. So he broke in and murdered the lady, placing her body under a blanket in an empty ground floor room. He put out a note for the milkman saying she was in hospital. He worked through the house over the next few weeks. When utility bills came in her post he took her cheque book and forged her signature on her cheques. When her body was discovered, on July 26th, the only insects present were the larvae of a species of scuttle fly, which ended up on my lab bench. I estimated that the eggs had been laid between 12th and 16th July. However, this clashed with the written evidence cited above. The police therefore called in one of new companies claiming expertise in forensic entomology. Unfortunately, they lacked any knowledge of scuttle fly taxonomy, especially with regard to their larvae. They merely looked up the chapter on Phoridae in a book (Smith, K. G. V., 1986. A Manual of Forensic Entomology. London: British Museum (Natural History. 205 pp)) and chose the species written about at greatest length – the coffin fly, whose larvae are characteristic of BURIED corpses. Thus they misidentified the genus and species and said the latest date the eggs could have been laid was June 26th. The police thereupon refused to pay their fee as the last recorded phone call by the deceased was on July 10th. They then asked Zak to comment on the two reports. He endorsed mine and declared the second to be nonsense. However, the police remained puzzled because of the written evidence of the note for the milkman and the cheques signed by the burglar as their dates clashed with my estimate. As the investigation progressed the evidence increasingly supported my estimate. They then called in a handwriting expert who quickly ruled that the note and writing on the cheques was not that of the deceased. The burglar was subsequently arrested and charged with murder.

As a consequence of my report having been challenged I was obliged to be called as an expert witness in court. After being examined in chief and cross examined, the prosecuting lawyer asked me to comment on the second forensic entomological report. I replied that I had shown the Crown Prosecution Service images of the larvae from the case and of those of the species claimed by the author of the second report. I said that if my two year old granddaughter were to be admitted to the court and she were to be shown these images, without telling her what they were, I would ask her "Are these little sausages the same as these other ones?" she would reply "Don't be silly granddad of course they are not!" I added that I thought that that would more readily convince the jury than Zak's rather more technical report. The judge replied "Thank you Dr Disney for enlivening a somewhat pedestrian review of the evidence. You may now step down"!

It was only because the written 'evidence' clashed with my report that I was obliged to go to court. Normally my reports were incorporated into that of a forensic entomologist or pathologist. Indeed for my reports for forensic cases from abroad (from Sweden to South Africa, from Chicago to Japan) this was taken for granted.

Following the conviction of the murderer I reported the fraudulent company to various relevant authorities. Only the Sussex Police responded positively by writing a report on the three entomological reports for the National Crime Faculty, highlighting the fraudulent nature of the second report. Otherwise the rest said it was not up to them to deal with the rotten company. I therefore wrote it up first for Nature, then for Science & Public Affairs and then the New Scientist. Each in turn after initial enthusiasm said their legal advisors said both they and I would be sued. I replied "Let them sue" but to no avail. So I published in a leading French journal instead: – Disney, R.H. L .,

2002. Fraudulent forensic scientists. Journal de Médecine Légale Droit Médical 45: 225-230. The offending company then spent three months trying to sue me but without success.

NO REGRETS? (GK)

A letter came to frighten me
With threat of law for telling truth
About inept report by man
Who falsely claimed proficiency
In field of science called upon
To help in murder case. It's sad
To see a decent man at heart
Resort to further lies to shield
The claim he knows is false. To save
His name he only need admit
He'd made a gaff, apologize,
Withdraw his flawed report and vow
To stay within the bounds of what
He knows for sure. But no. He thinks
He'll call what he believes is bluff
On my behalf. Oh foolish man.
I did not lightly raise my head
Above the edge of parapet.
I'd hoped he'd see his better way
To be regret expressed to those
He'd served so ill. Instead he's set
On course that's bound to harm himself
Above all else. I only wrote
About his fool's report when all
The other remedies had failed.
I wrestled long with doubts about
The right of what I chose to do.
I prayed. My friend endorsed the draft
Of what I wrote. But still I felt
A sadness at the need to act.
A little lie that's not renounced
Becomes the drop releasing flood
Destroying all. To choose the risk
Of owning up is surest way
To ever learn. Today, it seems,
We don't allow for errors by
The folk who strive to find a place
In sun and sometimes stray. Unless

We all admit we make mistakes
We'll never share in mercy's balm.

CONSEQUENCES (MC)

1. Market forces (MC)

A burglar killed, with brutal force,
A frail old lady for some pence
And twenty quid. He flung a coat
Across her prostrate corpse and left.
It's thus she lay in cold neglect,
Apart from female scuttle fly
Who laid her eggs and flew away.
At length police arrived on scene,
Along with those with special skills.
They found voracious maggots, gorged
And ready to pupate, as clue
To tell of time elapsed since death.
It's thus a specialist proposed
A term of thirteen days or give
Or take a two. To try to nail
A certain day another man,
Who advertised his skills for fee,
Was asked to view a sample too.
But he was ignorant of flies,
His fiction data lie for he
Had merely guessed by reading book
And choosing species often found
Before. Alas, he's wrong and gives
An estimate of thirty days -
When suspect burglar was away
In Spain. Confused police now ask
Another to adjudicate.
It's thus the phoney number two
Was shown to be a con. If he
Had been the only one, his gaffe
Would free a guilty man to strike
Again. So who's the biggest crook?
It seems that anyone can claim
An expertise when fancy fees
Suggest they must be sound. It's thus
The market favours fraud and spin -
Or what we used to label sin.

351

2. Adult child (CO)

Coercive letter came with threat
Of all the weight of law. But wait,
It's all assertion, not a fact
In sight. The threat's implied but not
Defined. It's clear it's all a bluff.
I bide my time before reply.
At length a bluster e-mail came
Demanding I address the charge
That I defamed the lousy rat
He calls his 'injured' client. Still
I let him sweat. At length I send
Him sample taken blind from file
Of black complaints against the toad.
And I advise he'd seal the fate
Of fool for sure by taking me
To court. His deeds exposed to world
Would spike his empty guns. Indeed,
If weren't for waste of time, I'd feel
Inclined to sue the scum myself.
But in my heart I feel for him,
Who knows he's truly in the wrong.
Denying all has set his feet
On road that's paved with endless lies
Until he's reached a point when truth,
Deceit and rage are now in mix
He can't escape. He's sinking fast
In mire he's made for self. His fate
Is dire unless he now recants
And vows to turn the page on past.
A loss of self-esteem and pride
Is tiny price to pay for peace:
Or is he adult child who still
Expects to get his selfish way?

3. April fool (TL)

A man on phone intones in slow
And measured voice
"This is P.C. Jones. I've news about
Your wife. She's had
A mishap...." Then the line goes dead.
I pause in shock.

I ring our home, but no reply.
I try police.
Their records note no thing amiss
With cherished spouse.
I ache for man to call again:
To no avail.
I head for home with thoughts now numb,
Besieged by fears.
Relief exceeds all bounds when there
She stands alive
And well. Although it's April 1st,
It's not a joke.
The swine requires a brain transplant.
Perhaps he lacks
That sense one's loved, which people need
To feel alive.
Perhaps corroding hate consumes
His sadist mind.
I faintly feel a tiny grain
Of pity calm
The fury burning out of hand
Within my soul.
May God forgive his hellish hoax
That drained my heart.

SEED OF DOUBT (GK)

Despite he knows I only wrote
The truth about a flawed report
This man submitted to police,
In which he falsely claimed his non
Existent skill allowed a clear
Conclusion that is plainly wrong,
He's now intent on saving face
By taking me to law. His case
Is not sustained by facts. Although
On paper I must win the day,
Our legal system stands or falls
Depending on the way the game
Is played in court by lawyers ranged
As rival teams. It seems the facts
Can be arranged in ways the mind
Rejects but feelings roused embrace.
The surface logic can conceal

A dastard ploy designed to twist
The words I wrote to show that when
A phrase is white it's really meant
To mean it's black. I need to keep
My calm, with nerves of finest steel.
I need to pause to ask myself
What dirty twist's behind the aim
Of ball he bowls. I'm smaller cat
Who's cornered by a tom with tail
Whose tip is slowly twitching side
To side. I wait to catch it off
Its guard with unexpected snarl
That punctures sense it thinks it's won.
As soon as seed of doubt is sown
The counter thrusts begin to tell
Until its tail is still, retreat
Begins to seem its better way
As triumph moves aside for fear.
At last my self-esteem revives,
Enhanced by clash endured to end.

UNEXPECTED CONSEQUENCES (CO)

As scientist I often seem
To be a trifle off my head
When viewed without a clue to what
I do and why. It's thus the shed
Beside my house is seen as den
For secret rites. It's full of shelves
Of bottles ranged in rows. In each
A tube of rotting meat that crawls
With restless maggots, or attached
To sides are pupae now at rest.
But these are not the heaving hordes
Of blowfly larvae culled to bait
A hook for catching perch. They're far
Below the size of those. Instead I farm
The tiny scuttle flies to learn
How long they take, in days, from egg
To fly. This helps police to know
The least it's been since death of those
Whose corpse contains a writhing batch
Of larvae left as tiny clocks
To mark the days since eggs were laid.

My gruesome game has helped to nail
A vicious beast who killed a child,
And cur who bashed an old and frail,
But wealthy, lady in her home
For sake of antiques worth a sum
Beyond his reach. Such men I view
As lower forms of life. Indeed
I wonder how a man can sink
So low to murder helpless folk
For sake of greed or else to rid
Himself of irksome child of she
He's lured from husband once she'd loved.
Her fall had triggered tragic tale.
They'd never dreamed such lowly flies
Would prove their alibis were lies.

Postscript to this whole affair.

I was subsequently invited to contribute to a special volume a journal was devoting to forensic science. My contribution being: – Disney, R. H. L., 2011. Forensic science is not a game. Pest Technology 5: 16-22. In this I updated the report of the Sussex case with subsequent events, including the attempt to sue me. The editors and publishers were clearly nervous about the risk of litigation so they inserted a lengthy disclaimer that ended by stating that their disclaimer "neither condones nor supports the message herein"!

My greatest disappointment was fellow scientists who privately applauded my stand against this fraudulent company, and another company with whom I subsequently clashed, but said it would not advance their careers if they publically supported me! In addition I picked up on the grapevine that my failure to procure a grant from NERC for my work on Phoridae had been partly influenced by comments by an Establishment scientist whom I had shown had evaded his opportunity to confront the evidence against the boss of the fraudulent company. His opinion was that I was a first class specialist on scuttle flies but I was 'somewhat unsound' when it came to acting in the public interest!

Another time I had to attend court was because the solicitor for the defence had failed to grasp the inescapable logic of my report. The case involved a woman who took a dog to a vet because it had several bruises and wounds. She claimed these afflictions had only been acquired that day. The vet disbelieved the woman and called in the RSPCA. Their inspector sent me maggots from the worst of the wounds. From the age of the maggots my report concluded that the wound was several days older than the day of the visit to the vet. The defence solicitor rejected my report and I was obliged to attend a magistrates' court. The solicitor for the RSPCA was excellent. He brought out the key points in my report in a very clear manner. It was then the turn of the defence solicitor. He started out with an extraordinary request "Dr Disney will you please tell the court your qualifications". I replied by pointing out that after my name at the head of my report it had added – MA, Cert. Ed, PhD, ScD. I then explained what these signified. The solicitor then said that was not what he had meant by his request and added "Did you obtain any GCE 'O' levels?"! I replied yes, eight in all, and I would see if I could recall them all. However, he realized the three magistrates were getting restless and so turning to face the astute lady in the Chair did an elaborate bow towards the Bench and requested that they may take it as read that I was qualified. "Get on with it" was the reply from the Bench! He then scrutinized the graph I had submitted to the court in which I had plotted temperature up the vertical scale and duration of development along the horizontal scale and the graph for the duration of development for the species of maggot in the case. The solicitor asked how to use this graph. I told him to select a temperature on the vertical scale and go across horizontally until he encountered the graph and then drop vertically to the bottom scale to read the relevant duration of development. He then asked as to what point on the vertical scale he should choose. I replied I had allowed for a range of temperatures, as the vet had not measured the temperature of the wound infested with the maggots. "So it could be right at the top?" he responded. I agreed but said I had stopped at that point because the temperature was now dangerously high according to the two references I had given in my report regarding temperatures in dogs. "So it could be at the bottom the scale?" was his reply. I agreed but pointed out that the dog would now have acute hypothermia! So his next request was to ask why my temperature scale was in Celsius. I replied it was so because I was a scientist. He then requested "Would you please convert it to Fahrenheit?" I replied "not off the top of my head. Besides it would only change the label. It would not change the inference that the dog's wound was invaded by maggots some days before the dog was taken to the vet". He then tried to pursue the question of healthy temperatures in dogs. I stopped him short and told him bluntly "I was called here as an expert on flies. I flatly refuse to answer questions on temperatures in healthy dogs. If he wished to pursue that line then would need to recall the vet." "Quite right" said the Chair of the magistrates. The result of all this nonsense was conviction for the woman with a suspended prison sentence of six months, a ban on keeping any animals for ten years and all costs were charged to the defence (I had told the RSPCA that they would have to pay my train fare but I would only charge a fee if their expenses were charged to the defence). If her solicitor had advised her to admit her guilt I would not have had to go to court and she would almost certainly have had a lighter sentence.

In another case, involving the murder of a man's stepdaughter, the defence called upon the services of a company essentially ignorant with regard to scuttle flies. The victim had been last seen in December but the body only discovered the following March when rain had exposed her knee by washing away the soil covering her carcass. The forensic entomologist called in by the police correctly concluded that the body had been buried many weeks before its discovery and rightly concluded that a species of blowfly had arrived only after the exposure of part of the body by the rain. Blowflies are usually the first insects to discover an exposed corpse, but will not penetrate the soil like many other insects. However, the defence's entomologist concluded that the blowfly indicated that the body had only been buried in March. This was despite the evidence of all the other insects present in the corpse. These included scuttle flies, which had been identified only as far as the family Phoridae in view of all the other insects present. On receiving the defence entomologist's report the scuttle fly specimens were sent to me. They included a species only added to the British List since Ken Smith's 1988 book on forensic entomology (cited above) had been submitted for publication (Disney, R. H. L., 1987. The undescribed male and holarctic status of Megaselia abdita Schmitz (Diptera: Phoridae). Entomologica scandinavica 18: 263-264) and its subsequent inclusion in my 1989 Handbook (cited in chapter 9). I had since then been sent this species from forensic cases from Britain, mainland Europe and the USA and data had been published by my colleague in Chicago on the duration of development of this species at different temperatures. These data proved the eggs of this species of fly had been laid in December. This helped to convict the stepfather of murder.

UNCONSTRAINED (GK)

For weeks I've put aside a chore
Of naming flies a man has sent
Without an aim that's clear to me.
But when at last I open tube,
And pour his sample into dish,
For viewing under microscope,
Among the dross I spot a gem,
A genus long I've dreamed to see.
It seems I often forge ahead
When others set agenda self
Has tried to shun. The plans I choose
Myself are often stalled, but then
Request has opened up a seam
So rich that tiresome trucks of coal
Have given way to diamonds large
As nuts or veins of gold beyond
My wildest hopes. Result is more
Achieved than sticking close to list
Of numbered tasks on page compiled
When seeking funding for my work.
By missing out on grants from NERC,

I'm free to follow hares I flush,
Without a sense of guilt. It's thus
I publish twice as much as those
Constrained to narrow paths prescribed
By rules that will insist one must
Outline one's plans in detail worth
A fiction's prize: or else, confined
By such a game, one plays it safe
With stodgy fare that lacks all flair.

Most policemen and lawyers I have encountered have been people of integrity concerned with getting at the truth. Only a few were otherwise. Most cases give rise to no unpleasant aftermath for expert witnesses brought by the prosecution. Some brought by the defence can be tiresome. For example:

MISJUDGED (CW)

A man accused of murder lied.
He told police the victim played
A game of darts in pub at time
Beyond the day a neighbour made
A call in vain, and noted still
In letter box a leaflet man
Delivered week before. Besides,
At scene of crime his tale began
To fall apart when insects found
Of corpse allowed a specialist
On tiny flies to estimate
The day their eggs were laid. The gist
Of clear report was victim died
A week before that game in pub.
The suspect man had never dreamed
A tiny fly would prove a snub
To fiction tale he'd bowled at cops.
Defence was less concerned with facts
Than how to aid the rich accused.
His bogus 'expert' now distracts
The jury using bluster, false
Or twisted novel claims about
The tiresome maggots found on corpse.
His artful story meant to rout
The prosecution's case was soon
Dispelled by questions putting guy
In spin of contradictions, so

358

He then resorts to rude and sly
Ripostes by means of which he hopes
To undermine the jury's trust
In opposition's case. But no. The twelve
Now one by one embrace disgust
At clot they now suspect has sole
Concern for fee he'll get for game
He plays. They rate his silly yarn,
Along with tale of darts, the same.
Indeed they start to wonder why
He's not in dock along with guy
Who's now on trial. They start to think
Between accused there's guilty link.
Defence is looking pretty grim
His deal 'no win no fee' was risk
He took in view of client's wealth.
His gain's now looking pretty slim.
His client seems not best in health
As jury's verdict's brief and brisk.

PARTNERS IN CRIME (GK)

A scientist of greedy bent
On making money was intent.
He joined commercial firm that aims
To offer expert skills to help
Police to solve assorted crimes.
But soon he learned to write reports
That suit the prosecution's case.
It's thus his reputation grew:
Until detective, cutting through
Confusing clues and complex clash
Of rival witness tales, with hunch
Proceeds to nail the crime on thug
He longs to put away despite
Some data giving alibi.
Our man invents a way around.
He's seen as 'sound'. It's thus he earns
Inflated fee for slipshod work
Selecting facts that fit the false
And flimsy case that's built by him
Who seeks to hike his clear-up rate.
Alas for them, the other side
Consulted scientist to whom

The truth was sole concern. In court
They clashed. The prosecution failed.
Our man's exposed as fraud and finds
Himself condemned. His peers delete
Him from their list of experts whom
They recommend. And he who used
His lies and favoured facts,
And shared his smutty jokes, is left bereft.
His record slips behind. He takes
To drink and slowly bungles more
And more. He moans about the good
Old days when scientists would serve
The cause of locking thugs away.

Not all forensic cases that came my way involved murder victims. Food contamination by insects were brought to me by Trading Standards officials or companies being threatened with litigation by a customer. For example a lady wanted to sue the Off Licence from whom she had purchased two cases of wine, one of red and one of white wine, when she found two bottles had a fly floating at the top. The Off Licence told her to sue the bottling plant instead. However, when pouring the red wine through a sieve I discovered specimens of a much smaller species of fly at the bottom. My problem became how come that a larger fly that floats and smaller flies that sink end up in the same bottle? The answer relates to the relative surface area to volume ratios of the two species. The larger fly possesses air sacs in its thorax to prevent overheating during flight. My conclusion was that the contamination occurred when filling the bulk container in France and not in the bottling plant in the UK. Anyway, this case prompted the following poem:

CONTAMINATED (CW)

I'm sent a bottle glowing gold
With finest wine from France. It feeds
Enticing dreams of bliss. But this
Is not to be. When lady bought
It hopes were high before she saw
A fly was bobbing just below
The cork. So I've been asked to name
The beast and say if drowning fall
Occurred before the tanker left
Or during bottling over here.
On pouring nectar through a sieve
On way to waste, I find in dregs
Some smaller flies as well as one

That caused complaint. Because they sink
But blowfly floats, though half submerged,
I can infer a likely scene
At time the drinking in excess
Had made them drunk before demise.
It's odd what tiny facts can tell
For those who never give them thought
Until a puzzle comes their way.
It's then one's forced to look at truths
Afresh and find that much of what
One thought was made one's own was filed
But not perceived in depth. The same
Applies to much I learned as child
And only slowly grasp anew
As age erodes the shallow views
That once had seemed all carved in stone
In heady days of prime. But time
Reveals them hollow husks long dead.
Imbibing shallow precepts shared
Among my peers I'd failed to spot
The deadly myths that lurked in files.
I'd clean forgot the wholesome milk
I'd drunk before I went to school.

An aspect of involvement in forensic cases has been the media contacting
me with queries or wanting to do a piece on my involvement in a case. I have
been surprised by those who come with a prepared agenda before questioning
me about the case in question.

CARICATURED (GK)

Reporter's busy setting scene
Before he signals time for take.
But first he wants to alter things
To fit assumptions. No mistake.
The story's fixed before he starts.
He only hears what sieve retains.
He's irked because I lack a coat
Of gleaming white, devoid of stains,
As sign to indicate I work
In lab. I'm not a chemist prone
To splash a dodgy brew! Again
He's thrown by tiny fly alone
On slide beneath the microscope.
He, lacking larger lens, now moves
To film some larger flies on pins,
But I object. Indeed he proves
My point. He's not reporting what
I do. He wants to make me play
A part to suit his script. There's more.
He chooses shots that don't display
The facts that tell it straight. Instead
The viewer sees my nostrils fill
The frame as I am peering down
The microscope. He vaunts his skill
With angled views, but loses point
Of how I help police to solve
A crime by use of insects culled
From corpse. He's driven by resolve
To show me off as way-out priest
Engaged in secret rites that pluck
The truth from arcane facts revealed
By maggots found in gruesome muck.
But worst of all he talks of proof
Instead of weighing likely tales.
I can't re-run the past. I choose
Account embracing all details,
Rejecting simple yarn to please
Police because of stubborn fact
That doesn't fit. Reporter sticks
With facile fiction still intact.

It is not only some reporters who ignore a 'stubborn fact'. I have had problems with some fellow Christians who object to my disbelief in the Virgin Birth. Apart from my reasons for my disbelief (see below), as I read the Gospels the incarnation took place at the baptism of Jesus by John the Baptist. Furthermore, our calling is to allow the Holy Spirit to enter our lives, albeit with little hope of it being as completely as was evidently the case with Jesus:

INCARNATION RULES O.K.! (GK)

When Buddha challenged ancient views,
And stripped away the myths, he found
The common core of ethics all
Religions teach. While much profound
Perception filled his mind, his sense
Of self dissolved and fell apart.
He's left with beastly drives, the dregs
Of former pains, emotions part
Perceived, and unfulfilled desires.
And some of these he thought had come
From former lives. The self as 'soul',
He taught his monks, was merely sum
Of all these things we label now
As evolution's means to stay
Alive in face of daily strife.
But when we heed the call of way
Our God would have us walk, his grace
Embraces all these basic fears and needs.
As Holy Spirit starts to feed
Our deepest inmost thoughts the seeds
Of love create emergent souls.
Incarnate selves are born to thrive
In paradise when flesh is dead.
For now it means we come alive.
Instead of shedding what we are,
Today we're meant to sanctify
Our secret selves and how we live.
It's thus our souls will learn to fly.

2004: Publication of my fourth collection of poems – COUNTERPOISE (Ronald Lambert Publications, 171 pages).

This collection included the following poem that in the eyes of a fundamentalist condemned me to damnation for eternity! However, it is precisely adherence to outmoded doctrines formulated many centuries ago that prevents most of my biological colleagues and the younger fellows of my college from taking religion seriously.

SPIN-DOCTORED? (CO)

It's in the Talmud we can read
Of Roman soldier's crime. His name,
Panthera, reeks of feline lust.
But it seems truth must not be told
When facts we'd rather not proclaim
Are part of story that we own.
We'd rather give a spin that adds
An extra sheen. A shocking twist,
For which our hero's not to blame,
Is quite taboo. Its thus I see
Fantastic tale of Jesu's birth
Of virgin pure, despite the fact
That only girls could be conceived
This way – if at all; besides, John
And Paul are silent on this score –
And Christ from cross entrusted John
With Mary's care. Perhaps greatest
Gift of Joseph, to lowly maid,
Before their joyous wedding day,
Was the secret of piercing rape
He strove to hide from prying world.
Perhaps her hasty trip to far
Away cousin's home was panic
Flight from malicious gossip's barbs?
And was the move to Nazareth,
On return from Egypt's refuge
From Herod's wrath, a move to flee
From corrosive whispering jests?
And was Panthera's wrong just used
By opportunistic God to give
A Christ for all who on the edge
Of hope are ditched? For Jesus sees
Our hidden selves. He will not bow
To privilege or praise a man
For noble birth, his wealth or fame.
A generous heart, a kindly act,

A secret gift, accepting blame
For lapse by friend in need of shield
From flaming row, or just to be
With she who mourns and wants to talk
Of happy memories or things
That might have been; it's these that Christ
Affirms in simple folk. It's these
That all are called to emulate.
Instead we tend to crave respect,
Affection's ambiguous embrace,
Or envy at the least, or else
The phony satisfactions won
From bitter-sweet success. We dare
Not face the truth that love for self
Corrupts the little love we get
Or give, unless we offer it
To God in simple trust, as once
Mary and Joseph gave their child.
Their love returned enhanced many
Times beyond their wildest dreams. She
Observed with growing puzzlement
It being spurned by those too blind
To see beyond their own conceits,
Too blind to truth about themselves.
And Pilate's riposte, "What is truth?"
Insistently reverberates;
As Christ beyond the cross becomes
Our Easter joy – our inner light.

Some object to my dismissal of the virgin birth as being contrary to the teaching of the church over many centuries. So I perhaps need to spell out the biological objection a bit more clearly. First one needs to highlight the pre-scientific view that the man planted his seed in the garden of the women's womb. Hence pre-scientific genealogies are all about the male lineage (as in the beginning of Matthew's Gospel). Since learning that half our genes come from the mother and half from the father such a distortion is no longer tenable. Next we need to consider the determination of the sex of a child. There are various sex determination mechanisms in nature. Thus ants have a haploid/diploid system and snails are hermaphrodite, but humans (like Drosophila fruit flies) have XX chromosomes for a female and XY for a male, so the father will have contributed either an X or a Y chromosome. If a women were to give birth to child without a contribution from a father then the child would have XX chromosomes, i.e. she would be female. If a male child were to result from a virgin birth he would be XX, a biological anomaly rather than a normal human being. Consequently if one were to insist on Jesus being the result of a miraculous virgin birth then one would be declaring that he was not born a normal human being, which would be contrary to the rest of the New Testament teaching. Hence I stand by the above poem. Furthermore, I think we should celebrate Joseph. He did not renounce his betrothal to Mary, following her rape, but went ahead with the marriage, contrary to the cultural tradition of the day. He not only genuinely loved her and stood by her but also cared for her illegitimate son. He was clearly a very remarkable man.

Also in 2004 on page 261 of The Ancestor's Tale by Richard Dawkins is reproduced one of my drawings (from the paper Disney, R. H. L. & Kistner, D. H., 1992. Revision of the termitophilous Thaumatoxeninae (Diptera: Phoridae). Journal of Natural History 26: 953-991). Several people have asked me what I think of the writings of Dawkins. Where I heartily agree with him, and with mainstream theologians, is that it is no longer acceptable to treat a Biblical text as authoritative. It must be evaluated in terms of its historical and cultural context. This is especially important with regard to the Old Testament. In terms of the New Testament we also need to be aware of the 'need' of writers to support their views by appeals to scripture. Thus St Paul is profound when commending Christ and the Gospel of grace and love (e.g. I Corinthians chapter 13). He is sometimes a dinosaur when he appeals to the Old Testament in support of cultural traditions now regarded as anachronisms or when he treats cultural attitudes of his day as normative. For example when in I Corinthians chapter 14 he wrote that women should be silent in church! But, when heeding the Holy Spirit instead, he wrote that for Christians 'there is no longer Jew or Greek, there is no longer slave or free, there is no longer male and female, for all are one in Christ Jesus' (Galatians 3: 28).

Returning to how I view Richard Dawkins, contrary to the media who refer to him as a 'top scientist', I rate his contribution as having been primarily as a writer dedicated to the public understanding of science. As far as his contributions to scientific knowledge are concerned, he did a good PhD and excellent postdoc. Subsequently, his one book primarily aimed at his fellow scientists was his 1981 book The Extended Phenotype: The Gene as the Unit of Selection. Leaving aside the issue as to whether it is the gene or the individual organism that is the target of selection, this book is an excellent synthesis and exposition of other people's ideas and conclusions. His other books concerned with explaining our modern understanding of evolution for the layman are extremely well written. They are marred, however, by his habit of including an exposition of his brand of fundamentalist atheism. This is odd in view of his admiration of 'Darwin's bulldog' T. H. Huxley, who coined the word agnostic, having argued convincingly that science, as science, could neither prove nor disprove the existence of God. Furthermore Dawkins coined of the word meme, which he then employed as a device for arguing that religious beliefs are untenable. But the meme has not stood up to critical scrutiny (e.g. Alister McGrath, 2005, Dawkins' God. Blackwell Publishing). The following poems reflect my perception of his promotion of atheism:

PARADIGM SHIFTS (MC)

The peacock's tail and orchid's bloom,
The insect's eye and desmid's form
Delight the artist each of us
Would be. In former days these spoke
Of God's design. Today we know
These wondrous things emerged, along
With microbes, viruses and AIDS,
By random variations pruned
By selection's greedy ruthless
Secateurs. And still these restless
Blades prevail, as drug-resistant
Pathogens emerge and pesticides
No longer work against the bugs
They're meant to kill. For some this fresh
Revealing truth has dethroned God.
For others it proclaims our view
Of Him was too constrained by
Our puny human minds. As man
In Dublin pub observed, "God, by
Definition, can't be defined"!
Only effects of grace divine
On human lives reveal the truth.
Thus only after weighty tomes
Galore did Aquinas truncate
His scheme of clever words. It seems
He glimpsed his cold allure of chains
Of logic had reduced our God
To item in a list of links
In philosophic game. Our Lord
Of love had been interred beneath
This pall of learning run amok.
Likewise only the God our thoughts
Had shaped was slain by Darwin's knife.
For still the Holy Spirit's fire
Awaits our quiet assent to flood
Our hearts with light divine. It's thus
I stand with Darwin's torch to guide
My mind while our Lord's gentle warmth
Begins to thaw the frozen crust
That blinds me to his boundless love.
It's thus I stand with those whose lives
Reveal compassion's gentle care,

Whatever crazy creed they hold –
Be it dogmas daft or crass claims
That God is dead – for Christ still bides
His time with patient, yearning, love.

FUNDAMENTALIST ATHEISTS (GK)

When God is expelled from our lives.
It seems that our brain then connives
At drivel espoused
As Chance is then housed
In place of His Grace that revives.

Or else a sceptic is born
Who views all beliefs with a scorn
Reducing our God
And all that seems odd
To juvenile jibes we'd outworn.

Selection of data to fit
A prejudice mind won't admit
Is greatest of sins
It ends where begins
Exposing our cynic as twit.

But fruit of the Spirit abounds
When loving compassion astounds
And truth of such facts
Negates the impacts
Of dogmas that Dawkins expounds.

FUNDAMENTALLY? (GK)

If God were dead I'd wonder why
Our Dawkins needs to preach the same,
As what's believed is scarce concern
If life is pointless, lacking aim.
If now alone is all that's real
Then past beliefs are merely junk
And future all too swift will come.
So if we're sober or we're drunk
Will matter not. And whether facts
And reason rule our lives or whims
And fancies fill our minds is just
Our choice. We maybe sing our hymns
To drugs, to crossword puzzles, maths
Or sports, but all is vain as soon,
Too soon, we'll die. Belief in Christ
And pilgrim's call one may lampoon,
But when one offers waffle in
Its stead one gives a stone in place
Of bread, or snake instead of fish.
I can't deny the gifts of grace.

A teenage youth proclaims his team,
Who lost the match, is still the best
Because the ref was biased rat
Who's blind or worse. It seems the same
When Dawkins argues God's demise
Because of Darwin's blaze of light.
He fails to mention mainstream church
Embracing Darwin too. The sacred texts
Enshrine abiding truths within
Their ancient myths. There's some who tried
Explaining evil in their lives
By tale of fearful devil ranged
Against the righteous Lord. But now
We guess the price of freedom's gift
Was march of nature drenched in blood.
When God allowed a universe
To run its course, apart from Him,
It maybe proved the means to make
Us free to hear the nagging call
To move from worship aimed at self
To focus all on Lord of hope.

By grace incarnate love can raise
Our deeper selves to heaven's gate.
Without this pilgrim aim to life
It's fleeting, pointless, ghastly joke.
But fruits of Spirit changing folk
Proclaim the Gospel truths anew.
But Dawkins still remains so blind
His mind precludes unwelcome facts.
He just ignores the winding roads,
The cul-de-sacs and theories now
Interred in middens long forgot,
As science climbed to present day.
He won't allow our thoughts of God,
And aim of life, the same so slow,
And error prone, attempts to see
The golden strands of truth concealed
Within the myths and culture-cloaked
Disguise. The pruning knife is tool
Required by all who seek the light.
But Dawkins uses axe to fell
The tree of faith instead, despite
The shoots of green the stump will feed
From roots alive, but out of sight.
As he reveres the truths derived
From what's observed, there's chance his zeal
Exposing errors may in time,
Unearth these deeper truths behind
The tale that science tells along
With source of fruits of grace we learn
Are changing lives of countless folk.
But still I share with Dawkins scorn
For ranting fools employing text,
From ancient times, against the gifts
That Darwin gave our minds. But next
I'll also scoff at claim that Darwin proved
That God is dead. He merely peeled
Away accretions based on dearth
Of facts that science since revealed.
As I engage in my research
I travel knowing not the end.
The same applies on pilgrim's road.
The worth of both I will defend.

IRRATIONAL ATHEISM (GK)

(Being a response to an article "infected with science" by Mark Ridley,
published in the New Scientist issue dated 25 December 1993. It was based
on the assumption that religious belief is irrational and is to be likened to a
virus infection afflicting society)

It seems analogies are out
When Paley's watch is up for grabs;
But Dawkins, Ridley and their ilk
Employ a pack of metaphors
When Darwin's dogs are used to hunt
The phantom they confuse with God.
It seems a virus of the mind
Has made them blind. It's very odd.

FLAWED (MC)

A man who denies there's a God
Declares he prefers on his tod
But when he was floored
He blamed the good Lord
Which logic decrees is most odd.

'NOW I ONLY KNOW IN PART...' (TL)
(1 Corinthians 13: 12)

It's like confessing one is gay
To say I place my trust in Christ.
It's not that one's ashamed as such.
But media seem to be enticed
By tales of fools rejecting light
With random quotes from ancient books
To trash what science teaches now.
But such are intellectual crooks
Who only heed the facts that suit
Conclusions reached before they start
Review of data now secured.
Indeed, like Dawkins preaching part
Of truth to fit belief that God
Is dead, their minds are closed so tight
That much of what is widely known
Is spurned as though it's deadly blight.
Unless beliefs are free to change
When shown that some of what we thought

371

We knew is now displaced by what
Is fresh, and so was never taught
Before today, we'll never grow.
With open minds, and inner ear
Attuned to Holy Spirit's prompt,
Researcher's finds can rouse no fear.

RESPONSE TO JOB 40: 8 (GK)

This earth of beauty, way beyond
What human minds may dare invent,
Is also world of dreadful acts
Of nature seeming quite intent
On wreaking havoc, pain and death.
But worse is freedom's gift abused
By human kind rejecting call
To rise above the process used
To slow evolve from cells to apes
Who serve their selfish selves alone.
We either yell 'a god who made
Us thus is mad, with heart of stone',
Or else confront the challenge faced
By all who glimpse the vision Christ
Proclaimed of Kingdom forged from peace
And justice, love that can't be priced.
Was freedom worth the costs involved?
Unless the universe were left
Alone to run its course, until
The such as us emerged, the weft
And woof of means would be sustained
By God who willed the blood and hurt
In each specific case. For such
My blunt rejection would be curt!
I'd join the ranks of those
Who relish Dawkins hurling stones
At fool rejecting reason's road
By choosing ancient texts he drones.

WITHOUT DOUBT! (GK)

Our Dawkins claims a leap of faith
Is just belief devoid of facts
In plain support. But faith is more
To do with trust and not with tracts
Expounding doctrines long consigned
To rubbish dumps of ancient flaws
And myths. Instead of swearing by
The Pentateuch, replete with laws
That few obey, we're called to place
Our faith in Kingdom based on love
In action, peace and justice: quite
Reverse of world of push and shove
For selves alone. The gifts of grace
Abound when faith inspires the ways
Of Gospel guiding hearts and minds.
So when our Dawkins loudly says
He can't believe in God because
He can't discern supporting facts,
He's showing world he's turned his back
On those who claim their kindly acts
Derive from fruits of Spirit's grace
Transforming lives of faithful folk.
His strident tone suggests a fear
Of being wrong requiring cloak.
Or does his seeming lack of doubt
Reflect a mind that's closed to need
For second thoughts? I swiftly learned
In science truth demands I heed
The slightest nagging doubt. The same
Applies with walk of faith. Unless
We will admit we lose our way
At times we'll fall for false success

EASTER JOURNEY (MC)

It's since we thinking apes evolved
That queues of troubles started. Doubts
About the point of all assailed.
Aspiring schemes, the thrust to stand
Above the herd, the lust for fruits
Beyond our reach, the wish to shape
The world for good, desire to lie
At ease while others tend to needs,
The fury goading on to war,
The striving after art sublime,
The ceaseless search for secret truths;
Our seething, ant-like, frantic work
And play allaying fears of night
And death's relentless call to rest
In peace, or else just cease to be,
Or enter realms beyond our dreams.
It seems it's here the great divide
Is found. There's those who know beyond
All doubt that grave is end. There's crowds
Who stand on Dover Beach* and fear
It's so. There's some, like Lyte** whose faith
Is built on Gospel's rock that death
Is mere horizon glimpsed beyond
The restless turbid ebb and flow,
The ups and downs of joys and woe.
For time I once embraced the cold
And stoic stance of those who think
They know that only life on earth
Is real. I relished freedom won
From fear induced by preachers steeped
In phoney dogma dressed in threat
Of judgement seen as price we pay,
Instead as purifying flame.
Then slowly creeping doubts began
To gnaw a gaping hole, until
Agnostic fog became the realm
In which I moved. But then a chink
Of distant light began to grow,
Until, beyond coercive screens
Of foolish claims, I stood beside
My soul mate Thomas in that room
When risen Christ appeared again

And cured his doubts – along with mine.
I found I'm on a journey bound
For state of being cleansed by love.

*Poem by Matthew Arnold
**Author of the hymn "Abide with me"

ENOUGH? (TL)

There's many lack belief in God
Today. For some it's little loss,
As deep ingrained they still adhere
To values freed from clinging dross
Of worn out creeds. But many lack
Concern for aught but self alone.
Their greed and lack of conscience means
They harbour hearts of hardest stone.
They live as forebear beasts intent
On mere survival. Come what may,
Desires and needs for self ensure
They're deaf to call to walk the way
Of serving cause or others less
Endowed with means to live their lives
Without a helping hand. They won't
Admit there's more than basic drives
That go to make us fully what
We're meant to be before we die.
Is pilgrim road the surest guide
To find the answer as to why
We're on this earth for fleeting stint?
We may perceive the merest hint
Of guiding light, but that's enough
To keep on track, however rough
The route may seem or steep the bluff.

As a postscript to my contention that Dawkins tends to dismiss relevant evidence I repeat the quote (in chapter 9) from the blurb about me on the back of my 1995 collection (Lapsed Atheist and other poems) – 'He regards observable facts and authenticated experiences as sacred, and all interpretation as provisional'. I contend that Dawkins turns a blind eye to relevant 'authenticated experience' of the fruits of grace transforming lives for the good. On the other hand he is correct in condemning much anachronistic and fundamentalist religious doctrine:

GIVE THANKS FOR ATHEISTS! (RE)

A ranting crank is claiming whole
Of Bible's varied mix of myth,
And garbled tales of past, along
With parts that still can heal the soul
(Despite that wrathful God), is true
Beyond dispute. He won't admit
The clash of rival thoughts displayed.
He sweeps aside the honest view
That Christ rejected some of what
Was taught of yore. The garbage preached
By fellow fools is why, at times,
I thank the Lord our nation's got
Outspoken folk who preach that God
Is dead. I don't agree, but wish
Them well. Their tireless toil to clear
The ground inters beneath the sod
The barmy weeds of dogmas killed
By knowledge gained by patient slog
Along with reason's ruthless fire.
It's humble people plainly filled
With Holy Spirit's gifts of grace
That show us Gospel's still alive.
It's lives of faithful pilgrims now
Reflecting light of God's own face.

LIVING GOD (MC)

'How strange that you believe in God'
A friend remarked. 'You must admit
It's very odd for one, like you,
With double doctor to your name,
With reputation long secure
On history's page of chosen field'.
But I replied that once I shared
His view that God was dead. But then
The deity supreme was just
An abstract noun, no image filled
My mind. Discarded function back
Of scheme of things we now explain
In other abstract terms concealed
Behind a screen of clever maths,
As priests of old behind the veil

For inner sanctum hid from crowd.
But then the love at work in lives
Of those who walked the way of Christ
Began to put a face on God,
And mind engaged with fruits of love
Redeemed from mere concern or gifts
To please. This love divine is flame
Of warmth and all consuming fire.
It purifies the mucky ore
Of common lives until the grains
Of gold appear and these are forged
To make a crown of lasting worth.
But more than that, this metal's not
Inert. A breath of life imbues
It with a living heart that throbs
With joy and praise for God who's real
Beyond our wildest wild surmise.

QUIRKY FAITH (MC)

My colleagues wonder why I go
To church. For them all talk of God
Is out of date – a worn out screen
Of sentiment preventing truth
Of world engaging thought. For me
Reverse is real. The love of God
Allows our darkest selves reprieve
As we confess our needs, the lamp
Of Christ permits we see the glow
Of hope concealed beneath the clouds
Of bleak despair. Besides, the folk
Who share my creed are like a shelf
Of fruits from many lands displayed
In local supermarket's spread.
There's nowhere else I get to know
Such diverse friends I'd trust with life.
Besides I've learned to see the flame
Of Holy Spirit's grace at work
In each and everyone, despite
Their quirks and stumbling, pilgrim, faith.

OUR ONLY NEED? (CW)

As youth I'd thought that mind would soon
Embrace and strive to fill the gaps
In knowledge still awaiting kiss
Of science on the march. Perhaps
I'd play a part in enterprise.
But now I know the holes in street
Of cobbled stones exceed the parts
Complete. The voids are not so neat
As once surmised. It's just the same
With abstract concepts meant to net,
Define and limit what we mean
By God. Concluding, with regret,
I binned attempts. The being Christ
Addressed as 'Father', urged us all
To claim as ours, is Lord supreme.
We only need to heed His call
To live the Gospel way of love.
Beyond the grave is when we'll start
To comprehend. For now our role's
To walk with Christ, to play a part
By means of grace, in making world
A place of trust, of peace and hope,
As justice ends compassion's drought.
We'll learn together awesome slope
Is not so steep as first we feared.
Forgiveness overcomes our self concern
When working for the greater good.
From Holy Spirit's prompts we learn
To set agenda for our day.
Forget the lofty urge to know
Extent of God's enigma now
Before we die. It's time to sow.
Our Lord will gather in the grain
When harvest days are due and all
Will find His welcome table laid.
We only need to heed His call.

THE LITTLE THINGS (CW)

There's tribe of writers some admire
Who never seem to reach the point
Of saying clearly what they mean.
They hint and juxtapose a thought,
An image, symbols, worldly things
Or phrase that's learned as sacred gem
Of paradox. It all implies
That depths beyond what common folk
Can comprehend are there to find
If one persists. But I've begun
To think they're imprecise because
They really can't believe that Christ
Had taught it's how we treat our friends,
Prepare a meal, perform the tasks
We're paid to do, relate to all
Who cross our path; in short it's how
We learn to love the humble things.
We'll find the holy in the most
Unlikely place or person met
By chance. The time for glory's show
Is when we've tried to live this way;
It's when we've learned our knowledge now
Is incomplete and must be so
As long as we abide within
The walls of time and space. Accept
That probing depths beyond our reach
Is mere escape from daily gift
Of chance to tend to little things.

Anyway, enough of all this sermonizing provoked by being asked what I thought of Dawkins! I just note that several of the above poems were included in my 2009 collection ('GUIDED BY KNOWLEDGE, INSPIRED BY LOVE') that was my contribution to the Darwin Bicentenary. Furthermore it was timely in view of the resurgence, during 2008, of 'Christian' fundamentalism in the media under its new guises of 'creation science' and 'intelligent design'. This was odd as one of the most persuasive lines of evidence for evolution is stupid design beautifully refined by selection, a supreme example being the eye of a fly. There are numerous lesser examples (such as the two cited in the following poem) where, trapped by inherited constraints, selection has been unable to eliminate what an engineer could have rectified in a matter of minutes. Despite this the letters sections of the house journals of learned societies started to be burdened with Creationist polemics.

When this happened in the Biologist the correspondence terminated with a note by myself (Disney, H., 2008. Creationism, Darwinism and ID. Biologist 55: 71 – Letterbox) and this later spawned the following poem:

UNINTELLIGENT DESIGN (MC)

The Bible tells a tale of slow
And tortured trials to understand
The ways of God by warring tribe
Intent on seizing fertile land
From neighbours scorned because they bowed
Their heads to idols made from wood
And bronze. It's not till Christ arrived
On scene at last we understood
The pearls concealed within the twists
And turns of muddled books that come
Before the Gospel's blaze of light.
But still there's those who treat the scum
And dregs as equal worth with wine.
Despite the thoughts of those who came
Before, explosive knowledge won
By science shows that much was lame
In views our forebears held, and much
Was nonsense posing as the truth.
The fools who cling to Genesis
As set in stone ignore the youth
Of knowledge then. The spot that's blind
In eye of man is bad design.
But octopus has got it right.
Recurrent nerve in neck is sign
Of same. In fish, whose neck is short,
It matters not it's back or front
A vessel bearing blood. But in
Giraffe it seems like stupid stunt
To travel down the neck and back.
For this 'designer' got the sack!

My antipathy towards these revamped fundamentalists was enhanced by their judgmental condemnation of those who didn't accept their ignorant neo-Puritan condemnations of homosexuals, unmarried partners, etc. (derived from an idolatry of texts plucked from the Bible regardless of their historical and cultural contexts). Furthermore the desire to prevent the splitting apart of the Anglican Communion caused the Church of England to avoid condemnation, without qualification, of those who stigmatized homosexuals as being not only 'wrong' but in failing to wholeheartedly welcome them as fellow human beings as much called to be children of God as themselves. The result was the C. of E. appeared to be irrelevant in the perceptions of the undergraduates and research students I encountered daily:

WE NOW BELIEVE (MC)

The Church of England's in a spin,
At risk of shedding outer fringe.
It's all because a priest who's gay
Was meant to get a bishop's crook.
What if he's stuck in boyhood's phase
When only other boys appeal,
Because of flaw in way he grew
Or stifling fears, induced in home
Of strains, had strangled steady growth?
With me it's only temper frayed
(And creeping time has tamed that beast).

We're surely meant to heed the fact
That those who blindly worship word
Of Bible 'free from error' (when
It's clear, to those who see, that parts
Are marred by ancient myths and mad
Taboos) are mired in mental world
Divorced from us who treat the text
As curate's egg. It's waste of breath
To talk of those whose minds are set
In permafrost of antique ways
Of thought before the patient work
Of scholarship and science chipped
Away accretions hiding gold
Of gospel half concealed beneath.
Besides, when Jesus taught 'you've heard
Of old an eye for eye and tooth
For tooth, but I declare....' He showed
Us all that we must only take
From ancient books the parts that fit
His view of God as love supreme.
He spurned the tribal god of wrath
Who's partisan, who stokes our qualms
With threat he'll punish straying sheep
In raw revenge. But I discern
A Christ who welcomes all, despite

Our quirks and scars from knocks we got
From other kids and novice dads
And mums. We now believe that God
Accepts us as we are before
He gently takes our hand to show
Us how to walk his ways of joy.

I will just add that I also took issue with some of my physicist friends who
had espoused the Anthropic Principle:

THREE ANTS AND THE GOLF BALL (MC)

*(A prose version of this parable of the three ants was originally published as
a letter in the New Scientist [1619: 118: – 30 June 1988] as a challenge to
adherents of the Anthropic Principle. Given only the velocity and trajectory
of the golf ball, nobody offered a solution to the argument engaging my three
ants!)*

Beside the clubhouse stand three pails,
Two with water and one with sand.
In the latter, strolling expanse
Of rolling dunes, there relax
Three happy philosophic ants.
Sue and her siblings Jean and Joan
Are relishing their Sunday chat
When suddenly, out of the blue,
A fearful thud and hail of stones
Announce a meteoritic ball
That misses them by gaster's length.
Deleted expletives conceal
Their quivering fright until, with
Their equanimity restored,
Our friends begin to speculate.
For Sue it was no fluke. The aim
Of he who hit the ball was good.
Indeed it was a stroke of one
Who is a master of the game.
But Joan objects. Why should he shoot
His ball at our bucket at all?
Or if he did, perhaps it was
Only after ninety-nine tries
He'd won. But Jean suggests he might
Have placed one hundred gleaming balls
In empty pail and thrown the lot,
In shower of hope, but just one

Had reached its mark. The three defend
Their rival views with growing heat.
Indeed they each become entrenched.
At length all three expire as each
Her dying desiccating last
Tracheal gasp expels. Perhaps,
In truth, the ball was ricochet
From tree from shot by novice who
Had aimed another way. Perhaps
This sorry tale will warn against
Nailing one's colours to a mast
That's insecure, such as the new
Form of Paley's watch in guise of
Anthropic Principle's allure!
Perhaps the dinosaurs all went
Extinct when cosmic golf was played.
Perhaps our fate will be the same.

It was evident to most that the common ground among most members of the mainstream religions and humanists was concern for the afflicted due to illness, ill fortune or some other cause of stress. The support for a plethora of charities and the response to fund raising events like Comic Relief testified to this. In other words the Gospel teaching of loving compassion and concern for the well-being of others commands wide support. Where there is divergence is with regard to the challenge of the Easter message that this life is a pilgrimage by which our emergent soul (brought into being through opening ourselves to the transforming grace gifted by the incarnation of the Holy Spirit) attains an eternal existence beyond the death of our physical bodies. In my experience the most committed to quiet, unobtrusive, service to the needs of others have been those who embraced this view of the purpose of our lives. It is all very well to jokingly dismiss the challenge of what might be the purpose of our lives with black humour, such as "I think I have discovered the meaning of life. You just hang around until you get used to it" (Charles Schultz, 1922-2000). But, as Václav Havel remarked (as quoted in The Wall Street Journal in 2014) "The tragedy of modern man is not that he knows less and less about the meaning of life, but that it bothers him less and less". Ministers of religion who focus on this perception have a far greater impact than those who defend discarded doctrines based on selected quotations from Scripture without regard to the immense, liberating, advances in knowledge during the last 400 years. It is this perception that pervades my 21st Century collections of poetry including the following.

2006: my fifth collection of poems published – A MUSING COG (Ronald Lambert Publications, 125 pages). Its cover showed four ants peering over the edge of a leaf watching army ants and looking out for one carrying prey as their target host for laying an egg as outlined in the following poem:

"OUT OF THE STRONG CAME SOMETHING SWEET" (MC)
(Judges 14: 14)

Consider photograph arrived
With e-mail from abroad. It gifts
An ordered row of little flies
Who peer from edge of leaf at stream
Of army ants below their perch.
They wait for one with prey of choice,
And then select a femur's bulge
As place for egg to hatch and thrive.
It seems the ants discard these limbs,
Like bones of fish we leave at rim
Of plate, before consuming rest.
Arrangements such as these induce
A sense of awe at diverse ways
The scuttle flies have found to make
A living in a world of threats
Of death without a pause. While most
Regard a march of army ants
With dread, a range of tiny flies
Perceive a chance to propagate
Their kind. Apart from those whose young
Are parasites of ants themselves,
A hundred species breed within
The midden trash these ants create.
There's others scan the fearsome front
Of raiding march as fleeing hosts
Of choice are flushed from cover. Thus
Is brought to mind those ruthless thugs
Who rose to rule by arms and blood
And then employed their loot to fund
The birth of lasting works of art.

It is not only ants who are unprepared for the unexpected. In 2006 I assented to a request from my GP to participate in a major NHS research programme on prostate cancer, expecting to be in the control group. However, it turned out that I had got prostate cancer.

SENTENCED (MC)

The weeks I wait results of tests
For cancer slowly eating flesh
Was like the months before demob,
But worse. For then I'd moved afresh
To life as student, filled with dreams
Of future promise. Now ahead
It's only fog, with plans on hold.
It's not the thought of pain I dread.
It's things not done, the time I've not
Allowed to show my real concern
For those for whom I deeply care.
But while it's sure I can't discern
What future months will hold, I feel
A sacred calm at thought of what
My fate might be. Because I know
I've lost control, there's not a jot
That I can do to alter what
Will be. I'll just embrace anew
My faith, as though my life will be
The same as when before I knew
This nagging threat. As crook who waits
For judge to hand his sentence down,
Before they ask the court to rise,
It seems I'm man about to drown
When ship has foundered in a storm:
And yet I feel it's just my boat
Has ceased to tack and now it's free
To run before the wind – afloat.
I'm cured of need to fill each blank
Before the call to walk the plank.

I was then booked for an operation to remove the prostate.

FRUITS OF GRACE (GK)

As slowly fiery dawn ignites
A winter's cloudy sky, so I
Engage in morning rite of stretch
And bend. It's by this means I try
To ease arthritic joints. Today
I'm due to place my life in hands
Of surgeon set to slice away
A cancer best excised. The strands
Of past neglects engage my mind.
While risks are small there's chance my end
Is nigh, but mind denies it's time
To die. Instead my thanks ascend
In silent psalm for life that's filled
With many joys eclipsing lows.
My wife and children, friends, and work
Have long dispelled the blackest crows
Foretelling gloom that in my youth
I'd feared would steal all sense of worth.
The news selects the wicked deeds
And random deaths, ignoring mirth
And countless acts designed to help
Improve the lives of those in need.
It adulates the shallow fools
Who reach the top impelled by greed.
The modest caring folk they just
Neglect. For those prepared to seek
The fruits of grace abound, which nails
The lie that preaches life is bleak.

The operation was a success and the cancer was found to have been confined to the prostate. Regular check-ups since confirmed the cancer had been successfully eliminated, with no evidence of it having spread beyond the prostate.

My first engagement after the operation was to attend an exhibition in which I had been asked to contribute some of my entomological drawings. Since a similar exhibit in York in 1980 (see chapter 8) even fewer entomologists executed their own drawings and photography was increasingly replacing drawing. I was still convalescing and briefly attended the exhibition in my pyjamas and a dressing gown! (Disney, R. H. L., 2006. Exhibit of entomological drawings. In exhibition "On the Way to things: drawing across the university". Churchill College, Cambridge. March 2006). The exhibition was such a success that it was extended and reassembled elsewhere in the summer (Disney, R. H. L., 2006. Exhibit of entomological drawings. In exhibition "Lines of Enquiry; thinking through drawing". Kettle's Yard, Cambridge. 15 July–17 September 2006). Following going three quarters blind in 2012 (see below), having previously executed many hundreds of drawings for my publications, I was obliged to switch to a digital camera on the microscope linked to a computer for the execution of my figures.

22 January 2008: Audrey's 80th birthday

Rachel organized members of the family and others to write tributes to Audrey along with photographs etc. for a large album. I got her to send it to the lab so that I could place it on the breakfast table as a complete surprise for her. She declared the tributes to be all over the top! But she was quietly grateful and treasured the album.

CELEBRATION (CW)

The scent of many blooms invades
The room, recalling glasshouse down
At Kew. Displayed as well are rows
Of cards on mantelpiece. The crown
Is orchid in ceramic pot
With label wishing all the best
For eighty years of birthdays passed
As milestones since she left the nest
Of baby's cot. She questions why
There's all this fuss. She finds it hard
To take it in. Embraced by young
And old alike, in high regard
She's held for kindness known to reach
Away beyond the norm. It's time
To tell her straight she's truly gold,
Even if in faltering rhyme!
Too long she's thought herself of small
Account, of little worth. Besides,
Of all who know her best it's she
For whom our love, for hers, abides.

I LOVE HER MORE (RE)

Her hair is white, her skin has lost
Its smooth and silky feel, but still
There's beauty in her face, despite
The loss of glamour fashion plates
Demand. Indeed an inner grace
Now emanates from deep within,
Revealing warmth that far exceeds
A facile surface elegance
Enhanced by makeup's doubtful mask.
I love her more as I perceive
Her honesty of soul and know
Compassion overflows her heart
And lack of pride reveals her gold.
Her autumn fruit exceeds the bloom
Of youth that first entrapped desire.
I prize her now as vintage wine.

EVENING YEARS (TL)

I'd put it somewhere safe but now
I can't recall exactly where!
It's like the time a student asked
About exquisite fly displayed
Beneath the microscope. Intrigued,
She'd wondered what its larva ate.
I searched the standard texts until
I'd found I'd published note myself
A score of years before! She'd laughed
Aloud and clearly thought I'd passed
My sell by date! Perhaps she's right!
Today I jot a dozen notes
A week to jog my mind about
The smallest things, but still there's some
I overlook or else postpone
Because I find another task
Escaped my lists. Perhaps it's time
I gently passed away. But no
I want to see my children's own
Discover life. Besides there's much
I've still to do, and still my wife
To cherish more than ever first.

388

2008: It was not realized at the time but this proved to be our last visit together to Australia. Trudy, having become interested in pain management, had decided to qualify in anaesthetics. She had completed her training in anaesthetics in Hobart, and passed the exams. Under the Australian system she was then obliged to spend a year of practical application of her new qualification in another hospital. So the family moved to Tweed Heads, on the border between New South Wales and Queensland. She and Andrew then were assigned to a hospital in the extreme south of Queensland, but Trudy spent the first six months with Careflight Queensland. This involved her going in a rescue helicopter to fetch an injured farmer in the outback or in an ambulance jet to Papua New Guinea to collect an ill Australian.

We joined them in their winter (our Summer). We were treated to a number of wonderful excursions, including watching migrating humpbacked whales migrating northwards. However, it was getting to know the grandchildren better that was the real highlight.

Incidentally I put out some simple water (pan) traps in the garden for scuttle flies and preserved the specimens in alcohol for processing back in Cambridge (Disney, R. H. L., 2008. Six new species of Megaselia Rondani (Diptera: Phoridae) from mainland Australia. Zootaxa 1899: 57-68). This small collection was made an exception in view of the backlog of generally collected specimens I had been obliged to decline, restricting myself to processing specimens with novel natural history data (e.g. reared from a known insect host or fungus, an adult visiting a named flower, etc.). My small collection was an exception as I was curious to know what an unexceptional suburban garden might produce. The fact that a collection of ten specimens at Tweed Heads in mid-winter represented nine species, of which six were new to science underlined our ignorance of the Phoridae of Australia! I named the first of the six new species Megaselia alisamorum, after my Australian grandchildren 'Ali' (Alistair) and 'Sam' (Samantha). Otherwise the one major exception to accepting a general collection without novel natural history data was when I was asked to identify 2767 specimens from the Galápagos Islands. There were twelve species of which nine, at least, were introduced by man (one from North America, six from South America, one from Africa and one from South East Asia) (Disney, R. H. L. & Sinclair, B. J., 2008. Some scuttle Flies (Diptera: Phoridae) of the Galápagos Islands. Tijdschrift voor Entomologie 151: 115-132). This project served to highlight the importance of considering the world fauna when one encountered specimens not keying out in the literature for the particular region from which a sample had been obtained. This collection from the Galápagos Islands provided a timely precursor to the following publication.

2009: my sixth collection of poems was published – 'GUIDED BY KNOWLEDGE, INSPIRED BY LOVE' (Eloquent Books, New York, 193 pages hardback). This collection was intended as my contribution to the Darwin Bicentenary. I thought by publication in New York I would reach a wider audience. However, it turned out that Eloquent Books were more concerned with spin than effective marketing. Indeed I had found their e-mails very tiresome:

INFECTED! (TL)

A routine e-mail's sent by guy
Assigned to edit disk with file
For book of poems. If the same
Were first, his condescending style,
Excessive length, perhaps would fit
The needs of novice just. For me
It's irksome waste of time to sift
From wordy flow the only three
Essential points he wished to make.
He'd had my life's synopsis, sent
At their request, in which it states
The proffered work is no event
Unique in my career. There's five
Collections on my list, along
With books and papers on the flies
I've studied over years. For long
I've worked on texts, corrected proofs.
As editor there's thirty books
That bear my name. And even if,
In charity, one overlooks
A learner new to game, it seems
The art of paraphrase was not
A part of training claimed, at great
Expense. There's more. I quite forgot
To mention crass remarks about
His joy and pride in helping such
A work as mine to see the light
Of day. It's over top and much
Is froth. It's trashy souvenir
They sell at Moslem shrines. I need
A pause to stem the scathing thoughts
That spring to mind. I just succeed
In curbing acid comments in
Reply. I wonder why he feels
Compelled to patronise. He's like
A leading chef who thinks his meals
Are far beyond what simple folk
Can even dream or let alone
Aspire to emulate. His own

Disease, to which he's clearly prone,
Is deadly virus goading on
His lengthy screed, his tiresome piece,
That's only served to generate
This spate from which there's no release!

The title poem of the collection is as follows:

"GUIDED BY KNOWLEDGE, INSPIRED BY LOVE"
(GK)

(Bertrand Russell's definition of the good life. He was expert on the basis of knowledge but seemingly blind to the true meaning of 'inspired', whose original meaning implied – being under the influence of the Holy Spirit)

Exchange of views on tele screen
Was pointless farce. They chose extremes
To titillate alone. Despite their claim
Debate was meant to find a way
To reach consent twas just a clash
Of rival views avoiding need
To heed the naked facts that smash
Their party lines proclaimed as truth:
Despite research has shown they're out
Of date, they've missed their sell by dates.
The same applies to doctrines taught
In times before advancing tides
Of knowledge changed the scene. Today
We're freed from superstition's blight
Concealing Gospel's golden light.
Transforming grace reveals the work
Of Hoy Spirit's gifts without
The need for dodgy creeds. It's lives
Reshaped, aflame with love that won't
Be brushed aside by sceptic caught
In trap of bleak demand we must
Restrain all truths with logic's chains.
Let reason rule our minds. Let love
Inspire the way we deal with all
With whom we interact each day.

The following three poems in this collection reflect similar and related concerns:

A CHILD'S DELIGHT (GK)

As child I relished nature's gifts.
When boy I once devoured a book
That Richard Jeffries wrote in praise
Of same. But now I scarce can look
At title page without I want
To squirm. It seems to me he'd claimed
A tot's beliefs, denying what
All adults know, as he proclaimed
A fairyland's enticing view
He knew was fancy free and lies.
His gift for words could not conceal
His phoney infantile surprise
At what he'd seen a hundred times
Before. I take for granted sight
That prompted tingling feeling surge
Of pure delight in past. With blight
Of spirit parched, I felt no urge
To stir that dormant sense of joy
That once was milk for nascent soul.
A brochure's praise just served to cloy
Until a child had paused to drink
A scene in silent gulps of awe.
She turns to say she thinks it's all
A dream come true. Her words restore
My dormant sense of wonder once
Was part of being true alive:
Before I'd learned of callous facts
By which the warring beasts contrive
To just survive another day.
Her pleasure helps my soul revive.

UNEXPECTED (GK)

With microscope I've drawn at least
A thousand figures used to show
The parts of tiny flies, to help
A novice recognise and know
The species found across the world.
It's while I draw I'm forced to view
Each little detail in its turn.
It's thus I stumble on the new
And unexpected facts, as mind
Is running free, as eye and hand
Engage in concentrated task.
It's thus I travel more than planned
When I embarked at start. Despite
I think I guess the score before
I first begin the outline sketch,
I nearly always, as I draw,
Discover something new. It's like
That journey when I asked a girl
I liked, to come for walk along
The river bank, and past the swirl
Of waters by the sluice where brace
Of swans were lazing at their ease
As bonded pair. But when we wed,
And still today, it's like a tease,
As I forever find my love
Revealing novel traits I'd not
Perceived before. Beyond the heat
Of first romance, I've found I've got
Myself a treasure rich indeed.
A tree has grown from tiny seed.

SUN AND SHADE (GK)

When I observe the fruits of grace
In other people, then I know
The Holy Spirit's real and God
Exists. And when I'm feeling low
I pause in silence. Then I may,
At times, become aware of sense
Of loving presence lifting soul
To light. At moments so intense
I feel at one with rest of world
And universe beyond. Too fast
The vision fades. I'm back on earth
Beset by sharp recall of past
And present pains, and conflicts, wars,
Injustice, nature's bloody strife
Beyond the beauty glimpsed before.
But then the warmth of lovely wife
Restores my will to carry on.
I hum a hymn of joyful praise
For kids, and theirs in turn; and thus
Disperse the fog of dark malaise.

Why did I feel a need to contribute a collection reflecting my belief that science has been a gift to Christianity? Science has helped to free the Gospel from past mistaken notions and unfounded myths. Most people, including atheists and agnostics, have assimilated the Gospel concern that we should strive to help the poor, the afflicted and those in need. To exercise compassion and to work for justice and peace has come to be accepted by most (but not all. The exceptions include various extremist Jihadist groups) as the hallmarks of a good society. While many advances have been achieved over the centuries much remains to be accomplished. The Gospel message that life has a meaning beyond our brief sojourn on earth remains to be accepted by most people in the West today, although the death of a loved one often leaves many wondering if, or hoping, it is true. The message of Easter remains a challenge and the recognition that incarnation is an option for all – see the poem INCARNATION RULES O. K.! (reproduced above), from this 2009 collection. Religion is about pilgrimage, conceived by Christianity as progressing from the legitimate self-centredness of the baby to the emergence of the progressively incarnate God-centred soul destined to survive the death of the body. The two great commandments – to Love God and to love our neighbour as ourselves – are the core of the Christian Gospel and to focus on one while neglecting the other is to miss out on the full vision of Christ's teaching and the message of Easter. This message retains the more ancient concept of life as a pilgrimage but rejects the notion of reincarnation as taught by Buddha (and Hinduism, but modern Hinduism is an amalgam of a number of similar but distinct traditions that British imperialism lumped together and labelled as one religion!). These musings resurfaced when reflecting on the In Memoriam event for Audrey, when I read a selection of poems at the Friends Meeting House in Jesus Lane in Cambridge (see below).

When the publication of 'GUIDED BY KNOWLEDGE, INSPIRED BY LOVE' was reported in the THE OLD DRAGON (2011, issue 1 page 15), despite a picture of the cover with my name, it was attributed to my late cousin Hugh instead. This prompted the following light hearted poem about the

AFTERLIFE! (TL)

To mark the second hundredth year
Of Darwin's birth, I published book
Of poems on the theme of faith
In Christ and science not at war.
Today my roving eye was brought to halt
By sight of short review of same
But then to my surprise I see
The author's Christian name is wrong.
They seem to think I'm cousin Hugh!
Among respectful tributes paid
To recent dead, is one for late
Lamented Hugh. Perhaps it's when
A poet dies the world at last
Acclaims his work!
Perhaps If I neglect to ask that lapse
Be publicised my sales will grow
Apace. Perhaps some readers will
Have paused, with musing slow recall
Of Hugh, to wonder why he'd not
Revealed he'd published poems since
The year of nineteen sixty three!
If only Hugh were still alive
We'd share a laugh at this mistake,
But we must wait till my demise!

Christmas 2010: Trudy, Alistair and Samantha were due to arrive in Cambridge on the Sunday before driving us all on the Thursday to South Wales for Christmas on the following Saturday at Rachel's. From Australia she had arranged to collect a hire car the next day. However, much of England, including Heathrow airport, came to standstill due to snow and ice. When they had set off from Hong Kong the pilot received a message to turn back to Hong Kong as he would not be able to land in England that day. They eventually arrived Wednesday evening. Sorting out the hire car, recuperating from jet lag, and last minute shopping demanded a change of plan. We hastily put together Christmas in Cambridge for us. We managed to book accommodation in Bath for a couple of nights after Christmas. Rachel and family, plus the postponed Christmas dinner Rachel had prepared, and Adrian joined us in Bath. Audrey much enjoyed showing our grandchildren around Bath and they photographed us outside the venue where we had had our wedding reception in 1963. We were not to know that it was the last time we, our children and grandchildren were all to be together.

RARE FAMILIARITY (RE)

The scenes we daily pass on way
To work we scarcely give a glance,
Unless we've been away for while.
It's then we greet with nod and smile
Those gentle pleasures now become
A part of what we claim as ours.
Indeed we've grown to be a piece
Of place that others see as strange.
With praise they notice things we take
For granted, see the detail we
Ignore as norm. They help us know
The gifts we never knew we owned.
The same, it seems, applies to those
We love. Since time and distance stole
A daily intercourse, we knew
As pleasing task or favoured coat,
We find our rationed meetings now
Are filled to brim with silent tears
And joyful smiles as we consume
The treasured crumbs of grace bestowed.

2011: my seventh collection of poems published – REITERATION (Pneuma Springs Publishing, UK, 151 pages). This collection primarily gathered together poems previously published in magazines or anthologies.

PREJUDGED (CW)

Reviewers mostly turned their backs
On latest book of poems sent
Because the blurb informs them straight
I look to Christ and serve content
In local church. It seems they just
Assume I'm soft in head and take
On board those dogmas long forgot
By most today. Their grave mistake
Is taking Bible Belt and likes,
Who preach their dinosaur beliefs,
As though they represent the norm
For mainstream pilgrims. But our brief
Is just allowing grace to fan
The inner spark of love to all
Consuming flame embracing life
And other folk; to heed the call
To build the Kingdom formed from peace
And justice wall to wall; to seek
The truth about oneself and what's
Required to help the strong and weak.
It's strange to learn that some dismiss
My poems just because I go
To church and others due to fact
Of reject doctrines I forgo.

Audrey had been taking medication for a heart condition diagnosed a few years before, but it had not been considered life threatening. However, she had subsequently slipped up on the pavement and badly dislocated her shoulder. Since then she had been feeling various pains but visits to the doctor had failed to produce a diagnosis:

INCURIOSITY FEEDS THE QUACK (GK)

For months my loving wife's been plagued
With pain in abdomen. The tests
On sampled blood and urine fail
To find a cause. A scan has drawn
A blank. So baffled doctor closed
The file, concluding nowt's amiss.
To me, as scientist, the fun
Has just begun when routine set
Of hunches bite the dust. For now
The hunt is really on for clues
To something strange. One cannot guess
Surprise awaiting turn of stone
Concealing novel beast. But no,
It seems in training doctors lose
Inquiring mind. The force-fed facts,
Appear to clog the brain until
All novel notions act as though
They're allergens that spark revolt.
A glance at time provides excuse
To end the consultation now,
In view of queue of those with ills
That fit the routine moulds that need
The eye of postman sorting mail
Alone. No wonder quacks
With crystals, herbs and powdered horn,
With talk of cosmic energies
Disturbed by jangled vibes, now thrive.
They mostly do no harm, or good.
But they believe ordeal is real,
And so do I – and she I love.
But words alone are not a balm.
So we must search on own for cure,
In ignorance of any blame
For what has caused her so much pain.

Despite the publication of the above in my 2009 collection, the following came as a complete shock.

1st March 2012: my beloved Audrey dies.

I received a phone call at the lab from a friend. A mutual acquaintance who suffered some condition related to Asperger's syndrome, had told him that he had just found Audrey dead in the garden. The paramedics and police were now at the scene. I raced home as fast as possible. Audrey was lying on her back still with a trowel in one hand. The paramedics said she must have died almost instantaneously from a massive heart attack. More often death from a heart attack is more like an earthquake. A series of minor tremors causes the patient to sit down and lean forwards before the fatal big attack. It was a relief to know she had not had a drawn out painful death, but it was an immense shock. With my medical history we had assumed I was more likely to die first.

In Wales Zoe and Max had gone to school with a daffodil attached to them as it was St David's Day. On return from School they learned that their much loved granny was no more.

The Funeral

The funeral was fixed for 12th March at the Church of the Good Shepherd.

Although it was Lent the vicar said that the idea of a funeral for Audrey without flowers would be unthinkable. Our daughters did a grand job with flowers and in particular with a superabundance of daffodils.

The ceremony at the crematorium was to have been on the same day. However, the doctor who signed the death certificate had departed forgetting it needed to be countersigned by a colleague. So the cremation had to be postponed until the 14th of March. A result was that following the funeral, which was attended by many, people stayed on and on sharing memories, etc. After four hours not only was I wilting but so were my daughters. So I started putting out the lights in the church!

For the order of service the following was printed on the inside cover.

ARTISTS (CW)

Delving, dissecting, plying paint
Artists explore our maze.
Those that succeed are those who find
A sight, a life, to praise.

Praising a stone, a rose, a man;
Showing a hope in acts
Hurled by a world of chance and pain;
Imparts a joy to facts.

Joy is a road to meet with love;
Love is a means to pray;
Prayer encounters God in all,
And He will blaze our way.

Jean Holloway's great hymn 'Lord we come to ask your healing teach us of love' (but leaving out the penultimate verse as the service did not include Holy Communion) was included as Audrey had written about the hymn in the Good Shepherd Newsletter for January 2010.
I subsequently adopted 'Teach us of Love' as the title of my next collection of poems (see below).
Before the tributes from our children and niece Jenny, I pointed out that 2013 was to have been our Golden Wedding. I then read the following poem:

RUBY WEDDING (CO)
(23 November 2003)

It's forty years ago today
We wed. The fires of youthful love
Consumed our fragile fears and doubts
As we embarked on unknown seas
Ahead. The sudden squalls, the joys
Of children, stormy nights, the days
Of calm, the sorrows shared along
With pure delights; from these we learned
The other's strengths and flaws: and how
To live with each as love embraced
Apprentice spouse we'd each become.
No longer simple labels can
Describe the depths of feelings now
We own or entertain alone.
Dissection only serves to kill

The very thing we would discern.
We'll just proclaim our simple thanks
For gift of years that leak away,
At ever faster pace, as we
Decline towards a Western sky
Aflame with richer hues than dawn.

On the day after the funeral our three children and I went to the undertakers, as I had put it to the children that if they did not view Audrey in her coffin they would regret it afterwards, even though it would be an emotional experience – as indeed it was. So in the afternoon we went over to Milton Country Park to unwind. While there we collected pondweed, water snails and other aquatic invertebrates to stock the small pond that Audrey and I had installed in the garden after our last long cycle ride together to order the thick plastic, bathtub shaped liner for the pond. We had many years before made a pond lined with thick plastic sheeting, but a vandal had climbed over the back wall of the garden and made holes in the liner. We were concerned about the loss of the breeding pool for the frogs and newts that we encountered in the garden. While in the Country Park Adrian took the photo of the greylag goose that I used on the cover of the following publication.

2012: my eighth collection of poems published – 'TEACH US OF LOVE' (Pneuma Springs Publishing, 273 pages), being my In Memoriam collection for Audrey.

Among the poems are these reflecting on my loss of Audrey:

'GOOD GRIEF!'? (TL)

I sit alone with mind a blank
Apart from sense of being lost
In whiteout waste of winter snow
With heart benumbed by biting frost.
And yet I know that Audrey, now
In paradise, would want me up
And getting on with rest of life.
But still, as I prepare to sup
Alone, I seem to lose the will
To carry on or else, with swing
Of mood, I work with little pause
For hours on end. It's strangest thing
When left bereft of daily warmth
Of lovely wife, it seems a part
Of self is set adrift on raft

On lonesome sea that's off the chart.
I'm told by those of good intent
I'll come to terms with present grief.
I don't accept their kind advice.
It goes against my heart's belief.
I hope with time I'll learn to keep
My sense of loss concealed from sight
And carry on with routine tasks
With outward calm. I know my plight
Is stony track that countless folk
Are daily walking on their own.
The pointless wars, disease and droughts
Ensure that many live alone
With hearts afflicted by the deaths
Of those they'd loved as constant pain.
Beyond my almost tears I know
I'll meet my treasured wife again,
When I have crossed from life to realm
Beyond demise. But now I must
Eject the moping fool who feels
He's just a speck of flotsam thrust
Ashore by blizzard gale. It's time
To shift the focus off myself,
To look to needs of others; time
To focus on the good in life
With grateful thanks in prose and rhyme.

WE'LL MEET AGAIN (TL)

It's since my truly treasure wife
Had died I find I'm often sat
At home with mind that's numb. Or else
A brief recall of this and that
We shared in past engages mind
Before the fog descends again.
I try to read but lose the plot.
I gaze at garden in the rain
And wonder if I'll feel caress
Of sun before it's time for me
To quit this life and move to where
My lovely Audrey now is free
From pain and worries suffered here
On earth. It's mainly thoughts of those
I love, my children, also theirs,

That gifts me any real repose.
For rest of time immersing self
In work is only way to ease
The grief that clouds my soul and chills
My heart. Is this a brief disease
That soon will fade? Or am I cursed
With slow decline until demise?
But no, my love, I hear you urge
I carry on and grow more wise.
You wouldn't want me staying down
And wishing now returned to time
We both were young and life was full.
You'd urge me on resuming climb
However weak my will and stumbling gait.
My path ahead is steep and age
Prevents a faster pace. But step
By weary step will grief assuage
Because I know we'll meet again
In realm beyond what human mind
Can only half conceive. I'm sure,
Also, I'll find you ever kind
And full of song. This faith alone
Is sacred truth I'll not disown.

After the family had departed I had two strange experiences. The first was when I was pondering with regret that I had not been of more help to Audrey with regard to her stress at Adrian's accident and its aftermath, and her consequent increasing pessimism about life (which she largely concealed from others but not from myself). I suddenly heard a voice "You were her rock". I turned around to see who had spoken, but there was nobody there. It was such an unexpected statement as it was I who had regarded her as my rock during the ups and downs of life.

The second experience was a brief, but amusing, vision. For some time before her death Audrey had been on at me to ditch an old pair of favoured trousers that I regularly wore to work. I agreed to do so when she ditched her old, somewhat faded, green coat that I reckoned was well past its sell by date. She agreed to ditch her coat as soon as I got rid of my old trousers! While rushing about preparing for the funeral I tore my old trousers and had to buy a replacement pair. That evening (when wide awake) my flow of thoughts was suddenly interrupted as I suddenly had a brief vision of myself dining at High Table in my College when I looked up to see Audrey momentarily standing in a fresh green coat and smiling at me! As with the unexpected vision following my mother's death (see chapter 8) this was no dream but an unexpected gift and confirmation that Audrey's gentle humour was fully intact!

5th May 2012: As an In Memoriam event for Audrey, I read a selection of poems at the Friends Meeting House in Jesus Lane in Cambridge

Many Quakers had attended Audrey's funeral. For about twenty years Audrey, with her friend Mary Hope, had prepared a cheap lunch each Wednesday at the Friends Meeting House. All were welcome regardless of their faith or none. I usually attended. We both found compelling the Quaker commitment to translating the Gospel teaching into practical action. The unstructured mode of worship was also a welcome antidote to anachronistic elements persisting in more formal worship in other Christian denominations. The strength of Quaker worship is its waiting upon the Holy Spirit. Their suspicion of trying to define the nature of God the Father reflects the Orthodox Churches emphasis on the mystery of God the Father. Indeed it is of sufficient concern in our earthly life to attempt to heed the promptings of the Holy Spirit as we endeavour to align our actions and relationships with the purposes of God, as was most fully revealed in the earthly life of Jesus. Time enough to contemplate the mystery of God the Father in our life beyond the grave. However, despite the attractiveness of traditional Quaker teaching, we were increasingly puzzled by the growing numbers of atheists joining the Quakers. The rejection of Easter by some 20th Century Quakers seems to have been the beginning of some Friends merging Quaker thought with agnostic humanism, which in turn caused some to espouse atheism. Without Easter we would never have heard of Jesus, let alone Christianity (including Quakers). Apart from Easter being the foundation event of the New Testament, if it had been all an invented myth, in terms of the culture of the day 2000 years ago, one would not have had women as the first witnesses of the Resurrection! Christian compassion, concern for justice and morality is essentially common to the mainstream of all the world religions. Easter demonstrates, rather than speculates, that there is a life for the emergent soul beyond death. Christians are the Easter people. Easter confirms that this life becomes a pilgrimage, from the legitimate self-centred concern of the baby to the God-centred focus of the redeemed soul, in a better life beyond the grave.

ON A DOWNWARD SLIDE? (TL)

For years the Quakers she'd admired
For living out the Gospel way
Of peace and justice, giving time
To misfits, hearing what they say
Without condemning ways of life
That seem astray or lacking sense
Of what is right. But when of late
There's some who've tried to now dispense
With Christian root, and thus with God,
She wonders why they shy away
From joining humanists. Their slick
But fluent preaching may gainsay
Belief in God, but seems to teach
A creed of reason on its own
As road to truth. Her love of spouse
Is not explained by such alone!
Is selfless sacrificial love,
Derived from faith in Christ, the same
As self delusion run amok?
Their smooth attempts to offer aim
For life, with death alone as end,
Is not for most of those whose lives
Are much constrained in terms of choice.
However much the rest contrives
To justify these new recruits
As Friends embracing all, they fail
To say what worship means when God
Is banned and praying can't avail.
It's good the Quakers open doors
To all who come. But pruning Christ
To give the atheists a home
It seemed to her the root was sliced.
Embracing need for open mind
Is not excuse for banning God.
He's source of grace preparing soul's
Ascent when corpse below the sod
Is laid to rot. Agreed the soul
Is only nascent hope at birth.
Emerging slowly during change
To person, fed from childhood's earth,
Our soul is born and slowly grows
As way of love's embraced. In youth

It swings from faith to doubts, before
With time it learns they gift us truth,
As when we heed our doubts we still
Progress towards the light. If, instead
We call a halt we're opting out.
We offer stones instead of bread.
To ditch the dated doctrines now
Perceived as past their sell by date,
By those with minds attuned to now,
Is only sense. It's not too late
To let the Quakers make the non
Believers welcome to attend,
But still insist on need to put
Their trust in God to be a Friend.

Apart from the atheists, some Quakers were calling themselves theists and others agnostics. For me, I would still be an atheist if I rejected belief in Easter and the implications that flow from that event. Too much philosophy (let alone rarefied theology) can obscure the significance of such a momentous historical event.

GRADUATION (GK)

With lustrous fresh degree, at end
Of grinding through the texts
From Plato, Russell, Ayer, much
Besides, she now concludes that life
Is either puddle after rain
Or else our loves, our high ideals
And hopes, displace these sterile games,
Where maths alone is merely tool
To follow through assumption's tale
But cannot say if it is true.
Indeed it's what she felt before
She ever opened books that seemed
Were built on solid rock. Those grand
And lofty schemes of words were piled
On sands and most have crashed as storms
Of mind, and spates of daily strains
And sudden deaths, have swept them all
Away. Her studies scoured the house
Of thought and scrubbed it free of grime.
They failed to furnish empty rooms.
The naked facts we use to run

Machines and reason orders schemes:
But when it comes to loves, that range
From racing pulse to quiet concerns
Sustained for years, it's then a faith
That life's a pilgrim's call must rule.
Whatever view we may espouse
Regarding life beyond the grave,
We learn emergent soul's the gain
No premise posed had ever dreamed.

The house and garden remained full of constant reminders of Audrey and our life together. One of the most treasured is of a painting of Flatford Mill, where we met and courted.

INDIVIDUAL PARTS (CW)

To me this painting on the wall
Is pure sublime. To most it's just
Another landscape daub that's good
But not of special note. I dust
Its glass with special care. The scene
Depicts where once I worked and where
I met my wife to be. So now
This view of Flatford Mill I swear
I'll cherish all my days, I'll rate
Above displays of greater works
Of art. It's thus perception's shaped
By odd events and other quirks.
It's thus we're each a novel tale.
We're each potential soul, unique
In loving light of Father God.
Our daily task is just to seek
The road we're meant to go, to hear
The call to play our tiny parts
In building Kingdom Christ proclaimed.
We lack a set of rules or charts.
Instead we pause to heed the voice
Of silent sound within the wells
Of inner selves, where sacred Word
Is seeking home beneath our shells
Of self concern and ancient drives.
We pray for grace to set aside
Distracting Siren lures. We pray
Incarnate love will be our guide.

PICTURES (CW)

I know this picture's not perceived
As art of highest grade by those
Whose role is using critic's eye
And pen to rule on what's 'okay'.
But in this gentle English scene
Of water mill and graceful swans,
Portrayed with loving strokes of brush
By painter few could name, I find
A sense of ease and silent praise.
Besides the view is one I know.
It's where I met the caring girl
Who then became the wife I love.
A work of art is dialogue
Between the artist's mind and skill
And what each viewer brings to bear
When stood before its silent stare.
I must conclude that some that hang
On walls of 'Modern' Tate reveal
That those who chose these daubs have minds
Devoid of sense of ease. Perhaps they feel
A need to stir up strife as means
Of screaming at the voids in life
That lack a sense of journey's end
As blissful state beyond the grave.
That guiding light sustains me when
I feel a chill in nights of stress.
It shines a torch on all that's good.
The art I like does just the same;
Or else portrays the dark to rouse
In me compassion's call to act.

Sometimes something would trigger more poignant memories:

MISFITS (TL)

I found your tattered shoes today,
My love, the ones you used to wear
When tending garden. Now their lack
Of fashion only speaks of care
For favoured flowers, children (three
Of ours, the four of theirs) and all
Who crossed your path in need of help.
You seemed to be at beck and call
Of some who took advantage more
Than once of kindness not restrained,
Despite your private view the same
Were on the make. You'd not complained
When later on you'd learned a tale
Of need had proved to be a lie.
To you their lack of sense of what
Is right was heard as lonesome cry
For love and self esteem impaired.
Your moral sense had been refined
By Baptist Church when you were child.
Its narrow creed had not confined,
As some of elders thought it should.
From Quakers later you had learned
To heed the Holy Spirit's prompts.
The local Parish Church had earned
Commitment too. Its favoured hymns
And sermons linked you back to when
You were a child. We both had shed
The rigid views, which like a wen,
Had marred our youthful faiths too quick
To judge. To walk the Way of Christ
We'd learned was just apprenticeship
In love. The Spirit's grace sufficed
To guide, without a scholar's game
With ancient text or rigid rule
Inducing sense of guilt alone.
We'd learned that God will ask a fool
To further Kingdom Christ proclaimed.
It's thus our selfish drives are tamed.

Having heard me read at the monthly CB1 poetry reading (originally held
in the CB1 café in Cambridge but subsequently in a series of pubs, etc.) a
publisher from the USA had expressed interest in publishing this 2012

collection. In the event he decided that, while he enjoyed my poetry, it was "too moralistic" for today's readership! At least that was a novel criticism for me. A more usual reaction was to consider my poems to be "too explicit". Subtle allusions, striking metaphors, similes and symbolism, however obscure, tend to be favoured by those conducting poetry workshops or lecturing on poetry in English. In my experience otherwise excellent poetry is too often marred by obscurities of this sort.

TWO CHEERS FOR T. S. ELIOT (RE)

When T. S. E. recoiled from shelves
Of sentiment and crafted verse
That posed as poetry in his day,
He sought retreat at first in pure
Abstractions Bradley* sieved until
Conclusions fled and paradox
Prevailed. Then clad in clever words,
Allusions gleaned from many texts
In several tongues, and collaged quotes,
He freed himself from fetters forged
By greatest poets past bequeathed.
But paradox prevailed, and most
Of readers still remain perplexed
Today, despite alluring way
With words and telling phrase. He'd cleared
The ground, but also launched a spate
Of acolytes inflicting poor
Attempts to imitate his style,
Without his wit and deep intent
To plumb the depths of spirit's reach
For things divine, in world where such
Concern is scorned or just ignored.
The challenge now is how return
To plainer speech and meaning once
Again restored to words of life
In complex world. A common, shared
Tradition now is not a base
From which we start. The polymath
Is now extinct. We each must dwell
In semi private niche, admit
Our knowledge only constitutes
A lucky dip. We share our loves,
And fractured bonds, our fears and hopes
For justice, peace and simple joys

That come our way. We yearn for gift
Of meaning. Doubt it's there to find
Remains as cloud, as cynics wrap
Religion's light in shrouds. There's some
Who steal its clothes for baser aims.
But when observing those who strive
To make the world a better place
We often find its grace divine
Is secret source and guide. But still
This blessing's flat denied by those
Who feel obliged to sell the case
That way to think is sceptic's view,
That's dead as desiccated bones.
They offer stones instead of bread;
Unlike our T. S. E. by end,
Despite attempts to hide his face.

*F. H. Bradley, whose philosophy was the subject of Eliot's doctoral thesis for Harvard University

2012: Award by the Entomological Society of Japan for the paper Maruyama, M, Komatsu, T. & Disney, R. H. L., 2011. Discovery of the termitophilous subfamily Termitoxeniinae (Diptera: Phoridae) in Japan, with description of a new genus and species. Entomological Science 14: 75-81. This paper was made possible by the publication of a monographic revision of these very aberrant scuttle flies found in termite fungus gardens in the Oriental Region (see chapter 9) which in turn followed the breakthrough leading to a radical reclassification of these extraordinary flies (see the paper by myself and Meg Cumming also cited in chapter 9). This, and other papers, including a monographic revision of the Afrotropical species (see chapter 9), that preceded the Oriental monograph had all been set in train by the realization that the 'missing' males of the Termitoxeniinae had been placed in a genus, whose females were 'unknown', that had been incorrectly assigned to a different subfamily! When one starts to suspect that the textbooks might be mistaken is when one may suddenly make a rapid advance in knowledge.

In 2005 I had been to my GP because of persistent pain in my left hip and frequently extending to my knee.

INCOMPLETE (GK)

My mind was slow maturing. Now
It hums with steady rhythm, strong
But silent in its prime. Today
The doctor told me aches and pains
Are now my daily lot as age
Is creeping up on me. My joints
Are wearing out, arthritis claims
Its time has come. My will is made
Of tungsten now as youthful fears
Were long ago all chipped away
By knocks and black events. Today
It's just my heart that still remains
In infants' class. But slowly, oh
So slowly, dearest wife and kids,
And theirs in turn, have brought me joy
That renders body, mind and will
A set of servant tools to use
To give the kiss of life to self
Of frozen stone. But as the ice
Begins to thaw a warming grace
Now starts to stir within its core.
An embryonic twitch of love
Suggests its birth is nearly due.
So by the time I enter grave
My slow emerging soul may find
The door to Kingdom Christ proclaimed.
It's then my faithful body, mind
And will, as well as heart at last,
Will choose to dissipate in death,
Releasing soul to God's embrace.

In the event this was not properly diagnosed until 2012:

MISDIAGNOSED! (CW)

A weary doctor late in day
A hasty diagnosis made
Of pains in hip and knee. He sent
Me off to physio to aid
The ease of joints he deemed was case
Of need to counter wear of years.
Prescribed regime of exercise
I strove to curb the urge for tears
As pain at times was more than just
A nuisance. Still affliction grew
Until at end of seven years
I went to G.P.'s place anew.
Another doctor than before
Dispatched me off for X-rays first
And other tests, before he said
It's not with ageing joints I'm cursed.
Sciatic nerve is cause of pains.
And furthermore my daily rite
Of exercise included some,
I'm told, would only worsen plight,
As not designed to ease the pain
Of angered nerve instead of joints
In need of daily drill. It's like
The need to earn sufficient points
A child was told that God required
To win his favour then and when
She dies! But in her teens she learned
That God is not a beast in den
Awaiting chance to pounce as soon
As sin's observed. Our Lord's desire
Is selfless love to rule our lives
Through gift of Holy Spirit's fire.

Following the correct diagnosis I underwent ten sessions of acupuncture. From session seven onwards the alleviation began to persist and by the tenth I was cured. What intrigues one is how was it discovered that a course of acupuncture was required if there is no persistent improvement until one has undergone several sessions!

December 2012

In the first week of December I realized something was amiss with my right eye. My left eye had been fogged since my time at Malham Tarn (see chapter 8). I went to Boots (my optician), from whom I had got my glasses. After a thorough examination they urged me to see my GP as soon as possible. I managed to get an appointment at the end of the afternoon. After a brief examination the GP phoned Addenbrooke's Hospital to say I was getting a taxi to Outpatients straight away. Two young doctors (one Chinese and the other from Sri Lanka) carried out a number of examinations and tests. With the MRI scan, which was excessively noisy, the Sri Lankan doctor told me to relax completely. I did so and dropped off to sleep! She rushed up, grabbed my hand and asked anxiously "Are you still alive?" As I woke up I replied "I was at the lumber mill on the Guatemalan border buying some mahogany planks!" It seems the racket of the MRI scan had triggered a memory from 1966 (see chapter 5). After the rest of the tests they said I could go but would receive an appointment with the senior consultant shortly. I had just sat down on the bus when the Chinese doctor jumped on, telling the driver to hold it, and said the consultant had glanced at the reports and said I must return to the hospital. By now the passengers had stopped talking and were gazing at this scene with astonishment! I was not released from hospital for a fortnight! Numerous examinations, scans and tests were carried out. One by one possible causes were ruled out. Having worked in tropical forests on three continents the tests ranged from tick borne infections to river blindness (Onchocerciasis), but all with negative results.

Soon after leaving hospital I tripped up over a protuberance of the pavement that I had not seen and I cut myself across my face. Cambridge was known to have some of the worst pavements of any city in England. This was partly because too many employed slabs that got cracked when lorries were forced by the narrowness of many roads to mount the pavement. Another cause was constant digging up to repair cables, pipes, etc. and then when these excavations were filled in and sealed with tarmac the new surfaces were frequently not smoothly contiguous with the rest of the pavement. I went into a shop to buy a suitable stick to support my weight if I stumbled again. At first I was offered a slender white stick. While the white serves to indicate to others that one has impaired vision, it was evident that its slenderness would not support my weight if I stumbled! Next very sturdy sticks used by mountaineers were offered but they were expensive and were only sold in pairs. Accordingly I selected a stick from a pile from where I had thinned some hazels at the end of the garden a year before. It was a little twisted but it was strong and when trimmed flat at each end was just the right height. I purchased a ferrule for the tip, painted part of it white (subsequently most of it was painted white by Tim, Rachel's father-in-law) and added a loop of cord just below the top to go around my wrist. Despite stumbling two to three times a day it prevented me from falling again. One day a teenage schoolgirl pulled up on her bike and called out "Hey man, your stick is real wicked". My grandchildren subsequently informed me that this was a compliment! Subsequently I frequently received comments from strangers about this stick.

After an outpatient session at the hospital a blood test suggested I should see a lung specialist. She showed that what had been thought to be an old, inactive TB lesion in my left lung was in fact a sarcoidosis. While it is not really understood they were known to be sometimes associated with blindness in one or both eyes. Furthermore, ten allergens were known to be associated with such. However, at a subsequent outpatient session all ten were ruled out, my only reaction being with the histamine control. Further investigations failed to identify a cause.

The consequences of becoming three quarters blind were a challenge not only with regard to coping with daily living but with respect to my research. I was no longer able to use the drawing attachment for making accurate measurements and for preparing drawings to illustrate the critical features used to distinguish similar species. If this had occurred a dozen years before I would have had to quit. However, advances in imaging and digital camera systems for the microscope enabled me to continue. I was enabled to purchase the MediaCybernetics Image Pro-Insight system by means of a gift from Stephen Salter, with whom I had shared rooms in my first year as an undergraduate (see chapter 3), after a friend had told him about my visual impairment. I subsequently thanked him by naming species after him and his partner Margaret (Disney, R. H. L., Nitta, M., Kobayashi, M. & Tuno, N., 2014. New records of Megaselia (Diptera: Phoridae) reared from fungus sporophores in Japan, including five new species. Applied Entomology & Zoology 49: 541-552). As this imaging system would not run on my iMac computer I had to acquire a PC, just for its operation. This system allowed me to make accurate measurements by clicking on two points and reading off the measurement in microns. The system for the camera allowed one to take several focal planes in succession and the software then combined these into a single image. It also added a scale bar in microns. In addition the use of a range of magnifying devices (one that throws up an enlarged image of a document onto a screen, a visor magnifier, a hand held magnifier, assorted watchmakers eyeglasses, etc., plus the Zoom facility on the computer) enabled me to carry on, albeit everything taking much longer.

However, my drawings in the past had combined a larger number of focal planes into a single image. Furthermore, I had found drawing was a powerful heuristic procedure. One is forced to examine the specimen closely and in so doing I acquired a detailed knowledge of the morphology and anatomy of scuttle flies. The following poem touches upon this:

DESPITE THE LEAKING HOURS (CW)

The rambling novel of the past
Was meal for those with time to kill.
Today we want our reading more
As snack. Besides the need to set
The scene in endless paragraphs
Of wordy wandering prose is not
Required in world exposed, without
A pause, to shifting image served
Along with processed spoken words.
Indeed for those who surf the Net,
Those glued to mobile phone all day,
They now subsist on pre-cooked packs
Of blended truths with fictions mixed.
It's those with minds like sieves that save
The central message fast, who win
In ceaseless race to leave the herd
Astern. To stand and stare is not
Advised if climbing ladder's main
Concern. But while I find myself
Immersed in work, for which the hours
Allowed are not enough, the saving grace
Is time I spend at microscope
Preparing drawings fit to show
The parts of insects that allow
Their recognition at a glance.
This task releases mind to go
On journeys unconstrained by need
To focus on the job in hand,
Beyond initial sketch before
Employing pen and ink. It's then
I think afresh and play with facts
In novel moves. I marvel too
At beauties found in what I draw.
It's thus, despite the leaking hours,
I find the time to sit and stare.

Furthermore, through concentrated attention when drawing I would observe anomalies with regard to the textbooks and classic monographs. An example was with regard to a feature of some scuttle flies termed the median furrow on the frontal region of the head. It had been assumed that this was novel acquisition by these phorid flies. But when drawing the heads of species in genera supposed to lack these furrows I realized that many had a vestigial furrow. I inferred, therefore, that the novel state during evolution had been the loss of the furrow in some of these flies. This in turn gave rise to the hypothesis as to the origin of a structure (the ptilinum) in later evolved families of flies (such as houseflies and fruit flies) which had been, until then, an unsolved mystery (see chapter 9).

Another problem with my impaired vision proved to be trying to navigate the websites that journals increasingly required one to use when submitting a paper. I had got used to sending them direct to editors as e-mail attachments or, if there were many figures, on a CD in the post. Too many journal websites are poorly designed, want irrelevant information (what were my academic qualifications? who was my PhD supervisor? – I didn't have one -, who is my employer? – I'm retired – what is my present position?, etc.), and too often key bits are in a small point size and in pale colours (green, blue, yellow) that are almost impossible for me to read without copying and pasting them into a document in order to change them to black and then Zoom to 200%. Also one had to acquire yet another username and password. However, just as the requirement to submit papers via these tiresome websites grew rapidly an alternative appeared – WeTransfer. This was far simpler. One put one's text file, covering letter and limitless figures, etc. into a folder and compressed it to a Zip folder. One then imported this to the WeTransfer website and typed in the e-mail address of the journal's editor and then sent it on its way. This was much easier for all concerned. However some journal publishers still preferred you submit via their website as they could then clutter it up with adverts for their journals, etc.

ILL CONCEIVED (TL)

For most of journals all I need
Is send my text, and figures too,
In e-mails quick and easy. So
It baffles me that just a few
Require a complex set of forms
To fill on website made to be
A challenge how to navigate.
Perhaps designer's devotee
Of legal contract forms one needs
To read a dozen times or more
Before their sense is fully grasped.
But soon it's all become a bore,
As stuck in loop again I must
Return to start once more, or choose
To quit the game, and hope, before
I'm driven quite berserk. I use
Computer most of time without

Complaint, but now and then I yearn
For days before it came to be
A drug. But no! I can't return
To papers penned in ink or else
Were typed with carbon copies filed
In bulky folders soon obese.
But now, before I get too riled,
I need a break. I feel at one
With plight of parents stuck with boy
Autistic since his birth. Their love
Is deep. They know he brings a joy
That's strange but rich. But every now
And then they feel the need for break
From constant care and fear he'll hurt
Himself if they neglect to make
A check that all is well. Refreshed,
They can return to routine days
And face demanding challenge posed
By boy whose genes prescribed his ways.

2013: Honorary Membership Freshwater Biological Association.
'For having made a significant specific contribution and, in addition, achieving fifty years continuous membership of the FBA'.

Following the move of Materials Science to West Cambridge, in September 2013, those of us based in the Museum of Zoology all had to move out to make way for the contractors to move in to redevelop the museum and the Materials Science building adjoining the north end of the museum. The latter building was to become a centre for conservation studies. I, my fellow entomologists and the support team for the Museum moved to the Austin Building of the old Cavendish Physics Department. I was allocated Room 118 (almost opposite the room where Watson and Crick built their model of DNA). This temporary move was programmed to last up to three years. To move into a larger room allowed accommodation for the primary collection of slide mounted world scuttle flies housed in a stack of sixteen wooden cabinets that I had amassed since the 1970s. Each cabinet held twenty-seven trays, with each tray accommodating thirty-six slides. Thus the stack as whole can contain 15,552 slides. This collection had become the most important collection of slide mounted scuttle flies in the world in terms of its coverage of genera and species. It includes about 1400 species of which about half are represented by type specimens (about 40% being primary types, i.e. holotypes or subsequently designated equivalents known as lectotypes or neotypes). Type specimens are those used to prepare the first published description of a species, comprising a holotype and paratypes. If it is subsequently discovered that a type series comprised specimens of two species then the name applies to species that includes the holotype and the excluded paratypes belong to the newly recognised species that had been confused with the holotype. In addition I have deposited duplicates in other museums (especially in the Museum Alexander Koenig in Bonn and the Natural History Museum in Los Angeles). The larger space also accommodated three steel cabinets which can house 13,500 slides. These cabinets house many duplicates that are available for studying variation or for donating to other museums.

The greater space in the Austin Building was also a blessing in view of my three quater blindness since 2012. The plans for the redesigned Museum of Zoology included space that would be allocated for my collection of world Phoridae. However, there would be much more limited working space for an established specialist taxonomist such as myself. This confirmed the assessment by colleagues and myself made in our correspondence to Nature in 1990 (see chapter 9). Had I been wise in making my collection the property of the Museum of Zoology in 1986? This decision had been prompted by referees based in the Natural History Museum in London recommending rejection of my papers on the grounds that I should not be depositing type specimens in a private collection! They were evidently trying to jump me in to stating that my private collection was destined for the NHM! I was particularly irritated by this recommendation of the referees as they seemed unaware that I had donated about 10,000 specimens to the NHM (mammals and insects from Belize, insects, crustacea, fish, etc from Cameroon and Dixidae from the British Isles). I responded by firing off a letter to Antenna (the house journal of the Royal Entomological Society) saying referees should assess the scientific merits of a paper not the habits of the author! The response gave rise to a second letter stating that my collection was now declared to be the property of the Museum of Zoology in Cambridge (Disney, R. H. L., 1986. Type specimens in private collections. Antenna 10(1): 4. +10(3): 106-107). I had pointed out that the most valuable collections I had consulted (or borrowed specimens from) in museums had all started as the private collection of an acknowledged specialist. My collection of world Phoridae, because of its large number of type specimens, is one of the most scientifically valuable collections for any family of insects in the Museum of Zoology. The NHM has important collections of pinned scuttle flies by earlier workers (especially Wood and Colyer – both originally private collections!), of which I have remounted many type specimens on slides.

An incomplete project that had stalled when I was no longer able to use the drawing attachment on the microscope was my revision of the world's species in the genus Chonocephalus (see chapter 9). With the new imaging system I was able to complete this project (Disney, R. H. L., 2015. Review of Australasian Chonocephalus Wandolleck (Diptera: Phoridae). Advances in Zoology and Botany 3(3): 51-168. Disney, R. H. L. (2016) Revision of Oriental Chonocephalus Wandolleck (Diptera: Phoridae). Annales Zoologici 66(2): 277-328.). The result of these revisions has been to add at least 100 species to the genus (many described females remain un-named until linked to their males, but some of these are probably new species but their males have yet to be described).

419

Hazards of being an obligatory pedestrian

22-24 November 2013: A memorable weekend.

Adrian phoned earlier in the week to say that after work (at Atlantic College) on Friday he was going to drive to Cambridge (being paraplegic his car was hand operated) for the weekend. He would be stopping off in Cardiff to pick up his new friend Catherine. This would be most welcome as it would add a positive new element to what would have been the Golden Wedding Anniversary of Audrey (had she lived) and myself on Saturday 23rd. On the Friday I left late for the lab (where I had an appointment at noon with a University disability officer in order to sort out some visibility problems with the computer) after first making Adrian's bed (a settee in the sitting room that could be turned into a bed) and to rearrange the furniture downstairs to allow wheelchair access. I returned early, in daylight, to finish preparing the house for Adrian and Catherine's visit. When crossing a road from the south side I successfully crossed the lane for traffic heading west and reached a refuge island half way. I paused until there was a lull in the flow of traffic moving eastwards in the lane ahead. I then headed for the far pavement. Unknown to me a taxi emerged from a cul-de-sac away to my right. Instead of taking the legal route to the lane of westward flowing traffic, by driving straight across to the middle, to a point to his left of the island refuge I had just left, and then turning right into the far lane he was aiming for, he decided to travel illegally by means of the hypotenuse (linking the further ends of his legal route) ending to his right of the island refuge I had just left. I was in the middle of this hypotenuse when he hit me. Being totally blind in my right eye I only knew about the taxi when bystanders picked me up off my back. An ambulance was quickly summoned and the excellent paramedics checked me out. My right knee was giving me agony (it swelled up greatly over the next few days and a doctor confirmed I had torn ligaments and muscles). The paramedics said my rucksack had absorbed the main impact of my fall. Without it I would have almost certainly have sustained spinal injuries (at the least) and I would have been in hospital when Adrian and Catherine arrived at my house later in the evening. In addition my glasses were broken with extensive scarring of the right lens. If the lens had been glass instead of toughened plastic it seems likely my blind eye would have been bombarded with splinters of glass. A policeman took me home and I was able, painfully, to complete some of my intended preparations for the visit of Adrian and Catherine.

Catherine Gourmelon proved to be very agreeable and she and Adrian were clearly very at ease in each other's company. She had been recently divorced but her former husband was minding the children during her weekend visit to Cambridge. There were four children – Jacques (aged eleven), Thibault (nine), Rémy (eight) and Malo (five). At home they spoke French but at school they spoke English and Welsh. With her obligations to her children and their schooling in Cardiff, Catherine and Adrian were obliged to live apart for the time being (for some years ahead at least).

On the Monday it took me about twice as long as usual to walk (waddle) to the lab, but I needed to be there as a forensic sample (of scuttle fly larvae) from a murder victim in Kent was due to be delivered to me that morning.

A few days later I received an answer-phone message from the policeman who had driven me home to ask how I was. I tried three times to reply but was told to leave a message or ring again before 11 pm. So next morning I handed in a detailed report to Cambridge Police station.

In this statement I had written that I did not wish to take legal action against the taxi driver. However, I suggested that he be asked to consider giving a generous donation to the charity SPINAL RESEARCH, Bramley Business Centre, Station Road, Bramley, GUILDFORD GU5 0AZ (www.spinal-research.org) Charity number 281325. If he were to confirm that he had accepted this suggestion I would be grateful.

An unwelcome postscript to this weekend came on the following Friday evening when I was walking very slowly, because of my painful swollen right knee, to friends a few streets away who had invited me to supper. A cyclist in black clothing, on a black bike and without lights, and riding on the pavement almost hit me head on. He neither stopped nor apologised, despite obliging me to lurch suddenly to my right and causing a painful wrench of a muscle in my neck (that took several weeks to settle back to normal).

The following letter, dated 12th December, was received from the Process and Collisions Unit of the Bedfordshire, Cambridgeshire and Hertfordshire police in Stevenage.

Dear Mr Disney,

Road Traffic Incident 22/11/2013 13:58
Location OUTSIDE CO-OP STORE, CHESTERTON ROAD, CAMBRIDGE

The collision that you were involved has been investigated. All of the available evidence has been reviewed and a decision has been reached by the case manager on behalf of the police.

In this instance it has been decided that **no further police action** will be taken.

The role of the police once a collision has been reported is to investigate the matter and to decide on the evidence obtained whether any offence has been committed; **it is not our role to apportion blame**, this to be decided by Insurance Companies.

Now that a decision has been made your insurance company are entitled to apply for a copy of the police report containing information collected during our investigation. Your insurance company should send a covering letter including the collision reference number to the address below.

If you have any queries regarding your collision, please do hesitate to contact us.

Yours sincerely [not signed and no named case manager or whoever]

Apart from this letter being unsigned and from a nameless person, two sentences that truly astonished me were the following in which I have highlighted in bold those statements that were the cause of my astonishment:

"In this instance it has been decided that no further police action will be taken.
The role of the police once a collision has been reported is to investigate the matter and to decide on the evidence obtained whether any offence has been committed; it is not our role to apportion blame, this to be decided by Insurance Companies."
Colleagues and friends assured me that much more minor offences routinely resulted in penalty points on a driver's licence. So the decision to take no action was inexplicable. Likewise they were equally astonished that it was not considered to be the role of the police to apportion blame when it was beyond dispute that the taxi driver had driven an illegal route. Consequently I decided to not let the matter rest with this unacceptable reply. I replied on 14th December taking issue with its unacceptable points. Having had no response I wrote again on 6th January 2014 at greater length with a copy to the Police Commissioner. To the latter I added that the Cambridge Police had a reputation for not reporting every crime and added as a postscript the following poem published in 2009 based on a true incident at Cambridge Station.

OFFICIAL STATISTICS (GK)

With suitcase stowed between the seats
On train, she talked to friend at ease.
But at the journey's end her case
Had gone. The thief had got her keys
To house, her pills for dodgy heart,
Her mobile phone and precious box
Of cedar wood with brooch and ring.
He must have been as cunning fox
To seize his chance when heads were turned.
Her tablets mimic shape of sweets
In form of tiny hearts. They pose a risk
To crawling child. At least the cheats
Had not obtained her purse. Police
Had merely shrugged, declaring chance
Of catching scum was nil. To log
The crime they felt would not enhance
Their clear-up rate required to meet
A target set by those remote
From scene and normal lives. So when
We heard a politician quote
'Statistics show that theft's declined'
We find ourselves to doubt inclined!

On 11th January I received a reply from the Process and Collisions Unit dated 7th January, and signed by a named person. I replied that 'because you took three weeks to respond you will be aware that I wrote to you again on 7th January and that your totally unsatisfactory response meant that I copied this second letter of mine to the Police Commissioner'. On 3rd February I wrote again to the Police Commissioner. On 4th February I received an e-mail from his office raising the question as to whether a letter from the P & C Unit, which is based in Hertfordshire, was of concern to the Commissioner. I replied that the accident had occurred in Cambridge, my report had been to the Cambridge Police and the P & C Unit in Stevenage was for the police of Bedfordshire, Cambridgeshire and Hertfordshire. On 17th February 2014 I received a reply from the Commissioner. It was essentially evasive waffle, including the sentence 'unfortunately as the Police and Crime Commissioner I cannot investigate individual operational matters, as these are in the remit of Cambridgeshire Constabulary'. I therefore copied the correspondence to my MP. He wrote to the Police Commissioner and received a totally unsatisfactory response amounting to evasion by him and the Process and Collisions Unit. My MP was unimpressed by this. So on 27th April 2014 I wrote to the Police Commissioner informing him that I had informally discussed the matter with legal acquaintances and a qualified and experienced driving instructor. They were agreed that the P & C Unit statement that 'there was insufficient evidence of any motoring offences having been committed' was fundamentally incorrect as it defies the inescapable logic of elementary geometry. Furthermore action would have been taken if I had been killed. As it was, according to the paramedics, my rucksack absorbed the principal impact of my fall and saved me from spinal injury most likely causing me to become paraplegic if not my death. The fact that only my right knee sustained serious injury has no bearing on the fact that the accident was caused by the taxi driver being in breach of the law. I added 'Perhaps the public ought to be informed that such a breach of the law by a driver of a vehicle is no longer considered to be a concern of the police. If you agree with this then should such information come best from The Home Secretary, from yourself or from the press?' I added the following P.S. 'Your assertion that all illegal acts are logged by the Cambridgeshire Police is incorrect. Following the theft of her case, my late wife received several accounts of mobile phones and of purses being snatched in the Cambridge Market and the nearest police saying there was no point in reporting it as the chances of recovery were nil. Furthermore, I had recently met a couple who had nearly been run down by a cyclist on the pavement but looking at his mobile phone instead of ahead. When the couple asked a pair of passing policemen whether they were going to apprehend the cyclist, they had replied that their beat for that day had been north of the last crossroads and they were now off duty on their way back to base! These incidents suggest that some police, when questioned, are not admitting to "failing to log all incidents"'. Having received no response, on 9th May 2014 I wrote to the Secretary of State for the Home Department, enclosing a copy of my most recent letter to the Cambridgeshire Police and Crime Commissioner and his reply plus the letter, dated 12th December, from the Process and Collisions Unit. I received a response dated 12th June 2014 from the Home Office Direct Communications Unit that stated that 'Law enforcement, including the enforcement of the law on the road is an operational matter for the police' and 'Any general policy within the force is a matter for the force's chief officer, who will decide how to deploy available resources in dealing with all the issues for which the force is responsible, taking into account any specific local problems and demands. It is not for the Minister to intervene in these decisions'. In my reply of 17th June 2014 I emphasised that 'It has at no time been disputed that the taxi driver, by driving westward in an east bound traffic lane, was in breach of the law. The Process and Collisions Unit for the Cambridgeshire Police stated that the reason they decided to take no action was because they did not regard it as the function of the police to apportion blame in the case of road accidents'. I added that 'By contrast, a lady living a couple of roads away was recently caught by a speed camera to be exceeding the limit on a nearby road. Nobody was inconvenienced or hurt by her breach of the law and yet the police unhesitatingly took action against her. Why the difference in police response?' As no reply was received I copied the key correspondence to the Chair of the

Parliamentary Committee concerned with the Home Office. However, he did not reply to several e-mails followed by a letter to the House of Commons. So much for the evasions and buck passing by the Establishment!

Another postscript to this accident.

I wrote to the taxi driver on 11th January 2014 with a copy of my report to the Cambridge Police (of 5th December 2013) and inviting him to give a donation to the charity Spinal Research. Having received no reply, I wrote again on 3rd February 2014. After some weeks, having received no reply again, I agreed that a firm of solicitors would sue him for damages on a 'no win no fee' basis. My intention was to achieve a more generous donation to Spinal Research than he might have done if he had complied with my request. When it seemed that an agreed settlement had been agreed his solicitor suddenly decided, in September 2014, to argue that I was to blame for the accident! He therefore applied for a court hearing in Northampton. His submission for the court was essentially stupid. I therefore reiterated the essential points to my solicitor and added "It seems his solicitor did not grasp the difference between plausible inferences derived from clues (such as maggots in a corpse) or witness statements, and the contrasting irrefutable deductions derived from the geometry of the scene of an accident. When a rapid sequence of events culminates in a nearly static endpoint scene the human mind is apt to come up with the most plausible explanation of what caused the outcome." I illustrated this with reference to the true event of a dog, a hare, and a car ending up in a ditch in the following poem.

'NO DOUBT' (GK)

A man was driving home at dusk,
With dog behind and hare he'd bought
From local butcher on the seat
At front, when all at once a tyre
Was pierced by nail and car in skid
At speed was thrown in ditch. Displayed
To passers by were yapping cur,
A corpse of hare on verge and bloke
Extracting self from slime. Police
Appeared to hear a witness swear
The hare, pursued by hound, had caused
The Ford to swerve. It seems our minds
Must always make coherent sense
Of tangled scenes. Perhaps that's why
Some experts still cannot admit
They do not know, despite a lack
Of facts they need to grasp to craft
A story we can trust. It seems
A sense of pride prevents a halt
To flow of words when none suffice
To bridge a gulf of ignorance.
An academic holding forth,
When claret's going rounds at end
Of ample meal, may do no harm.
But I have known a self proclaimed,
But conman, 'expert' witness lie
In court to cover gaps in tale
He's made to reach conclusion cops
Desired. It seems the prospect fee
Imparts a certainty where none
Exists. For me persistent doubt
Has often proved the key to truth
Concealed so well from common sense
That only dogged toil revealed
It naked, shining bright, exposed
To light when lifting hundredth stone.
I often feel that disbelief
Is only road to faith that's real.

In response, I was told I would be obliged to attend court as the taxi driver was denying his guilt, despite also simultaneously admitting his guilt by trying to blame me for not looking to my right for oncoming illegal traffic! However, when I sent my solicitor a colour print of a Google Earth satellite image of the scene of the accident, with the taxi driver's legal route marked in black and his illegal route in red with the accident spot half way along it, his solicitor called off the court hearing, having grasped that he would be laughed out of court. The settlement obtained by my solicitor was a far larger donation to Spinal Research than what the taxi driver might have paid if he had responded to my two letters, apart from the cost of his fee paid to his solicitor. I did wonder whether the latter knew there was no chance of his winning for his client, but knew that he would still gain financially whatever the outcome. Or was he really so grossly incompetent?

The dropping of this court appearance reinforced my confidence in my interpretation of the accident and, having had no acceptable reply from the Establishment, I e-mailed a summary of this affair and the fruitless correspondence to the Independent Police Complaints Commission on 9th January 2015.

Another incident: 16th January 2014

I was walking along the pavement a little after 5 pm when a teenager, riding her bike on the pavement without lights and paying more attention to her mobile phone than the way ahead, ran into the back of me. I fell over backwards. My bottom landed in a puddle of muddy water, but again my rucksack absorbed the main impact of the fall. This was clearly evidenced by the rupture of some fine clementines in a bag in my rucksack that I had purchased in Cambridge market at lunch time! The road has cycle only lanes both sides.

Before I had gone blind in my right eye, in 2004 I had published the following poem!

GENERATIONS GAP? (CO)

As I'm hard of hearing, also
Being purblind in one eye,
I choose to walk to work along
A path from which all bikes are banned,
As clearly signed. But still each day
There's always one or two for whom
The law, it seems, does not apply.
When I dissent at being asked
To move aside they're only rude,
Declaring they're beyond the reach
Of traffic wardens or police
With better things to do. While true
As far as gravity of sin
Applies, I feel their lack of thought
For all but selves betokens deep
Contempt for other folk beyond
Their own self-centred clique. It makes
One wonder whether sense of life
As pilgrim's hike has crossed their minds.
Perhaps, for them, it's all a game
Without an aim and older men
Are merely obstacles in way
As they pursue their petty ploys.
If so it's odd because it's plain
They're mostly students blessed with brains,
And prospects bright, above the norm.
But if they don't respect the rights
And needs of others now, what hope
Have we of building better lives
In which we mutually support
Both strong and frail? Or am I now
Becoming bore they pigeon hole
Beyond concern because of age?
If so they can't complain at rage
I feel when tactful plea receives
Abuse in place of straight assent.
Instead, I step aside for peace!
Or am I coward caving in?

Returning to the accident caused by the taxi, I received a letter dated 27th May 2015 from a Detective Sergeant of the Camera, Tickets and Collision Unit. This was said to be the 'final letter' reiterating their original position. In addition he added that as my injury was only 'slight' it supported their case for not taking action against the taxi driver! He had neither contacted myself, my GP or Addenbrooke's Hospital (who had been dealing with my persistent uneven gait resulting from the accident). So on what basis had he decided my injury was slight when I was still suffering its effects some eighteen months later? How serious had an accident caused by an illegal act to be before it was regarded as worthy of action by the police? I replied to his letter that I had already put the matter into the hands of the IPCC. I copied the letter from the C, T & C Unit to the IPCC. They copied this to the Professional Standards Department for the Cambridgeshire Police (whose mission statement is: creating a safer Cambridgeshire!). I received a response dated 8th September 2015. It amounted to two and half pages of evasive waffle upholding the first totally unacceptable letter received from the Process and Collisions Unit of the Bedfordshire, Cambridgeshire and Hertfordshire police in Stevenage, which was dated the 12th December 2013. So I then sent a summary of this saga (so reminiscent of the fatuities encountered when dealing with the authorities in Central America and West Africa!) to the Sunday Times (which had recently written about some current questionable police priorities), then to the Guardian and then to my local newspaper, the Cambridge News. None of these even acknowledged my submission, let alone requested fuller details. Too many political events, scandals and bigger failings by the police were dominating their concerns at the time.

This prolonged correspondence following the accident in November 2013 was essentially an irritating diversion from my normal life.

March 2014: my ninth collection of poems published – COME WHAT MAY (Pneuma Springs Publishing, UK, 308, pages).

The title poem was as follows:

COME WHAT MAY (CW)

Within a lapse of less than year
From time my treasured wife had died,
I'm struck by loss of sight in eye
On right, on which I've long relied.
As more than thirty years ago
The eye on left was dimmed by mist
Induced by dam to blood supply
To part. This recent sudden twist
Derailed my normal way of life.
I strive to concentrate on what
I still can do and leave alone
Concern for tasks that now are not
On options list. Support of friends,
Of children, theirs and kin now keep
Alive a sense of being blessed;
So when my mood is at a neap
A sense of God's embrace restores
A surge of gratitude. Recall
Of hordes of folk around the world
Deprived of food, of peace, in thrall
To wars, ensures my thanks that small
Affliction merely mars my days
As, come what may, my life is full.
The death of Christ on cross conveys,
Beyond a doubt, that come what may
Beyond the grave there's Easter's hope.
So even when a child is blind
We dare not blame our God or mope
At present plight. Ignore the sects
Who still insist that God controls
The smallest moves of universe.
The cross denies that claim, extols
The freedom, thus confirmed by Christ,
Who wouldn't shun the ghastly price,
Of love incarnate risking way
Emergent souls escape the dice
Of random acts and evil plots.
The Easter joy transforms the past,
Despite apparent black defeats.
So come what may remain steadfast.
It's when we heed the inner light
We find our lot to be, to know,

We're on the road to heaven's gate.
Of course we're free to say a no
To call to join the pilgrim band,
To live the Kingdom Way, despite
Whatever plight, or blight, impedes,
Restricts our youthful hopes. In spite
Of those who think we dream, or those
Applauding way I cope, in truth
We've merely grasped that God is love.
Despite my faith is that of youth
Confused by ups and downs of life, ,
By loss of eye and lovely wife.
If given choice I'd opt for she
Who's gained her peace ahead of me.
But I rejoice she's now complete.
At my demise in bliss we'll meet
For then the dark will be no more.
Our infant faiths will be mature.
So, come what may, I say rejoice
And praise our Lord with joyful voice.

LASTING GAIN (GK)

With Internet we're nearly swamped
By regiments of facts now logged
In books and also only on
Computer disks. But when I work
At microscope I daily learn
How little science knows of all
The teeming forms of life this earth
Sustains. I add my pennyworth
For future tomes on scuttle flies.
These tiny beasts all act as though
The biosphere is meant for them
Alone as means to propagate
Their kind at its expense. Besides
Myself, there's few who share delight
At varied ways of life, at range
Of delicate designs that fit
Each fly for chosen role in scheme
Of things upon this lonely orb,
In lesser spray of stars in grand
Expanse of space. Perhaps my time
Upon this earth has been a game

Of child, escaping all that's real
To realms of make believe.
Perhaps it's same for all who strut upon
A public stage or quietly work
Behind the scenes in modest niche.
Our diverse roles will all be filled
By others when we've moved ahead.
It's what we learn of loving grace
Within our hearts that will abide.

EASTER (RE)

*(First published in 1990 in a 278 page Collins anthology THE RURAL
SPIRIT edited by Mervyn Wilson. The dust-jacket reproduced John
Constable's picture THE CORNFIELD. Walking this landscape became the
occasion for much of the courtship of Audrey and myself!)*

Weaving a world of meaning from the joys
And interactions of a home we screen
Ourselves from the screaming blank of a cold
And pointless life. One that keeps hurling back
The cry of Jesus from the cross – "My God,
My God, why hast thou forsaken me?"
The echo of that cry is with us still.

We lie like pebbles smooth upon the beach
Of time, while the historian's eye selects
A ruby, notes a wetted gleam of red
That fools the hunter's eye, but dries to naught;
While the geologist perceives the slow
Relentless trituration pulverize
Those timeless stones to sand, that forms a rock
Again in ceaseless cycles mocking all.
What is man that Thou art mindful of him,
O Lord, what fleeting specks in time are we?

But as we now peer back from the far bank
Of the baptismal river of our youth's
Absorption with self, having walked the plank
Of love, of marriage, of accomplishment
In our careers, we pace an ordered lawn
Beholding morning-glory blooms at dawn.
Each day the spiralling tip ascends, each
Day immaculate flowers form to die.
Generation upon generation.

432

An endless repetition of splendid
Striving for perfection. Our own children
In the bud, while our youthful visions wilt.
Will the struggle achieve a fertile seed?
Will fruits develop from the tortured stem?
Or, silted by experience in excess,
And inundated by insignificance,
Will they lack the trace element of faith?
Will they, will we, ascend in Easter praise?
Will we at last perceive beyond the grave?
Beyond the chains of time and pace we'll raise
Our songs, as Christ does us with love enslave.

KEEPING GOING... (CW)

This month demands upon my time
Are heaping extra stress it's hard
To bear. This seeds the fear I'll start
To crack or else collapse, discard
My queue of tasks by quitting lab
To take my ease. But then surprise
Of novel gain in knowledge brings
A joyful calm, a precious prize
That compensates for weeks of grind.
Besides I sense an idle life
Would slowly snuff my will to live
As boredom, more than strife,
Descending like a deadly smog
Would bring about a slow descent
To black despond, if not demise.
I'm eager hound who's on the scent
Of quarry, knowing not how long
The chase, and even if the prey
Is real or just a phantom spawned
By burning, strong desire. I'll stay
The course as long as strength allows.
The hunt reflects my faith in God
Sustaining hope my soul will thrive
When flesh decays beneath the sod.
For now it's still a sapling tree
As love incarnate comes and goes
Because of self concern and doubts.
But gifts of grace will set it free.

433

EXPECTATIONS (RE)

I've travelled much of world and met
A range of folk. I've done some things
That few have had the chance to do.
I've known the good and evil men
Can instigate. I've tasted pain
And joy, and triumph's fleeting gain
And failure's bitter pill. But still
I hope for best in those I meet
And in the days to come. Perhaps
It's just that I'm a kid at heart,
Except I'm now inclined to want
To stay at home and fall asleep
In front of box. In fact it seems
My youthful drive has given way
To dogged toil in one small field.
But you should see the blooms I tend.
They're not the Chelsea Show, they're not
A grand display, but each is gem
In gentle way for those with eyes
To see. I've few regrets at how
My world has shrunk to routine ways,
To faithful friends and those I love.
I'm filled with thanks for what remains
Of autumn days before my end.
I'm near prepared for what comes next.

LYRIC'S ECHO STILL (GK)

As boy I relished sight of hawk,
Of dragonflies, and glimpse of deer.
When first I watched the blackcock lek
The pure delight gave no compare.
And then as student I was fed
A meal of abstract concepts, meant
As discipline but choking joy.
A mechanistic monocle
Became the means of building house
Of knowledge, piling naked facts
In edifice abducting mind.
So now I find content in view
Of walls I've helped to build. As each
Small brick of novel truth has come

My way I've hummed a ghost of song
I sang as child. Indeed at times
When I've beheld a strange new fact
I've been a kid again with toy
From Christmas tree. But now the time
To stand and gaze in awe has gone
The way of snow in spring, I sing
No more in lilting lyrics filled
With praise. A quieter psalm proclaims
A deeper sense of gain – wisdom,
Oh so tardy won by patient toil
And pain, as insights slowly grasped
Conferred a humbler tone in face
Of how minute is what we know.
As I behold the vast expanse
Of what remains to be explored,
As now I hand the baton on
To younger folk with eager minds,
I relish once again a bird
At nest, a perfect rose, a cat
Who stalks its prey with twitching tail.
Or else I doze and dream I'm boy
Beside a stream, in silent hills,
Intently watching dipper hunt
It's prey with concentrated skill
And zest, as youth I used in quest
For puzzle's long elusive prize.

PETER, PATRON SAINT OF FOOLS (RE)

In youth I thought the choice was mine.
I tried to go my Peter way,
But life insisted on its say;
Until I learned to not decline.
In middle years I held the reins
And tried to drive within constraints.
My life it seemed had few complaints,
But still I bridled at the chains.

But now I find myself quite free
Requests besiege me every day,
And I no longer have a say
As I respond and ask no fee.

435

Perhaps the road of folly rules
Our youth as means to tame our wills;
And only after several spills
May God then use us stubborn mules.

REALISTIC ASSESSMENT (GK)

At times the tasks ahead are weights
I'd rather shed. They're largely toil
And little fun. But then the joy
Of novel truth, revealed beneath
The microscope, revives my will.
Besides, when I behold the shelf
Of papers filed I know I've made
Advance within my chosen field.
But when I look beyond I see
I've only just begun. We pride
Ourselves on knowledge gained, despite
The fact we've only plucked an ear
Or two of wheat at edge of spread
Extending out of sight. I could
Have made a bigger splash with dash
Of fashion's craze for theories plucked
From air without regard for weird
And complex webs that nature weaves.
When clothed in maths they dazzle folk
For spell, but slowly shrink as facts
Erode their claims to cover more
Than tiny square of patchwork quilt
We strive to stitch. We're here to clear
A little ground and sow a seed
Or two. The harvest comes when we
Are gone and others claim the spoils,
And we are long forgot. For now
A job well done is prize enough,
Despite we know it's far from best.
Suffice to say we tried to serve.

CARRY ON (GK)

I tinker at the margins, part
In groundless hope I'll leave my field
An ordered spread when I am gone.
In truth I've found a dozen bits
Of thousand piece design whose rich
And complex theme I've scarcely glimpsed.
Perhaps I should have tuned my mind
To cleaning up a minor part
Of mess the world's become. Perhaps
Such toil is merely bailing boat,
While others, splashing oars, defeat
All efforts meant to save from wreck.
But still I will proceed with task
Begun and give a helping hand
To others sharing in my game.
At end of day it scarcely rates
A jot the type of job we do.
It's how we rub along with those
We meet, with whom we interact.
It's here my blindness often caused
Unwitting slights and even hurts.
As child I often served myself
By choice; but since, neglect has been
The cause of most of lapses now
Recalled with sense of shame. But now
I know forgiveness underlies
The love derived from give and take,
And mercy comes as holy grace
That gives me strength to carry on.

In July 2014 Emily Hartop, from the Natural History Museum of Los Angeles County, spent a couple of weeks learning my methods and how to decide whether some of the species of the giant genus Megaselia collected in backyards (gardens) and public parks in Los Angeles were species previously unknown to science. Together we added a European species to the American list, and more than thirty species were new to science. She became convinced I had not been joking when I had declared that the majority of the species in this huge genus remained unknown to science! Indeed this proved to be the case (Hartop, E. A., Brown, B. V. &. Disney, R. H. L., 2015. Opportunity in our ignorance of urban biodiversity: study reveals 30 new species and one new Nearctic record for Megaselia (Diptera: Phoridae) in Los Angeles (California, USA). Zootaxa 3941(4): 451-484). This paper was commented on in Science

(8 May 2015), as well as being cited on Twitter and other social media, as though this was an astonishing report rather than yet another routine indication of our ignorance of the world's fauna. I had previously noted that urban and suburban habitats in England are rich in phorid species (see chapter 9).

Another visitor to my lab in 2014 was Dr Raja Muhammad Zuha from the Program Sains Forensik (Pusat Pengajian Sains Diagnostik & Kesihatan Gunaan, Fakulti Sains Kesihatan, Universiti Kebangsaan, Malaysia). He came for a fortnight in November 2014 to learn my methods. This visit followed on from having previously shown there were more than the then documented species of scuttle flies involved in forensic cases in Malaysia (Thevan, K, Disney, R. H. L. & Ahmad, A. H., 2010. First records of two species of Oriental scuttle flies (Diptera: Phoridae) from forensic cases. Forensic Science International 195: e5-e7). Raja's specimens caught visiting rabbit carcasses likewise added new species and other known species that may feature in future forensic cases. Were these visits to learn my methods hinting that I might not be long for this life and they had better come before my demise?!

What these diversions emphasised is that our knowledge of the world's scuttle flies is in its infancy. Perhaps my dream of a definitive monograph on the British species in the context of the European fauna was premature. It would seem that by making a priority trying to help others has been not so much a diversion as a sensible procedure in terms of advancing knowledge. Furthermore it has caused me to use my gradually growing knowledge to foster collaboration with an extraordinary diversity of fellow scientists from a range of countries, many of which are in political turmoil or at odds with each other. I summarise the numbers of my publications below:

SCIENTIFIC PUBLICATIONS

My publications of books, chapters in books, scientific papers, abstracts of lectures and posters, comments, etc. in scientific journals total more than 650. More than 500 publications deal with Phoridae. For more than 400 I am sole author and I am first author of more than 100 of those of which I am a co-author.

My co-authors were from the following countries: Angola, Argentina, Australia, Austria, Azores (Portugal), Belgium, Brazil, Bulgaria, Canada, Canary Islands (Spain), China, Czech Republic, Denmark, Ecuador, Estonia, Finland, France, Germany, Hungary, India, Iran, Ireland, Israel, Italy, Japan, Java (Indonesia), Kenya, Kuwait, Malaysia, New Caledonia, Nigeria, Norway, Panama, Poland, Russia, Saint Helena, South Africa, South Korea, Spain, Sulawesi (Indonesia), Sweden, Taiwan, Thailand, The Netherlands, Turkey, United Arab Emirates, United Kingdom, United States of America, Uruguay, Yugoslavia and Zimbabwe.

In addition to this list of the nations occupied by my co-authors I have published papers that referred to specimens sent by others who had made collections in a further list of locations: Afghanistan, Aldabra, Algeria, Antarctica (Casey Station), Arctic (N.W. Russia), Ascension Island, Bahamas, Bangladesh, Barbados, Belize, Bolivia, Borneo (Indonesia), Botswana, Brunei, Burma (Myanmar), Cameroon, Cape Verde Islands, Central African Republic, Chad, Chile, Colombia, Comoros Islands, Costa Rica, Cuba, Dagestan (Russia), Dominican Republic, Egypt, Ethiopia, Falkland Islands (Malvinas), Fiji, Galápagos Islands (Ecuador), Ghana, Greenland (Denmark), Guatemala, Guyana, Hawaii (USA), Honduras, Ivory Coast, Jamaica, Kamchatka (Russia), Laos, Leeward Islands, Liberia, Madagascar, Madeira (Portugal), Malawi, Mexico, Mozambique, Nepal, New Zealand, Nightingale Island, Oman, Pakistan, Papua New Guinea, Peru, Philippines, Puerto Rico, Réunion Island, Romania, Sabah (Malaysia), Sarawak, Saudi Arabia, Sénégal, Seychelles, Sierra Leone, Sri Lanka, Sudan, Sulawesi (Indonesia), Sumatra (Indonesia), Switzerland, Tanzania, Tonga, Trinidad, Uganda, United Arab Emirates, Venezuela, Viet Nam, Yemen, Zaire and Zambia.

Some requests to identify specimens did not result in publications in which I was at least a co-author but I was merely thanked or acknowledged in a paper by the person requesting my help. The more I tackled the scuttle fly world fauna the more I was able to help others by naming (often describing as new) the species encountered in their ecological, pest, forensic, etc., studies; coupled with relating their observations to what was already documented in the scientific literature. My gradually acquired taxonomic expertise was essentially a means to the end for the pursuit of my primary research interest – the advancing of our knowledge of the natural histories of these extraordinary insects. By helping others to publish their novel observations I was not only advancing my primary objective thereby but was providing a service for others. This service is likely to prove to be my enduring scientific legacy. That I was able to provide this service, indeed the development of my entire scientific career has resulted from a series of unexpected events: – the army mixing up two reports resulting in my posting to Cyprus. Audrey declining to choose a birthday present on behalf of her boss leading to her move to Flatford Mill and hence our meeting and us having to leave (but our marriage providing the sustaining relationship of my life). My military experience leading to my appointment by the Ministry of Overseas Development. A burglary leading to my appointment to the Overseas Staff of the Medical Research Council on the basis of my performance in Belize. An attempt to sack me without cause leading to my move to Cambridge; with a resulting increase in my scientific output. The latter being increased by me slowly learning that in seeking to serve others before my own ambitions in fact enhanced my scientific expertise and output. Service is at the heart of the Gospel of Christ! Perhaps it takes a lifetime to grasp this simple guide to living life to the full. Indeed our lives are winding trails of pilgrimage, whether we recognize it or not. Hence the title of this meandering tale – REGAINING LIFE'S WINDING TRAIL. In retrospect the succeeding titles of my collections of poems serve as signposts along the way: FINDING MYSELF – QUESTINGS – LAPSED ATHEIST – COUNTERPOISE – A MUSING COG – 'GUIDED BY KNOWLEDGE, INSPIRED BY LOVE' – REITERATION – 'TEACH US OF LOVE' – COME WHAT MAY – 'WAR IS A FAILURE OF POLITICS'.

In April 2015, at the annual meeting of The Friends of the Rural Development Movement in Birmingham, I think some thought my end was nigh when I unexpectedly experienced a severe allergic response to one of the spices in the delicious Tamil curry served at lunch. However, after dozing in the car for much of the journey back to Cambridge and following a prolonged night's sleep I gradually returned to normal over the next week. It was a timely reminder that our lives are fragile and I was no longer a youth!

In March 2016 an examination at Addeenbrooke's Hospital of my damaged hearing (see Chapter 2) revealed in sophisticated detail the persistence of the extensive damage to the upper third of my hearing range due to two terrorist bombs in 1958, thus refuting the Ministry of Defence's deceitful denial of the extent of this damage (see Chapter 9), but revealed a subsequent deterioration in the lower two thirds of the range. However, recent software advances in the programming of hearing aids, which differentially enhance one's hearing in different parts of the range individually for each ear separately, provided some improvement. While not a return to acuteness of my hearing in my youth, it certainly made life a little easier.

FINAL LAP (CW)

As I begin to master field
Of chosen work at end of years
Of toil, I find my body bit
By bit is wearing out. At height
Of powers faults accrue. So now
I have to change to lower gear
To climb the smallest hill. I see
An older friend who meant to fill
Retirement days with projects, left
For years on shelf at back of shed,
In fact consume the hours with dwarf
Concerns instead of what he planned.
I hope I don't regress like that
Before I die. I'd rather go
On crest of wave in reach for sky.

DEPARTURE (CO)

As darkness beckons see the glow
Of distant fuse's fast approach.
The reach of youthful dreams is spent.
The years of breathless climb to peak
Are dead. I pause to order tasks
Desired before my days are done.
The trail of triumphs now seem few
In face of what remains to do.
We merely add a stone or two
To edifice we hope to build
Before we die. A human heart
Has slowly grown from wrecks of hopes.
Indeed compassion's creeping gain
Is worth a wagon load of cheap
Success. The love of wife is best
Of lasting treasures I'll retain
As ferryman applies his oars
And children wave from fading shore.

LITTER (CW)

This lovely park is marred
By litter in excess.
The empty cans and stubs
Of fags, the paper bags,
The plastic bottles strewn
Along with glossy ads
From magazines, the peel
Of fruits, the turds of dogs,
Or condoms left to tell
Of other drives than food.
Perhaps our lives are like
This spread of green when we
Are gone and other folk
Recall ourselves and deeds.
Or will they see a lie -
Expanse all neatly mown
And free of flotsam's blight?
When I by love am known,
The truth's both black and white:
So do not pick me clean,
The litter's part of scene.

THE SOURCE (CW)

A newborn spring is born beneath
A slab of slate on mountain's slope
That sweeps aloft to wayward clouds
Aglow with rising sun's display.
Its waters hold the cold of night, but taste
As pure as promised days ahead
For which they've sought when still beneath
The ground. They gather speed as they
Descend as tiny stream that soon
Is joined by trickles oozing one
By one from right or left, before
They merge and gather speed until
A sill of rock induces plunge
Of foaming, laughing joyous fall
Of awesome, youthful force that holds
One's gaze entranced. By now the freight
Of floating junk along with dance
Of swirling roll along its bed
Of shifting stones, is borne along
To plain where larger boulders, then
The smaller pebbles, settle out
As river slows to steady flow.
By now suspended silt conceals
Its floor and flotsam rides beneath
The sky, along with ducks and swans
Who glide in graceful calm. It seems
Its final chance of shedding load
Will be when sea is reached at last.
For then it joins the ceaseless swell
Of praise, the source of all our hopes.

July 2015: publication of my tenth collection of poems – WAR IS A FAILURE OF POLITICS. Pneuma Springs Publishing UK (118 pages). Sold in aid of the Anglican Pacifist Fellowship.

This collection was prompted by my growing disquiet at the apparent failure of politicians in the West to grasp that military involvement in the Muslim world of the Middle East and North Africa was not just stupid but was the principal cause of the rise of extreme jihad movements in the 21st Century. My disquiet was based on a mixture of history and personal experience. My GCE 'A' level in modern history (see chapter 1) had ignited a continuing interest in history that had made me familiar with the fact that the imperial powers had imposed boundaries that disregarded pre-existing boundaries between different cultures prior to their conquest. Consequently, when an empire ended, there tended to be a period of agitation until more rational boundaries were agreed. If not, then trouble was likely to arise at a later date. In Cameroon we had experienced the impact of the Biafran war, which was essentially a southern Christian-Animist culture against a northern Muslim culture. In West Africa prior to the days of the European empires the boundaries between these cultures had been essentially East-West. The boundaries between nations bequeathed by these empires run North-South instead, and frequently divided tribes between two counties as well. My problem with the Nigerian Consul in Buea was a minor example of the folly of a northern Nigerian being posted to a southern Cameroonian consulate (see chapter 7). The more recent division of the Sudan is a similar example of a post empire redrawing of the boundaries. My father would have been appalled by the actions of the extreme northern Sudanese Government that had precipitated this split. The belated discovery of rich oil fields straddling new boundary was an additional complication.

Returning to my disquiet at Western involvement in the Muslim world of the Middle East and North Africa, we need to consider three elements. There are the different cultures and there are the ludicrous boundaries following the defeat of the Ottoman Empire. On top of this has been the subsequent impact of the exploitation of the rich oil fields after the Second World War. When Colonel T. E. Lawrence, backed by the British Government, helped get the Arabs to contribute to the defeat of the Ottoman Empire in the First World War it was on the understanding that boundaries would be redrawn after the war in accordance with the wishes of the Arabs. However, in 2016 the Sykes-Picot agreement was drawn up in total disregard of this undertaking given to the Arabs. In this ultimate act of imperial arrogance Sykes and Picot sat in Europe with a small scale map and drew a line of about 500 miles in length and declared to the left would be French and to the right would be British when the war had ended. At the Treaty of Versailles conference after the war this agreement was adopted and the prior undertakings to the Arabs were rejected. Lawrence returned to Britain in disgust. He renounced his commission as a colonel and signed up as 352087 A/c Ross in the RAF (see his subsequent account of his RAF service in THE MINT published in 1935 by Jonathan Cape). The rightly acclaimed film LAWRENCE OF ARABIA ended prematurely. It should have concluded with the betrayal of the Arabs by the post war adoption of the Sykes-Picot Agreement.

With regard to the different cultures the imposed boundaries, following the defeat of the Ottoman Empire, divided the Kurds between Iraq, Iran and Anatolia in Turkey, and with substantial numbers of Kurds in Syria and Armenia. Otherwise the principal divisions are between the Shiite and Sunni Muslim traditions. The post imperial boundaries throughout the Middle East and North Africa had disregarded the principal dispositions of these two, often antagonistic, cultures. The only role of the West should be to encourage and

444

facilitate diplomatic discussions that would redraw boundaries that give rise to nations reflecting the wishes of these different cultures and which reduced conflicts between them. I make no apologies for my tenth collection of poems being 'political'!

By 2014 charity appeals were being received at the rate of two to three a day rising to three to four in the run up to Christmas. These were being received as cold calls by phone, by mail, as other deliveries by hand to my house, as loose inserts in magazines I received and by e-mails. Regrettably most were junked straight away as I already had a number of standing orders for charities and could not commit to yet more on my modest pension. The appeals that came in the mail that were junked straight away were those that included a gift such as a pen (which I pocketed without further ado). The worst were those that included coins, seemingly to cover the postage, as a means of putting on the pressure to respond. The coins, however, went instead into the collecting box on my kitchen table. This was for the Children's Society, and routinely received the 5p and copper coins obtained in change when shopping. Otherwise I gave to occasional special appeals (usually for some recent disaster in the news) at church or to people with collecting tins in the street for approved causes. I regretted not being able to give to some of the appeals. However, I give the background below to being suddenly and unexpectedly being in a position to give a number one off donations to some of these.

Audrey and I had obtained our mortgage from the Britannia Building Society (a mutual building society) in 1984 and had paid it off in 2004. We had then continued with Britannia with a modest savings account into which Audrey's old age pension was paid (and to be drawn upon only for unexpected expenses), but we banked with another bank, into which my pension was paid (and we used for our regular needs, utility bills, Council tax, etc.). Subsequently the Britannia was merged with the Co-operative Bank, so we transferred our bank account to the Co-op Bank. However, the latter had failed to take in that the Britannia had got into financial difficulties in the recession in the first decade of the 21st Century. The merger had contributed to the near collapse of the Co-op Bank before a new directorship and management was installed. I have sketched this as being the background to the following surprise. In September 2015 I was checking my latest bank statement when I nearly fell off my chair with astonishment. There was a payment in of £29, 341.90. I had never envisaged ever having such a sum of money in my life. It seemed to me that there had clearly been some mistake! So I went into the local branch of The Co-operative Bank, and suggested it had been paid into my modest account in error. After twenty minutes online it was confirmed that it was not an error but was a payment from my Britannia Building Society account that was now incorporated into the Co-op Bank. So I suggested the decimal point must be in the wrong place. But they were adamant that that was not so. The Bank, however, insisted that the payment was correct. It then transpired that the Department of Work and Pensions had made three payments into my account having belatedly caught up with the changes due following Audrey's death in

March 2012. Audrey's pension had ceased but the DWP had continued to deduct the tax from a non-existent pension for a further three years until they realized their error! Anyhow the result was that I was able to make donations to some charities, especially those trying to cope with the massive refugee problem due to the mayhem in the Muslim world. In addition I was able to deposit £7000 each into the bank accounts of our four grandchildren to help with future university fees or other post school training courses.

Having got this sorted in October I received another financial surprise, but negative this time. The background was as follows. A few years back I had received a Government grant to install loft insulation. Next on offer in 2012 was a grant towards the cost of installing solar panels. I was duly measured up for this but when it came to filling in the form I was asked "I presume your income exceeds £15,000 a year?" I replied that it was just less than that (at the time). I was told I was therefore not eligible for the grant, which was only available to the better off! Then early in 2015 I was told that the conditions pertaining to these grants had changed, besides which my income was now exceeding £15,000 due to a combination of it being linked to an index of the cost of living and a change in the level of taxation. However, I was now told I was still ineligible for a Government grant for solar panels because I had exceeded the age of 75! However, in 2015 Cambridge City Council launched a scheme to give grants of up to £6,000 for external wall insulation for houses lacking cavity walls. The work was to be assessed by the green energy company Climate Energy, who would sign up a suitable contractor to undertake the job. I was all measured for this and told that the cost would be £9,420-08. I was duly awarded the full grant of £6,000 and paid Climate Energy the balance of £3,420-08 with the work to start 'in the summer'. As the summer gave way to autumn I made several calls to ask when the work would start, but with no response. Then on the evening news on BBC Radio 4 on 8th October I learned that Climate Energy had gone bust. It seemed the Government's sudden withdrawal of grants to green energy companies, in order to cut the budget deficit, had driven the company into the red. I immediately contacted the City Council with concern over the £3,420-08 I had paid the company. The Council was confident that the job would be completed as the subcontractor had already been signed up for the agreed sum that I had already paid. Others entering the scheme at a later date might not be so fortunate. I was understandably relieved. However, this tale of my attempts to be green with respect to energy left me being extremely sceptical of the Conservative Government's genuine commitment to green policies designed to curtail global warming!

On a more positive note, in the same week in October 2015 I received a copy of the just published anthology THE POETRY BUG edited by John Tennent and published by Parthian. This 405-page collection of poems about insects and spiders, published over several centuries, included the following two poems of mine.

CHANGING PERCEPTIONS (CO)

Oh thirsty fly, who sipped from cup
Of William Oldys* long ago,
I wonder whether you were clean:
Or had you dined on turd of dog
Before you sought to quench your need?
And did you spring from larva raised
On rotting meat? Before the eye
Of microscope revealed this world
As home for microbe hordes one could
Delight in humble fly who shared
One's drink. But now we know the risk
Of germs that hitch a ride on feet
Of such as sampled William's wine,
We're wise to swat, as swift as can,
As soon as seen. The same applies
To outworn creeds our current facts
Repudiate. As knowledge grows
We shift our course, like lowland stream
That ever feels its way to sea
Whose boundless truth extends beyond
The line our gaze can hope to reach.

*William Oldys (1696-1761) published his poem "On a fly drinking out of his cup" in 1732.

LOWLY ORIGIN (RE)

When apes began to groom their mates
In hunts for lice and fleas, they found
They liked the interchange of grunts
At each success, enjoyed caress
Of mutual combing bouts. These stunts
Became the start of talk for fun,
Apart from calls to warn of death
From eagle's swoop or pounce of lion.
It's thus I seize elusive words
To share my thoughts and feelings felt
To be of worth beyond the fog
Of blanket fur of daily noise.
Perhaps our reach for truths and light
Began with quest for vermin hid
From sight or out of range apart
From help of mate. So let us praise
The humble flea and thank the louse
Who chose our forebears as their house.

Of the numbers of my poems featuring insects that were considered for this anthology perhaps these two made it because neither alludes to my Christian faith!

As I come to the end of this rambling set of anecdotes and poetic reflections on my unusual life, I increasingly return to the task of trying to complete my monograph on the scuttle flies of the British Isles and Western Europe. Whether or not I achieve this matters less than the fact that keeping busy and my mind active, continues to make living a daily challenge.

Finally, to those who regard my faith is all very well but my life has been rewarding unlike the lives of many. My good fortune, my 'success', has been despite unexpected setbacks. I have come through my snakes and ladders life to end on a ladder and being recognized as an accomplished scientist who had the good fortune to marry a wonderful wife. While this perception has a point it misses out on my understanding that everyone is involved in a pilgrimage, although many do not recognize this for much of the time. So I will end this meandering mixture of prose and poetry with a poem that explores this perception. It incorporates fragments from my own life (e.g. the regatta at Overy Staithe – chapter 1, and the rescue of a drowning sergeant – chapter 2) along with my observations of the lives of a great diversity of people I have encountered. Each of us is called by God, whether we recognize this or not. The Holy Spirit does not only impinge on the overtly religious, let alone on those more concerned with dogma than with embracing the Gospel of love.

SECRET EDDIES (CO)

The tide approached its flood as two
Were crouched in bows of straining boats
With eager hands on anchor ropes,
The younger lad had looped his line
To suit the depth. His rival fumed
As hand to hand he raced the cord
Before the metal ring emerged.
He grabbed his oars and heaved a swirl
Of water fast astern as flecks
Of foam were boiling in his wake.
The smaller boy had seized the lead
And, using knowledge gleaned in hours
Afloat on moody creek, he nudged
The secret eddies, holding gain
Despite his youth and lack of brawn.
The prize was his, but sweeter far
The local bully's boast was drowned.
The latter spat abuse at all
In sight as, spoiling for a fight,
He sees his girl has slipped her chain.
He later left to wed the ranks
Of local regiment; and time,
And dogged thrust, have yielded stripes
And sergeant's role. He strutted proud
And cursed aloud. He drove his men
With mean contempt. They feared his tongue,
Admired his strength. At length they sailed
For distant land to curb a tide
Of terror launched by ruthless men,
In name of hope. With secret joy
He hurled his hate against the foe,
As all alone he hid his hurt,
His friendless self, from men he scorned.

At tether's end of weeks with gun
And pack on mountain tracks in glare
Of sun by day and insect whine
By night, the powers-that-be draft
Them to the sea for ordered peace.
In cooling swim in faithless waves
He finds himself in sucking swirl
That whirls him fast between some rocks.

At once a dozen men now plunge
To pull him clear. As grasping hands
Uphold his gasping head and bring
Him face to face with those who strive
To save his life, he views his squad –
So long despised. They ring around
His nearly water-grave. With tears
He thanks them on the shore. He finds
Within his mind a skinny boy
Who never cursed the tide, but linked
His skill to fickle flow in team
Of silent wills – to win the cheers.
His gratitude includes the lad,
Whose face contrived to drive him mad,
But who as blessing now appears.

But he had wandered aimless ways
Of hostile nights awash with fates,
Whose scheming skills ensured the wreck
Of every role he'd claimed as his.
He'd proved this earth was still the home
Of those who worked to quench the light,
Conspired to nail our Lord anew.
He'd learned that good was doomed to fail.
His 'call' concealed delusion's blight.
The secret eddies lost to view.

Too long his night concealed the grace
In those who ply their patient skills;
In him who'd crouched in dank and draughty cell.
An ancient monk by candle's flame
Curling twirls of filigree
Around the 'J' of sainted John
Lighting every page with gold
To praise his God beyond the grave.

In her who's crouched beside a microscope.
A scientist pursuing truth
Counting pollen grains from peat
And plotting graphs that penetrate
Mists of past before the trees
Were laid to waste by fire and axe.

In him who's crouched on rail beside a bin.
A farmer heeding bidding tune

Wheat he'd tended since the seed
Is valued now in pounds per tonne
Feeding distant nameless folk
And keeping wife and kids content.

In her who's crouched within a cage of toil,
Without explicit craftsman's goal
Cog in someone else's scheme
Living life without a theme
Faceless number on a sheet –
But faithful soul who'll be redeemed.

As potter crouched above his wheel he sculpts
The flowing forms that grow and die and rise
Again; until he stays his hand as eye
Declares a halt. But now it's fired, his gaze
Discerns the need to try again. The voice
Within is goading lonely climb anew
Of peaks he half perceives ahead, but fears
He'll never reach before he's brought to rest.

Perhaps he's doomed to wrestle with himself
Till death. His art demands he concentrate
His lonely light within the shrinking space
On sinking ship. Abandoned long ago,
By those who seek for warmth away from him
Whose soul is lost to view beyond the rim
Of focussed mind, his raft of hope is when
He's working once again to find his dream.

A backward glance reveals a million ways
He might have come with greater ease. Perhaps
The route he chose is linked by grace to genes
Entrusted long ago by birth and God's
Redeeming call to use a talent, won
At throw of dice. Perhaps he'll build a wall
In Kingdom Christ sustains, proclaims, for all.
He may perhaps – perhaps he may too late.

Enslaved to wheel by talent's goad
The soothing grace of fickle clay
Devours the doubt that aim of life
Is not achieved by making vase.
Deluding ease delights the eye
And brings recall of Bible text

Of man not turning head from plough.
And yet a whisper in his mind
Insists he hear the cry of need
From folk who reach imploring hands.
But now the clock beside his kiln
Demands he's midwife to his pots –
Resplendent in their new born glaze.

His girl was swept away by call
For flood of refugees who starve.
Her ceaseless reassuring words
Become an endless running tape.
Although she tries to feed her Lord
In each and every one, she fears
She scarcely sees beyond their want.
She finds her eye intrigued by sun
Caressing rainbow glaze from hair
Of hungry child who waits at tail
Of winding queue of slow despair:
Or else the wrinkles wrought by woe
On ancient woman's face entrance.

Her gift she bought from craftsman's wife
Adorns his wall. A wooden face
To mask his pain and toil and tears
Behind a peace; despite his fears,
His grief for children laid to rest,
His hopes in holes. And yet he knew
The sun as light that shines upon
Our wooden wills – revealing joy;
As warming love redeeming dark
Despair and bearing hopes renewed.
It's strange that he who carved this face
Has left behind a nameless grave.
He never dreamed that you or I
Would be so moved by what his skill
Had launched upon our sea of awe,
To cleanse who thought themselves above
Whose schooling used no book or pen,
Whose wisdom used no words but wood.

On makeshift alter in a tent
His vase with roses stands sublime
Beside a loaf of bread and glass
Of wine. At touch of candle's light

The polished table's top reflects
The mingled reds, and perfect forms
Of potter's art and baker's craft
Inverted so the eye believes
The truth extends below, above –
Beyond constraints of space and time.
Caressing glaze of flicker flame
On bread and thorn, on vase and wine,
Unite to wing her will aloft.

At home the potter plies his craft,
Exploiting skill with growing art.
His secret sorrows only shared
With pliant clay and cunning brush.
His wares are sought by folk from far
Who don't redeem his love foregone.
His lonely journeys bearing fruit
As silent pots become his words.
He daily sheds his self-esteem,
Until his growing crust of gloom
Is burned to glaze of joy in kiln
Of lost girl's note – that fills his vase.

Whirling and gusting as lightning struck,
Twirling and twisting in dance of love,
Swimming in floods of an awesome force,
Joining their hands in an act of trust.

Their hopes that each would quickly grow
To fit the image each desired
Had slowly waned, along with faith
In caring God and saving grace.

For long 'twas blank within his heart
Despite the neons in the dark.
Despite the city's ceaseless throb,
He numbly passed each bridge alone.

Learning that hope is ahead,
Leading him into the way
Held by the dance of lights
Cast by the lamps of fresh trust.

Holding the hand of his wife
Sharing her watch in the night.

Peering ahead and astern
Each is engulfed by her gloom.

Learning that love here on earth
Burns with a guttering flame.
Finding that each is alone,
Hoping their link is of steel.

Seeking the Way on their own,
Now they touch Christ in their pain
Healing the scars of their spills,
Cleansing in pools of new grace.

Now that their spring is all spent,
Finding their faith is restored,
Rejoicing in new-found peace,
Secure in a new-born love.

Resting at end of river's rage
Slowly they drift on gentle lake.
Fearless they glide to setting sun
Beckoning trials of exit falls.

Disaster strikes when storm erupts.
Their craft is split against a rock.
Her half is hurled across the sill.
Beneath the falls her breath is still.

His howl of anguish rends the night.
He's haunted by the time their cat
Was felled by pain and they'd decreed
Its end. And its dying eye reproached
The hypodermic needle – that death
Stained bayonet in his hands. 'It had
To be done' he mumbled and stumbled
Into the dark. He felt sick and drained.
'Who were they to choose the right to live,
Dogged by pain, or the release of death?'

Soft 'mee-owl' of a feline spectre
Padded into his perception, prowled
Around his apprehension and sprang
Upon his sense of guilt: cat-and-moused
Around his conscience and purred a sleek
Ripple of fur against his tremble

Of sensitivity. Clutching claws
Probed his feelings with deft taunting pats.

In time that phantom's form had faded,
But lingered as recurring purring:
A mocking ripple of laughter that
Preyed upon his peace of mind: a noise
That fouled the reception of his soul.
He thought he'd laid that corpse to rest
As new humility was bequest.

But now his grief is full of cat.
He sees it curled against the stove
Amidst the chaos strewn around
Their house alive with kids, who seemed
To feel a home is where you drop
A sock upon the stair, or leave
A mug beside a chair. A green,
Exotic bottle stands in calm
Atop their rented tele box.
From slender, graceful neck a rose
Is spreading softly tinted flakes
Of purest tone. A dance of light
Adorns the glass of ocean hue,
That swells its curving belly round
The shadowed forms of thorny stems.
This perfect bloom redeems the room.
Its fragrance seems an incense gift,
To lift our gaze above the grind
Of daily chores and spiky quirks
Of growing child and hungry cat.
Its severed life restored his faith.

But then that cat insinuates
The rose is really his dear love
Returned to haunt his restless nights
And lonesome days of empty hours.

Cursing a wind that plucked the leaves
Sweeping the fallen shuffling flakes
Burning an endless pile of days
Coughing in curling smoke from heart
Resting his mind in timeless task
Scornful of sitting down in ease
Clinging with grip of drowning man

Work had become his raft of life
Toil had become his anchor rope
Fouled in the spokes of autumn's wheel
Striving to speed the seasons round
Hoping to keep the flames alive
Feeling his sun was nearly set
Wishing the night would never fall
Doubting that dawn would ever come
Fearing to raise his eyes to east
Denying buds could burst anew
Desiring trees with evergreen leaves.
At dawn he roams deserted streets.

Clamped in paving stone's embrace
Roots explore beneath the slabs.
Purple blooms of thistle head
Crowning stem that finds the sun,
Laughing at the concrete maze,
Scorning feet of restless men.

Only eyes of mourning man
Drink from spiky cups of hope.
Since reprieve for friendly weed,
Rooted deep in childhood's past,
Many gems besiege his sight
Waiting thread of loving glance.

Christ's own flock are like these gifts,
Drawing strength from hidden depths,
Overlooked by passers-by.
Flashy, sterile, hybrid blooms
Set no head of fertile seeds.
Glamour fades while weeds rejoice.

In youthful rush he'd not conceived
Our Lord might seek him as a means
For grace to enter shadowed nooks.
Beneath the simple surface facts,
Today in many little things
He hears in many daily acts
A joyful sound of worship's wings.
The love of God has broken through:
And now he knows the 'call' was true.
And now he makes his pots in peace
And gives his profits for the cause

That took his wife to distant shores.
And now a former sergeant minds
His sales and lives at ease with all.
And both acknowledge, deep within,
The secret eddies words conceal.

"THEREFORE DO NOT LOSE HEART. THOUGH OUTWARDLY WE ARE WASTING AWAY, YET INWARDLY WE ARE BEING RENEWED DAY BY DAY. FOR OUR LIGHT AND MOMENTARY TROUBLES ARE ACHIEVING FOR US AN ETERNAL GLORY THAT FAR OUTWEIGHS THEM ALL. SO WE FIX OUR EYES NOT ON WHAT IS SEEN, BUT ON WHAT IS UNSEEN. FOR WHAT IS SEEN IS TEMPORARY, BUT WHAT IS UNSEEN IS ETERNAL." (2 Corinthians 4: 16-18).

Father, the Gospel of Christ is perceived as paradox by the world, but it is our calling. To bind ourselves to Thy service is to commit ourselves to perfect freedom. Descent into humility and self-abandonment is our ladder to Thee. When we empty ourselves we are filled by Thy grace. Enable us to dwell at the point of tension between stability and change between the personal and the community between obedience and initiative between the desert and the market place between action and contemplation in order that Thy purposes may prevail. In darkness we see Thy light. In death we discover Thy eternal life.

(The conclusion of my contribution to Prayers of Pilgrimage. An Anthology of Prayers from the people of the Church of the Good Shepherd, Chesterton, Cambridge, 1997; 44 pages).

APPENDIX

Some other professional involvements

A. Editorial work

1973 – 2000 Editorial Panel of Field Studies.

1974 – 1987 Editorial Adviser Transactions of the Royal Entomological Society London (which became Ecological Entomology).

1975 – 1992 Editorial Board of Natural History Book Reviews.

1976 – 1998 Member of AIDGAP Committee (Aids to Identification in Difficult Groups of Animals and Plants)

1979 – 2013 Co-founder and co-editor (with Dr. S. A. Corbet) of Naturalists' Handbooks (Cambridge University Press / Richmond Publishing Co. Ltd/ Company of Biologists)/Pelagic Publishing) (see Appendix G).

1995 – Editorial Panel of Studia dipterologica (Germany).

1999 – International Advisory Board of Fragmenta Faunistica (Poland).

B. Membersips of learned societies, etc.

Fellow of the Royal Entomological Society of London (elected 1964)

Fellow of the Linnean Society of London (elected 1984)

Member of Systematics Association

Life Member of Freshwater Biological Association

Life Member of Marine Biological Association

Chartered Biologist and Fellow of the Royal Society of Biology (formerly the Institute of Biology) (elected 1989)

Member of the Company of Biologists

Honorary Research Fellow of the Field Studies Council (elected 1999)

Life Member of Field Studies Council

1999 – 2002 Member of UK Systematics Forum.

C. Memberships of public bodies, etc.

1972 – 1975 Member of the Yorkshire Council for the Environment

1975 – 1981 Ministerial Appointee on Yorkshire Dales National Park Committee of North Yorkshire County Council

1974 – Scientific Advisory Panel, Onchocerciasis Control Programme (World Health Organisation)

1977 – WHO Scientific Working Group on Filariasis

1978 – Adviser to Sri Lanka Ministry of Education on their Field Studies Centres Programme (under auspices of British Council)

1981 – 1984 Governor of Kirkby Malham Primary School, North Yorkshire

1983 – 1987, 1989 – 1996 Pastoral Selector for Advisory Council for the Church's Ministry (subsequently Advisory Board for Ministry)

1985 – 1990 Wicken Fen Management Committee (National Trust)

1997 – 2005 Director of Dervish Mine Clearance Limited, Edinburgh (SC181198).

D. Poetry collections

FM – FINDING MYSELF (Outposts Publications, 1963 – 20 pages).

QU – QUESTINGS (Chester House Publications, 1982 – 54 pages)

LA – LAPSED ATHEIST and other poems Rockingham Press, 1995 – 40 pages).

CO – COUNTERPOISE (Ronald Lambert Publications, 2004 – 171 pages)

MC – A MUSING COG (Ronald Lambert Publications, 2006 – 125 pages)

GK – 'GUIDED BY KNOWLEDGE, INSPIRED BY LOVE' (Eloquent Books, New York, 2009 – 193 pages hardback edition. Pneuma Springs Publishing, UK, 2014 – 168 pages, paperback edition).Also available on KINDLE

RE – REITERATION (Pneuma Springs Publishing, UK, 2011 – 151 pages). Also available on KINDLE

TL – 'TEACH US OF LOVE' (Pneuma Springs Publishing, UK, 2012 – 273 pages). Also available on KINDLE

CW – COME WHAT MAY (Pneuma Springs Publishing, UK, 2014 – 308 pages).

'WAR IS A FAILURE OF POLITICS' (Pneuma Springs Publishing, UK, 2015 – ☐☐ pages). Also available on KINDLE

E. Flies I have named after Audrey, our children and grandchildren

1. Simulium audreyae (Garms, R. & Disney, R. H. L., 1974. Eine neue Simulium-Art aus Kamerun (S. audreyae n. sp., Simuliidae, Diptera). Zeitschrift für Tropenmedizin und Parasitologie 25: 128-133). [see chapter 7].

2. Megaselia audreyae (Disney, R. H. L., 1978. A new species of Afrotropical Megaselia (Diptera: Phoridae), with a re-evaluation of the genus Plastophora. Zeitschrift für angewandte Zoologie 65: 313-319). [see chapter 7]

3. Clitelloxenia audreyae (Disney, R. H. L. & Kistner, D. H., 1997. Revision of the OrientalTermitoxeniinae (Diptera: Phoridae). Sociobiology 29: 3-118). [see chapter 9].

Dohrniphora adriani (Disney, R. H. L., 1983. Four new species of Dohrniphora (Diptera: Phoridae) from Panama. Entomologica scandinavica 14: 452-456.

Dohrniphora rachelae

Dohrniphora trudiae (but later synonymised with D. anterospinalis Borgmeier, whose original description had proved to be misleading)

Aphiura alistairi (Disney, R. H. L., 2003. Tasmanian Phoridae (Diptera) and some additional Australasian species. Journal of Natural History 37: 505-639).

Megaselia alisamorum (Disney, R. H. L., 2008. Six new species of Megaselia Rondani (Diptera: Phoridae) from mainland Australia. Zootaxa 1899: 57-68).

Megaselia maxi (Disney, R. H. L., 2009. Insects of Arabia scuttle flies (Diptera: Phoridae) Part II: the genus Megaselia. Pp 249-357 in Krupp, F. (Editor-in-Chief) Fauna of Arabia 24. 405 pp. Senckenbergische Naturforschende Gesellschaft, Frankfurt a.M, Germany and King Abdulaziz City for Science and Technology, Ryadah, Kingdom of Saudi Arabia. ISBN 978-3-929907-80-3).

Pilosaphiura samanthae (Disney, R. H. L., 2003. Tasmanian Phoridae (Diptera) and some additional Australasian species. Journal of Natural History 37: 505-639.

Megaselia zoeae (Disney, R. H. L., 2009. Insects of Arabia scuttle flies (Diptera: Phoridae) Part II: the genus Megaselia. Pp 249-357 in Krupp, F. (Editor-in-Chief) Fauna of Arabia 24. 405 pp. Senckenbergische Naturforschende Gesellschaft, Frankfurt a. M, Germany and King Abdulaziz City for Science and Technology, Ryadah, Kingdom of Saudi Arabia. ISBN 978-3-929907-80-3).

F. Organisms I know to have been named after me.
1. Elassoneuria disneyi (Gillies, M. T., 1974, J. Ent. (B) 43: 73 – 82).
2. Chiloglanis disneyi (Trewavas, E., 1974, Bull. Brit. Mus. Nat. Hist. 26(5): 331 – 419).
3. Empis (Disneyempis) hirsutipennis (Smith, K. G. V., 1975, Entomologist's mon. Mag. 111: 189 – 192 (1976)).
4. Atherigona (Acritochaeta) disneyi (Deeming, J. C., 1979, Entomologist's mon. Mag. 114: 31 – 52).
5. Genus Indet., 'Disney's Xenomyia' (Skidmore, P., 1985, The Biology of the Muscidae of the World. W. Junk, Dordrecht. (on p. 375 – 377).
6. Lutzomyia (Coromyia) disneyi (Williams, P., 1987, Mem. Inst. Oswaldo Cruz. 82: 525 – 529).
7. Sarcophaga disneyi (Blackith, R. & Blackith, R., 1988, Japan. J. Sanit. Zool. 39: 301 – 311).
8. Macrocheles disneyi (Fain, A. & Greenwood, M. T., 1991, Bull. Inst. Roy. Sci. Nat. Belg. Entomol. 61: 193-197).
9. Metopina disneyi (Liu, G., 1995,Proc. 2nd Natl Ann. Symp. Young Agronomists. Peking: Chinese Academy of Agricultural Sciences. Pp. 482-6.
10. Tonnoiriella disneyi (Withers, P., 1997, Dipterists Digest 4: 61-64).
11. Uroseius disneyi (Fain, A., 1998, Internat. J. Acarol. 24: 213-220).
12. Megaselia henrydisneyi (Durska, E., 1998, in Disney & Durska, Europ. J. Ent. 95: 437-453).
13. Dohrniphora disneyi (Mostovski, M. B., 2000, Zool. Zh. 79: 312-320).
14. Pseudacteon disneyi (Pesquero, M. A., 2000, J. New York Entomol. Soc. 108: 243-247).

15. Megaselia disneyella (Brenner, S., 2006, Entomologist's Gaz. 57: 119-135).

NAMED (GK)

In life involving global range
Researching tiny flies, I've come
Across a range of other weird,
Intriguing creatures, including some
Unknown before. A dozen such
Their experts named them after me!
It's thus some flies, a fish, a mite
Or two and other beasts agree
In sharing species name. Perhaps
In years to come the only trace
To indicate I walked this earth
Will be this odd assort race
Of beings linked to faceless me
By whim. It's worst of rogues, the likes
Of Stalin, Hitler, rest of pack,
The hordes who lived by swords and pikes
Besmirched with blood, that fill each page
Of history's log. The countless host
Who tried to live in peace and serve
The common good, who'd never boast,
Who quietly carried on despite
The random knocks and mundane tasks
That chance had dealt, it's they deserve
Our praise. Beneath their modest masks
Were silent saints who hid their lights.
Their names are lost, but not their gifts
Of sense of duty, justice, care
And trust in grace that still uplifts.

G.NATURALISTS' HANDBOOKS

Co-founded and co-edited in 1979 by Dr S. A. Corbet and Dr R. H. L. Disney
Initially published by Cambridge University Press, then Published by the Richmond Publishing Co. Ltd, then by The R.P.Co for the Company of Biologists, then by Pelagic Publishing.
1. Insects on nettles. By B. N. K. Davis. 1983. Second edition 1991.
2. Grasshoppers. By Valerie K. Brown. 1983.
3. Solitary wasps. By Peter F. Yeo & Sarah A. Corbet. 1983. Second edition 1995.

4.Insects on thistles. By Margaret Redfern. 1983. Second edition 1995.

5.Hoverflies. By Francis S. Gilbert. 1986. Second edition 1993.

6.Bumblebees. By Oliver E. Prÿs-Jones & Sarah A. Corbet. 1987. Second edition 1991. Third edition 2011.

7.Dragonflies. By Peter L. Miller. 1987. Second edition 1995.

8.Common ground beetles. By Trevor G. Forsythe. 1987. Second edition 2000.

9.Animals on seaweed. By Peter J. Hayward. 1988.

10. Ladybirds. By Michael Majerus & Peter Kearns. 1989. Second edition, by Helen E. Roy, Peter M. J. Brown, Richard F. Comont, Remy L. Poland, & John J. Sloggett, 2013

11. Aphid predators. By Graham E. Rotheray. 1989.

12. Animals of the surface film. By Marjorie Guthrie. 1989.

13. Mayflies. By Janet Harker. 1989.

14. Mosquitoes. By Keith R. Snow. 1990.

15. Insects, plants and microclimate. By D. M. Unwin & Sarah A. Corbet. 1991.

16. Weevils. By M. G. Morris. 1991.

17. Plant galls. By Margaret Redfern & R. R. Askew. 1992. Second edition 1998.

18. Insects on cabbages and oilseed rape. By William D. J. Kirk. 1992.

19. Pollution monitoring with lichens. By D. H. S. Richardson. 1992.

20. Microscopic life in Sphagnum. By Marjorie Hingley. 1993.

21. Animals of sandy shores. By Peter J. Hayward. 1994.

22. Animals under logs and stones. By C. Philip Wheatear & Helen J. Read. 1996.

23. Blowflies. By Zakaria Erzinclioglu. 1996.

24. Ants. By Gary J. Skinner & Geoffrey W. Allen. 1996.

25. Thrips. By William D. J. Kirk. 1996.

26. Insects on dock plants. By David T. Salt & John B. Whittaker. 1998.

27. Insects on cherry trees. By Simon R. Leather & Keith P. Bland. 1999.

28. Studying invertebrates. By C. Philip Wheater & Penny A. Cook. 2003.

29. Aphids on deciduous trees. By Tony Dixon & Thomas Thieme. 2007.

30. Snails on rocky sea shores. By John Crothers. 2012.

31. Amphibians and reptiles. By Trevor Beebe. 2013.

In 2013/2014 Sally and I handed over the editorship to Dr William Kirk.

INDEX